The Philosophy of Friedrich Heinrich Jacobi

Bloomsbury Studies in Modern German Philosophy

Series Editors:
Courtney D. Fugate, American University of Beirut, Lebanon
Anne Pollok, University of South Carolina, USA

Editorial Board:
Desmond Hogan (Princeton University, USA)
Ursula Goldenbaum (Emory University, USA)
Robert Clewis (Gwynedd Mercy University, USA)
Paul Guyer (Brown University, USA)
Brandon Look (University of Kentucky, USA)
Eric Watkins (University of California, San Diego, USA)
Corey W. Dyck (University of Western Ontario, Canada)
Stefanie Buchenau (University of Paris, France)
Paola Rumore (University of Turin, Italy)
Heiner Klemme (Martin-Luther-Universität Halle-Wittenberg, Germany)

Central and previously overlooked ideas and thinkers from the German Enlightenment Era are showcased in this series. Expanding research into areas that have been neglected particularly in English-language scholarship, it covers the work of lesser-known authors, previously untranslated texts, and issues that have suffered an undeserved life on the margins of current philosophical-historical discussion about eighteenth-century German thought.

By opening itself to a broad range of subjects and placing the role of women during this period center stage, the series not only advances our understanding about the German Enlightenment and its connection with the pan-European debates, but also contributes to debates about the reception of Newtonian science and the impact of Leibnizian, Kantian, and Wolffian philosophies

Featuring edited collections and single-authored works, and overseen by an esteemed Editorial Board, the goal is to enrich current debates in the history of philosophy and to correct common misconceptions.

Titles in the series include:
Tetens's Writings on Method, Language, and Anthropology, edited by Courtney D. Fugate, Curtis Sommerlatte and Scott Stapleford
Kant's Rational Religion and the Radical Enlightenment, by Anna Tomaszewska
The Human Vocation in German Philosophy, edited by Anne Pollok and Courtney D. Fugate

The Philosophy of Friedrich Heinrich Jacobi

On the Contradiction between System and Freedom

Birgit Sandkaulen

Translated by Matt Erlin

BLOOMSBURY ACADEMIC
LONDON • NEW YORK • OXFORD • NEW DELHI • SYDNEY

BLOOMSBURY ACADEMIC
Bloomsbury Publishing Plc
50 Bedford Square, London, WC1B 3DP, UK
1385 Broadway, New York, NY 10018, USA
29 Earlsfort Terrace, Dublin 2, Ireland

BLOOMSBURY, BLOOMSBURY ACADEMIC and the Diana logo are trademarks of Bloomsbury Publishing Plc

First published in Great Britain 2023
This paperback edition published 2024

Copyright © Felix Meiner Verlag, 2019

English Language Translation © Matt Erlin, 2023

Birgit Sandkaulen has asserted her right under the Copyright, Designs and Patents Act, 1988, to be identified as Author of this work.

Cover design by Louise Dugdale
Cover image: Portrait of Friedrich Heinrich Jacobi. 1780.
The Picture Art Collection / Alamy Stock Photo

All rights reserved. No part of this publication may be reproduced or transmitted in any form or by any means, electronic or mechanical, including photocopying, recording, or any information storage or retrieval system, without prior permission in writing from the publishers.

Bloomsbury Publishing Plc does not have any control over, or responsibility for, any third-party websites referred to or in this book. All internet addresses given in this book were correct at the time of going to press. The author and publisher regret any inconvenience caused if addresses have changed or sites have ceased to exist, but can accept no responsibility for any such changes.

A catalogue record for this book is available from the British Library.

A catalog record for this book is available from the Library of Congress.

ISBN:	HB:	978-1-3502-3571-7
	PB:	978-1-3502-3575-5
	ePDF:	978-1-3502-3572-4
	eBook:	978-1-3502-3573-1

Typeset by Integra Software Services Pvt. Ltd.

To find out more about our authors and books visit www.bloomsbury.com and sign up for our newsletters.

In memoriam Stephan Otto

Contents

Preface	viii
Note on Translation	xi
List of Abbreviations	xii

Part One Leitmotifs

1	Life and Work	3
2	Jacobi's "Spinoza and Antispinoza"	15
3	Groundless Belief: A Philosophical Provocation	29
4	Does Spirit Have *Esprit*? On the Figures of Soul, Spirit, and Reason in Jacobi's Philosophy	45
5	Between Spinoza and Kant: Jacobi on Freedom and Persons	61
6	That, What, or Who? Jacobi and the Discourse on Persons	75
7	Brother Henriette? Deconstructions of Friendship in Derrida and Jacobi	93
8	"I am and there are things outside me": Overcoming the Consciousness Paradigm with Jacobi's Realism	105
9	The "Tiresome Thing in Itself": Kant – Jacobi – Fichte	129

Part Two Critical Relations

10	I-hood and Person: The Fichtean Aporia and the Debate with Jacobi	153
11	Fichte's *Vocation of Man*—A Convincing Response to Jacobi?	169
12	This Individual and No Other? On the Individuality of the Person in Schelling's *Freedom Essay*	183
13	System and Temporality: Jacobi Contra Hegel and Schelling	203
14	Third Position of Thought toward Objectivity: Immediate Knowing	215
15	Metaphysics or Logic? The Importance of Spinoza in Hegel's *Science of Logic*	235

Bibliography	248
Proof of First Publication	256
Index	258

Preface

Heinrich Heine, like Friedrich Heinrich Jacobi (1743–1819) a son of the city of Düsseldorf, called Jacobi a "whining old woman," and "nothing but a quarrelsome sneak, who, disguising himself in a philosopher's cloak, made his way in among the philosophers, first whimpering to them about his love and his tender soul, and then letting loose against reason."[1] It was a fatal lapse of judgment, one that anticipated an entire series of later mischaracterizations and marginalizations. In scraping away the many layers of this distorted reception history, however, we discover one of the most prominent and most interesting representatives of classical German philosophy.

In his role as public intellectual (he never held an academic appointment as professor of philosophy), Jacobi intervenes in all of the major philosophical debates of his day, or rather, he himself initiates these debates, ensuring that his contemporaries remain constantly on their toes. The story of his impact begins with a pioneering reconstruction of the philosophy of Spinoza that electrifies the intellectual landscape "like a thunderbolt from the blue" (Hegel) and is ultimately responsible for elevating Spinoza to the status of canonical philosopher. He goes on to make seminal contributions to debates surrounding Kant's critical philosophy, further elaborating the critique he develops in that context in subsequent disputes with Fichte and Schelling, where he once again advances a series of highly influential claims. And these thinkers are not the only ones upon whom Jacobi made a lasting impression. Hegel's philosophy is equally unthinkable without Jacobi's inspiration, as Hegel himself repeatedly attests. Described by Fichte as a "reformer in philosophy simultaneously with Kant," Jacobi is in fact the éminence grise of the epoch.

The long history of misinterpretation that has cast such a shadow over his work would be a relevant subject for a future investigation. Apparently, Jacobi neither fit the mold of those nineteenth-century histories of philosophy that emerged from the context of an increasingly professionalized academic discipline, nor did authors like Heine find it easy to give him due credit. His work was simply too rebellious and too provocative, as the double role he consistently plays in these debates makes clear. On the one hand, he admires and supports the explanatory potential of a rigorous systematic philosophy, but through a contradiction in the form of a "salto mortale," he also reveals himself to be one of the most astute and insightful critics of this philosophy, bringing its weaknesses to light long before Kierkegaard. With an eye toward this double role, Jacobi referred to himself in the debate with Fichte as a "privileged heretic": privileged, because he is a philosophical insider whose profound conceptual and linguistic impact

---

[1] Heinrich Heine, *On the History and Philosophy in Germany and Other Writings*, ed. Terry Pinkard, trans. Howard Pollack-Milgate (Cambridge: Cambridge University Press, 2007), 59.

on the entire canon of classical German philosophy is undeniable, and yet still a heretic whose analyses, in their existential commitment to personal freedom, deliberately challenge more than a few fundamental philosophical convictions.

While Jacobi has mostly been rewarded for such provocations with a countless series of misunderstandings, a number of more recent developments have begun to remedy the situation. His works are now available in a complete critical edition. The completion of the critical edition of his letters, which comprise the richest corpus of philosophical correspondence in the entire epoch and which forms an integral part of his works, has been taken up as part of the research program of the German Academies of Sciences. In this same context, the compilation of an online dictionary is also underway. With contributions from a host of international scholars, it aims to elucidate, on the basis of a selection of key concepts, Jacobi's entire oeuvre—the philosophical writings, the two novels, *Allwill* and *Woldemar*, and his extensive correspondence—together with his reception during the period. This effort will no doubt be facilitated by a range of recent publications that reflect the current state of research. Jacobi, then, has long since ceased to be an insider's tip, but in contrast to Kant or Hegel, his works have certainly not circulated in the millions. The task of unlocking their full historical and systematic potential remains to be completed.

*

The original German edition of this volume was published with the Felix Meiner Verlag in Hamburg on the occasion of the 200th anniversary of Jacobi's death.[2] I am extremely pleased that an English edition is now also available. *The Philosophy of Jacobi: On the Contradiction between System and Freedom,* the title of which encapsulates the brief description of Jacobi's position given above, contains a selection of my previously published essays as well as an additional biographical chapter on Jacobi's "Life and Work" that was written specifically for the English edition. Following upon this introductory chapter, the first part of the book elucidates a series of "leitmotifs" in Jacobi's philosophy, and the second contains a discussion of "critical relations" that considers Jacobi's impact on some of the central works of Fichte, Schelling, and Hegel.

The book is aimed at readers seeking an introduction to Jacobi's thought and his role in the period around 1800 as well as scholars working in the field of classical German philosophy. The conceptual and thematic organization of the volume means that the reader can work through the chapters in sequence, as with a conventional monograph, or approach them as stand-alone essays, choosing a selection that speaks to their particular interests. The cross-references in each chapter are intended to assist the reader in charting a path through the work. The critical apparatus of the German edition, including citations from and references to the secondary literature consulted, has been reproduced unchanged in the English translation and supplemented with citations from the available English versions of primary texts.[3] Quotations from

---

[2] Birgit Sandkaulen, *Jacobis Philosophie. Über den Widerspruch zwischen System und Freiheit* (Hamburg: Meiner, 2019).
[3] For the texts and English translations of Kant, Fichte, Schelling, and Hegel, see the detailed bibliography at the end of the volume.

Jacobi are taken from the standard English edition by George di Giovanni: *The Main Philosophical Writings and the Novel* Allwill.[4] In the few instances where it seemed desirable, for example, for consistency with the main text or to clarify certain points, di Giovanni's translation has been tacitly modified. Where no published English translation was available, as for example in the case of Jacobi's novel *Woldemar* or his text *On Divine Things and Their Revelation*, an English translation of the relevant passages appears here for the first time.

*

Many people worked together to make the publication of this book possible, and I would like to sincerely thank all of those who contributed their energies. My heartfelt thanks go to Sally Sedgwick, Karl Ameriks, Brady Bowman, and Fred Neuhouser, who encouraged me from the start to publish an English edition and supported my efforts to this end in a variety of significant ways. I am delighted that the book is appearing with Bloomsbury and grateful to Colleen Coalter for her decision to include it in their catalogue. I would also like to thank Ulla Hansen from the Felix Meiner Verlag, whose intensive personal engagement in working with Bloomsbury helped ensure a smooth transfer of the project from Hamburg to London. Sincere thanks are also due to the jury of "Geisteswissenschaften International," which selected the book for translation and provided the requisite funding. Matt Erlin took on the complex task of rendering the text into English. I thank him from the bottom of my heart for his excellent work as well as for our intensive and fruitful collaboration. I would also like to express my gratitude to Brady Bowman and Dan Breazeale for the invaluable suggestions on the translation that they contributed along the way, including, in the case of Brady Bowman, an initial English version of Chapter 2 that served as a model for the entire project. Last but not least, I am greatly indebted to my students Nadine Schönemann, Alice von Franz, and Tilman Schmidt for their careful attention to all of the detail work required for the English edition, from the tracking down of English sources to the compilation of the final bibliography.

Berlin, March 2022
Birgit Sandkaulen

---

[4] *The Main Philosophical Writings and the Novel* Allwill, ed. and trans. George di Giovanni (Montreal & Kingston: McGill-Queen's University Press, 1994), quoted parenthetically throughout as MPW.

Note on Translation

The translation of this work was funded by Geisteswissenschaften International—Translation Funding for Work in the Humanities and Social Sciences from Germany, a joint initiative of the Fritz Thyssen Foundation, the German Federal Foreign Office, the collecting society VG WORT, and the Börsenverein des Deutschen Buchhandels (German Publishers & Booksellers Association).

Abbreviations

Friedrich Heinrich Jacobi

BK — "Drei Briefe an Friedrich Köppen" (1803). In JWA 2,1, 332–72.

DH — "David Hume über den Glauben oder Idealismus und Realismus. Ein Gespräch" (1787). In JWA 2,1, 5–112.

"David Hume on Faith, or Idealism and Realism, A Dialogue" (1787). In MPW 253–338.

GD — "Von den göttlichen Dingen und ihrer Offenbarung" (1811). In JWA 3, 35–136.

JBW — *Briefwechsel. Gesamtausgabe.* Founded by Michael Brüggen and Siegfried Sudhoff, edited by Walter Jaeschke and Birgit Sandkaulen. Stuttgart-Bad Cannstatt: Frommann-Holzboog, 1981 ff.

JF — "Jacobi an Fichte" (1799). In JWA 2,1, 187–258.

"Jacobi to Fichte" (1799). In MPW 497–536.

JWA — *Werke. Gesamtausgabe.* Edited by Klaus Hammacher and Walter Jaeschke. Hamburg: Meiner, 1998 ff.

MPW — *The Main Philosophical Writings and the Novel Allwill.* Edited and translated by George di Giovanni. Montreal & Kingston: McGill-Queen's University Press, 1994.

Spin — *Schriften zum Spinozastreit* (1785–1819). In JWA 1,1.

"Concerning the Doctrine of Spinoza in Letters to Herr Moses Mendelssohn" (1785) and "excerpts" (1789). In MPW 173–251 and 339–78.

WL — "Ueber eine Weissagung Lichtenbergs" (1811). In JWA 3, 7–31.

Other Abbreviations

AA — Immanuel Kant. *Gesammelte Schriften.* Edited by the Königlich-Preußische Akademie der Wissenschaften. Reprint, Berlin: De Gruyter, 1968.

AA — F. W. J. Schelling. *Werke. Historisch-Kritische Ausgabe.* Edited by Thomas Buchheim et al. Stuttgart-Bad Cannstatt: Frommann-Holzboog, 1976 ff.

CPR   Immanuel Kant. *Critique of Pure Reason*. Edited and translated by Paul Guyer and Allen W. Wood. Cambridge: Cambridge University Press, 1998.

E   Baruch de Spinoza. *Ethics*. In *The Collected Works of Spinoza*, edited and translated by Edwin Curley. Vol. 1. Princeton: Princeton University Press, 1985.

FW   *Fichtes Werke*. Edited by Immanuel Hermann Fichte. Reprint, Berlin: De Gruyter, 1971.

GA   J. G. Fichte. *Gesamtausgabe der Bayerischen Akademie der Wissenschaften*. Edited by Reinhard Lauth et al. Stuttgart-Bad Cannstatt: Frommann-Holzboog, 1964 ff.

GW   G. W. F. Hegel. *Gesammelte Werke*. Edited by the Nordrhein-Westfälische Akademie der Wissenschaften und der Künste, in cooperation with the Deutsche Forschungsgemeinschaft. Hamburg: Meiner, 1968 ff.

JR   G. W. F. Hegel. "Friederich Heinrich Jacobi's Werke". In GW 15, 7–29.

– "Review, Friedrich Heinrich Jacobi's Works, Volume III." In *Heidelberg Writings. Journal Publications*, edited and translated by Brady Bowman and Allen Speight, 3–31. Cambridge: Cambridge University Press, 2009.

KrV   Immanuel Kant. *Kritik der reinen Vernunft*. Edited by Jens Timmermann. Hamburg: Meiner, 1998.

SW   F. W. J. Schelling. *Sämmtliche Werke*. Edited by Karl Friedrich August Schelling. Stuttgart/Augsburg: J. G. Cotta'scher Verlag, 1856–61.

TWA   G. W. F. Hegel. *Werke in zwanzig Bänden*. Edited by Eva Moldenhauer and Karl M. Michel. Frankfurt a.M.: Suhrkamp, 1970 ff.

VE   G. W. F. Hegel. "Wissenschaft der Logik. Vorbegriff. Dritte Stellung des Gedankens zur Objektivität. Das unmittelbare Wissen". In GW 20, 100–17.

– "Science of Logic. Preliminary Conception, Third Position of Thought towards Objectivity. Immediate Knowing." In *Encyclopedia of the Philosophical Sciences in Basic Outline. Part 1: Logic*. Edited and translated by Klaus Brinkmann and Daniel O. Dahlstrom. Cambridge: Cambridge University Press, 2010, 109–25.

Part One

Leitmotifs

1

Life and Work

Departures (1743–79)

Friedrich Heinrich Jacobi is born in Düsseldorf on January 25, 1743, as the second son of a wealthy merchant. While his older brother Johann Georg, a future poet and publicist, is allowed to freely pursue his interests, Jacobi spends his childhood and adolescence in what appear to have been highly oppressive circumstances. As he explains in the autobiographical interlude contained in his dialogue *David Hume über den Glauben oder Idealismus und Realismus* [1787; *David Hume on Faith, or Idealism and Realism*][1] he was "continually being accused of stupidity, and quite often of being frivolous, or obstinate and antagonistic" (DH: JWA 2,1, 40; MPW 279). And in a letter to Goethe on November 6, 1774, Jacobi remarks on

> how many chains were forged to bind my heart and spirit when I was a child; how every possible effort was made to disperse my powers and to twist my soul. Nonetheless, much of that which God had entrusted to me was preserved, and for this reason I know in whom I believe. I hearken only to the voice of my own heart. To hear this voice, to distinguish it, to understand it—this is my definition of wisdom; and to follow it courageously is virtue. And so I am free; and how much more enticing is this blissful freedom than the comforts of tranquility, of security, of saintliness! (JBW I,1, 268)

Jacobi's use of the term *freedom* here alerts us to the central focus of his life's work. This is true in the double sense that considerations of freedom are fundamental for his own life decisions and that freedom figures as the main theme of his entire philosophical project, one whose metaphysical, ethical, and political implications Jacobi spends a lifetime unfolding. Freedom, he writes, is the "fundamental article of my thought."[2]

---

[1] The title of Jacobi's works is given in German the first time it is used and then followed with the English in square brackets. If Jacobi's work in question exists in a published translation, then the English title is italicized and capitalized; if it has not been translated, the English title is not italicized, or is not enclosed in quotation marks in the case of an essay. The date appears at the start of brackets followed by a semicolon.
[2] Letter to Jean Paul from May 11, 1817 in *Friedrich Heinrich Jacobi's auserlesener Briefwechsel*, ed. Friedrich Roth, vol. 1 (Leipzig: Gerhard Fleischer, 1825), 463. "All of my convictions are based on my one most fundamental conviction: that human beings are free," in F. H. Jacobi, *Werke*, ed. Friedrich Roth and Friedrich Köppen, vol. 6 (Reprint Darmstadt: Wissenschaftliche Buchgesellschaft, 1980), 231.

It is typical for Jacobi's productive strategy of connecting these two dimensions that passages from the letter to Goethe reappear shortly thereafter in the epistolary novel *Eduard Allwills Papiere* [1776; Edward Allwill's Papers], having clearly been subject to a critical reconsideration in the meantime. After all, how can we distinguish the freedom of the heart from mere capriciousness that threatens to infringe upon the freedom of others? Such questions will give rise to many further discussions, the contents of which are also shaped by a series of formative personal experiences.

Jacobi seems destined to pursue a life in commerce, succeeding his father in the family business despite his wishes to the contrary. He completes a short apprenticeship in Frankfurt and is sent in the same year to Geneva for additional training (1759–61), at the conclusion of which he is prevented from fulfilling his desire to study Medicine in Glasgow. Instead, following his father's decree, Jacobi returns from Geneva to join the Düsseldorf trading house, taking over the reins in 1764 and leading the business until 1772. The experience brings with it certain advantages, inasmuch as it gives him practical knowledge of economic affairs—Jacobi never becomes an ivory tower aesthete—and it also almost immediately opens up new career prospects. De facto, however, he claims that these "commercial matters" transform him "into a completely different person than I usually am."[3]

Behind this assertion one can discern what is perhaps the most important of experience of Jacobi's entire life, an experience of liberation that occurred during his time in Geneva. With an enthusiasm bordering on euphoria, Jacobi refers to this period as "two of the happiest, and certainly most fruitful years of my life" (DH: JWA 2,1, 42; MPW 280) because it is there that he first makes the acquaintance of the mathematician and physicist Le Sage, a teacher and mentor who instills in him the basic confidence he lacks and strengthens his belief in his own intellectual abilities. "That evening a new chapter of my life began." (DH: JWA 2,1, 41; MPW 280) As a result of the support from Le Sage, Jacobi begins to believe in his "grands talens," a phrase that appears several times in later letters from his mentor. Meanwhile, his philosophical studies as well as his encounters with Voltaire and the circle of intellectuals around Rousseau initiate him into the world of philosophy and the radical French Enlightenment. Diderot and many others will later pay their respects to Jacobi in Düsseldorf-Pempelfort.

It is worth noting in this context that Hegel opens the Jacobi chapter of his *Lectures on the History of Philosophy* by calling attention to this French background, leaving religious matters entirely out of the equation. Only in later accounts did it become commonplace, as is still often the case today, to begin a discussion of Jacobi with a reference to his pietistic roots. An autobiographical remark from his correspondence with Mendelssohn also comes to mind here, in which he explains that already as a child he began "to worry about things of another world" (Spin: JWA 1,1, 13; MPW 183). While this statement appears to give the impression that he was wrestling with the question of his eternal salvation, we would be mistaken to rush to such a judgment. In Supplement III to the expanded second edition of his book *Über die Lehre des Spinoza in Briefen an den Herrn Moses Mendelssohn* [1785/1789; *Concerning the Doctrine of Spinoza in Letters to Herr Moses Mendelssohn*], Jacobi elucidates this

---

[3] Letter to Sophie von La Roche, June 1, 1771 (JBW I,1, 107).

passage with reference to "a representation of endless duration, quite independent of any religious concept" (Spin: JWA 2,1, 216f.; MPW 362), that is to say, to a profound sense of metaphysical terror capable of re-occurring at any time—definitely *not*, in other words, a religious experience, but rather a *cosmological one*.[4]

Whatever specifically religious fears Jacobi might have experienced in his protestant home—fears about which, it should be noted, we know nothing—in order to understand his philosophy, it is crucial that we maintain a consistent separation between these two categories and resist the temptation to ascribe to his philosophy a foundation in Christian doctrine. Our understanding of Jacobi, as well as our assessment of his aims and of his ongoing relevance, will be greatly enhanced if we take seriously his objection to *"religious materialism"* (GD: JWA 3, 46) and thus help lay to rest once and for all the peculiar religious fixation that characterizes many interpretations of his work. To this end, one should also take seriously his expressed desire to study medicine, which forms a stark contrast to the theological training pursued by so many of the other protagonists of the classical period of German philosophy.

Nonetheless, while the presumption that Jacobi is motivated by fundamentally Christian concerns leads to a deeply flawed if not entirely erroneous interpretation of his philosophy, it is certainly correct and appropriate to point out his deeply rooted inclination for metaphysics. This inclination was not acquired by way of an engagement with contemporary academic philosophy or theology; it was *existential* in nature and manifested in an uncompromising search "for the truth out of inner need," which is how he himself characterizes the interest in fundamental metaphysical questions (Spin: JWA 1,1, 14; MPW 184).

The encouragement Jacobi receives in Geneva to begin this search has a lifelong impact, but one that also has two immediate consequences upon his return to Düsseldorf. First, he quickly establishes contact with the Amsterdam bookseller Rey and begins to amass what will become an enormous private library, which he uses throughout his life for both comprehensive reading and intensive studies. Indeed, we must always keep in mind the fact, perhaps best demonstrated by his so-called *Denkbücher*,[5] that the philosopher of existence Jacobi is also an exceptionally well-read scholar, one who, because of his sheer passion for knowledge, usually begins "by tirelessly retracing the historical threads" (DH: JWA 2,1, 44; MPW 282). These book purchases were also facilitated by his marriage in 1764 to Betty von Clermont, the daughter of an Aachen textile manufacturer who contributed considerable financial resources to their union.

Second, thanks to his studies in Geneva, Jacobi is well positioned to intervene in the contemporary philosophical discussion in Germany. The essay competition sponsored by the Berlin Academy of Sciences in 1763 brings Mendelssohn and Kant to his attention. Already at this point his reservations with regard to Mendelssohn's submission lead him to an initial analysis of Spinoza's *Ethics,* meaning that by the time

---

[4] See also Jacobi's letter to Baader of November 11, 1798 (JBW I,11, 320).
[5] See the newly published complete edition: *Die Denkbücher Friedrich Heinrich Jacobis*, ed. Sophia Victoria Krebs (Stuttgart-Bad Cannstatt: Frommann-Holzboog, 2020).

of Spinoza controversy and its enormous resonance in the 1780s, Jacobi is able to build on some twenty years of study of Spinoza. It is thus no surprise that when Lessing asks about his familiarity with Spinoza, Jacobi replies: "I think I know him as only very few can ever have known him." (Spin: JWA 1,1, 17f.; MPW 187) His reported reaction upon reading Kant's *The Only Possible Argument in Support of a Demonstration of the Existence of God* (1763) is also significant in this context, namely, that he was highly gratified to discover that Kant's deliberations served to confirm the correctness of Spinoza's proof of God's existence (DH: JWA 2,1, 42–47; MPW 282–285). Decisive here is Kant's concept of "Absolute Being," which—in contrast to Mendelssohn's approach—does not entail a rationalist operation of inferring actuality from possibility (DH: JWA 2,1, 44; MPW 283).

What we can ultimately glean from the autobiographical reflections in *David Hume* is, on the one hand, an awareness of the philosophers and texts that were central to Jacobi's development, together with a recognition of certain basic philosophical concerns. The latter include, for example, the fundamental distinction, central to all his future deliberations, between *Grund* and *Ursache,* ground and cause, which he develops on the basis of the difference between *theory and practice* and which we will address in detail in subsequent chapters.[6] On the other hand, through his reference to the pleasures taken in conclusively substantiated positions as well as in identifying substantive connections between viewpoints that seem completely opposed to one another, such as those of Spinoza and Kant, Jacobi also reveals his unique way of thinking. It is a mindset that strongly privileges consistency of thought over half-hearted equivocations and yet is simultaneously capable of separating an admiration for radical consistency from the approval of the positions elaborated with this rigor. This intellectual profile provides the foundation for the development of Jacobi's later philosophy, whose appeal and provocative power stem from its twofold character as a double philosophy, one that does not espouse a single viewpoint but rather simultaneously occupies two opposing *and* correlated positions.

The activities of the 1760s bear visible fruit in the 1770s. The year 1771 marks the beginning of Jacobi's journalistic ventures as well as his friendship with Christoph Martin Wieland. Following the example of the *Mercure de France*, the two develop a plan for the journal that comes to be known after 1773 as the *Teutscher Merkur,* with Wieland serving as editor while Jacobi contributes a number of articles. The appearance of Wieland's essay "Über das göttliche Recht der Obrigkeit" [On the Divine Right of Government] in 1777, however, leads Jacobi to end both their collaboration and their friendship as a matter of principle. Apparently Wieland had crossed a line in Jacobi's eyes, an interpretation that finds additional support in Jacobi's repeated subsequent criticisms of platitudinous "tolerance" as well as his refusal to accept his friend Stolberg's conversion to Catholicism.

A notable change in Jacobi's professional life occurs in 1772 with his appointment as court chamber councilor responsible for the reform of trade and customs policy in the duchies of Jülich and Berg. While in this position, Jacobi complements his practical

---

[6] I provide an initial explanation of this crucial distinction in Chapter 2.

efforts in the arena of economic reform, which finally enable him to withdraw from the family business, with theoretical studies. Not least under the influence of Adam Smith, he articulates a program of progressive liberalism that finds expression in the political writings from the end of the 1770s and the beginning of the 1780s, including "Zwei Politische Rhapsodien" [1779; Two Political Rhapsodies] and a response to Wieland's previously mentioned essay, which he titles "Über Recht und Gewalt" [1781; On Right and Power]. His liberal attitude, however, eventually comes into conflict with his professional goals. He obtains a ministry appointment in 1779 in Munich, where he serves as privy councilor in charge of customs and trade policy for all of Pfalz-Bayern, but he is forced to give up the position in the same year. Both his publications and his efforts at economic reform—including his participation in efforts to abolish serfdom—had met with disfavor. He does, however, remain in the court chamber until his retirement in 1802.

By this time, his estate at Pempelfort near Düsseldorf has become a renowned center of hospitality and sociability. This reputation develops in no small part thanks to the support of his wife Betty, with whom Jacobi leads a happy marriage and fathers numerous children (four of eight children survive; Jacobi's "favorite" dies shortly after Betty's premature death in 1784). Their beautiful home and the large, park-like garden, which can still be visited today, host many prominent guests, including Sophie von La Roche, Heinse, Forster, Diderot, and Goethe, as well as, later on, Hemsterhuis, Herder, Hamann und the Humboldt brothers. In a letter to Jacobi from May 5, 1786, Goethe conveys an impression of Jacobi's life that is as vivid as it is ambivalent:

> One has so many reasons to be envious of you! House, grounds, and Pempelfort, prosperity and children, sisters and friends and a long pppp. For that, however, God has also punished you with metaphysics [Metaphisick] and thereby placed a thorn in your flesh, whereas he has blessed me with physics [Physick] so that I can find comfort in the observation of his works. You are also, by the way, a good person, such that one can be your friend without sharing your opinions. (JBW I,5, 196)

This friendship with Goethe, enthusiastically entered into by both parties, plays a prominent and sometimes complicated role in Jacobi's biography. With Goethe's encouragement, Jacobi publishes *Eduard Allwills Papiere* (1776) and *Woldemar* (1779), becoming an acclaimed novelist. Both texts are distinctive for their multiperspectival narration. Jacobi situates his protagonists within a larger constellation of figures whose own reflections often cast a critical light on their views, without, however, turning them into one-dimensional monsters. Instead, and in far more complex and interesting fashion, the author shows how these self-proclaimed moral geniuses ultimately fail to grasp the true challenges of freedom. Because these novels are concerned with what we would today call the *meta-ethical* question of how to ground moral positions, rather than merely with the positive depiction of moral enthusiasm, Jacobi is able to return to both projects in the 1790s. In what can be seen as a realization of the aim stated in the preface to the second edition of *Eduard Allwills Briefsammlung* [1792; *Edward Allwill's Collection of Letters*]—"depict as conscientiously as possible humanity as it is, whether explicable or not" (JWA 6,1, 89; MPW 383)[7]—he effectively expands the novels into textual laboratories for the investigation of complex moral situations, and it is thus no surprise that the new editions attract the attention of both Fichte and Hegel.

From the very beginning, however, Jacobi's efforts fail to find favor with Goethe. On the contrary, in 1779 Goethe causes a scandal with the so-called "Ettersburg Crucifixion," in which, to the delight of the Weimar court society, he nails a copy of *Woldemar* to a tree. Their friendship survives this crude caper thanks to Jacobi, whose goodwill is manifest in his amiable response to a note from Goethe that he receives some three years later.[8] Nonetheless, a fundamental disagreement remains, as Goethe's remarks cited above illustrate. With the juxtaposition of "Metaphysics" and "Physics," Goethe adopts a standpoint in the Spinoza controversy that is opposed to that of Jacobi, just as many years later, in response to the dispute between Jacobi and Schelling, he will declare himself to be on the side of nature.

There is, however, also another reason why the friendship with Goethe proves to be problematic. From a cultural and literary historical point of view, it has played a central role in the tendency to categorize Jacobi as a figure of the "age of sensibility" or "Storm and Stress," and the corresponding restriction of scholarship to an assessment of his moderate literary success while completely ignoring his reputation as a philosopher. Bollnow's pioneering account pushes back against this tendency in the sense that it considers precisely these novels to be Jacobi's most significant philosophical accomplishment. But he also considers Jacobi's later philosophical efforts as misguided aberrations in comparison with the "*Lebensphilosophie*" of the "Storm and Stress," and for this reason his analysis, despite offering some valuable insights, ultimately proves to be inadequate.[9]

The Spinoza Controversy and its Consequences (1780–9)

In the 1780s Jacobi achieves his decisive breakthrough and makes his debut on the philosophical stage. While unintended, with regard to its intellectual substance the basis of this breakthrough is also not surprising. Two major works appear in rapid succession, both of which are pioneering and have an impact that is every bit as powerful as that of Kant's *Critique of Pure Reason*. In 1785, Jacobi publishes *Concerning the Doctrine of Spinoza in Letters to Herr Moses Mendelssohn* (with a second, expanded edition in 1789), followed in 1787 by the dialogue *David Hume on Faith, or Idealism and Realism*. In terms of content, these two, or rather three texts together constitute a sequence of enormous complexity.

---

[7] "So entstand in seiner Seele der Entwurf zu einem Werke, welches mit Dichtung gleichsam nur umgeben, Menschheit wie sie ist, erklärlich oder unerklärlich, auf das *gewissenhafteste* vor Augen stellen sollte." (JWA 6,1, 89)

[8] Goethe writes, "As we get older and the world becomes more narrow, we cannot help but occasionally recall in amazement those times in which we ruined friendships as a form of diversion and, thanks to our frivolous arrogance, neither felt the wounds we inflicted nor made any effort to heal them" (Goethe to Jacobi on October 2, 1782, JBW I,3, 54). Jacobi responds on October 17, 1782.

[9] Otto F. Bollnow, *Die Lebensphilosophie F.H. Jacobis* (Stuttgart: Kohlhammer, 1933).

It all begins with Jacobi's visit to Lessing in Wolfenbüttel in 1780. He gets along brilliantly with Lessing, a longtime admirer of his novels. This mutual affinity is on full display in their fascinating and spirited discussion of Spinoza, in which Lessing argues in favor of the philosopher and Jacobi argues both for and against him. This encounter comes to be remembered as one of the most famous philosophical conversations in the history of modern thought, an event that inaugurated the so-called Spinoza renaissance and established Spinoza's reputation as a canonical figure in the history of philosophy. Before any of this occurs, however, Jacobi sends a record of the conversation to Mendelssohn in 1783, following up on his previous inquiry as to whether Mendelssohn was aware that his recently deceased friend Lessing was, in fact, a "Spinozist." The correspondence that grows out of this initial contact follows a highly peculiar path, but one that is nonetheless characteristic for the symptomatology of the so-called Spinoza controversy.

The initial question of whether or not Lessing was a Spinozist quickly mutates into an entirely different question, the question of what, precisely, the doctrine of Spinoza actually entails and whether it permits a degree of hermeneutical latitude large enough to allow for a less radical interpretation (Mendelssohn) or not (Jacobi). This question gives rise to a serious antagonism between Jacobi and Mendelssohn. Their conflict crystallizes around Spinoza's *Ethics*, a work that had until that point been maligned as atheistic and fatalistic and suppressed from the official discourse of philosophy, and its stakes involve nothing less than the *constitution, scope, and validity of reason itself*. Let it be noted that this debate is anything but academic. On the contrary: at its core is the very self-understanding of modernity as it takes shape around 1800, that watershed period which Reinhart Koselleck has memorably designated the "Sattelzeit."[10]

When Jacobi makes his dispute with Mendelssohn public, revealing the sensational news of Lessing's Spinozism as well as his assertion that "the orthodox concepts of the Divinity are no longer for me" (Spin: JWA 1,1, 16; MPW 187), he thus launches a debate in which virtually the entire intellectual world of the era will participate. The first reactions come from representatives of the orthodox Berlin Aufklärung, who, siding with Mendelssohn, accuse Jacobi of being an enemy of enlightenment. They even go so far as to insist that he bears some responsibility for Mendelssohn's untimely demise in 1786, and they appeal to Kant in Königsberg for a statement on the matter, which Kant ultimately provides (1786; "What Does it Mean to Orient Oneself in Thinking").[11]

Upon returning from a two-month journey to London in the summer of 1786, Jacobi, for his part, develops the plan for his dialogue *David Hume*, with which he hopes to clarify his views. Against the accusations of the Berlin circle that his position "promotes Catholicism, and denigrates the use of rational enquiry in the justification of the truth of religion" (DH: JWA 2,1, 18; MPW 263), he intends to demonstrate, as he had already done in the dispute with Mendelssohn in the *Spinoza Letters*, that the supposed alternative of enlightenment or religious fideism is in no way the central

---

[10] Reinhart Koselleck, "Einleitung," in *Geschichtliche Grundbegriffe. Historisches Lexikon zur politisch-sozialen Sprache in Deutschland*, ed. Otto Brunner, Werner Conze and Reinhart Koselleck, vol. 1 (Stuttgart: Klett-Cotta, 1979), XV.

[11] See the collection of documents in the commentary to Jacobi's correspondence JBW II,5, 699–727.

issue. At this point the complexity and philosophical significance of the debate become even more pronounced, as Jacobi decides to bring Kant's *Critique of Pure Reason* (in the first edition of 1781) into the analysis. In opposition to idealism he invokes the concept of a "resolute realism" [entschiedener Realismus], bringing his argument to a climax in a Supplement entitled "On Transcendental Idealism," in which he offers a critique of Kant's concept of the thing in itself that continues to be discussed to this day.

This dual focus on Spinoza *and* Kant becomes constitutive for the second edition of the *Spinoza Letters*, as is shown by the two most important new additions: the treatise on freedom and *Supplement VII*, both of which now also take Kant's *Critique of Practical Reason* (1788) into consideration. With his distinction between two types of reason, the reason of which "man is in possession," and the reason that "is in possession of man" (Spin: JWA 1,1, 259f.; MPW 375), Jacobi makes especially clear in *Supplement VII* that he does not in fact intend to abolish reason in favor of irrationality as was being claimed by the Berliners. Rather, he aims to subject it to a substantial revision and to gain in the process a new and greatly enriched understanding of reason, one that integrates its discursive and intuitive aspects with an eye toward practical consequences.[12]

Against this backdrop, it becomes clear that the responses to Jacobi that appear after 1790 take shape under entirely different conditions and must be understood as part of the post-Kantian era of German philosophy and literature. A notably younger generation of philosophers now enters the scene, born in the 1760s and 1770s and including such figures as Fichte, Hegel, Hölderlin, Schelling, and Novalis. These thinkers have little interest in the stale preoccupations of the Berliners, certainly not in their accusations of irrationalism and fideism, which continue even much later to be leveled against Jacobi, as if by default and without any reflection on their origins in the particular orthodoxy of this group. For the new generation it is clear that Kant's and Jacobi's critique of reason has banished Mendelssohn's rationalism to an irrecoverable past. In contrast, Jacobi's position as both for and against Spinoza in the *Spinoza Letters,* which are now consistently being read in the second, expanded edition of 1789, completely reframes the entire complex of ontological and epistemological questions. Jacobi now comes to be seen, in the words of Fichte, to be "a reformer in philosophy simultaneously with Kant."[13]

A third group of responses, appearing in the mid-1780s, is in some respects the most peculiar of all. It comprises the reactions of Jacobi's friends and closest acquaintances, including Goethe, Herder, Lavater, Hamann, and Claudius, with whom he discusses

---

[12] From this perspective, the not uncommon division of Jacobi's thinking into an early and a late phase proves to be untenable. Grounded in the notion that it is only late in life that he finds his way to a positive concept of reason, this division seems to stem from a false backward projection from the retrospective commentary on *David Hume* that he includes in the *Introduction to the Author's Collected Philosophical Works* of 1815. This particular *Supplement VII* to the *Spinoza Letters* is actually one of Jacobi's most important texts and has generally received far too little attention in the scholarship. The standard translation of Jacobi's works into English unfortunately includes only excerpts.

[13] J. G. Fichte, "A Crystal Clear Report to the General Public Concerning the Actual Essence of the Newest Philosophy: An Attempt to Force the Reader to Understand," trans. John Bottermann and William Rasch, in *Philosophy of German Idealism: Fichte, Jacobi and Schelling*, ed. Ernst Behler (New York: Continuum, 1987), 47 (translation amended).

the initial publication of the *Spinoza Letters* in statu nascendi. Some of these reactions are to be found in the extensive private correspondence to which the *Letters* give rise, but they also appear in published form, as for example in Herder's *God* (1787/1800), to which Jacobi offers an extremely critical response in Supplements IV and V of the 1789 edition of the *Spinoza Letters*. While all of these figures side with Jacobi against the Berlin circle, they nonetheless disagree with him on substance, albeit for the most various reasons. Goethe and Herder simply cannot understand what Jacobi has against Spinoza; Hamann and Claudius, on the other hand, cannot understand why Jacobi would ever advocate for Spinoza or why he decided to engage in this debate in the first place. Although Goethe and Herder do contribute to the Spinoza renaissance in their own way, the members of this group remain largely unaware of the truly explosive force of the *Spinoza Letters*, as can also be seen in the fact that Claudius coins the title "Spinozabüchlein" (Spinoza Booklet) for one of the major works of the entire tradition of classical German philosophy.

The Privileged Heretic (1790–1819)

Among Jacobi's inner circle, it is really only Jean Paul who later develops a sympathetic understanding of his position. Their friendship begins in 1798 at Jean Paul's initiative, shortly after he reads *David Hume*, and it quickly acquires special significance as a consequence of their joint participation in the confrontation with Fichte. This confrontation inaugurates the next major period of public prominence in Jacobi's life, which had recently taken a dramatic turn. In 1794, the advance of French revolutionary troops forces him to flee Pempelfort and take up temporary residence in Hamburg and Holstein. It is only in 1798 that he is again able to settle down permanently, this time in Eutin, where he remains until his relocation to Munich in 1805. Jacobi's generally critical view of the French Revolution finds expression in a contribution to Schiller's *Horen* that he wrote while still in Pempelfort, "Zufällige Ergießungen eines einsamen Denkers" [1793; Occasional Outpourings of a lonely Thinker]. While disapproving, however, the essay is much more than a one-sided condemnation of the event. It includes not only a sharp critique of the *Ancien Régime* but also a compelling social theory of the power of public opinion.

In the 1790s Jacobi begins an intensive study of Fichte's writings; at the same time he undertakes the previously mentioned revision of *Edward Allwill's Collection of Letters* (1792) and *Woldemar* (1794 and 1796). These two activities form a crucial backdrop to the 1799 publication of his *Letter to Fichte*. This simultaneity is especially noteworthy in light of the central role played by the novels in their intellectual exchanges. Fichte references the novels in repeated enthusiastic assertions of the "striking conformity of their philosophical convictions,"[14] and Jacobi includes a collection of excerpts from the novels with his epistle. The occasion for Jacobi's letter is Fichte's entanglement in the

---

[14] Fichte's letter to Jacobi from 30 August 1795, JBW I,11, 55. In this context see also the letters of September 29, 1794, and April 26, 1796.

so-called atheism dispute in Jena, in regard to which he asks Jacobi for a statement. We will turn later to the implications of Jacobi's famous diagnosis of Fichte's *nihilism*, and specifically to the question of how his analysis of the *Wissenschaftslehre* recapitulates the basic structural constellation of the *Spinoza Letters* while simultaneously surpassing it through the incorporation of *David Hume*. For now we will simply note that with this highly influential letter, the "privileged heretic" Jacobi (JF: JWA 2,1, 198; MPW 505), who follows and critically comments on his own influence, establishes himself as a key player in the post-Kantian philosophical context.

This engagement continues with a renewed and extensive critique of Kant (*Über das Unternehmen des Kriticismus, die Vernunft zu Verstande zu bringen, und der Philosophie überhaupt eine neue Richtung zu geben* [1802; On the Efforts of Critical Philosophy to Bring Reason to its Senses, and to point Philosophy as a whole in a new Direction]) as well as with the *Drei Briefe an Friedrich Köppen* [1803; Three Letters to Friedrich Köppen]. In the latter Jacobi offers a response to Hegel's *Faith and Knowledge, or the Reflective Philosophy of Subjectivity in the complete range of its forms as Kantian, Jacobian, and Fichtean Philosophy* (1802). Although the text had appeared anonymously, Jacobi accurately attributes it to Hegel on the basis of stylistic features. Jacobi's rejection of Hegel's radical polemics is certainly a rhetorical *tour de force*, but in its substance, his argument takes aim at Schelling's philosophy of nature and philosophy of identity. Perhaps because Schelling is so close to Jacobi in so many respects, having successively adopted one after the other of Jacobi's motifs into his own philosophy, Jacobi's controversy with Schelling turns out to be the most unpleasant of all for both parties.

Following Jacobi's appointment to the Munich Academy of Sciences in 1805, for which he serves as the inaugural president from 1807 to 1812, Schelling and Jacobi meet personally in Munich. After Schelling delivers his address "Concerning the Relation of the Plastic Arts to Nature" (1807) to the academy, however, Jacobi turns his back on what he sees as Schelling's Spinozistic naturalism. In the subsequent theism controversy, he criticizes Schelling in *Über die Göttlichen Dinge und ihre Offenbarung* [1811; On Divine Things and Their Revelation] for a profound ambiguity in his position. This attack leads in turn Schelling's *Denkmal auf Jacobi* [1812; Monument to Jacobi's Work on the Divine Things], a text which, while it may not raise the culture of philosophical debate to new heights, nonetheless does succeed in forcing Jacobi to withdraw from the Academy. In the "statum controversiae between the men of nature and freedom," Goethe takes the side of Schelling.[15]

Jacobi devotes the time remaining to him to the publication of the collected edition of his works, which he expands through the addition of a number of important texts, including the *Einleitung in des Verfassers sämmtliche philosophische Schriften* [1815; Introduction to the Author's Collected Philosophical Works] and the preface to the final edition of the *Spinoza Letters* (1819). It remains an open question how the dispute with

---

[15] Goethe in a letter to Knebel from April 8, 1812 in Walter Jaeschke, ed., *Religionsphilosophie und spekulative Theologie. Der Streit um die Göttlichen Dinge (1790–1812). Quellenband*, Philosophisch-literarische Streitsachen 3.1 (Hamburg: Meiner, 1994), 319. In this context see also the documents on this dispute written in support of Jacobi by Friedrich Schlegel and Jakob Friedrich Fries.

Hegel would have unfolded. Jacobi himself expressed regret about a missed opportunity after reading Hegel's Heidelberg assessment of his work from 1817. As Jacobi puts it, "I would have welcomed one more chance to try out on him everything of which the power of thought is capable, if only my old mind had been up to the task."[16] Jacobi dies on March 10, 1819. "One always feels a sense of abandonment," writes Hegel on March 26, 1819 to Niethammer,

> whenever one of these old lineages, which we have admired from a young age, comes to an end. He was one of those men who marked a turning point in the intellectual formation of the age and its individuals, and who provided a source of stability in the world in which we conceive our existence.[17]

---

[16] Letter to Neeb from May 30, 1817, *Auserlesener Briefwechsel*, vol. 2, 468.

[17] "Er war einer von denen, die einen Wendepunkt der geistigen Bildung der Zeit sowie der Individuen formierten und die für die Welt, in der wir uns unsere Existenz vorstellen, einer der festen Halte waren," in *Briefe von und an Hegel*, ed. Johannes Hoffmeister, vol. 2, 3rd ed. (Hamburg: Meiner, 1969), 213.

2

Jacobi's "Spinoza and Antispinoza"

"As to my *Spinoza and Antispinoza* …" (Spin: JWA 1,1, 274): in this single phrase, Friedrich Heinrich Jacobi captures the essence of his philosophical approach. And we see at once that the presentation of this philosophy is no simple task. Things are relatively simple if a philosopher advocates for a *single* theory or a *single* point of view. But when that philosopher is committed to pursuing a *double philosophy*, then the situation inevitably becomes more complex. Precisely herein lies the exceptional character of Jacobi's position.[1] At one and the same time, he speaks both *for* and *against* Spinoza. On the one hand, he adopts Spinoza's standpoint; on the other, he is Spinoza's opponent—and these two contrasting positions cannot be separated from one another; rather, they are indivisibly connected in the form of a double philosophy. How, then, are we best to understand it?

In framing a response to this question, I will proceed in three steps. In the first step, I briefly recall the circumstances of the historical event that was the publication of Jacobi's *Spinoza Letters*. In a second step, I bring out the substantive commitments that inform Jacobi's double philosophy, in order then finally, in the third step, to explicate what I understand to lie at the heart of his conception.

The *Spinoza Letters* as an Historical Event

Jacobi's double philosophy of "Spinoza and Antispinoza" is highly unconventional and provocative, and its impact was enormous. This point must be acknowledged at the outset. Indeed, Jacobi's significance can hardly be overstated. Not only is he to be credited with the so-called Spinoza renaissance toward the end of the eighteenth century—to the extent that we study Spinoza today as a classical modern philosopher, this too can be traced back to Jacobi, who succeeded in anchoring him in the official discourse of philosophy. Beyond his role in the Spinoza renaissance, Jacobi also had a seminal influence on the formation and ongoing development of post-Kantian philosophy as

---

[1] For detailed discussion of the following, see Birgit Sandkaulen, *Grund und Ursache. Die Vernunftkritik Jacobis* (Munich: Wilhelm Fink Verlag, 2000). It was Dieter Henrich who first characterized Jacobi's thought in terms of a "double philosophy" (Dieter Henrich, "Der Ursprung der Doppelphilosophie. Friedrich Heinrich Jacobis Bedeutung für das nachkantische Denken," in *Friedrich Heinrich Jacobi. Präsident der Akademie, Philosoph, Theoretiker der Sprache*, ed. Dieter Henrich (Munich: Beck, 1993), 13–27.

a whole. Fichte, Schelling, and Hegel, to name only the most prominent philosophers of the post-Kantian era, would be unconceivable in the absence of Jacobi's intellectual provocations and their own engagement with his double philosophy. Jacobi's enormous significance is therefore comparable to that of Kant. In their own distinct ways, Kant and Jacobi both heralded the beginning of a new epoch in philosophy at the close of the eighteenth century: Kant with his foundational work, the *Critique of Pure Reason*, and Jacobi with a book entitled *Concerning the Doctrine of Spinoza in Letters to Herr Moses Mendelssohn*.

This book, which I will refer to subsequently simply as the *Spinoza Letters*,[2] caused an immediate sensation upon its appearance in 1785. In 1789 Jacobi published a second, expanded edition with substantial additions of new texts. Jacobi himself refers to these additions as "Supplements," but we should not be misled. Though the term might ordinarily suggest a mere addendum, an afterthought to the far more important main text, here the "Supplements" are a constitutive part of the main text itself. *Supplement VII* is of special importance, and I will return to it later in more detail.

For now, however, it suffices to note that even just the title of the book and the character of its so-called "Supplements" already suggest that not only its *content*—that is, the double philosophy of "my Spinoza and Antispinoza"—but also its very *form of presentation* is unusual. Indeed, it is unlikely that a comparable effect has ever been achieved by a book that is not really a book at all in the strict sense of the word. Far from offering a systematically organized set of arguments, to say nothing of an extended demonstration *more geometrico*, Jacobi's text is in its structure comparable neither to Kant's *Critique of Pure Reason* nor to Spinoza's *Ethics*. Instead, the text is constituted by a collection of diverse "building blocks," a structure that stems first and foremost from its particular history of its composition. The publication arose largely (though not entirely) from a series of letters Jacobi exchanged with Moses Mendelssohn concerning—as the title indicates—the doctrine of Spinoza.

The occasion for this correspondence between Jacobi and the most prominent representative of the rationalist Berlin Enlightenment and close friend of G. E. Lessing was a potentially explosive question on the part of Jacobi: is Mendelssohn aware that the recently deceased Lessing was a "*Spinozist*"? (Spin: JWA 1,1, 8; MPW 181) Since Mendelssohn is aware of nothing of the sort, Jacobi forwards him the notes from his conversation with Lessing, which took place in Wolfenbüttel in 1780 and which, with the publication of the *Spinoza Letters,* was soon to become famous. Jacobi's account leaves no doubt as to Lessing's Spinozism, and the essential features of Jacobi's own double philosophy also find expression here. I will come back to this central text, which constitutes, as it were, the *Spinoza Letters*' oldest and deepest stratum. Important for now is that this conversation sparked the confrontation with Mendelssohn that has come to be known as the "pantheism controversy," the first of three major controversies in which Jacobi was to be embroiled. The equally consequential "atheism controversy"

---

[2] I deliberately refrain from using the term Matthias Claudius introduced to refer to the book, the *Spinozabüchlein*, which unfortunately became established usage in older scholarship on the subject. Jacobi's text is obviously no mere "booklet," but a foundational work of towering importance for the whole of classical German philosophy.

surrounding Fichte and the "controversy concerning divine things" with Schelling would later follow. Mendelssohn, in other words, is the first—after Lessing—to experience *in statu nascendi* the provocative potential of Jacobi's double philosophy. And the process reveals that he possesses neither an adequate knowledge of Spinoza himself, nor is he in a position to make sense of Jacobi's double-position of "Spinoza and Antispinoza." The dispute between Mendelssohn and Jacobi thus mainly revolves around the question of wherein, precisely, the "doctrine of Spinoza" consists, and which options exist for responding to it. And even though Jacobi undertakes a series of additional attempts to clarify the situation (including a fictive dialogue with Spinoza and a densely packed, forty-four-paragraph presentation of the main ideas of the *Ethics*), he remains unsuccessful in his efforts. Ultimately, Mendelssohn proves to be too ill-equipped for this debate. With the tools at his disposal, namely, the rationalist ideas of Christian Wolff and his school, he is simply not in a position to grasp what is for him an entirely new conceptual constellation.

It is for this reason as well that the publication of the *Spinoza Letters* in 1785 causes such a sensation. The world learns of Lessing's Spinozism; it encounters Jacobi's double philosophy; and it finds Spinoza placed center stage as an attractive philosophical alternative. And all at once the world also discovers that Mendelssohn's rationalism has been definitively overcome. Kant had himself already offered a thoroughgoing critique of this style of rationalism. Now, however, and in an entirely different manner than was the case with Kant, Jacobi demonstrates beyond any doubt that the rationalist school of thought has failed. To keep pace with the times—such is the message of the *Spinoza Letters*—one must return to the past, to a time before the emergence of Wolffian scholasticism, and to a work that had been mocked and declared dead: Spinoza's *Ethics*.

An exceptional story, all things considered, and one that never ceases to amaze. And it is only against the backdrop of this event, comprising the origins as well as the impact of the *Spinoza Letters*, that one can really speak about Jacobi's book. The same can be said, incidentally, for all of Jacobi's later writings. He never wrote "pure" monographs, always choosing instead to engage dialogically with other positions. He engaged in very public controversies, and precisely through this participation drove the philosophical discussion forward. As far as the study of Jacobi is concerned, however, his public prominence has also given rise to a dangerous temptation, one to which the scholarship on classical German philosophy has, to its own detriment, frequently fallen victim. To the extent that Jacobi, despite his tremendous influence, has not been simply been excluded from the canon, he has mainly been considered only as a source of inspiration, that is to say, only in relation to the many contemporaries who were caught up in the drama of the Spinoza-event, not as a substantive philosopher in his own right. In consequence, Jacobi's own position has, by and large, been conflated with the mere image of it as reflected in the eyes of his contemporaries (e.g. Mendelssohn, Kant, Goethe, Herder, Fichte, Schleiermacher, Novalis, Reinhold, Schelling, Hegel, and others, all of whom engaged with his thought).

This is no way to go about understanding a philosopher. The reception of Jacobi is tremendously important, as I myself have repeatedly stated, but we must be on guard not to confuse the reception of the *Spinoza Letters* with Jacobi's own *authentic* position. We will never acquire an adequate grasp of Jacobi's thought in this manner, for the simple reason that his contemporaries were not interested in truly *understanding* Jacobi's reflections but rather in *defusing* the provocative potential of his "Spinoza and Antispinoza." Their efforts to do so unavoidably gave rise to misunderstandings, omissions, and reinterpretations of Jacobi's double philosophy, which have shaped the reception of the *Spinoza Letters* in multifarious ways. It can certainly be fruitful to retrace this long line of misreadings, all of which stem from the attempt to avoid confronting the problem he diagnoses. Such a reconstruction can open up entirely new lines of inquiry. These can only be successfully pursued, however, if we first establish a fundamental distinction between Jacobi's authentic concerns and the reception of his book. With this in mind, I propose to bracket for now the various appropriations and transformations of Jacobi's "Spinoza and Antispinoza" that followed in the wake of its initial presentation, and to turn my attention instead to the arguments of Jacobi himself.

System and Freedom

"As to my *Spinoza and Antispinoza* ..."—what motivates Jacobi to speak both for and against Spinoza? Why does he adopt Spinoza's standpoint and yet in the same breath insist that one must switch to the side of the Antispinozist? How, furthermore, do these two positions relate to each other? The constellation is clearly structured such that we cannot begin to determine the position "Antispinoza" until we have gained clarity regarding the position "Spinoza." This in itself already gives us an important insight into Jacobi's thinking. His interest in Spinoza's *Ethics* is by no means merely historical. He views Spinoza's philosophy not as a philosophy of the past, but as one that justly demands an effort to grasp and appropriate it in the present. But how does he justify this assertion?

Jacobi's answer is that Spinoza's immanentist metaphysics is the very paradigm of rigorously consistent, thoroughly systematic thought. It is the epitome of a self-contained, complete system—a "philosophy of *one piece*."[3] This was an entirely novel view; before Jacobi, no one had ever said anything of the kind about Spinoza's *Ethics*. On the contrary: according to Christian Wolff's well-known verdict, Spinoza's doctrine was as a whole basically unsound. It was indeed Wolff himself who, by his alleged "refutation of Spinoza," had been chiefly responsible for ousting Spinoza from the official discourse of philosophy. But Wolff had focused his attention exclusively on the *Ethics*' geometrical method. He had examined only the letter of Spinoza's proof procedure and found it to be insufficient.

Jacobi takes an entirely different approach. What enables his novel perspective on Spinoza is precisely his lack of interest in the *Ethics*' geometric form. Rightly or

---

[3] Jacobi coins this phrase ("Philosophie aus *Einem* Stück") in his *Letter to Fichte* (1799) (JF: JWA 2,1, 200; MPW 507), in which he interprets Fichte's *Wissenschaftslehre* as a reconfiguration of Spinoza's substance monism. Jacobi's translation, in the Fichtean context, of the "Spinoza and Antispinoza" constellation into an alternative between *Alleinphilosophie* and *Unphilosophie* sheds further light on the basic structure at issue in both cases. On the relations between Jacobi and Fichte, see Chapters 9, 10, and 11 in this volume.

wrongly, he regards this form as an exterior coating that must be peeled back in order to uncover the *inner cogency* of Spinoza's monism. This innovative approach to Spinoza's text becomes clear in Jacobi's conversation with Lessing. When Lessing asks him what he takes to be the "spirit of Spinozism," "the one that inspired Spinoza himself," he replies:

> It is certainly nothing other than the ancient: *a nihilo nihil fit* that Spinoza made issue of, but with more abstract concepts than the philosophers of the cabbala or others before him. In keeping with these more abstract concepts he established that with each and every coming-to-be in the finite, no matter how one dresses it up in images, with each and every change in the infinite, *something* is posited *out of nothing*. He therefore rejected any *transition* from the infinite to the finite […] and in place of an emanating *En-Soph* he only posited an *immanent* one, an indwelling cause of the universe eternally unalterable *within itself*, One and the same with all its consequences. (Spin: JWA 1,1, 18; MPW 187f.)[4]

Jacobi is deeply familiar with the text of the *Ethics* (and with Spinoza's correspondence, as well); he can provide citations to support each and every interpretive claim—he is, without exaggeration, the period's foremost authority on Spinoza and the first to reconstruct the compelling internal logic of Spinoza's philosophy. But to repeat, in doing so he does not follow the geometric sequence of propositions. Rather than reproduce the steps by which Spinoza argues for the uniqueness of the one substance and its corollary, namely that everything else is merely an internal, "modal" differentiation of the divine substance and its attributes, Jacobi goes straight to the heart of Spinozan monism: the conception of the divine *causa immanens* "as the *pure* principle of the actuality in all that is actual, of the *being* in everything existent [als das *lautere* Prinzipium der Würklichkeit in allem Würklichen, des *Seyns* in allem Daseyn]" (Spin: JWA 1,1, 39; MPW 199).[5]

---

[4] "Das ist wohl kein anderer gewesen, als das Uralte: *a nihilo nihil fit*; welches Spinoza, nach abgezogenern Begriffen, als die philosophirenden Cabbalisten und andre vor ihm, in Betrachtung zog. Nach diesen abgezogenern Begriffen fand er, daß durch ein jedes Entstehen im Unendlichen, unter was für Bilder man es auch verkleide; durch einen jeden Wechsel in demselben, ein *Etwas aus dem Nichts* gesetzt werde. Er verwarf also jeden *Uebergang* des Unendlichen zum Endlichen […] und setzte an die Stelle des emanierenden ein nur *immanentes* Ensoph; eine inwohnende, ewig *in sich* unveränderliche Ursache der Welt, welche mit allen ihren Folgen zusammengenommen—Eins und dasselbe wäre." (Spin: JWA 1,1, 18)

[5] Like many other passages from his works, Jacobi's phrase: "the being in everything existent" or "the being in all beings" (*das Sein in allem Dasein*) quickly gained wide currency. It plays a central role for instance in the first part of Hegel's Logic, "The Doctrine of Being" (cf. GW 21, 100 and GW 20, § 86; G. W. F. Hegel, *The Science of Logic*, ed. and trans. George di Giovanni (Cambridge / New York: Cambridge University Press, 2010), 87; G. W. F. Hegel, *Encyclopedia of the Philosophical Sciences in Basic Outline. Part I: Science of Logic*, ed. and trans. Klaus Brinkmann and Daniel O. Dahlstrom (Cambridge/New York: Cambridge University Press, 2010), 137). Phrases such as this demonstrate the extent to which, in translating Spinoza's scholastic terminology into more contemporary philosophical parlance, Jacobi was also creating new concepts and indeed a new language of philosophy. Jacobi was, it is important to recall, not only a philosopher, but also the author of two highly regarded novels (*Allwill* and *Woldemar*)—a writer in command of impressive stylistic resources.

There is nothing arbitrary in the way Jacobi proceeds, nor does his approach distort Spinoza's philosophy. Jacobi reflects on the motive that gave rise to this philosophy, and he rightly identifies that motive as a fundamental interest in presenting *a universal and wholly rational explanation* of how the world hangs together in its totality and how human life fits into it. Spinoza's *Ethics* not only arises from this interest in total explanation, it also uniquely satisfies this interest. Any metaphysical theory must aim at inner coherence as a condition of its success. It must therefore provide an account of the finite that avoids any ontological gap or need for "transition" between the infinite and the finite.[6] It must likewise detach itself from ways of thinking—theories of divine creation, for instance, no less than Neoplatonist theories of emanation—that posit a rationally incomprehensible beginning of the world. Thanks to his uncompromising faithfulness to the axiom: *a nihilo nihil fit*, Spinoza proves singularly successful in his endeavor.

Seeing this helps us recognize one of the key implications of Jacobi's new approach to Spinoza. Because he discerns the paradigm of explanatory rationality at the heart of Spinoza's metaphysics, he also understands how immediately the doctrine's propositions all flow from it and how directly their content depends on it: here the *ontological commitments* are inseparably bound up with the *epistemic interest in explanation*. This onto-logical nexus constitutes Spinoza's monism and, as Jacobi recognizes, this is precisely the source of its unique intellectual strength and persuasiveness. As a consequence of his underlying commitment to explanation, all of Spinoza's characteristic doctrines prove to be derivable from the fundamental theorem of divine immanence—particularly the parallelism of thought and extension at the level of the attributes, of mind and body at the level of finite modes, and the concomitant denial of final causation. Intentional action, that is, action grounded in freedom of the will and undertaken for a consciously chosen end, can be attributed neither to God nor to human beings. Indeed, as Jacobi emphasizes, Spinoza's basic commitments leave him no choice but to identify the belief in final causes as the most deeply seated of all human prejudices and to exclude it categorically from his thinking.

Jacobi's insight into the foundations of Spinoza's metaphysics not only enables him to elucidate the unprecedented logical rigor of Spinoza's system; it also leads him to express his profound admiration for this rigor. Jacobi is fascinated by Spinoza's systematic thinking and his uncompromising attitude. We find a telling instance in his response to Lessing's observation that "people always speak of Spinoza as if he were a dead dog." "And so they will go on speaking of him," replies Jacobi:

> To understand Spinoza requires too great an effort of mind and too much determination. And no-one can be said to have understood him to whom the meaning of even a single line in the *Ethics* is still obscure; nor anyone who does not comprehend how this great man could have as firm an inner conviction in his philosophy as he so often and so emphatically professed to have. Even at the very

---

[6] On the question of such a "gap" between the finite and infinite and its central importance to systematic philosophy, cf. for instance Hegel, *Science of Logic*, trans. George di Giovanni, 122, and Chapter 15 in this volume.

end of his days, he wrote: "... *non præsumo, me optimam invenisse philosophiam; sed veram me intelligere scio.*"—Few can have enjoyed such a tranquility of spirit, such a heaven of the intellect, as this clear and pure mind did. (Spin: JWA 1,1, 27; MPW 193)[7]

Lessing's incredulous response is thus hardly surprising: "And you, Jacobi, are no Spinozist?" (Spin: JWA 1,1, 27; MPW 193). For Jacobi shows all the signs of being a committed Spinozist. There can be no greater admirer and defender of the *Ethics* than he. Despite that fact, however, or indeed because of it, Jacobi now turns the tables. It is at this very point that Jacobi rejects Spinozism and embraces the "Antispinoza" position. Here, verbatim, is how he explains his surprising yet principled reversal:

> I love Spinoza, because he, more than any other philosopher, has led me to the perfect conviction that certain things admit of no explication: one must not therefore keep one's eyes shut to them, but must take them as one finds them. I have no concept more intimate than that of the final cause; no conviction more vital than that *I do what I think,* and not, that *I should think what I do.* Truly therefore, I must assume a source of thought and action that remains completely inexplicable to me. But if I want to have absolute explanation, then I must fall back upon the second proposition, and hardly any human intellect could countenance the application of it to individual cases, taken in its full compass. (Spin: JWA 1,1, 28; MPW 193f.)[8]

Three aspects of this explanation are especially important to note. First, Jacobi informs us of the crux of his disagreement with Spinoza, namely *the reality of intentional action.* He is fully aware that Spinoza denies the reality of final causation, rejecting belief in it as a deep-seated human illusion. But this has no bearing on the fact that it is for Jacobi the "most vital conviction" of all. We thus also come to understand, in the second place, that Jacobi's objections to Spinoza are not purely intellectual or theoretical in nature but have their source instead in the *praxis of the lifeworld.* Spinoza's metaphysics may open the gates to a "heaven of the intellect," but for precisely that reason his system of ethics touches on the very nerve of life as we live it. Spinoza demands a revision to our belief in the freedom of our actions that is so radical, a revision to our conception of ourselves as agents and of the lifeworld we inhabit that is so fundamental, that the prospect of actually putting his conception into practice proves to be entirely unbearable.

---

[7] "Eine solche Ruhe des Geistes, einen solchen Himmel im Verstande, wie sich dieser helle reine Kopf geschaffen hatte, mögen wenige gekostet haben." (Spin: JWA 1,1, 27)

[8] "Ich liebe den Spinoza, weil er, mehr als irgend ein andrer Philosoph, zu der vollkommenen Ueberzeugung mich geleitet hat, daß sich gewisse Dinge nicht entwickeln lassen: vor denen man darum die Augen nicht zudrücken muß, sondern sie nehmen, so wie man sie findet. Ich habe keinen Begriff der inniger, als der von den Endursachen wäre; keine lebendigere Ueberzeugung, als *daß ich thue was ich denke,* anstatt, *daß ich nur denken sollte was ich tue.* Freilich muß ich dabey eine Quelle des Denkens und Handelns annehmen, die mir durchaus unerklärlich bleibt. Will ich aber schlechterdings erklären, so muß ich auf den zweyten Satz gerathen, dessen Anwendung auf einzelne Fälle, und in seinem ganzen Umfange betrachtet, kaum ein menschlicher Verstand ertragen kann." (Spin: JWA 1,1, 28)

A third point remains to be mentioned, and it is perhaps the most important of all. For it bears on the epistemic implications of these reflections. If Spinoza's denial of intentional action is indeed the logical consequence of his commitment to a thoroughly rational system of explanation, then, by the same token, one cannot defend the reality of such action by appealing to the principles of rationality. It is impossible in principle to ground my "vital conviction" that, in "doing what I think," I am acting freely. It is a necessarily "inexplicable" fact of life-worldly praxis itself. For as Spinoza himself has conclusively shown, as soon as we undertake to provide rational ground for it, it can only appear as an irredeemable illusion.

These, then, are the basic, defining features of Jacobi's "Spinoza and Antispinoza" and the philosophical provocation it represents. On his side, Spinoza has the ideal of complete rational consistency, the paradigm of a rigorously formulated system of metaphysics. On the opposing side, we have the experience of human praxis—what Habermas and others will later refer to as the "participant perspective." Returning to Spinoza's side again, we have the fact that his *Ethics*, precisely by virtue of the rigor with which he follows out the ontological implications of a total commitment to rational explanation, can serve as a springboard to the all-important insight that such a commitment is fundamentally incompatible with the praxis-constitutive belief in human freedom: "Every path of demonstration leads to fatalism" (Spin: JWA 1,1, 123; MPW 234). Or, to put it in another way, according to Jacobi's problem-diagnosis there can be no *system of freedom*. Putting it this way should already suffice to indicate how and why Jacobi's framing of the problem of rationality was to become a source of continual agitation for the efforts of Fichte, Schelling, and Hegel to build a post-Kantian system of reason and freedom.

To bring Jacobi's provocation fully to light, I turn now to his infamous *salto mortale*—Jacobi's *leap* from the side of "Spinoza" to that of "Antispinoza." "I extricate myself from the problem through a *salto mortale*," says Jacobi in his conversation with Lessing. And when Lessing responds by asking Jacobi what he means by this, he replies: "Just watch and see me do it. The whole thing comes down to this: from fatalism I immediately conclude against fatalism and everything connected with it" (Spin: JWA 1,1, 20; MPW 189).[9] This leap represents precisely the point that I have just been trying to convey. The leap is essentially *practical* in nature, something real only in the enactment, the meaning of which is to come to the defense of the convictions that constitute human praxis in the lifeworld. It is necessary to take a *leap* because it is impossible to argue logically against a consistently rational system. Jacobi sought to express this fundamental state of affairs by saying that, while the "doctrine of Spinoza" is indeed "irrefutable" [*unwiderleglich*], it is not for that reason "uncontradictable" [*unwidersprechlich*] (Spin: JWA 1,1, 290).

Hence we must distinguish between *refutation* und *contradiction*. We cannot refute Spinoza's metaphysics; that is, we cannot hope to counter his conclusions by raising rational, purely logical objections—if we could, then his metaphysics would not be the

---

[9] "Sie mögen mir es immer absehen. Die ganze Sache bestehet darin, daß ich aus dem Fatalismus unmittelbar gegen den Fatalismus, und gegen alles, was mit ihm verknüpft ist, schließe." (Spin: JWA 1,1, 20)

unique paradigm of perfect systematicity that it is. If Jacobi's diagnosis is correct, then we cannot, in the final analysis, hope to "improve" Spinoza's conception or "modify" this or that feature of it, much less to construct an equally rational and self-enclosed, but philosophically more palatable alternative to vie with Spinoza's substance monism. All of that is ruled out by the very nature of the case. This does not mean that we can raise no objections whatsoever. Such objections can only be plausibly raised, however, in the form of a *practical contradiction*. It ultimately comes down to making a *decision*, and this is precisely Jacobi's point. *Either* one stands with Spinoza and embraces the system together with all it implies. *Or* one embraces the reality of volitional freedom and enacts this contradiction in the very leap that propels one *out of the system* and onto the side of "Antispinoza."

There is no mistaking the provocative character of this alternative. That Jacobi's contemporaries declined to follow his invitation to take the leap is, in the end, hardly surprising. Yet be that as it may, it would be a misunderstanding to regard the leap as *irrational*. What Jacobi aims to establish here is not an originary irrationality, but rather the *limits of rationality itself*. Not everything that is meaningful or whose meaningfulness life compels us to acknowledge is capable of rational explanation. Coining yet another of those expressive phrases that gained entry, through the *Spinoza Letters*, into the wider vocabulary of German philosophy (this one recurs, for example, as well in Feuerbach), Jacobi declares to Lessing:

> In my judgment, for the seeker after truth there is no higher accomplishment than to disclose *existence* and to reveal it ... To him, explanation is a means to an end, a path to where he is headed, a first stop and never a final goal. His final goal is that which is beyond all explanation: the unanalyzable, the immediate, the simple. (Spin: JWA 1,1, 29; MPW 194)[10]

To disclose—literally, to uncover or unveil. Only thus do we ever gain access to the vital underpinnings of our lives, of this Jacobi is convinced; only thus do we gain assurance and certainty of our agency and freedom.

Grounding versus Causing: A Founding Confusion

To this point, I have spoken of Jacob's leap as a leap out of "fatalism," but the *Spinoza Letters* also contain a statement I have not mentioned up till now: "Spinozism is atheism" (Spin: JWA 1,1, 120; MPW 233). The book's early reception was shaped by the sensation which it (understandably) caused. On the face of it, to lodge the charge of "atheism" against Spinoza was no less conventional than to accuse him of "fatalism"; both positions had frequently been ascribed to Spinoza by his detractors. In Jacobi's

---

[10] "Nach meinem Urtheil ist das größeste Verdienst des Forschers, *Daseyn* zu enthüllen, und zu offenbaren ... Erklärung ist ihm Mittel, Weg zum Ziele, nächster—niemals letzter Zweck. Sein letzter Zweck ist, was sich nicht erklären läßt: das Unauflösliche, Unmittelbare, Einfache." (Spin: JWA 1,1, 29)

analysis, however, they take on a completely new weight and significance. From his perspective, we can no longer dismiss Spinoza's denial of free will and a transcendent God as the reprehensible but idiosyncratic opinions of a single individual; rather, we must recognize them for what they truly are: the necessary and inevitable concomitants of a total commitment to rationality. The philosophical provocation entailed by this conclusion becomes even more apparent when compared to Kant's comparatively modest critique of reason. Although Kant denies that God and freedom can ever become objects of rational insight, he nonetheless accords them the status of "ideas," objects that reason must inevitably encounter in its pursuit of a highest, unconditional, explanatory ground and about which we may at least *think* without falling into blatant contradictions. Jacobi, by contrast, denies that even this option remains. Fully consistent rationality does not lead us to Kant's "critical" metaphysics, it lands us instead with Spinoza's metaphysics of immanence.

I have thus far deliberately avoided any mention of what might be styled Jacobi's "charge of atheism" for a particular reason. It was just this statement that occasioned one of the most consequential misunderstandings of his position, namely, that Jacobi's response to Spinozism is to reassert a traditional Christian worldview. Nothing could be further from the truth. Reference to an "intelligent personal cause of the world" (Spin: JWA 1,1, 20; MPW 189)—as a contrasting figure to Spinoza's *causa immanens*—is no doubt integral to the "Antispinoza" position. However, it has nothing to do with any kind of appeal to traditional religion. The opposite is the case, as should be evident from my account of Jacobi's manner of proceeding in the second step above: without exception, the "beliefs" he embraces as incompatible with Spinoza's doctrine are rooted one and all in the *experience of human action*. Everything depends on the foundational role of human praxis and the lifeworld in his thought.

In order to provide additional support for this claim, I turn now in my third and final step to the aforementioned *Supplement VII*, which takes us to the very center of Jacobi's double philosophy. In this text Jacobi once again highlights the paradigmatic stature of Spinozan metaphysics, a thesis he further supports through the inclusion of a brief review of the entire history of philosophy. Spinoza, Jacobi asserts, was able to solve all of the major philosophical problems that had remained unresolved from antiquity down to the time of Descartes. And yet, he continues, Spinoza's true goal, namely "*a naturalistic explanation of the existence of finite and successive things*, was no more likely to be realized by his new way of thinking than by any other" (Spin: JWA 1,1, 251).[11]

At first glance, this assertion might seem blatantly to contradict everything we have been saying so far. Did Jacobi not credit Spinoza's monism with furnishing just such a *naturalistic* explanation of finite existence as a modification of the divine substance and its immanent causality? He did indeed, and Jacobi still stands by that view in *Supplement VII*. Now, however, and much more radically than in his original conversation with Lessing (where the issue comes up only briefly), Jacobi foregrounds a problem that

---

[11] Aber was Spinoza "eigentlich zu Stande bringen wollte: *eine natürliche Erklärung des Daseyns endlicher und successiver Dinge*, konnte durch seine neue Vorstellungsart so wenig, als durch irgend eine andre erreicht werden" (Spin: JWA 1,1, 251).

is fatal even to—or indeed especially to—a perfect system of metaphysics, precisely because of its success in grounding all finite things in a single *causa immanens*. This problem stems from the fact that the finite world, the world of nature as well as the human lifeworld, are *temporally constituted*. The phenomenon of time is the downfall of all metaphysics, including Spinoza's—this is Jacobi's radical thesis.

Jacobi does not argue that Spinoza simply denies the reality of time, dissolving everything into timeless eternity. On his analysis, the problem is actually much more dramatic: Spinoza's ontology is implicitly committed to the paradoxical, self-contradictory notion of an *"eternal time"* (Spin: JWA 1,1, 251), which, however, it also fails to acknowledge, thereby falling into self-deception. Here I can merely gesture at the brilliant description of the problem that Jacobi pairs with his diagnosis.[12] For Spinoza, finite things have both an *eternal essence* and a *temporal existence*. If, however, a consequence of his monism is that nothing can either be or be conceived *outside of God*, then neither can temporal existence fall outside the sphere of divine immanence. And this in turn means that time cannot flow along an open path. We must therefore conceive temporal succession, that is, the phenomenon of finite things *coming to be* and *passing away*, in the same way we conceive the eternal essence of things within the unity of God; and that, effectively, is to remake the phenomenon of temporal change in the image of an *"eternal time,"* where "things come to be without coming to be; […] change without changing; [and] precede or follow one another without being before or after one another" (Spin: JWA 1,1, 256; MPW 372).

With his general diagnosis of the problem, Jacobi not only strikes at the core of Spinoza's *Ethics*; he also gives a trenchant account of how and why the specifically Spinozan aporia of an "eternal time" inevitably arises. Spinoza, he argues, has confused the concept of *cause* with that of *ground—ratio sive causa*, as the *Ethics* literally has it. This identification or confusion of the two is, on the one hand, integral to the way Spinoza conceives his system of metaphysics; on the other hand, though, it is also the source of intractable problems. Jacobi finds that Spinoza has failed to respect the "essential difference" (Spin: JWA 1,1, 256; MPW 372) between the two terms: *Ground* is a logical concept, denoting the relation of *logical* dependence between *ground and consequence*; *cause*, on the other hand, denotes something entirely different, namely the relation of *real* dependence between *cause and effect*, whose *temporal difference* it therefore also entails. As a determination belonging not to logic, but to the temporal constitution of reality, causation is a *"concept of experience"* and one that originates more specifically in the consciousness we have of our *actions*. We experience ourselves as agents, as acting persons who causally produce an act—an effect—in the world (Spin: JWA 1,1, 255ff.; MPW 371ff.).[13]

Based on the aforegoing elucidation, we can make the following five concluding observations on Jacobi's position. First, with a view to *causation*, we see that Jacobi once again insists on the *experiential dimension of action* itself, which he now explicitly links

---

[12] See Chapter 13 in this volume.
[13] It will be interesting on another occasion to compare Jacobi's argument with Michael Della Rocca's and Jim Kreines's interpretation of Spinoza, insofar as they focus on Spinoza's commitment to a version of the PSR.

to the *phenomenon of time*—for "an action that does not happen in time is an absurdity" (Spin: JWA 1,1, 257; MPW 373). Secondly, in terms of the structure of Jacobi's double philosophy, this insistence in turn sheds additional light on the "Antispinoza" position. In seeking to defend our understanding of ourselves and our world, Jacobi champions a conception that is inseparably bound up with the experience of time. In this he clearly anticipates the concerns that will define twentieth-century existentialist thought.

Thirdly, and by contrast, we see that for Jacobi, the position "Spinoza" is defined by the philosopher's confusion of the purely logical relation of ground and consequence with the experience of real causation. This confusion makes it seem as though one were licensed to treat real causation as equivalent to logical grounding and to introduce the latter's structure into the temporal succession of cause and effect, as though it were equivalent to the relation of ground and consequence. Hence the paradox of an "eternal time." Spinoza's confusion of these two categories, moreover, his insertion of a "*sive*" between the concepts *ratio* and *causa*, is not an incidental feature of his thought but is rather constitutive of his entire system. The anchoring of his metaphysics in a notion of a divine *causa immanens* follows directly from his failure to distinguish between ground and cause.

Had Spinoza confined himself to the relation of ground and consequence, he would have produced a work of pure logic devoid of any reference to reality. Conversely, had he focused exclusively on causal determination, he would have been forced to sacrifice his commitment to total explanation and make room for a conception of God as an intentionally acting, personal agent. But nothing could have been further from Spinoza's mind. Putting the same point slightly differently: The only way for the *Ethics* to have the onto-logical import Spinoza ascribes to it, the only way it can be both completely rational in its argumentation and simultaneously engage with reality, is for Spinoza to construct his monism around the conflation of these two categories. Mixing up grounding and causation is the condition of his success—and yet also of his failure, for it prevents him from gaining conceptual purchase on the genuine reality of the temporal world. At the center of the *causa immanens* lies confusion: The divine substance is the ground from which everything follows (*sequi*); at the same time, God also figures as a cause and action is ascribed to him (*agere*). In drawing his conclusions, Jacobi therefore characterizes Spinoza's God as a "blindly actuose being" [ein blind actuoses Wesen] (Spin: JWA 1,1, 265). As I mentioned, I find this to be an exceptionally astute analysis of the *Ethics*,[14] and it is worth noting that if Fichte, Schelling, and Hegel had paid closer attention to the details of Jacobi's *Supplement VII* they might have been somewhat less assured of their ability to create an alternative, subject-centered system that could replace Spinoza's system of substance monism while also meeting the objections Jacobi articulates there.

This brings me to my fourth observation: I have just said of Jacobi's double philosophy that, on its "Antispinoza" side, his concern is to defend experience of action in its temporal dimension. This is certainly true, but it is nonetheless necessary

---

[14] In this connection we should note Jacobi's structurally exact and detailed discussion of Giordano Bruno, to whom he dedicates Supplement I of the second edition of the *Spinoza Letters*. See Stephan Otto, "Spinoza Ante Spinozam? Jacobis Lektüre des Giordano Bruno im Kontext einer Begründung von Metaphysik," in *Friedrich Heinrich Jacobi*, ed. Walter Jaeschke and Birgit Sandkaulen (Hamburg: Meiner, 2004), 107–25.

to revisit the specifics of this defense. Upon considering the matter more closely, we see that Spinoza would *never have had occasion* to confuse the concepts of ground and cause in the first place, had he himself not implicitly *presupposed*—in the guise of causation—the experiential fact of human action (which he then recasts in an explicitly logical form). Indeed, precisely this insight is what lends Jacobi's interpretation its tremendous significance. His double philosophy of "Spinoza and Antispinoza" offers far more than a simple juxtaposition of two opposing positions. Rather, it discloses the unacknowledged role of human action at the foundations of the "Spinoza" side itself, revealing the process of rationalization to which it has been subjected in the interest of systematicity. The disclosing of existence, which, as we have heard, Jacobi praises as the highest a seeker of truth may hope to accomplish, is thus the same goal he sets for his own examination of the "Spinoza" position.

My fifth and final observation concerns Jacobi's conviction, developed in detail in *Supplement VII*, that a *metaphysical dimension* inheres in our experience of ourselves as acting. To act and thus to be a free cause is to *initiate* a process of change within the world. As finite beings, we are no doubt subject to the conditions of nature; and yet, in acting freely we also come to the awareness of something *unconditioned*, something whose ground lies beyond the conditions of finitude and whose inexplicable facticity points human existence toward something absolutely unconditional, *the beginning made by an absolute cause*. Jacobi is thus drawing on the consciousness of agential freedom—and by no means traditional religion—in disclosing one of the essential elements of the "Antispinoza" position, the relation to God as the "intelligent personal cause of the world." But that is not all that remains to be said, lest we forget the characteristic dynamic of double philosophy itself. To frame it as a question: What led Spinoza to believe that he could provide a universally valid explanation of how the world hangs together in its totality by grounding it in a divine substance he explicitly conceived as *absolute*? As to Jacobi's answer, there can be no doubt. Whenever and however metaphysical systems aspire to apprehend the dimension of the absolute, their efforts ultimately rely on the consciousness of the unconditioned that humans gain through their experience of agency.

3

Groundless Belief: A Philosophical Provocation

In 1780, one year before the initial appearance of Kant's *Critique of Pure Reason*, the tiny German town of Wolfenbüttel played host to one of the most memorable and momentous philosophical conversations in history. The interlocutors are Lessing and Jacobi, and the topic of conversation is the philosophy of Spinoza. None of these three is a professor of philosophy, and this has significant implications for the discussion. Primarily scholastic questions are not of interest here, and the circumstances of the conversation bear witness to the casual elegance of eighteenth-century customs. According to Jacobi's notes, the most important exchanges take place during the morning rituals of dressing and grooming. One might wonder whether it is really possible to concentrate on a serious subject in such circumstances, but clearly, the answer is yes. The tone ranges from lighthearted to ironic, and the participants' mutual enjoyment of such an uninhibited *tour d'esprit* crackles between the lines of Jacobi's report. The subject matter, however, is anything but trivial.

It is in fact so significant that it shortly thereafter leads to an extended dispute between Jacobi and Moses Mendelssohn. Mendelssohn responds in shocked disbelief when he hears what his recently deceased friend Lessing has allegedly said and what Jacobi claims to have said in response. And when Jacobi then publishes the Wolfenbüttel conversation together with documents related to their dispute in 1785, German intellectual life is shaken to its very foundation. Goethe, whose poem *Prometheus* also played a role in the controversy, remembers the event years later in his autobiography *Poetry and Truth* (1811–33) as a veritable "explosion"[1]; along the same lines, Hegel speaks in his *Lectures on the History of Philosophy* of a "thunderbolt from the blue" that electrified the intellectual landscape of an entire era.[2] From this point on, nothing is the same as before. It is not only Kant's critique of reason but rather the combination of Kant's writings *and* Jacobi's publication, *Concerning the Doctrine of Spinoza in Letters to Herr Moses Mendelssohn* (republished in 1789 in a substantially expanded edition), that inaugurates a new era in the history of philosophy. What could Lessing and Jacobi possibly have wanted to discuss that was capable of causing such a sensation?

---

[1] Johann W. Goethe, *From my Life: Poetry and Truth*, Parts One to Three, trans. Robert R. Heitner (New York: Suhrkamp Publishers, 1987), 469.

[2] Hegel, *Vorlesungen über die Geschichte der Philosophie*, TWA 20, 316f.; G. W. F. Hegel, *Lectures on the History of Philosophy*, trans. Elisabeth S. Haldane and Frances H. Simson, vol. 3 (Lincoln: University of Nebraska Press, 1995), 412. The "thunderbolt" was all the more powerful for the fact that Jacobi also drew Kant's Critical Philosophy into the discussion. At various points in this volume I address Jacobi's relation to Kant in more detail.

The *Handbuch Deutscher Idealismus* informs us of the facts of the case in an entry of a little more than a page in length. Jacobi, we learn, was "surprised" by "Lessing's declaration of enthusiasm for the philosophy of Spinoza." Jacobi himself

> was an opponent of all of the existing rationalist systems of philosophy and especially of the system of Spinoza. To be sure, he considered Spinoza's philosophy as offering the most consistent example of a rationalist metaphysics, but precisely this consistency meant that it led directly and inevitably to fatalism and atheism, from which belief in divine revelation offered the only possible refuge.[3]

Whether intended by the author or not, the impression conveyed by this description is that of an anecdote from the distant past—hardly a matter capable of moving us today. After all, the "rationalist systems" of the seventeenth and eighteenth centuries hold little interest for us; Kant has thoroughly convinced us of their "dogmatism." Nor do we find the question of divine revelation to be an urgent matter in our own lives, and thus we are even less concerned with the fact that Jacobi, according to the *Handbuch*, found it necessary to take "refuge" in this Christian belief. As depicted here, the entire constellation of concerns strikes one as so foreign that it hardly seems worth the trouble to investigate why this exchange gave rise to such a scandal, shaking the world with the force of an "explosion" or a "thunderbolt from the blue." From this perspective, only the briefest overview is required before one can turn to more important questions and problems. But is this the proper perspective on the matter?

As my question suggests, I do not think so. Indeed, I would argue that the synopsis I have just cited is not only insufficient but also misleading. By creating the impression that we are dealing with an episode from the days of long ago, the entry obscures the fact that current debates regarding the relation between belief and knowledge are actually revisiting a set of problems that was already exercising the minds of leading philosophers at the beginning of the modern era. Even more importantly, by providing information that is factually incorrect as well as perpetuating one of the stereotypical misrepresentations of Jacobi's position, it also hinders any substantive illumination of the complex relation between belief and knowledge, which—and precisely this is the crux of the debate between Jacobi and Mendelssohn—certainly cannot be reduced to a simple opposition between "rationalism" and "belief in divine revelation."

Against this backdrop, my goal in this chapter will be to offer an alternate perspective on the matter. As already intimated, I will be guided in this effort by two primary assumptions. From a genealogical point of view, I believe that we are best served by retracing what has since become a diverse set of inquiries back to the original nexus of problems as it took on paradigmatic form around 1800. And from a systematic point of view, I combine this genealogical approach with a typological clarification of the relation between belief and knowledge, one that culminates in a new interpretation of this relation. This interpretation poses a challenge to the conventional religious

---

[3] Detlev Pätzold, "Die Vernunft und das Absolute," in *Handbuch Deutscher Idealismus*, ed. Hans J. Sandkühler (Stuttgart/Weimar: Metzler, 2005), 25f.

associations of the former term, but precisely in doing so, it also opens a path for the integration of religious concerns. In order to do justice to the complexity of the material, I will proceed in three steps. In each, I will discuss the various interpretive options before concluding with the version that I not only find to be the only adequate one but also the one that is the most interesting philosophically.

Step One: Belief in Divine Revelation

For the purposes of this first step, but only here, I assume for the sake of argument that at least one piece of information from the *Handbuch* is correct: the assertion that Jacobi responds to Spinoza's metaphysics with the conviction that "belief in divine revelation offered the only possible refuge." We should note at the outset that this assessment can be traced back to Mendelssohn's own appraisal. After reading the notes from the Wolfenbüttel discussion, he had interpreted Jacobi's position as a "noble retreat under the banner of faith" and thereby simultaneously relegated him to the status of a "Christian philosopher" (Spin: JWA 1,1, 179; MPW 355). This interpretation subsequently made its way into countless depictions, without, however, the inclusion of any specific reference to the actual source. Whatever ones general position on this reading, it seems to find support in one (and only one, it should be noted) of the revelations made by Jacobi in his conversation with Lessing: "I believe there is an intelligent personal cause of the world" (Spin: JWA 1,1, 20; MPW 189).[4]

A careful reader should immediately be struck by the fact that Jacobi does not say "I believe *in* a (or the) personal God, who created the world," but neither does he say "I believe *that* the world has a cause." A reformulated version would have to read roughly as follows: "The reality of a creative cause of the world reveals itself in the consummation of my thought and action." We will return later to these crucial distinctions. Leaving them aside for the moment, however, and taking the statement at face value, one would be hard-pressed to find anything in it that could be considered scandalous, whether in our current circumstances or those of the late eighteenth century. Why shouldn't one believe that the world has a creative origin? After all, Mendelssohn himself shares this belief, basing it, of course, not on the Christian but on the Jewish tradition. The potential for such a statement to engender conflict only becomes clear when we consider its corollaries. Most significant in this regard is, first, the fact that what is said to be *believed* in this context cannot simultaneously be *known*, and secondly, that this latter claim is not arbitrarily made but rather follows with absolute necessity from Spinoza's metaphysics.

Without wanting to exaggerate, it is important to underscore the tremendous shock Mendelssohn experiences when Jacobi confronts him with this twofold assertion. At the height of the eighteenth-century German Enlightenment, Jacobi has done nothing less than demonstrate the irreversible demise of the era of philosophical rationalism. At the heart of this rationalism was the conviction that reason is capable of both

---

[4] "Ich glaube eine verständige persönliche Ursache der Welt." (JWA 1,1, 20)

rationally grounding and of demonstrating, through proofs of God's existence, the essential contents of traditional religion. Operating under the assumption that belief has a religious connotation, the rationalist reading of the relationship between belief and knowledge (applicable to Descartes as well as to Leibniz) argues for a continuity between these two terms rather than an opposition, insofar as they pertain to the same contents and are equally certain of the validity of those contents.

It is precisely in relation to this view that the core of Jacobi's position comes into sharper relief. To start with, the question of whether or not he takes refuge in "belief in divine revelation" is entirely irrelevant in this context. Rather, the crucial point to be made here is that Jacobi, despite what the *Handbook* suggests, definitely does not begin by first classifying Spinoza under the general rubric of rationalism in order to then express a critical view of his *particular* version of it. On the contrary: Jacobi's opponent in this context is not Spinoza but Mendelssohn, who figures here as a prominent representative of a popular-philosophical Enlightenment incapable of seeing past its own self-satisfied adulation of reason. Such complacency has led this group to bury Spinoza like "a dead dog" (Spin: JWA 1,1, 27; MPW 193), a thinker who, far from being merely the "most consistent" rationalist philosopher, created something unprecedented: an absolutely "pure," which is to say thoroughly consistent metaphysical system (Spin: JWA 1,1, 128; MPW 236). In demonstrating what happens when we radically and uncompromisingly rely on the capacity of reason alone, accepting any and all consequences that this reliance entails, Spinoza definitively severed the bond between the substance of traditional religious belief and that of knowledge.

"There is no other philosophy than the philosophy of Spinoza" (Spin: JWA 1,1, 18; MPW 187). Although he certainly shares the assessment of Spinoza's philosophy contained in Lessing's statement, Jacobi is more than a mere admirer. As he rightly claims, he has not only undertaken an exhaustive study of the *Ethics* but also offers the first adequate reconstruction of its essential arguments, thereby thrusting it into the foreground of philosophical interest.[5] Significantly, his analysis does not focus attention on the geometric method. The unity and coherence of Spinozan system are not to be found in the logical unfolding of its propositions but rather in its overall "spirit," which emerges from Spinoza's consistent application of "the ancient: *a nihilo nihil fit*" (Spin: JWA 1,1, 18; MPW 187). The necessary consequence of this approach is a metaphysics of immanence that denies any and all attribution of origins to final causes, and that explains the world and the subjects acting within it as an internal and also necessary modification of the divine *causa immanens* and its energetic potential.

Against this backdrop, we can see that Jacobi's characterization of Spinoza's conclusions as atheistic and fatalistic requires some additional clarification. As far as the intellectual brilliance of Spinoza's thought is concerned, Jacobi's attributions are simply analytical *observations* that find support in Spinoza's own assertions. Especially the notes to the *Ethics* imply the destruction of all traditional conceptions—philosophical as well as

---

[5] Comparing Jacobi's interpretation to earlier discussions of Spinoza (Bayle, Budde, Wolff), Ulrich J. Schneider argues that Jacobi's account is "probably the first critical-rational reconstruction of a philosophy in the history of European thought" (Ulrich J. Schneider, *Die Vergangenheit des Geistes. Eine Archäologie der Philosophiegeschichte* (Frankfurt a.M.: Suhrkamp, 1990), 177f.).

religious—of God, the world, and humanity, as a consequence of the definitive rejection of a *causa finalis* together with the concomitant possibility of free will. Jacobi's *critical assessment* is another matter entirely, with regard to which he explicitly distinguishes the possibility of contradiction [*Widerspruch*] from the necessarily futile attempt at a logical refutation [*Widerlegung*] (Spin: JWA 1,1, 290). In other words, Jacobi's assessment is made possible as a result of a decision, one driven not by theoretical concerns but by the practical question of how to live.

What sort of "ethics" does Spinoza's *Ethics* propound? What implications does his system have for our lives? For Lessing as well, these are the decisive issues. It is his own self-image or, even better, his general attitude toward life that he finds reflected in Spinoza, something which comes through in the intriguing claim that, as "an honest Lutheran" he does not "crave a free will" (Spin: JWA 1,1, 28, 21; MPW 194, 189). The opposite is true for Jacobi: Spinoza does not resonate in Jacobi's case with any sort of "Lutheran" disposition. On the contrary, his philosophy demands that one view the very conviction which Jacobi considers to be most essential as a fantastic illusion: the conviction that we are the free and accountable originators of our actions and that, in Jacobi's words "*I do what I think*, and not, *that I should think what I do*" (Spin: JWA 1,1, 28; MPW 193).

Hardly an anecdote from the distant past, then. The only thing that has receded into the past is Mendelssohn's version of Wolffian rationalism, in large part as a result of Jacobi's analysis. Spinoza's *Ethics,* on the other hand, now seen as *the* foundational text of modernity, encompassing its entire range of theoretical and practical problems, acquires a relevance that has never been called into question since. Certainly all of the post-Kantian philosophers hold this view. They fully adopted Jacobi's assessment as their own—one need only think of Hegel's claim: "But the fact is that Spinoza is made a testing-point in modern philosophy, so that it may really be said: You are either a Spinozist or not a philosopher at all."[6] In the process they also immediately incorporated the problem that Jacobi had made visible into their own deliberations, asking whether we must choose between a rigorously consistent system of reason and our existential expectations with regard to freedom. And in the versions of this question posed by later thinkers one can see the ongoing impact of this fascination with Spinoza, which has animated philosophers ranging from Nietzsche to Deleuze and also finds expression in contemporary debates about naturalism.[7] Jacobi's assessment also helps us to understand why Spinoza has had such a lasting influence on modern philosophy even after the appearance of Kant's critique of reason. After all, Kant's critique of rationalist "dogmatism" was not undertaken with this metaphysics of immanence in mind. In formulating his theory of ideas and his doctrine of the moral postulates, he was in fact himself trying once again to "rescue" the traditional worldview, albeit in the form of a reason that no longer *knows* its metaphysical concepts on the basis of demonstrative

---

[6] TWA 20, 163f.; Hegel, *Lectures on the History of Philosophy*, vol. 3, 283.
[7] Particularly interesting in this context is the appeal to Spinoza in António R. Damásio, *Looking for Spinoza. Joy, Sorrow, and the Feeling Brain* (London: William Heinemann, 2003). See Birgit Sandkaulen, "Selbst und Selbsterhaltung. Spinoza im Blick der Neurowissenschaft," *Studia Spinozana* 15 (2006a): 231–44.

evidence but rather *believes* them on moral grounds. In contrast to rationalism, then, belief and knowledge diverge in Kant, with the crucial condition that belief loses its association with religion and becomes part of reason itself.

Are we really to believe that Jacobi's alternative to this conception was the Christian doctrine of divine revelation? Insofar as he is clearly not advocating for a Kantian rational faith, this interpretation might still seem plausible. The question, however, is what such a position could actually mean in the context of the discussion just described. It should first of all be borne in mind that when he objects to Spinoza, the status of the divine is hardly Jacobi's only interest. He is no less concerned with the constitution of finite beings and their self-understanding as free agents, which makes clear at the very least that rehabilitating religious tradition as such is not his primary motivation. Secondly, and on a related note, we should recognize that Jacobi's declaration of his belief that there is an "intelligent personal cause of the world," which he offers as the alternative to Spinoza's *causa immanens*, can be understood as the common heritage of the Jewish and Christian traditions. The actual "essentials" of the Christian religion—Trinity and Incarnation—play no role here. And it is thus all the more important to remember, thirdly, that the evaluation of these statements as those of a "Christian philosopher" was originally introduced into the discussion by Mendelssohn. The precise character of his assertion is of crucial importance here. Rather than referring to specific statements made by Jacobi whose *contents* are identifiably Christian, Mendelssohn focuses exclusively on the *epistemic status* of Jacobi's remarks. For it is here that Mendelssohn believes the difference between the two religions finds expression. The Christian "duty of suppressing doubt through faith" is completely absent from the Jewish religion, which "knows no duty to resolve doubts of this kind otherwise than through reason; it commands no faith in eternal truths" (Spin: JWA 1,1, 179f.; MPW 355).

It would no doubt be interesting to investigate further the background to this assertion, that is to say why Mendelssohn attributes to Judaism a capacity for rationalism that stands in contrast to that of Christianity. Presumably such an investigation has already been undertaken by scholars in the philosophy of religion. For our current purposes, however, the key question is how Jacobi responds to this epistemic reproach, namely, with an epistemic argument of his own. Two aspects of this argument are of crucial importance. On the one hand, it should be noted that Jacobi draws an explicit distinction between two uses of the category of belief—between the concept of belief as he intends it to be understood and the "other belief" of Christianity (Spin: JWA 1,1, 116; MPW 231). On the other hand, we should also note that, without neutralizing this distinction, he also points to a peculiarity of belief that is common to both perspectives and that effectively calls into question the relation of doubt, belief, and knowledge as depicted by Mendelssohn. Whether the doubt is "defeated" by belief or eliminated "by reason" is thus not the critical issue, because belief is not a *theoretical* attitude at all, neither in the sense that it provides a propositional response to doubt nor in the sense that it could itself be justified propositionally in turn. My earlier reformulation alluded to precisely this point. According to Jacobi's understanding, belief is a *practice* that precedes all reasoning. On the one hand, the Christian religion encourages us to actualize this practice by pursuing a certain way of life, while, on the other hand, it remains independent of any specific religious conceptions in the sense that we are always already "born" into it. In this sense, the belief that Jacobi wants to defend denotes a pre-reflective "immediate certainty," the groundless evidence for which is also presupposed by reason itself in its own search for grounds, at least as long as reason wants to avoid the abyss into which its striving after certainty threatens to lead it:

> My dear Mendelssohn, we are all born in belief, and in belief we must remain, just as we are all born in society, and must remain in society: *Totum parte prius esse necesse est.*—How can we strive for certainty unless we are already acquainted with certainty in advance, and how can we be acquainted with it except through something that we already discern with certainty? This leads to the concept of an immediate certainty, which not only needs no proof, but excludes all proofs absolutely, and is simply and solely *the representation itself agreeing with the thing being represented.* Conviction by proofs is certainty at second hand. Proofs are only indications of similarity to a thing of which we are certain. The conviction that they generate originates in comparison, and can never be quite sure and perfect. But if every *assent to truth* not derived from rational grounds is belief, the conviction based on rational grounds must itself derive from belief, and must receive its force from belief alone. (Spin: JWA 1,1, 115f.; MPW 230)[8]

Truth on the basis of groundless belief: as can still be recognized in the often-invoked phrase "justified true belief," falsely attributed to Plato,[9] any such belief will appear deficient in a rationalist context, requiring justification through reason in order to transform it into legitimate knowledge. Jacobi turns this hierarchy on its head. Here knowledge is justified by the immediate certainty of belief, which is itself in no need of justification but is rather revealed for what it is by the very absence of any rational

---

[8] Translation amended according to the translation of William Hamilton, "On the Philosophy of Common Sense," in Thomas Reid, *The Works of Thomas Reid*, ed. Sir William Hamilton, vol. 2, 6th ed. (Edinburgh: Maclachlan and Stewart, 1863), 793. It is highly interesting that Hamilton chooses "belief" rather than "faith" to translate Jacobi's concept of "Glaube," all the more given that the context is a treatise on the philosophy of common sense. This provides additional support for the decision to translate "Glaube" uniformly as "belief" here and in all further chapters of this study. "Lieber Mendelssohn, wir alle werden im Glauben gebohren, und müssen im Glauben bleiben, wie wir alle in Gesellschaft gebohren werden, und in Gesellschaft bleiben müssen: *Totum parte prius esse necesse est.*—Wie können wir nach Gewißheit streben, wenn uns Gewißheit nicht zum voraus schon bekannt ist; und wie kann sie uns bekannt seyn, anders als durch etwas das wir mit Gewißheit schon erkennen? Dieses führt zu dem Begriffe einer unmittelbaren Gewißheit, welche nicht allein keiner Gründe bedarf, sondern schlechterdings alle Gründe ausschließt, und einzig und allein *die mit dem vorgestellten Dinge übereinstimmende Vorstellung selbst ist.* Die Ueberzeugung aus Gründen ist eine Gewißheit aus der zweyten Hand. Gründe sind nur Merkmale der Aehnlichkeit mit einem Dinge, dessen wir gewiß sind. Die Ueberzeugung, welche sie hervorbringen, entspringt aus Vergleichung, und kann nie recht sicher und vollkommen seyn. Wenn nun jedes *für Wahr halten*, welches nicht aus Vernunftgründen entspringt, Glaube ist, so muß die Ueberzeugung aus Vernunftgründen selbst aus dem Glauben kommen, und ihre Kraft von ihm allein empfangen." (Spin: JWA 1,1, 115f.)
[9] With reference to the debate sparked by Edmund Gettier, see: Peter Ptassek, Birgit Sandkaulen, Jochen Wagner, and Georg Zenkert, *Macht und Meinung. Die rhetorische Konstitution der politischen Welt* (Göttingen: Vandenhoeck & Ruprecht, 1992), 12ff.

foundation. In its structure, this point is reminiscent of an argument already advanced by Aristotle, according to which every demonstration must always be based on something that is itself not demonstrable. Unlike Aristotle, however, Jacobi is not thinking here of something like an unprovable axiom. Rather, in keeping with his sense of belief as a form of living practice, he has in mind the immediate certainty of being, the original disclosedness or "presentation" [Darstellung] of reality, and in this we can at the same time see the central difference between his position and Kant's rational faith.[10]

One can still insist on calling this reality-disclosing and reality-confirming belief a belief in "divine revelation." In this case, however, the label can refer to no more than the fact that Jacobi here very consciously invokes a realm that eludes rational explanation, whether it is a question of physical reality or the metaphysical reality that encompasses the conviction of human free will. Indeed, it is this realm that provides an existential foundation for all rationality in the first place and is thus also not to be understood as the basis for any sort of axiomatic derivation.[11] If this position has been dismissed—in the first but by no means only case by the representatives of the Berlin Enlightenment—as not only fideistic but as the epitome of counter-enlightenment irrationality,[12] such dismissals serve only to reveal the explosive power of investigations

---

[10] Noteworthy in this context is the curious fact that Jacobi, already in his conversation with Lessing and then later in the previously cited reply to Mendelssohn, had based his insistence on immediate certainty on none other than Spinoza himself. See E II, prop. 43, scholium: possession of a true idea entails absolute certainty of that idea. Otherwise, as Spinoza persuasively argues, our ideas would resemble mute portraits on the wall rather than acts of intellectual insight. It is thus in this connection that Spinoza utters his famous assertion: "veritas norma sui et falsi est." Jacobi's recourse to this remark has repeatedly led to questions about the consistency of his position, because it also appears to require full acceptance of Spinoza's ontological presuppositions. This includes acceptance of the parallelism of mind and body, which would, however, invalidate precisely that belief in the reality of the *causa finalis* which constitutes the centerpiece of Jacobi's objection to Spinoza (cf. Hermann Timm, "Die Bedeutung der Spinozabriefe Jacobis für die Entwicklung der idealistischen Religionsphilosophie," in *Friedrich Heinrich Jacobi. Philosoph und Literat der Goethezeit*, ed. Klaus Hammacher (Frankfurt a.M.: Vittorio Klostermann, 1971), 35–8 and Brady Bowman, "Notiones Communes und Common Sense." On the Spinozan backdrop to Jacobi's reception of the philosophy of Thomas Reid, see *Friedrich Heinrich Jacobi*, ed. Walter Jaeschke and Birgit Sandkaulen (Hamburg: Meiner, 2004), 159–78). Such an assumption is by no means necessary, however. First of all, in presenting the evidential specificity of convictions, Jacobi has recourse to a state of affairs that Spinoza himself explicitly described as not requiring proof and that he highlighted instead as a generally familiar phenomenon. Indeed, in order to ensure that the self-referentiality of the spirit possessed a dignity of its own, Spinoza had no choice but to describe the matter in this way. Secondly, this point should be distinguished from Spinoza's simultaneous interest in restricting the scope of the phenomenon of immediate certainty, which is to say in grounding it ontologically in such a way as to cast any certainty of the *causa finalis* as nothing but a form of human prejudice. From the start, Jacobi takes issue with precisely this operation. Against the ideal of absolute rigor in the pursuit of a consistent explanation of lifeworldly phenomena, he proposes the no less consistent assumption of a "source of thought and action that remains completely inexplicable to me" (JWA 1,1, 28; MPW 193).

[11] Also relevant in this context is Jacobi's assertion: "We can only demonstrate similarities. Every proof presupposes something already proven, the principle of which is revelation. Belief is the element of all human cognition and activity." „Wir können nur Aehnlichkeiten demonstriren; und jeder Erweis setzt etwas schon Erwiesenes zum voraus, wovon das Prinzipium Offenbarung ist. Das Element aller menschlichen Erkenntniß und Würksamkeit, ist Glaube." (Spin: JWA 1,1, 124f.; MPW 234)

[12] Especially, for example, in the work of Isaiah Berlin, *Against the Current: Essays in the History of Ideas* (London: Hogarth Press, 1979) and Frederick C. Beiser, *The Fate of Reason. German Philosophy from Kant to Fichte* (London: Harvard University Press, 1987).

into the relationship between belief and knowledge. Presuppositions regarding the meaning of the term "belief" are just as unlikely to be productive in this context as unreflected preconceptions regarding what counts as knowledge.[13]

Second Step: The Philosophy of Reflection

As the initial step has shown, religion tends to spring to mind whenever the term "belief" is mentioned. This tendency is worth noting, but the situation is really no different today than it was in Mendelssohn's time. A case in point is the much admired speech delivered by Habermas upon receiving the peace prize of the German Book Trade in 2001.[14] It is notable with regard to the discussion at the time that all of the participants drew freely from the resources of traditional religion, using them to reinforce or even to help legitimate whatever emancipatory causes they sought to advance. In a sense, the same strategy can be attributed to Jacobi. When provoked by Mendelssohn's reproach, he does indeed distinguish between two dimensions of belief, but his explication of Christian belief places it at least within the same general vicinity as his own version. This line of argument, however, is not without consequences for religion itself. For the sake of our understanding of ourselves and our world, Jacobi wants to draw our attention to the primordially practical and, as such, non-propositional disclosedness of reality, which precludes any attempt at explication and thus also any objectification. From this perspective, however, religion is also relieved, as it were, of the positivity of its tradition. In its essence, religion is transformed into a disposition rather than a collection of propositions, which, in Mendelssohn's view, are accepted only at the insistence of a religious authority seeking protection from demands for rational examination and justification.

In his famous critique in *Faith and Knowledge* (1802), Hegel works up a second version of Jacobi's ostensible position. Despite the prominence this version acquires in the course of Hegelian philosophy, it has curiously never made its way into those handbooks that provide information on Jacobi. Perhaps the matter is just too complicated. After all, how is it possible that the same person who allegedly saved himself from the threat of Spinoza's metaphysics by recklessly abandoning reason in favor of divine revelation—an interpretation that remains prevalent even today—simultaneously appears in the company of Kant and Fichte as a major representative of the philosophy of reflection? It is clearly not possible, which is why Hegel initially refrains from even engaging with Mendelssohn's assessment.

---

[13] See also Gottfried Gabriel, "Von der Vorstellung zur Darstellung. Realismus in Jacobis 'David Hume,'" in *Friedrich Heinrich Jacobi*, ed. Walter Jaeschke and Birgit Sandkaulen (Hamburg: Meiner, 2004), 145–58, who counters such ingrained reflexes by drawing attention to similar figures of thought in Jacobi and Wittgenstein.

[14] Jürgen Habermas, "Faith and Knowledge," in *The Future of Human Nature*, trans. Hella Beister and Max Pensky (Cambridge: Polity Press, 2003), 101–15. The same can be said of Derrida's contribution (Jacques Derrida, "Faith and Knowledge," in *Religion*, ed. Jacques Derrida and Samuel Weber, trans. Samuel Weber (Stanford, CA: Stanford University Press, 1998), 1–87), notwithstanding the fact that neither Habermas nor Derrida are eager to make the case for religious tradition.

His diagnosis instead presupposes that the long-standing conflict between belief and knowledge has resolved itself. Modernity has absorbed the traditional contents of positive religion, with the result that the previously external relation between knowledge and belief has become a matter internal to philosophy itself. It is typical for Hegel that in making this diagnosis, he relegates Spinoza entirely to the background, something that occurs again and again in his thought all the way up through the programmatic introduction to the *Science of Logic*. Spinoza's "secularization" of the transcendent Creator God into a *causa immanens* forms not a moment *within* but rather the very *framework of* the modernity that Hegel seeks to lead to the true concept of itself.

As far as the figure of belief is concerned, however, Hegel sees clearly and correctly that it no longer pertains to an outside authority, a source inherently external to reason, but rather takes on meaning entirely within philosophy as a contrast to knowledge. If one then begins to wonder, however, just who or what was responsible for this split between belief and knowledge in the first place, then, according to Hegel, the only answer is that it was none other than reflection itself. That which is inaccessible to reflection has been posited as inaccessible by reflection, and for this reason everything that it assigns to belief remains merely a subjective projection without any real content. The problem is no longer the irrational blindness of belief, as it was for Mendelssohn, but rather its formalistic emptiness.

Hegel clearly crafts his critique of Jacobi with the help of Jacobi's own tools, and it is just as clear that the organization of his text as a whole has benefitted from the objections previously leveled by Jacobi against Kant and Fichte. To pursue this matter here, however, would take us too far afield.[15] What interests me in the current context is the fact that Hegel's criticisms only appear convincing if we completely ignore the practical foundations of Jacobi's approach. It is hard to imagine that Hegel was unaware of this. He did, after all, follow in Jacobi's footsteps in his early writings, where he attempts to cast belief as an attitude in which the reality of practical life announces itself, and which cannot be re-presented in the form of propositional knowledge.[16]

In his effort to grasp the specific "spirit of Christianity," however, Hegel seems to have fused the two facets of belief that Jacobi seeks to differentiate (despite their shared non-propositional status) into a single concept of religion. It would be worth examining more closely whether it isn't this very conflation and "Christianization," so to speak, of Jacobi's concepts that leads the Frankfurt Hegel to diagnose an aporetic loss of reality as the "fate" of Christianity, which he then polemically projects back onto Jacobi himself in the 1802 text, albeit now in the form of de-Christianized philosophy of reflection. Together with his commitment to a philosophical system that he had in the meantime adopted from Fichte and Schelling and which does indeed presume that the tension between belief and knowledge has been overcome, this could explain why his critical presentation of Jacobi goes so oddly awry. It is significant that nothing

---

[15] See Birgit Sandkaulen, "Das Nichtige in seiner ganzen Länge und Breite. Hegels Kritik der Reflexionsphilosophie," *Hegel-Jahrbuch* 2004 (2004): 165–73.

[16] See especially Text 42 "Glauben ist die Art ..." in GW 2, 10–13.

about this changes in his later works. Starting with *Phenomenology of Spirit,* Hegel does depart from his practice in *Faith and Knowledge* and begin to refer explicitly to the figure of "immediate certainty." His presentation of this figure, however, runs directly against the grain of Jacobi's intentions. Rather than the reality-disclosing and reality-confirming ground of our practical life activity, it appears as merely the theoretical attitude of a consciousness that makes a statement *about* something but lacks the categorical resources to say concretely what it means. Abstract inwardness/empty longing and the failure of reference/a lack of concrete actuality thus form two sides of the same problem in the "metaphysics of subjectivity" to which Hegel stylizes Jacobi's position, before proceeding to use this stylized version as a foil for his own conception of a "mediated immediacy."[17]

Third Step: The Metaphysics of Action

What, then, is the true character of the belief in which Jacobi sought "refuge" from Spinoza?[18] Hegel's contemporary interpretation, which gains additional plausibility when one considers his diagnostic interest in the problems of modernity as well as his theological training, provides support for my assertion that it cannot be the Christian belief in divine revelation. Lest I be misunderstood, let me make clear that there is nothing at all contradictory in principle in declaring one's adherence to a religion, nor in positing a relation between *fides* and *ratio* that keeps the autonomy of reason within certain limits. Such declarations have a long and venerable tradition. These positions, however, presuppose that traditional religion continues to exercise a binding force, and this force, as Hegel rightly states, has been dramatically weakened in the wake of the Enlightenment. This certainly does not prevent one from insisting on this binding force even under these new conditions. One can, for example, avoid any real engagement with the challenges posed by Enlightenment thought, or one can simply decide, these challenges notwithstanding, to attribute a *sui generis* validity to religion. Hamann is representative for the first option, and the late Friedrich Schlegel or Kierkegaard for the second. The fact that Jacobi's position does not line up with either of these options becomes apparent precisely to the extent that all three of these thinkers, although they acknowledge Jacobi's contribution, nonetheless maintain a certain critical reserve. Hamann cannot understand why Jacobi so doggedly insists on immersing himself in his Spinoza studies; Schlegel laments the absence of the "positive revelation" of Christianity[19]; and Kierkegaard complains that Jacobi only performed a "subjectivizing

---

[17] This approach also shapes the structure of the two texts that Hegel devoted to a renewed confrontation with Jacobi in the wake of *The Science of Logic*. The difference between the friendly tones of the Heidelberg review of Jacobi's works and the largely polemical style that characterizes the "Third position of thought towards objectivity" in the "Preliminary conception" of the *Encyclopedia of the Philosophical Sciences* is only a superficial one. See Chapter 14 in this volume.
[18] On the following, see also Chapter 4 in this volume.
[19] Friedrich Schlegel, "Über F.H. Jacobi: Von den göttlichen Dingen und ihrer Offenbarung," in *Kritische Schriften und Fragmente*, ed. Ernst Behler and Hans Eichner, vol. 3 (Paderborn: Schöningh, 1988), 160.

act" with regard to Spinoza but did not effectuate the "transition from the eternal to the historical" content of religion.[20] Hegel's own critique of reflection echoes in the evaluation of Kierkegaard, which is all the more striking given that Kierkegaard sought with his *Fear and Trembling*—the "paradox" of Christianity—to establish his distance from Hegel.[21] And thus, inasmuch invocations of a "belief in divine revelation" do not in fact advance our understanding in this context, it would seem that the diagnosis from the perspective of the philosophy of reflection offers the more convincing version of Jacobi's standpoint. At least it would if Jacobi had derived the Other of reflection out of reflection itself by way of a theoretical procedure.

What is really going on here can probably best be described as a *paradigm shift*. Hereafter philosophy and religion can no longer be understood simply as matters that *concern* our lives, but rather, according to Jacobi's basic impulse they must be understood as they emerge *out of* life itself. "The principle of all cognition," as he states at a central point in the programmatic *Supplement VII* of his *Spinoza Letters*, "is living being; living being proceeds from itself, it is progressive and productive" (Spin: JWA 1,1, 248; MPW 370). What does it mean to make the productivity of living being into a "principle," into the absolute basis of things? It is worth pointing out in this context that the philosophical tradition has not exactly prepared us to make sense of such a position or of the challenge it entails. For this reason, it will be helpful at the beginning of this third step to explain briefly how Jacobi's approach runs counter to no fewer than three different ways of thinking.

First, by referring to the fundamental importance of our practical life activity, he distances himself from a model that restricts itself to an internal analysis of cognition. This distinction remains valid even if we choose not to limit cognition to forms of discursivity but rather, following the current custom, declare the capacity for intuitive insight to be the foundation of discourse. For despite some structural parallels, which I have already pointed out in the Aristotelian example, the difference is that Jacobi does not locate the evidence base within cognition but ties it to the practice of life. Connected to this, secondly, is the fact that his approach nullifies the observer perspective that is an almost inevitable consequence of the privileging of cognition. The act of cognition always presupposes distance from its object. This premise is also confirmed by the argument from the philosophy of identity that cognition and its object should coincide, that they are "in truth" identical. Jacobi has been misunderstood precisely along these lines, that is to say as also seeking, *within* the framework of an observer model, to establish a unity of cognition and object derived from the philosophy of identity. For this reason, it is all the more important to recognize that his foregrounding of practical life activity entails an entirely different perspective. Life is certainly not characterized by unity but rather by a multiplicity of difference—the decisive factor is that life is *experienced* here and not representationally generated by the mind of an observer.

It goes without saying that this point has significant consequences for the presentation as well as for the reading of the Jacobi's texts. For insofar as the logic of

---

[20] Søren Kierkegaard, *Concluding Unscientific Postscript to the Philosophical Crumbs*, ed. and trans. Alastair Hannay (Cambridge: Cambridge University Press, 2009), 85.
[21] Kierkegaard, *Concluding Unscientific Postscript*, 89.

the matter requires one to speak *from* life rather than *about* it, then Jacobi can neither present life as an object of observation, nor can the reader take up the position of an observer vis-à-vis Jacobi's statements. A fitting expression of this state of affairs, one in which we can also discern the evocative appeal to the reader or listener to adjust her own attitude accordingly, can be found in his conversation with Lessing. There, it will be remembered, he asserts that "for the seeker after truth there is no higher accomplishment than to disclose *existence* and to reveal it" (Spin: JWA 1,1, 29; MPW 194).[22] Nothing mysterious or even "mystical" is intended here, although such intentions have been attributed to Jacobi on numerous occasions. To put it in ironic terms, Jacobi simply asks his desk-bound readers to temporarily abandon their observation posts and consider for once, at least in their imaginations, what means to live a vital, "productive" life.

Jacobi's insistence on this engagement with life means that new concerns take center stage, and this brings us to the third intellectual model from which we need to distinguish his approach. In claiming that life is the "principle of all cognition," Jacobi is not calling for a simple inversion of the previous hierarchy, that is, he is not claiming that an irrational structure of instincts, or what Schopenhauer referred to as "blind will," should be our starting point instead. This is not to say that Jacobi objects to the premise that all living things are driven forward by "desire," namely, by the drive for self-preservation. He does, however, object to the idea that *human* life can be reduced to this interest in self-preservation. On the contrary, according to his analysis, a reductionist thesis of this sort must always be understood as already the result of an explanation, an explanation that has only been able to establish the state of affairs it claims to elucidate by way of a prior process of rationalization.

Jacobi's analysis is remarkable in many respects, not least when considered in light of current philosophical debates. It may seem like a grand gesture to unmask the luminous sphere of cognition as the mere product of blind desire, and to challenge "western" conceptions of the "animal rationale" in the process. Upon a closer analysis, however, we find that it is none other than this same "animal rationale" who makes such naturalizing argumentation possible in the first place. The invitation that Jacobi extends to his readers follows from this: to adopt a perspective that is prior to such rationalizing explanations, the perspective from which we proceed in the practical pursuit of our lives. In this case we understand ourselves neither as detached observers nor as mere instruments of blind instinct, but as *agents of our actions*.

Insofar as Jacobi's approach cannot be explained by way of the operations of the philosophy of reflection, nor in terms of the adoption of a belief in divine revelation, scholars have sought to find other models that can help clarify his position. In this context, associations with the life philosophy of the early twentieth century have come

---

[22] The statement in its entirety reads as follows: "In my judgment, for the seeker after truth there is no higher accomplishment than to disclose *existence* and to reveal it ... To him, explanation is a means to an end, a path to where he is headed, a first stop and never a final goal. His final goal is that which is beyond all explanation: the non-decomposable, the immediate, the simple." [Nach meinem Urtheil ist das größeste Verdienst des Forschers, *Daseyn* zu enthüllen, und zu offenbaren ... Erklärung ist ihm Mittel, Weg zum Ziele, nächster—niemals letzter Zweck. Sein letzter Zweck ist, was sich nicht erklären läßt: das Unauflösliche, Unmittelbare, Einfache.]

up repeatedly.[23] On this reading, Jacobi is best understood as a precursor to Dilthey and the modern hermeneutic tradition that he helped shape. At least as far as the required change in perspective is concerned, such an association is not entirely misguided. Indeed, in making the distinction between "understanding" and "explanation," Dilthey is similarly exhorting his readers to think from the position of life itself rather than in terms of a confrontation with an object of representation. Continuing along this path, one could even place Jacobi's undertaking into a productive dialogue with Heidegger's fundamental-ontological "Phenomenology of Dasein." Here, however, we must also take note of a crucial difference. What Jacobi intends to demonstrate in shifting from the observer to the participant perspective is not primarily the *productive interconnectivity* of life, not the thrownness of a Dasein that always already contains the understanding of Being from which it proceeds. Jacobi instead places the emphasis on the personal consciousness of our actions, on the "consciousness of our spontaneous self-activity in the exercise of our will," which underlies our actions "regardless of our finitude and our slavery to nature" (Spin: JWA 1,1, 262; MPW 377).

With this we have returned to the point with which we began our considerations. Spinoza's dismissal of this conviction as a mere illusion—that is, the conviction that we are the intentional agents of our actions—follows necessarily from his program of a "pure," which is to say uncompromisingly rigorous metaphysics. But this is truly the sticking point for Jacobi, giving rise to the leap of his practical contradiction, and, on the basis of the foregoing discussion, we are now in a position to recognize a crucial motif in this regard. As has just been shown once again, it is clear, on the one hand, that Jacobi consistently argues in an *ex negativo* fashion. In his contradiction of Spinoza, he reclaims our experience of acting in the modality of immediate certainty as a fundamental parameter of our self-understanding. And for this reason he also counters Spinoza's program of universal explanation with the perspectival shift toward a disclosure of existence, a shift that seeks to account for our fundamental self-understanding by way of the participant perspective of our own practical life activity. If, however, one thinks this figure through to its logical end, then one sees that the *ex negativo* method of contradiction in no sense means that philosophy and life, knowledge and belief, simply exist side by side in a state of mutual independence. Instead, what we find in regard to the structural relation between belief and knowledge is that the convictions informing our practical life activity *constitute the foundation* of all philosophy.

They constitute, in a sense that is anything but trivial, that basis which is presupposed to the exact extent that it is claimed to be subject to rational explanation. The consequences of this insight are extraordinarily far-reaching. Along the horizon of our actions, we discover the actuality of ourselves and the world prior to any propositional transformation. Our understanding of our own free self-activity is revealed to us and along with it our understanding of the world around us, into which we act and in which we experience ourselves as finite entities who have no choice but to respond as active beings to the resistances we encounter. But this is not all that is disclosed to us in the consciousness of our actions. Only here, and only insofar as we act with

---

[23] See Otto F. Bollnow, *Die Lebensphilosophie F.H. Jacobis* (Stuttgart: Kohlhammer, 1933).

the conviction of having the freedom to begin something new—despite our natural entanglements—are we able to access the metaphysical reality of an origin that is per se absolutely unconditioned.[24]

Against this backdrop, it becomes apparent that it is not a genuine achievement of traditional metaphysics to have opened a horizon to the unconditioned or the absolute. Its contribution consists rather in subjecting that which has always already been disclosed to a process of rationalization. In the wake of Spinoza's system, moreover, any certainty regarding the possibility of a causal beginning has been declared illusory. And yet, without the presupposition of such certainty, no metaphysician would ever have come up with the idea of constructing an entirely self-contained system from the process of rational justification, as opposed to continuing to extend this process *in indefinitum*. If we follow Jacobi's train of thought here, however, then it also becomes clear that the opening up of a metaphysical dimension cannot be seen as an original achievement of religion either.

It may indeed seem to be the case that the traditional contents of religious worldviews have been *de facto* transferred to philosophical concepts and, thanks to a consistent process of "secularization," ultimately been substantially transformed. Nonetheless, in turning his attention back to our practical life activity, Jacobi intends to highlight something else. According to his reasoning, which emerges particularly clearly in his later discussion with Matthias Claudius, we actually confront with the same structural situation in the case of both religion and philosophy. After all, humans would have never accepted revealed religion in the first place had they not already grasped beforehand just what it was that the "teachings" of religion were appealing to. Strictly speaking, they would have been incapable of even understanding what was at stake or what they were being called upon to do (GD: JWA 3, 42).

The applicability of this insight, moreover, extends beyond the case of the Christian belief in divine revelation. The point at issue here is actually valid in a universal sense—as Jacobi emphasizes throughout, it applies as well to all natural religions and their fetishistic practices. Although these may be viewed as mere superstitions held by "raw peoples," they nonetheless offer similar evidence of how all human beings, in experiencing themselves as agents, are confronted with the basic experience of an unconditioned cause, an experience that then finds expression in any number of forms (Spin: JWA 1,1, 262; MPW 377). From an anthropological point of view, this experience can also be seen to mark the boundary between the human and the animal. Jacobi does not doubt for a moment that animals demonstrate exceptional intelligence.

---

[24] Cf. the late *Introduction to the Author's Collected Philosophical Works* (1815): "The concept of freedom is inextirpably rooted in the human mind as true concept of the unconditioned, and compels the human soul to strive after a cognition of the unconditional that lies beyond the conditioned. Without the consciousness of this concept, nobody would know that the limitations of what is conditioned really are *limitations*." [Der Freyheits-Begriff, als wahrer Begriff des Unbedingten, wurzelt unvertilgbar im menschlichen Gemüthe, und nöthigt die menschliche Seele nach einer über das Bedingte hinaus liegenden Erkenntniß des Unbedingten zu streben. Ohne das Bewußtseyn dieses Begriffs würde niemand von den Schranken des Bedingten wissen, daß sie *Schranken* sind] (JWA 2,1, 412; MPW 572). With this argument Jacobi takes direct aim at Kant and his epistemological claim that reason proceeds from the understanding to strive toward an unconditioned totality of knowledge.

Were one to surprise them in the act of communicating with a fetish, however, then it would no longer be possible to refer to them as animals.

None of these reflections imply that we must take leave of religion entirely. In analogy to the previous interpretation of philosophical worldviews as a *rationalization* of that which is non-propositionally inscribed into our practical life activity, one can understand (and appreciate) religion as a *visualization* of the same immediate certainty. Jacobi is convinced that our status as corporeal beings makes us dependent upon visualization. Not surprisingly, then, his sympathy for the image-world of religion comes through in subtle ways as well as in explicit statements, not to mention in his own use of religious images in order to illuminate the matters with which he is concerned. But to reiterate: What Jacobi says about the religious imagery also applies to his own approach. Images do not reveal themselves *as* images. In order to understand them *as* images, we require a standard that is derived not from the images themselves but from manifestation of the unconditioned in our consciousness of action.

In order to counter Mendelssohn's assertions and especially the accusation of blind submission to the dictates of religion, Jacobi begins in the second edition of the *Spinoza Letters* to speak of reason rather than belief. As genuine or substantive reason, which "is in possession of man" [die den Menschen hat], this capacity is to be strictly distinguished from *reason-seeking* rationality, of which man is "in possession" [die der Mensch hat] (Spin: JWA 1,1, 259f.; MPW 375ff.).[25] It is the former, practical reason that enables us, in the consciousness of our action, to access the dimension of the unconditioned. This reason, Jacobi asserts, "poetizes truth," [*dichtet Wahrheit*] a phrase that aptly encapsulates his challenge to modern philosophy in the form of a paradox (GD: JWA 3, 49). But if this is in fact the case, then there is nothing to keep us from understanding the poetic truths of reason as the achievement of an original *religious energy*, an energy that exists prior to any particular manifestation of metaphysics or religion and that moves human beings, as distinct from animals, throughout the course of their lives. It is toward this phenomenon and not merely toward positive religion that we must direct our attention, should we venture to claim that these matters are no longer of any concern to us.

---

[25] "*Hat der Mensch Vernunft oder hat Vernunft den Menschen?*" (Spin: JWA 1,1, 259). For a detailed discussion see Chapter 4 in this volume.

4

Does Spirit Have *Esprit*? On the Figures of Soul, Spirit, and Reason in Jacobi's Philosophy

Of Spirit and Esprit

To be praised by Hegel is always an ambivalent pleasure. For no one is impervious to the effects of "sublation," an operation that tends to transform even the moment of a position deemed to be worth preserving into something no longer entirely recognizable. A particularly fraught example of this ambivalence is the case of the predicate "spirited" or "having esprit" [*geistreich*], which Hegel uses to describe Jacobi on two separate occasions. He not only attributes this quality to Jacobi in the angry polemic contained in his early Jena publication *Faith and Knowledge*, but also in the more serene and generally positive review of Jacobi's works written during his later Heidelberg period. In 1802, Hegel writes,

> The utterances of experience and about experience have esprit because there is the allusive echo of speculative Ideas in them. The interest of Jacobi's writings rests on this musical consonance and resonance of speculative Ideas. But the music remains an echo; for the Ideas are refracted in the medium of reflection's absoluteness; the music must not blossom into Logos, the scientifically articulated word which is what one expects where the issue is philosophical.[1]

In 1817, Hegel returns to this idea. Here, "having esprit" is described as "a kind of surrogate for methodically cultivated thought and for the reason progressing in it."

> Jacobi's style is only distracting when it comes to speculative matters and then especially when Jacobi uses it to polemical ends. For though the speculative is the inner, hidden, motivating force behind philosophical *esprit*, the speculative as such reveals itself fully only in the form of the concept. If the glow of the idea is what makes the twilight of *esprit* so sweet, it forfeits this merit when the light of reason itself shines forth, leaving only darkness to distinguish twilight from it.[2]

---

[1] Hegel, *Glauben und Wissen*, GW 4, 360. G. W. F. Hegel, *Faith and Knowledge*, ed. and trans. Walter Cerf and Henry S. Harris (Albany: State University of New York Press, 1977), 115.

[2] In the following, Hegel's *Jacobi-Review* will be cited parenthetically in the text as JR with an indication of the page number in GW 15 as well as of the corresponding page in the English translation G. W. F. Hegel, "Review, Friedrich Heinrich Jacobi's Works, Volume III," in *Heidelberg Writings. Journal Publications*, ed. and trans. Brady Bowman and Allen Speight (Cambridge: Cambridge University Press, 2009): JR 24; 25f.

Over the years, despite the evolution of Hegel's own thought and despite the change in his attitude toward Jacobi, both the attribution and assessment of "having esprit" remain the same. And this single, seemingly context-independent predicate more or less captures the entire range of Hegel's thinking about Jacobi: praise and blame, recognition and criticism, admiration and fundamental irritation are all condensed into this one phrase. On the positive side, Hegel remarks that thinking and speaking with esprit opens up a dimension that is "far superior to the understanding" (JR 23; 25). Something unanticipated becomes visible, a horizon appears of which the understanding, content with itself and its insights, remains entirely unaware. The spirited free play of ideas can thus help put one in a productive frame of mind. It can stimulate the intellect and help to counter intellectual rigidity, by literally taking one's mind off things. Only a witless barbarian would question the value of this musical stimulation of the spirit. Hegel's characterization, however, also reveals the alleged limits of esprit. It can and must not aspire to be more than stimulation. Whenever, therefore, such spirited thinking and speaking fails to acknowledge its own limits but rather strays into the "polemical," it becomes "distracting." It can only ever set the mood, so to speak, for a knowledge that remains the exclusive domain of the systematic investigations of science. Logos and concept are the actual forms of thinking, they articulate reason and reason articulates itself in them. It is at this moment at the latest, the moment when speculative science aligns itself entirely with these modalities of thought, that its light begins to shine so brightly as to cause everything else to recede into darkness. Having esprit is definitely not the same as having mastery of spirit.

Hegel alludes to this relationship between spirit and esprit in his discussion. When he emphasizes, for example, Jacobi's "great conviction that the absolute must be received as spirit" (JR 14; 13), he is well aware that in thinking and speaking with "esprit," Jacobi fully intends to say something substantive about spirit and not simply to stimulate a thought-provoking discussion of some arbitrary topic. For Hegel, however, esprit and spirit are not equivalent terms; rather, they relate to one another hierarchically. An individual who has a wealth of esprit does not in fact have more spirit but less of it, because he is unable—and, for polemical reasons, also unwilling—to harness his wealth for the production of systematic, scientific knowledge. And in making these assertions, Hegel is certainly right on two counts.

First, it was in fact Jacobi, far more so than Kant, who made the meta-rational dimension of spirit the focus of his attention, thereby providing post-Kantian philosophy with a potential source of inspiration whose significance can hardly be exaggerated. In contrast, Kant first uses the expression "spirit" not in his fundamental program of transcendental philosophy but only in the aesthetic context of the *Critique of Judgment*.[3] For Jacobi, however, and later also for Fichte, Schelling, and Hegel, *spirit* serves as a key concept, one that not only expands the lexicon of terms pertaining to subjectivity, the subject, the I, or self-consciousness, but also modifies the semantics of these expressions in a particular way, such that they come to denote an *integral*

---

[3] For a detailed discussion, see Birgit Sandkaulen, "'Was geht auf dem langen Wege vom Geist zum System nicht alles verloren.' Problematische Transformationen in der klassischen deutschen Philosophie," *Deutsche Zeitschrift für Philosophie* 50 (2002): 363–75.

self-relation rather than one that is limited to theoretical or cognitive concerns. Hegel, however, is also right in regard to a second point. Because Jacobi is indeed firmly convinced that *spirit,* on the one hand, and the interests of science, on the other, are fundamentally incompatible, even that they stand in a hostile relationship to one another. In a text that he attached to his *Letter to Fichte* in 1799 and later published separately under the title *Ueber die Unzertrennlichkeit des Begriffes der Freyheit und Vorsehung von dem Begriffe der Vernunft* [On the Inseparability of the Concept of Freedom and Providence from the Concept of Reason], he states unambiguously that "*spirit* does not tolerate scientific treatment, *since* it cannot *become letter*. Spirit must therefore stay outside, before the gates of its *science*. Where that science is, there *spirit itself* is not allowed. For this reason we can be sure that whoever believes himself to be spelling out spirit, in fact always spells out something else, whether knowingly or unknowingly" (JF: JWA 2,1, 233; MPW 529).

It is easy to see why such an assertion would prompt Hegel to invoke his distinction: the distinction between esprit, on the one hand, as the mere "surrogate for methodologically trained thinking," and scientific thought on the other. To *attune* oneself to spirit by way of esprit is one thing. It is even a necessary first step, if the *speculative* science at issue here is to be more than a science of the understanding. When Jacobi, however, insists in his polemical excess on decoupling spirit and science once and for all, then it is no longer a matter of intellectual stimulation but of a powerful provocation, one that must be countered with equal force. Then one is called upon to highlight the inadequacy of esprit. Instead of truly opening a path to dimension of spirit, esprit remains bound to the very context that it seeks to transcend. It is refracted in the medium of reflection, as is made clear in Jacobi's case by "his disjointedness, leaps, bold expressions, intellectual acuity, and his exaggerations and persistence, his use of sensuous images, and appeals to emotion and common sense" (JR 24; 26). To cordon off the procedures of science from the activity of esprit thus means assigning esprit an intermediate position—reflecting its rights as well as its wrongs—between mere understanding and a reason that is conceptually articulated.

Hegel's concept of spirit as it relates to his own scientific aspirations is not up for discussion here, nor is the question of whether he succeeded in refuting Jacobi's objection.[4] One significant strength of his analysis is definitely worth highlighting, however. To the extent that Hegel describes Jacobi's thought in terms of "esprit," he at least avoids the mistake of mischaracterizing it as a sentimental or even irrational countercurrent to enlightenment. Jacobi later, in the *Introduction to the Author's Collected Philosophical Works* of 1815, complained bitterly of how he had been labeled a "philosopher of *feeling* or of *sentiment*" in order to discredit his position (JWA 2,1, 379; MPW 542). Hegel cannot be accused of such intentions. On the contrary, Jacobi's esprit, which, in his diagnosis, oscillates between understanding and reason, between reflection and speculation, appears rather as a characteristic feature of modern thought. The modern intellect, insofar as it does not align itself with the self-satisfied optimism of the understanding, is characterized by conflict and disunity. It is thus no coincidence that Hegel again employs the predicate "having esprit" (and

---

[4] I address these matters in Chapters 13, 14, and 15 in this volume.

with an analogous valuation) in *The Phenomenology of Spirit,* where it characterizes the language of the "disrupted consciousness." The appearance of this consciousness, as exemplified in this case in the work of Diderot, serves as a crucial prelude to the modern world of spirit and is thus clearly superior to *"simple consciousness"* in its innocence and naiveté.[5]

Toward a New View of Reason

Jacobi's remarks on spirit must be viewed a part of a broader constellation of reflections on the intellectual and cultural upheavals of modernity. The foregoing entreé into the fraught relationship between spirit and "esprit" as reflected in Hegel was intended to draw attention to this fact. In the name of spirit, Jacobi reveals new ways of seeing and thinking and develops new presentational forms that challenge the conventions of exclusively discursive reasoning. Precisely because he is not simply perpetuating tradition but rather opening up innovative new perspectives; however, each new insight must be painstakingly wrung from established ways of thinking and speaking. Everything Jacobi says therefore presupposes, as Hegel rightly notes, a peculiar brokenness, the implication of which is that there can be no direct and frontal access to the essential aspects of spirit.

To put it another way, we can hardly expect a conventional treatise on spirit to result from a discourse defined by "esprit." An obvious and exemplary case in point is the text in which Jacobi for the first time thematizes the elusive dimension of spirit *as such.* I am referring here to *Supplement VII* from the second, substantially expanded edition of 1789 of his book *Concerning the Doctrine of Spinoza in Letters to Herr Moses Mendelssohn.*[6] This is the text to which Jacobi himself refers later, in the aforementioned addendum to his *Letter to Fichte,* and there as well he reiterates his claim that the crucial observation to be made about spirit is contained in the answer to a "strangely sounding question": *"Does man possess reason, or does reason possess man?"* (JF: JWA 2,1, 232; MPW 528).[7]

This question, toward which the entire analysis in *Supplement VII* builds, serves as a kind of subheading in the text, under which the following is then formulated as an answer:

> If we understand by reason the **soul** of man *only* in so far as it has distinct concepts, passes judgments, and draws inferences with them, and goes on building new concepts or ideas, then reason is a characteristic of man which he acquires

---

[5] Hegel, *Phänomenologie des Geistes,* GW 9, 284. G. W. F. Hegel, *The Phenomenology of Spirit,* ed. and trans. Terry Pinkard (Cambridge: Cambridge University Press, 2018), 303f.
[6] I have described this *Supplement VII* as Jacobi's "secret magnum opus" (Birgit Sandkaulen, *Grund und Ursache. Die Vernunftkritik Jacobis* (Munich: Wilhelm Fink Verlag, 2000), 64–76): The leitmotifs developed by Jacobi in the 1770s and 1780s converge here in an analysis that also incorporates his views on Spinoza and Kant and that subsequently informs all of his later works. The distinction one occasionally finds in the scholarship between Jacobi's early and late work is thus unfounded.
[7] "Hat der Mensch Vernunft, oder hat Vernunft den Menschen?"

progressively, an instrument of which he makes use. In this sense, *reason belongs to him*. But if by reason we mean the principle of cognition in general, then reason is the **spirit** of which the whole living nature of man is made up; man *consists* of it. In this sense man is a form which reason has assumed. (Spin: JWA 1,1, 259f.; MPW 375).[8]

Both what Hegel admires and criticizes in Jacobi's philosophical contributions as well as Hegel's own efforts to move beyond Jacobi's "allusive echo of speculative ideas" have as their precondition the innovative, exploratory features of this text. In order to relate the crucial implications of Jacobi's approach and intentions with the greatest possible precision, it will be helpful to provide a step-by-step review of his essential arguments.

First and foremost, we must take note of the following: As is the typical for the condensed "manner" (to use Hegel's term) of speaking characteristic of esprit, in which relations and connections are established across dissonances and divides, two discourses are interwoven here and thereby cast in a new light: *the discourse on reason and the discourse on soul and spirit*. But this does not simply involve identifying soul and spirit as two different forms of reason. Keeping in mind that the determinations formulated here are to be understood as an *answer to the question of reason*, then the key point is rather that reason functions as the superordinate category, and the categories of soul and spirit only enter into the equation and acquire their specific contours as subordinate elements. In other words, to say anything valid regarding soul and spirit not only requires us to take reason into account; such statements also presuppose that we have already established what reason truly is.

I have already mentioned that the concept of spirit becomes a keyword of the epoch, one that acquires particular significance in the context of reflections on subjectivity. We can now see that the determination of this concept is only possible on the condition of having previously clarified the features of reason. Precisely this fact, however, heightens the complexity of the philosophical task. If it is indeed true that, in the case of soul and spirit, traditional definitions are no longer valid and we must instead view these concepts as belonging to the basic configuration of reason (elucidating their status and substance in terms of this primary context), then this requirement applies all the more so to the superordinate category of reason itself. To suppose, in other words, that one already knows what reason is, what is meant by this expression, would be even less defensible. Rather, the meaning of reason must itself be subject to a fundamental reexamination. What is thus required as the basis for all further statements is nothing less than what Kant demanded—a *critique of reason*. In referring to Jacobi's project in these terms, we are in no way distorting it. On the contrary: it is unimaginable that Fichte could have admired Jacobi as "a reformer in philosophy simultaneously with Kant,"[9] or that Hegel could have discerned in Jacobi's texts the "allusive echo" of

---

[8] Boldface corresponds to letter spacing in original.
[9] Fichte, *Sonnenklarer Bericht an das grössere Publicum*, GA I,7, 194. J. G. Fichte, "A Crystal Clear Report to the General Public Concerning the Actual Essence of the Newest Philosophy: An Attempt to Force the Reader to Understand," trans. John Bottermann and William Rasch, in *Philosophy of German Idealism: Fichte, Jacobi and Schelling*, ed. Ernst Behler (New York: Continuum, 1987), 47. Translation amended.

speculative ideas if Jacobi had not intended to pursue a fundamental critique of reason, one undertaken both in alignment with and in opposition to Kant. And this contrast with Kant's *Critique of Pure Reason* is a matter of some significance, as is shown by the fact that whereas Kant does not refer to the concept of spirit, Jacobi's own critique of reason has spirit as one of its central emphases. We will be able to see this more clearly if we temporarily bracket the investigation of soul and spirit and turn in our next step to a more detailed consideration of the question of reason itself.

By positing one reason that man possesses and another reason that possesses man, Jacobi introduces a distinction that he later designates as one between an "*adjective*" and a "*substantive*" reason (JF: JWA 2,1, 232; MPW 529). In assessing his argument, it is critical first of all to acknowledge the significance of his decision to make a *distinction* at all, and secondly, to be clear about the *nature of this distinction*. In neither case can he have expected to be met with appreciation and approval. Rather, on both counts, his approach appears as a sharp challenge to the prevailing practice in philosophical investigations of reason. With regard to the decision to introduce a *distinction* in the first place, Jacobi is responding to a particular discourse on reason that had become largely entrenched over the course of the eighteenth century. In this discourse, reason has congealed into a one-dimensional category that serves to denote the rational capacities of concept formation, judgment, and inferential reasoning. Interestingly, this reduction of reason to the practice of discursive rationality, which continues to be its conventional meaning in ordinary speech even today, is characteristic of both Wolffian rationalism and Lockean empiricism. What has been lost in both cases is any connection to the substantially richer and more complex understanding of an older tradition, which insisted on differentiating between *nous* and *dianoia*, *intellectus* and *ratio*, and thus also between *intuitive* and *discursive* aspects of reason. As an alternative to the one-dimensional usage of his epoch, with its corresponding reduction in the scope of the meaning of reason, Jacobi posits his substantive distinction between two forms. Against this backdrop, it is not wrong to claim that Jacobi in certain respects reconnects to this older tradition—albeit not without significant modifications—or even that he is responsible for reminding his contemporaries that it exists at all.

This brings us to the second question, that of the *nature of the distinction* between these two forms, and from this perspective Jacobi's critical engagement with Kant becomes visible. After all, there can be no denying that the *Critique of Pure Reason* already aims to counter the one-dimensional "rationalism" of the prevailing discourse with its own more differentiated conception. For Kant this means distinguishing between the capacity of understanding on the one hand and that of reason on the other. The difference between them consists in the fact that the understanding, as the capacity of concepts or rules, combines with sensible intuition to enable empirical cognition, whereas reason, as the capacity of principles, generates the ideas that provide the horizon for its orientation toward the unifying framework of the unconditioned. Thus, under the rubric of reason and the ideas proper to it, Kant brings a metaphysical dimension into play, even going so far as to invoke Plato in this context.[10]

---

[10] CPR A 314, B 370f.

This is not the place for an exhaustive discussion of just how substantively and thoroughly Jacobi engages with Kant's propositions here. It will have to suffice instead to identify the point at which the paths of Jacobi and Kant definitively diverge. It is certainly true that in making the distinction sketched out above, Kant attributes to reason a *sui generis* dimension that transcends the understanding. Crucially, however, this dimension is nonetheless conceived and described in *relation* to the understanding and as *determined* by its competencies. In other words, the analysis presented by Kant under the guise of a *critique of pure reason* is actually a "critique of the understanding," the results of which are only subsequently applied to reason. Ultimately, the ideas proper to reason appear in this analysis merely as a particular class of concepts, whose scope encompasses the unconditioned, but for which the same limitation holds as for all concepts, namely, that in the absence of a reference to sensible intuition they remain empty and without any objective content.

With this, we are able to acquire a more precise sense of what Jacobi is aiming at. As we have seen, Jacobi insists on the need to reach an understanding of exactly what is "meant by reason," and he introduces in this context the distinction between an adjective and a substantive reason, which is conceived both in opposition to the prevailing one-dimensional view of reason and to Kant's conception of a reason whose meaning derives from the understanding. Jacobi thereby frees substantive reason, which now appears as reason in the proper sense and thus also as the reason to be considered in conjunction with spirit, from any obligation to adhere to the standards of rationality associated with the understanding. This does not mean, of course, that he intends to dispute the existence of the standards of discursive rationality. Nor would he in any way want to dispute that these standards are important. However, Jacobi limits the scope of their applicability, whereby he simultaneously ascribes to reason in the emphatic sense a separate purview and its own proper forms of evidence, placing it not simply alongside but above adjective reason. This is no arbitrary gesture. After all, Jacobi's position is actually far less puzzling than the failure of Wolff or Locke to justify their decision to restrict the scope of reason exclusively to the jurisdiction and the procedures of discursive rationality, and of Kant to explain why the criteriology of the understanding should be applicable to the dimension of reason as well. Kant instead unquestioningly adopts this approach and, as a result, not surprisingly ends up in what he himself refers to as the "awkward situation" of speaking of reason as a dimension *sui generis* while depriving it of its special status in the very same moment.[11] Jacobi, on the other hand, reveals the features of substantive reason on the basis of *phenomena* that testify to its existence.

Such phenomena are characteristic of *human existence*. And this directs our attention once again to the initial and therefore decisive question of reason, which appears now in a different and expanded light. Whether man possesses reason or whether reason possesses man, this is what we are asking. And this means in turn that however the question with regard to the two distinct forms of reason is to be answered, the determination of reason is always immediately and inseparably bound to the determination of human existence. If reason were to be detached from this latter

---

[11] CPR A 299, B 355.

determination, it would be a completely empty concept in either of two forms posited here. Reason would be nothing but the abstract hypostatization of an anonymous capacity of cognition. The cultivation of such "reason" may typify discourses of theoretical philosophy, but these discourses—and in such moments Jacobi's "esprit" becomes, to quote Hegel, distractingly "polemical"—are really nothing more than "games" to pass the time.[12] Breaking the spell of such games and anchoring the question of reason to the contexts of experience, to the anthropological-existential certainties of human life, thus constitutes an indispensable feature of the critique of reason as conceived by Jacobi. And here we can see that the significance of his project extends well beyond the limited domain of a theory of knowledge with exclusively epistemic relevance.

Of Existential Things: The Representation of the Conditioned and the Unconditioned

It should be apparent that only by framing the problem in this way can one integrate the perspectives of soul and spirit into the question of reason. And we are now in a position, as our next step, to consider the two forms of reason posited in more concrete

---

[12] In order to convey a better sense of Jacobi's "esprit" and its "polemical" employment, which irritated others besides Hegel, it is worth quoting the relevant passage from the *Letter to Fichte* in its entirety: "Taken *simply as such*, our sciences are games that human spirit devises to pass the time. In devising these games, *it only organizes its non-knowledge* without coming a single hair's breadth closer to a cognition of *the true*. In a sense it rather moves away from it thereby, for in thus busying itself it distracts itself from its non-knowledge, ceases to feel its pressure, even grows fond of it, since the non-knowledge is *infinite*, and the game that it plays with the human spirit becomes ever more varied, engrossing, extended, and intoxicating. If the game thus played with our non-knowledge were not infinite, and not so constituted that at its every turn a new game arose, we would fare with science just as with the so-called game of tic-tac-toe: would be sick of it once all its moves and possible turns are known and familiar to us. The game is spoiled for us because we understand it entirely, because we *know* it. So I don't understand how one can be satisfied with scientific cognition; how one can sacrifice all truth apart from the scientific, and rejoice at the insight that there is no other, *if* one has attained to this truth (*to scientific knowledge*) at its foundation as Fichte did, and sees just as clearly, or at least as clearly as I do, that in purely scientific being we only play a game with empty numbers." ["Unsere Wißenschaften, *blos als solche*, sind Spiele, welche der menschliche Geist, zeitvertreibend, sich ersinnt. Diese Spiele ersinnend, *organisiert er nur seine Unwißenheit*, ohne einer Erkenntniß des *Wahren*, auch nur um ein Haar breit näher zu kommen. In einem gewißen Sinne entfernt er sich dadurch vielmehr von ihm, indem er bey diesem Geschäft sich über seine Unwißenheit blos zerstreut, ihren Druck nicht mehr fühlt, sogar sie lieb gewinnt, weil sie—*unendlich* ist; weil das Spiel, das sie mit ihm treibt, immer mannigfaltiger, ergötzender, größer, berauschender wird. Wäre das Spiel mit unserer Unwißenheit nicht unendlich, und nicht so beschaffen, daß aus jeder seiner Wendungen ein neues Spiel entstünde: so würde es uns mit der Wißenschaft, wie mit dem Nürrenberger, so genannten *Grillenspiel* ergehen, das uns anekelt, so bald uns alle seine Gänge und mögliche Wendungen bekannt und geläufig sind. Das Spiel ist uns dadurch verdorben, daß wir es ganz verstehen, daß wir es *wißen*. Und so begreife ich denn nicht, wie man an wißenschaftlicher Erkenntniß genug haben, auf alle Wahrheit außer der Wißenschaftlichen Verzicht thun, und der Einsicht, daß es keine andre Wahrheit gebe, sich erfreuen kann—*wenn* man dieser Wahrheit, *dem wißenschaftlichen Wißen*, wie Fichte auf den Grund gekommen ist, und es eben so klar, zum wenigsten, wie ich, vor Augen hat: daß wir im rein wißenschaftlichen Wesen nur ein Spiel treiben mit leeren Zahlen." (JF: JWA 2,1, 206f.; MPW 511f.)]

detail. Here we see that Jacobi's *existential approach*, by evoking to a certain extent the relation between *ratio* and *intellectus* that was familiar to the older tradition, or between the discursive and the intuitive moments of reason, opens up an entirely new and unconventional perspective on the matter. This is true not only with regard to the case of substantive reason, but also and especially with regard to adjective reason. For what are the most salient characteristics of this form of reason, the reason that man possesses? As far as its competencies as such are concerned, the essentials have already been conveyed in the previous discussion of the truncated, one-dimensional discourse on reason. Jacobi, as well, highlights precisely these capabilities as the capabilities of discursive rationality: concept formation, judgment, and inferential reasoning. In the broader contexts of *Supplement VII* and the *Spinoza Letters* as a whole, the spectrum of these rational capabilities and actions is amalgamated under the operational rubric of the search for *sufficient reason*. Certain phenomena can be adequately explained by establishing sufficient reasons for the "mediations" through which they arise. In such cases, explanation takes the form of a rational reconstruction of the sequence of these mediations:

> We comprehend a thing whenever we can derive it from its proximate causes, or whenever we have insight into the order of its immediate conditions. What we see or derive in this way presents itself to us as a mechanistic connection. [...] The construction *of a concept as such* is the *a priori* of every construction; and at the same time our insight into its construction allows us to cognize with full certainty that it is not possible for us to comprehend whatever we are not in a position to construct. (Spin: JWA 1,1, 258; MPW 373f.)

In highlighting this constructivist aspect of rationality, Jacobi has undoubtedly identified something crucial, an aspect of rationality that has become ever more apparent and ever more widely recognized as modernity has progressed. But this is not all. Jacobi actually goes a step further, in that he understands the competencies of this rationality as "adjective," that is to say as an *attribute*, by which he clearly intends to invoke the figure of the so-called *animal rationale*. The specific attribute of rationality is ascribed to a living being or, to be more precise, to a particular type of animal. If this relation is taken literally, as Jacobi intends, then the expression "animal rationale" loses its traditional aura, insofar as the phrase now captures only one particular aspect of reason, and not even the essential one.

Even more significantly, however, the illumination of this relation goes hand in hand with the idea that this specific attributive dimension of discursive rationality should be viewed in connection with the *life* that serves to ground it. As animalia rationales, human beings have reason at their disposal—but they do not always already have it at their disposal, as some kind of "eternal truth" that lacks any existential locus in lived experience. Rather, according to Jacobi, this attribute is only formed "bit by bit" in the course of a "natural history," a historiogenesis of rationality. It emerges, moreover, as a necessary "instrument," employed and progressively refined relative to the specific circumstances that humans have confronted and continue to confront in the course of their history.[13] These pioneering efforts by Jacobi to elucidate a category of adjective reason are clearly deserving of attention, not least in light of current discussions, which have highlighted the significance of natural and cultural evolution for understanding cognition. In harnessing his "esprit" to break free from traditional modes of thought as well as from the program of Kant's new critical philosophy, Jacobi manages to reveal discursive rationality as simultaneously *constructivist* and *instrumental-pragmatic*, and thus also *evolutionary* in character. In doing so, he anticipates approaches that will only become commonplace in the course of the nineteenth century, for instance among the successors of Nietzsche and the early pragmatists.

It is no less important, however, to note the crucial difference between Jacobi and these later thinkers. For Jacobi, this specific attribute of the animal rationale must not be conflated with reason in its entirety. To distinguish reason in its substantive and therefore emphatic meaning from adjective reason is to posit a "principle" that is not at the disposal of humans in either a constructivist or instrumental sense, and for the very reason that is not the specific *product* of their natural circumstances but rather forms the *basis* of their "whole living" existence. This brings a completely different idea into play, according to which human existence can never be adequately conceived simply as the existence of an animal with advanced rational capacities. The reason is that such a reduction runs counter to our phenomenal experience, though the phenomenon in question here is of a different type than those described above. Jacobi presents this phenomenon as the characteristic feature of human consciousness—that it "is composed of two original representations, that of the conditioned, and that of the unconditioned. These two representations are inseparably connected, yet in such a way that the representation of the conditioned presupposes the representation of the unconditioned and can only be given with the latter" (Spin: JWA 1,1, 260; MPW 375).

Jacobi clearly adopts the term "unconditioned" from Kant, but one can see how differently it is employed here. For one thing, Kant ascribes the search for the unconditioned to the systematic interest of a hypostatized reason, which seeks to complete the conditions of possibility of cognition in the unified horizon of the unconditioned. Furthermore, in the course of this epistemic search, the unconditioned inevitably ends up being conceptualized from the perspective of the conditioned, namely, as its unfettering. Jacobi, on the other hand, inverts this theoretical framework. First, he is referring here not to a pursuit of speculative reason but to a fundamental feature of human consciousness. And, secondly, as his reflections also make clear, the representation of the unconditioned particular to human consciousness is, no less than that of the conditioned, an *original* representation. It cannot be derived from or traced back to something prior to it; indeed, in its primordial quality it in fact *precedes the representation of the conditioned*. Jacobi's thinking here is, to be sure, thoroughly metaphysical. But it is not especially complicated, let alone characterized by overheated speculation.

Humans share the fate of being finite or natural beings with all other living creatures; this is simply a fact. Their potential and ability, as animalia rationales, to consciously shape their life circumstances through the constructive application of

---

[13] *Supplement VII* presents this story as one of progressive disenchantment, see Sandkaulen, *Grund und Ursache*, 103ff.

instrumental rationality change nothing in this regard. The crucial and thus *qualitative* rather than quantitative difference between humans and other creatures lies in the fact that humans have a "representation of the conditioned"; they have, in other words, an *awareness* of their status as finite beings. This articulated or unarticulated knowledge of finitude and conditionality, however, cannot be explained by the condition of finitude itself, because it necessarily implies a distancing from this condition. We know that we are finite beings, therefore, solely because we are not consistently finite, but are rather beings whose ability to even consider our own finitude depends on something more fundamental, on an "original representation of the unconditioned."

Jacobi's reflections, insofar as they engage with the meta-rational dimension of reason, have been repeatedly misconstrued. Even those who have not gone so far as to associate him with some sort of mystical and thus presumably "irrational" position have tended to see him as advocating something like an "intellectual intuition" of the unconditioned, which, as such, is liberated from all finite conditions. Not least in his reception by the German idealists, one finds assertions that such figures can be found in Jacobi, when in fact they have merely been read *into* his texts on the model of an "allusive echo of speculative ideas." As one can see, being engaged with substantive reason certainly does not mean detaching oneself from all finite conditions for the sake of an exclusive view toward the absolute. We are and remain finite. Nonetheless, the consciousness of our finitude has always been accompanied by a representation that cannot originate from the conditioned as such, but from which it would be equally misguided to try to derive the conditioned "scientifically." This representation instead serves as the basis or precondition for our ability, as finite beings, to maintain a *self-relation*. This fundamental self-relation, which, unlike adjective reason, we do not have at our disposal, because there is no operation by means of which we could reach behind this basis of "our entire living nature," is what Jacobi terms *spirit*.

The Pragmatism of the Soul and the Personal Freedom of Spirit

As the final step in our presentation, we can now offer some concluding reflections on the implications and contours of the *spirit-Being* of human existence, always also keeping its phenomenological features in mind. Turning first to the relation between *spirit* and *soul*, we can see in light of the previous discussion that Jacobi depotentiates the determination of the soul in a unique way. It is unique in the sense that his own critique of reason, which links the "human soul" to the determination of instrumental reason, poses a challenge to a wide range of analyses that purport to explain the conspicuous diminution of the soul in modernity. Such analyses seek to trace this loss of significance back to the new paradigm of the philosophy of subjectivity and/or to the collapse of the traditional ontology of substance that long provided the foundation for the concept of the soul. In the course of such reconstructions, they attribute the decisive break with tradition to Kant, for whom, as a consequence of his transcendental-philosophical revolution, it is indeed the case that the only way the soul can still be considered is through the lens of a paralogical fallacy.

However, one should not overlook the fact that Kant's apparent derogation is far from the last word in discussions of the soul. Kant does not attack the dignity that has traditionally been ascribed to the soul in its role as the locus of immortality. He only denies that the soul, as a simple and thus indivisible substance, can ever become an object of cognition, which necessarily depends on the interplay of concept and intuition. As long as the soul appears as an idea of reason, however, to which the practical postulate of immortality can then be linked, the discussion of it can continue unimpeded. With Jacobi, on the other hand, we confront an entirely different situation. Here the potential for religious and metaphysical interpretations of the soul is truly diminished. In the context of the reason that man possesses, "soul" is nothing more than an expression for the natural constitution of a living being which, as animal rationale, develops the specific attribute of rationality. One could say that the soul is thereby drawn into the current of a thoroughgoing naturalization and disenchantment, carried out by the instrumental rationality of adjective reason itself.

With Jacobi, however, this diminution of the soul is not accompanied by a turn to the paradigm of subjectivity in an effort to find a substitute for traditional conceptions. In this respect as well, his reflections are at odds with conventional frameworks for understanding the epochal shift that occurs around 1800. References to the "subject" or to "self-consciousness" are few and far between in his works. And the term "I" as well, to the extent that he uses it, has a meaning entirely different than the one that tends to be associated with Fichte's foundational project of a Wissenschaftslehre. The distinct usage that informs Jacobi's approach becomes apparent precisely in the criticism he levels against Fichte's principle, where he refers to "that *impersonal personality*, that naked *I-hood* of the I without *self* [...] in other words, *pure and bare inessentialities*" (JF: JWA 2,1, 212; MPW 516f.). Subjectivity and I-hood are per definitionem universal, epistemically grounded structures. What they lack (and must always lack) is the self—the unmistakable and irreducible individuality and identity of *personal existence*, in a word: spirit. "Through his spirit man becomes something utterly incomparable, an individual for himself and without otherness, his *unique* spirit constitutes him as the One who he is, this One and none Other" (GD: JWA 3, 26).[14]

Using the expression "spirit" to refer to the individual constitution of a personal existence makes good sense. It ensures from the start that one cannot ascribe the status of an exclusively *empirical* phenomenon to the concrete individual or the concrete person, an ascription that would lead once again to an entanglement in the paradigm of subjectivity. In the latter, the concrete I, in contrast to the universal structure of subjectivity, is conceived as something along the lines of an empirical occurrence, about which, however, it remains entirely unclear what actually distinguishes such a manifestation from other empirically existing phenomena, say, stones or trees. If one assumes that the I is indeed something different than a stone or tree, then there is no way to avoid imputing to such a manifestation the *interior perspective* of a self-relation, which can be discerned in certain utterances but which cannot be identified entirely

---

[14] "Ein Unvergleichbares, ein Eines für sich und ohne anderes ist der Mensch sich selbst durch seinen Geist, den *eigenthümlichen*, durch welchen er *der* ist, der er ist, *dieser Eine und kein anderer*." See Chapter 6 in this volume.

with these utterances. If, however, one then goes so far as to grasp this self-relation as the instantiation of a universal structure of "I-hood," then the unique individuality of the I has again been bypassed but from the other direction, without coming one step closer to its "explanation."

The futility of such efforts leads Jacobi to conclude that spirit is not and cannot be an object of science. What is astonishing, however, is that this was his position from the beginning; he had no need to wait for the results of post-Kantian forays into the philosophy of subjectivity. Against the backdrop of his distinction between two forms of reason, spirit, as is clear from its designation as the form that possesses man, is situated outside the scope of rational explanation, assured of its own dignity in being inaccessible to any explication in terms of sufficient reason. Because if it is indeed the case that "is not possible for us to comprehend whatever we are not in a position to construct," then it follows from this that "we have no concept of qualities as such, but only intuitions or feelings. Even of our own existence, we have only a feeling and no concept" (Spin: JWA 1,1, 258; MPW 374). The evidence of spirit provided by feeling or in the form of immediate knowledge expresses a fundamental self-relation that is only accessible from the perspective of interiority. This evidential confirmation, which, in contrast to discursive explanation, must be articulated ex negativo, can certainly be linked to the motif of *intuitive evidence*. This motif, as we have seen, is familiar from the older tradition, where it is associated with the meta-rational dimension of the *nous* or the *intellectus*.

The parallel with this older tradition, however, makes it all the more important to emphasize once again the existential foundation of Jacobi's reflections, according to which the concerns of spirit are concerns of the "whole living nature of humans." The expression "spirit" has nothing to do with cognitive phenomena, but neither does the alternative it offers to the empirical occurrence of the I point to something *spiritual* in the traditional sense.[15] Moreover, and quite apart from this fact, the existential grounding of the discourse on spirit also implies that the modality of intuitive confirmation cannot be detached from it and treated, so to speak, as an independent epistemic object. Interestingly, however, this is precisely what Hegel does in order to then accuse Jacobi, in his later critique of immediate knowledge, of falling prey to the arbitrariness of mere assurances, products of an esprit that generates only the "allusive echo of speculative ideas," whose arbitrariness is only overcome when the logos of science takes matters into its own hands. Certainly, if one adopts this approach, then Jacobi's insistence on intuitive evidence may very well seem indistinguishable from that of Descartes,[16] but in fact this approach misses the point entirely. Jacobi's recourse to the modalities of feeling or immediate certainty presumes the *performative* realization of an individual self-relation that acquires its existential foundation not epistemically but rather *practically*. This means that the original representation of the unconditioned, which is linked in human consciousness to the original representation of the conditioned (even though it precedes the latter) is once again grounded in the phenomenal—in the *experience of action*. The instrumental-pragmatic orientation of the soul corresponds to the practical

---

[15] The English term for "Geist"—spirit—must therefore be understood as completely unrelated to the "spiritual."

[16] On this point see Chapter 14 in this volume.

orientation of spirit. The substantive impulse toward freedom that characterizes this orientation enters into the adjective construction of mechanistic connections and, in the same moment, counterbalances it.

In the context of *Supplement VII* and the *Spinoza Letters* as a whole, one consequence of this line of reasoning is the elevation of the concept of *cause* to the status of a central fundamental concept, but in a meaning that has absolutely nothing to do with the concept of causality as projected onto objects. For Jacobi it instead implies that we only have this concept at our disposal at all because we use it to designate a type of action initiated in the awareness of a freely projected, intentional capacity to begin. Continuing in the vein of the analysis presented thus far, this means that the freedom of spirit is for Jacobi a fact in the original sense of an "act," a f(act), one that must be considered *metaphysical* precisely to the extent that it transcends the justificatory horizon of a graspable datum. From this perspective, however, it is also clear that the concept of "autonomy," regardless of how one construes it, cannot be invoked here. Because it considers the acts of individual agents within a framework of universal reasons and structures, the concept of autonomy again fails to capture precisely that existential disposition toward action which we experience as foundational. In light of the fundamental reflections on reason contained in *Supplement VII*, it thus comes as no surprise that Jacobi in the previously mentioned text *Ueber die Unzertrennlichkeit des Begriffes der Freyheit und Vorsehung von dem Begriffe der Vernunft* refers to "the unification of natural necessity and freedom in one and the same being" as an "utterly incomprehensible fact, a miracle and a mystery equal to creation itself":

> From its side reason, whose being consists *only in what can be conceptualized*, strives to deny the *reality* of this mystery and the *truth* of this miracle. As the representative of a necessity that has already determined everything with violence, and that will not let anything happen that has not *already happened*, though fundamentally *never did happen*, reason busily endeavours to clear that mystery and miracle out of the way, as a deception due to *temporal lack of knowledge*. It repels them step by step, annihilating time and eventuality. But from the other side, the inner *certitude* of spirit equally proclaims the reality and the truth of the same mystery and miracle. It compels us to heed its witness with the power of an authority that no rational inference can outface. It attests to what it proclaims *with its deed*, for no action, not even the least one, can happen without the influence of the faculty of freedom, without the *contribution of spirit*. (JF: JWA 2,1, 234f.; MPW 530)[17]

---

[17] Jacobi did not fail to consider the question that presents itself here, namely, the question as to how one can recognize this "contribution of spirit," and he answered it as follows: "If you were teasingly to request me that in any work whatever, or action, or human character, I separate what pertains to nature from what pertains to freedom, and indicate how the one must be distinguished from the other, so I request to you in reply, *without* teasing, that you do *not* draw this distinction in any instance whatever in which you feel admiration, respect, gratitude, or love; that you do *not* represent a faculty of freedom alongside the efficacy of nature, and do *not* refer the feelings thus aroused in you to that faculty alone. I know that it would be impossible for you. You would immediately forgo the feelings the moment you think the free faculty away, the moment you truly dispense with the assumption of it." (JF: JWA 2,1, 237; MPW 532)

Against this backdrop, we can now fully appreciate what it really means for Jacobi to tether his discussion of spirit from the start to a reason *that possesses man*, and to address in this context alone the unique self-relation that qualitatively distinguishes humans from other living creatures—their consciousness of themselves as free agents. Indeed, what is ultimately being expressed here is the idea that the freedom of spirit as a metaphysical f(act) can only be a *human experience* to the extent that it is at the same time experienced as *happening to us*. The original representation of the unconditioned that arises from the experience of freedom, although it is here inseparable from the fact of our finitude, thus always already points to something absolutely unconditioned, an absolute cause, a God that is spirit. About this divine being, however, or the nature of its relation to the world of finite entities, no statements can be made that could ever constitute an adequately grounded explanation. On this point as well Jacobi breaks radically with conventional ways of thinking, in this case with the traditions of metaphysics. The only metaphysics that can now be discussed under the rubric of a metaphysics of spirit is a metaphysics of freedom, which consciously foregoes the pursuit of any theoretical knowledge and instead reflects on reason as an *organ of apprehension or "taking hold of"*: "'Taking hold of' is the root of reason." "'Taking hold of' presupposes something capable of being taken hold of; reason presupposes the *true*: it is the faculty of presupposing the true" (JF: JWA 2,1, 201, 208; MPW 507, 513).[18]

The constellation outlined here is as interesting as it is topical. Regardless of whether one considers reason to be capable of less than this "taking hold of," or whether one has significantly more confidence in its competencies, we can be certain in both cases that science "always spells out" something other than the meaning of spirit as personal selfhood.

---

[18] "Von Vernunft ist die Wurzel, *Vernehmen*." "Vernehmen sezt ein Vernehmbares; Vernunft das *Wahre* zum voraus: sie ist das Vermögen der Voraussetzung des Wahren." (JF: JWA 2,1, 201, 208)

5

Between Spinoza and Kant:
Jacobi on Freedom and Persons

I.

To address the topic of "freedom after Kant" as it pertains to the immediate post-Kantian period is inevitably to grapple with the legacy of Spinoza. To what degree Kant himself developed his philosophy in dialogue with Spinoza remains a matter of debate even today.[1] In the case of Kant's direct successors, however, there can be no doubt that their engagement with his philosophy of freedom is always also mediated through their response to Spinoza. At first glance, this response appears to entail a decisive break with Spinoza. Schelling, for example, in proclaiming that "the beginning and the end of all philosophy is—*freedom*,"[2] is clearly conceiving of his project as "a counterpart to Spinoza's *Ethics*."[3] If we look more closely at this alleged "counterpart," however, we also find Schelling's explicit assertion that Kant's theory of morality only ever applies to the finite, empirical I, certainly not to the I as principle of philosophy, which as "*absolute* power"[4] [absolute Macht] successively unifies into itself all the characteristics of Spinozan substance. In other words, and the reference to early Schelling is but one example of this, the status of freedom after Kant is rather complicated.

This claim holds true for Jacobi as well—the philosopher who first established Spinoza's *Ethics* as a paradigmatic point of reference in the official discourse of philosophy. In view of his unequivocal claims regarding Spinoza's so-called fatalism, one would expect Jacobi of all people to embrace Kant's philosophy, to see it an attractive alternative to be unconditionally endorsed in the interests of freedom. But it is not that simple, as Jacobi himself explains in a letter to Kleuker from 1788:

> I am currently studying Kant's *Critique of Practical Reason* [...]. You can imagine how strange it must be for me to find that Kant grounds the belief

---

[1] Most recently, Omri Boehm has provided us with a highly interesting set of reflections on the matter (Omri Boehm, *Kant's Critique of Spinoza* (Oxford: Oxford University Press, 2014)).
[2] Schelling, *Vom Ich als Princip der Philosophie*, AA 2, 101. F. W. J. Schelling, "Of the I as the Principle of Philosophy or On the Unconditional in Human Knowledge," in *The Unconditional in Human Knowledge. Four Early Essays (1794-1796)*, trans. Marti Fritz (Lewisburg: Bucknell University Press, 1980), 82.
[3] AA 2, 80. Schelling, "I as Principle," 69.
[4] AA 2, 122. Schelling, "I as Principle," 95. See also § XIV in its entirety.

in God in the fact of the causality of human reason, just as I do, and like me can conceive of no remedy for Spinozism unless one accepts and presupposes freedom. And yet our ways of conceiving the matter and our principles are completely different. (JBW I,8, 72f.)

How are we to understand this assertion? What view of freedom is being presented here, which shares certain commitments with Kant's position on the one hand, but, on the other, differs "completely" from it?

In order to answer these questions, the reflections that follow will focus primarily on a text entitled "Concerning Man's Freedom," which Jacobi inserted into the second, 1789 edition of his book *Concerning the Doctrine of Spinoza in Letters to Herr Moses Mendelssohn*. Kant is never mentioned by name in the text, but ten years later, in the *Letter to Fichte* of 1799, Jacobi explicitly notes that it constitutes (among other things) a critical engagement with Kant's practical philosophy, and he also includes the text among several Supplements to the letter, referring to it here as "The Aphorisms concerning Non-Freedom and Freedom" (JF: JWA 2,1, 213; MPW 518).[5] The use of the term "Aphorisms" is fitting here, insofar as the text is not a treatise in the conventional sense. But neither is it merely a loosely related collection of thought fragments. What Jacobi has composed is rather a carefully arranged sequence of fifty-two dense paragraphs, which are divided into two main sections: "FIRST SECTION: *Man does not have Freedom*," "SECOND SECTION: *Man has Freedom*" (Spin: JWA 1,1, 158–69; MPW 341–9).

It should be clear by this point that we must be wary of taking these section headings to imply a straightforward antithesis between Spinoza and Kant. In fact, the complexity of Jacobi's argumentation means that both Spinoza and Kant appear together in the first as well as in the second section. In Jacobi's view, it follows just as necessarily from Kant's philosophy as from Spinoza's that freedom is an illusion. And conversely, the thesis that human beings possess freedom is as much a consequence of Spinoza's position as it is of Kant's. Against this backdrop, and considering that the subsequent generation of post-Kantians all read Jacobi's *Spinoza Letters*, it should come as no surprise that seemingly clear-cut attributions are abandoned in their work in favor of new constellations. With regard to Jacobi himself, as I aim to demonstrate in the course of this chapter, his astute analysis of the problem points to a conception of freedom which has much to commend it.[6]

---

[5] Jacobi not only makes explicit reference to "Kant's ethical law" in these aphorisms, he also claims to have undertaken a deduction of the categorical imperative in his earlier text: "I have never understood how anyone could find something mysterious or incomprehensible in the categorical imperative, which is in fact so easy to deduce *(Spinoza Letters*, Pref. pp. xxxiii and xxxiv)" (JF: JWA 2,1, 214; MPW 518).

[6] See also Jürgen Stolzenberg, "Was ist Freiheit? Jacobis Kritik der Moralphilosophie Kants," in *Friedrich Heinrich Jacobi*, ed. Walter Jaeschke and Birgit Sandkaulen (Hamburg: Meiner, 2004), 19–36, and Oliver Koch, *Individualität als Fundamentalgefühl. Zur Metaphysik der Person bei Jacobi und Jean Paul* (Hamburg: Meiner, 2013), 80ff.

II.

I will begin with three brief points by way of orientation, after which I will jump *in medias res*, so to speak, in order to reconstruct Jacobi's *Treatise on Freedom* from the inside out. With regard to form—this is the first thing to be noted—the antithetical structure of the text bears a certain similarity to that of Kant's third antinomy, also in coming to the conclusion that neither of the two possible positions is simply to be declared the winner. We are neither free nor unfree beings, but constitutively both; we have a "*double* tendency," as Jacobi writes toward the end of the text (Spin: JWA 1,1, 168; MPW 348). For this reason, the reader would do well to accept the statements made about human unfreedom in the first section as indicating Jacobi's actual position, albeit only in a restricted sense.

Second, however, and with regard to content, Jacobi disrupts the constellation of the third antinomy in the most fundamental way. Neither Kant's opposition between *determinism and freedom* nor its compatibilist dissolution has any purchase here. The line of argumentation that leads to Jacobi's diagnosis of "mechanism" in the first section of the text (Spin: JWA 1,1, 162; MPW 344) is simply far too complex, which is partially, though not entirely, the result of the fact that in both sections, he never fails to combine the *cosmological* aspect of the discussion of freedom with the *moral* dimension of the problem. In this sense, Jacobi incorporates Kant's transition to the *Critique of Practical Reason* into his argumentation from the outset. What freedom is and what it means, whether it can be ascribed to us or not—such questions cannot be decided theoretically, only practically.

Moreover, from within the framework of this practical point of view—and this is the third point—a series of additional concrete questions emerge in conjunction with the performance of our actions, questions of *how* we act, *who* it is that acts, and *toward what end* the actor directs his activity. From a Kantian perspective, this framework also simultaneously invokes the ethical law of practical reason, what Kant refers to as the "ratio cognoscendi" of freedom.[7] The essential nature of freedom as an indispensable ingredient of ethical action becomes clear on the basis of the law which demands that we subject the maxim of our action to a test of universalizability. And this leads in turn to a contrast between free action, as lawful action motivated by duty, and unfree action, which follows not the *ought of reason* but the *heteronomy of inclination*. With this distinction, we have arrived at the point where Jacobi's position becomes radically opposed to that of Kant, and so I will now proceed *in medias res*.

III.

According to Jacobi, the proposed dichotomy of reason and sensuality, of duty and inclination, is fundamentally inadequate for coming to a sufficient understanding of freedom, and in a double sense. On the one hand, as we will soon see, the evidence

---

[7] Kant, *Kritik der praktischen Vernunft*, AA V, 4 Anm.; Immanuel Kant, *Critique of Practical Reason* (1788), in *Immanuel Kant: Practical Philosophy*, ed. and trans. Mary J. Gregor (Cambridge: Cambridge University Press, 1996), 140.

for unfreedom, what Jacobi refers to as "mechanism," extends well beyond what is indicated by inclination. To this corresponds, on the other hand, the fact that our moral consciousness, to the extent that it involves freedom, is undergirded by a distinction far more fundamental than the one invoked by an awareness of duty, and whose realization in action is accompanied by a unique experience of *joy*.[8] Following Jacobi, then, we are entirely justified in formulating the question of freedom as follows: When do we truly *feel* free? Do we feel free when we consider ourselves to be subject to the obligations of the categorical imperative? Or do we feel truly free at those moments when we have the impression, an impression that manifests itself in an experience of joy, of being entirely *at one with ourselves*?

From a Kantian perspective, of course, the counter question immediately presents itself, namely, what could this joyful feeling of being at one with myself possibly have to do with an adequate moral consciousness? Even Schiller, who some years later also sought to implement an emotional reform of duty based ethics, nonetheless remains reliant on Kant's premises in his efforts to resolve the opposition between duty and inclination through the figure of the beautiful soul. Doing ones duty *gladly*, however, until it has become so habituated that it is no longer experienced as the strict compulsion of unconditional obligation, is not what Jacobi has in mind. For this reason, it is best to set aside Schiller's beautiful soul as an ideal of ethical perfection here, especially since Jacobi himself offers a very different perspective on this topic in his novel *Woldemar*. There, with regard to the question of moral consciousness, the beautiful soul as embodied in the figure of Woldemar appears as a highly problematic case. I will return to the novel at the end of the chapter. For now, we are faced with the following question: What does the feeling of being at one with myself have to do with the moral content of freedom?

Jacobi's answer to this question turns on a crucial distinction that grounds his entire discussion of freedom at the most fundamental level: our moral consciousness in the proper sense is based on the intuition that there exists a qualitative difference between the orientations toward action provided by the *pleasant and the useful*, on the one hand, and, on the other hand, by the *good*. From this perspective, to be completely at one with myself in the free orientation toward the good also means eo ipso to be at one with the other.[9] Jacobi calls this ethical disposition *religion*, a term that must here be viewed as entirely free from any association with positive religion and also, we should note, from any thought of an exclusive relationship with a transcendent divinity. What is meant

---

[8] The pleasure at issue here is one which, according to Jacobi, "cannot be compared to any other joy: *this is the joy that God himself has in his existence*" (Spin: JWA 1,1, 168; MPW 348). This statement clearly reflects the influence of Spinoza. I will return to the question of Jacobi's proximity to and distance from Spinoza below.

[9] The classical distinction between the pleasant, the useful and the good informs the reasoning of the entire second section. Platonic, Aristotelian and stoic influences are clearly visible, sometimes in the form of explicit references to individual thinkers (Spin: JWA 1,1, 164f.; 167; MPW 345f., 348). The implications of an appeal to Aristotle are explicitly treated in the novel *Woldemar*. The virtue-ethical concept is expressed with particular intensity, as in the following passage: "They all want to be lovers of virtue, not of the advantages connected with it; and they all want to know of a *beauty* that is not just a source of *pleasure; a joy that is not mere titillation*." (Spin: JWA 1,1, 168; MPW 348)

is rather an ethical practice among human beings, which expresses itself in the form of *"pure love"* (Spin: JWA 1,1, 167; MPW 347). In this context, and in anticipation of a point to which I will briefly return at the end of the chapter, it also bears mentioning that among all of the successors of Kant and Jacobi, Hegel strikes me as the thinker who best understood that Jacobi's line of reasoning leads to a completely new concept of freedom, a concept which he later incorporates into his own work in the figure of being with oneself in another (Im-Andern-Beisichselbstsein).

Before considering such questions of influence, however, we must first further elucidate Jacobi's own position, which centers on the fundamental distinction mentioned previously: the qualitative difference between the useful and the good, on the basis of which the distinguishing quality of freedom becomes visible. Unless we attribute freedom to ourselves, we cannot draw this distinction or even begin to understand it—in this case the good is identical to the useful. "By good," Spinoza writes, "I shall understand what we certainly know to be useful to us."[10] It is clear that Jacobi has precisely this utilitarian orientation of Spinoza's *Ethics* in mind in the first section of his text. But wouldn't Kant himself object that this matter has already been resolved? Doesn't his presentation of the ethical law and the freedom that it presupposes demonstrate precisely that moral action is to be distinguished in principle from all forms of instrumental action, that a good cause is always an end in itself and not a means to something else?

Jacobi has no intention of contradicting Kant on this matter. On the contrary, he wants to emphasize that Kant's primary concern is to draw this very distinction. Against the backdrop of this agreement, however, Jacobi's objection becomes all the more pointed. Instead of expressing our genuine interest in the good, the categorical imperative distorts it.[11] Interestingly, according to Jacobi's argumentation, the same holds true for Spinoza, but from the opposite direction. The further Spinoza progresses in his *Ethics*, the more the instrumental perspective fades into the background, to the point that happiness no longer appears as the reward of virtue but as virtue itself.[12] As we have just seen in his use of the term "joy," Jacobi expressly incorporates this position into his own concept of freedom, but he simultaneously combines this gesture with the objection that the premises of Spinoza's own theory fail to provide any basis for

---

[10] Spinoza, *Ethics*, E IV, Def. 1.

[11] In order to minimize any possibility that this subtle analysis could be superficially interpreted as reflecting a misunderstanding of Kant, Jacobi also adds to the Supplement attached to the *Letter to Fichte* an "Excerpt from a Letter to a Friend Concerning Kant's Moral Doctrine" (JF: JWA 2,1, 257f.; MPW 535), from which one can conclude that his understanding of Kant's *intention* is entirely correct. The focus is on the idea of an end-in-itself, which Jacobi shares with Kant but which he insists can never be adequately grounded with Kantian arguments. In fact, according to Jacobi's analysis, the way Kant's reasoning unfolds actually points to an instrumental perspective. In its substance, the idea is similar to one found in Tugendhat: in order to be certain that the categorical imperative expresses something more than instrumental contractualism, one has to read the second formulation, that is, the idea of the end-in-itself, into the first (Ernst Tugendhat, *Vorlesungen über Ethik* (Frankfurt a.M.: Suhrkamp, 1993), 80ff.). This means that, in the absence of such an inverted interpretation, there are good reasons for Jacobi's critical reading. On this point, see the subsequent discussions in this chapter.

[12] E V, prop. 42.

rendering such a view of ethical life comprehensible. In fact, Jacobi already formulates this objection in his conversation with Lessing:

> Spinoza also had to wriggle quite a bit to hide his fatalism when he turned to human conduct, especially in his fourth and fifth Parts [of the *Ethics*] where I could say that he degrades himself to a sophist here and there. —And that's exactly what I was saying: even the greatest mind, if it wants to teach all things absolutely, to make them rhyme with each other according to distinct concepts and will not otherwise let anything stand, must run into absurdities. (Spin: JWA 1,1, 28f.; MPW 194)

By splitting the text into two sections, Jacobi incorporates this diagnosis—of the inconsistency of rigorously consistent theories—into the structure of his *Treatise on Freedom*.

IV.

Turning now to the first sequence of paragraphs with the previous discussion in mind, we find an arrangement that is as astute as it is provocative. Under the heading "man has no freedom," Jacobi offers a consistently instrumental view of our actions, taking what appear to be the two diametrically opposed positions of Kant and Spinoza and combining them under *the rubric of a naturalistic ethics*. The categorical imperative is decoded as a highly sublimated form of the striving for self-preservation that underlies Spinoza's approach, with the result that one of the problems in Kant's model also falls away, namely, how the obligation of reason can become volition, that is, how it becomes an actual motivation for action. By the same token, Jacobi allays the suspicion that a focus on self-preservation lacks all moral substance and simply encourages blind egoism.

One can already see from the structure of the argumentation just how important it is for Jacobi to demonstrate precisely this convergence between self-preservation and (instrumental) morality. First, the section begins with the third part of Spinoza's *Ethics*, from which it follows that Jacobi, the inaugurator of the Spinoza renaissance around 1800, must be exempted from one of the criticisms that is frequently (and mostly justifiably) directed toward its participants. While it is true that the Spinoza renaissance was generally focused too intently on Spinoza's metaphysics of substance and therefore ignored the analysis of the affects so central to his system, this accusation cannot be leveled against Jacobi himself. All of the documents that comprise the *Spinoza Letters*, including the initial conversation with Lessing, attest to the fact that Jacobi considers the *Ethics* to be an integrated whole. It is thus all the more noteworthy, and this is the second point, that the theorem of self-preservation in the *Treatise on Freedom* is detached from its foundation in divine potency. This enables the transformation of Spinoza's approach into an empirical naturalism, the scope of which is extended beyond that of human life. It begins with the observation that in the case of all finite things, existence always involves a relation to coexistence. With regard to "living nature," this relation expresses itself in the sensations of desire and repulsion, which together attest to a more foundational striving. This "desire a priori" is the striving for self-preservation (Spin: JWA 1,1, 158; MPW 341).

What Jacobi thereby reformulates in empirical terms is Spinoza's image of an infinite interweaving of modes. Crucially, this network cannot be understood as a purely extrinsically determined causal nexus; rather, every individual point in the network involves the inner determination of an active relation to itself. For this reason, the arguments Jacobi presents in making the case for unfreedom, arguments he relates with exceptional acuity, have nothing to do with any straightforwardly deterministic scenarios. And such scenarios are transcended altogether in the next step, in which Jacobi, precisely because he has first expanded Spinoza's model into a naturalistic theory of the living as such, is all the better positioned to highlight a difference that pertains to the specific characteristics of human nature.

Unlike animals, humans are "rational beings." This does not mean that humans drop out of the universal web of existence and coexistence, but it does imply that the basic striving for self-preservation is sublimated here into the "rational desire" of the will, a capacity which consists in being able to rationally justify action and, by doing so, ensure that it serves the interests of reasonable self-preservation (Spin: JWA 1,1, 159; MPW 342). It is apparent that Jacobi understands "rational beings" in this context quite literally as "animal rationale." The critical significance of this move comes into better focus if we reintroduce the distinction between two types of reason first articulated in *Supplement VII* to the *Spinoza Letters*—the distinction between a reason (later referred to as *adjective*) that man possesses, and a reason (later referred to as *substantive*) that possesses man (Spin: JWA 1,1, 259f.; JF: JWA 2,1, 232; MPW 375, 528). Here we are clearly dealing with a case of adjective reason, which humans use as a "tool," that is, with the epitome of *instrumental rationality*.[13] In this context, human action is normatively oriented toward "practical *principles*" (Spin: JWA 1,1, 160; MPW 342), whereby individuals evaluate alternative courses of action according to the criterion of whether they serve the cause of successful self-preservation, and, in the process, also attribute to themselves those actions in which irrational impulses had the upper hand. In view of the palpably unpleasant consequences of such actions, they are forced to confront the realization that they could and should have done better (Spin: JWA 1,1, 160; MPW 343).

In pursuing this line of argumentation, Jacobi ends up aligning himself with Spinoza's approach, in the sense that the internal formation of moral consciousness through the cultivation of inclination[14] is made into a prerequisite for intersubjective cooperation (Spin: JWA 1,1, 161; MPW 343). The argument is a strong one irrespective

---

[13] See Chapters 4 and 6 in this volume, where I show that in his description of a naturalistic ethics grounded in instrumental rationality, Jacobi also incorporates elements of a Lockean empiricism.

[14] In view of the "official" antithesis between duty and inclination in Kant, my use of the formulation "cultivation of inclination" is intended to be somewhat pointed.

of its connection to Spinoza. Once again the shortcomings of a simple determinism are avoided, which on this level would have to assert something like the compulsory internalization of predetermined moral norms but without being able to explain how we could even understand the normative appeal to orient our actions toward specific ends, not to mention why we would seek to incorporate these norms—more or less successfully—into our own lives. With this in mind, it is fascinating to note how Jacobi's thought process culminates in a reference to "the moral laws that we call *apodeictic* laws of practical reason," thereby indicating, as previously shown, that it is indeed Kant's categorical imperative which he intends to target here (Spin: JWA 1,1, 162; MPW 344).[15] Insofar as it is reattached to the fundamental interest in self-preservation, Kant's idea of autonomy, including the difference between the hypothetical and the categorical imperative is, on the one hand, subverted and—from a Kantian perspective—heteronomously defamiliarized. But on the other hand, it is at the same time preserved in subtle fashion, because the moral law is interpreted as an expression of our inner normative disposition and not as some sort of external coercive mechanism.

Ultimately, then, instrumentally grounded morality in the service of self-preservation can be freed entirely from purely strategic considerations. We do not cooperate with others because it is advantageous to us on the whole, which is in fact what Kant's examples of the principle of universalizability rather forcefully suggest. Rather, "a natural love and obligation to justice towards others" flows directly from our striving for self-preservation. "A rational being cannot distinguish itself *qua* rational being (abstractly) from another rational being. The *I* and *Man* are one; the *He* and *Man* are one; *therefore the He and I are one*. The Love of the *person* therefore limits the love of the *individuum,* and necessitates my not holding myself in high regard" (Spin: JWA 1,1, 161f.; MPW 343f.).[16]

Driven to the furthest point of its rational sublimation, the self bound up with the aim of self-preservation finally fades away. Upon the perfect realization of the ought, its addressee disappears, the ought transforms itself into the purest form of volition, and instrumentally rational naturalism necessarily tips over into *nihilism*—this is the new, even more dramatic conclusion that Jacobi, on the basis of his *Treatise on Freedom*, draws in his *Letter to Fichte* in reference to Fichte's own Wissenschaftslehre.

However, one need not pursue every twist and turn of the nihilistic logic of an approach "built on one fundamental impulse alone" (Spin: JWA 1,1, 160; MPW 343) to appreciate the complexity that characterizes Jacobi's diagnosis of human unfreedom and, by the same token, the sophistication of his position on freedom, both of which have significant relevance for contemporary discussions. It is not a question of a simple causal determinism here, nor of a purely affective desire, but rather of the

---

[15] In the *Letter to Fichte*, where Jacobi makes both his engagement with Kant and his critical intent explicit, the pursuit of self-preservation is described as the "necessary urge to be consistent with ourselves, i.e. the *law of identity*" and is identified with Kant's "moral law" (JF: JWA 2,1, 214; MPW 518).

[16] On Jacobi's use of the concept "person," see Chapter 6 in this volume.

rational control of our natural interest in self-preservation. What this means is that the conventional distinction between causes and reasons or grounds can no longer serve as the basis for distinguishing a form of action that is qualitatively free. Accordingly, in Jacobi's description of "mechanism" one finds neither a lack of good grounds nor a shortage of alternatives for action, which, on the contrary, come into view and are normatively evaluated here. The notion that we merely carry out that which has been predetermined by a seamless set of causal relationships, in other words, is *not* what is being asserted in this context.

Therefore, to the extent that we are the authors of our actions and also consider transgressions against our principles as acts for which we are responsible, it would be completely inconceivable to revert back to a line of argument based on a disjunction between determinism and arbitrariness. In no way, according to Jacobi, does freedom consist "in some absurd faculty to make decisions without grounds" (Spin: JWA 1,1, 164; MPW 345). A well-founded moral naturalism has long since moved beyond the opposition between contingency and necessity. In light of this state of affairs, it would be banal to claim that freedom consists in being able to do whatever strikes my fancy. But then what does an adequate concept of freedom actually look like?

V.

I have already pointed to the answer above. Freedom—this is the central message of the second section—manifests itself in an orientation toward the good that is free from all instrumental considerations. Given that Jacobi rightly claims to share this basic conviction with Kant, we should not be surprised by the rather Kantian character of his claim that "this freedom consists essentially *in the independence of the will from desire*" (Spin: JWA 1,1, 164; MPW 345). This means that unlike animals, with which we share a natural interest in self-preservation, humans are fundamentally capable of distancing themselves from this interest (also in its sublimated form of "rational desire"). And in so doing, they disclose a genuinely moral world in which the good, rather than being identical to the useful, constitutes a distinct orientation for action. In contrast to Kant's claim, however, it should be clear in light of all that has been said thus far that the moral law cannot be the ratio cognoscendi of such freedom. On the one hand, we have seen that Kant's imperative can be decoded as a form of instrumental rationality, while, on the other hand, it is apparent that the moral surplus Kant intends to provide through the ethical law presupposes that a genuine dimension of the good has already been understood. In other words, and Jacobi's argumentation culminates in precisely this claim, freedom is always already *actual*, which is to say, *active*.

Jacobi thereby directly links a cosmological consideration to a matter of practical concern. From a cosmological point of view, he attacks the premises of naturalism, objecting that the living totality of relations of existence and coexistence, of action and passion, cannot be understood if it is considered to be entirely relational. On the contrary, to assert (correctly) that living beings actively re-act to their environment is always already to presuppose a general capacity for action as such, a *"pure self-activity"* [reine Selbstthätigkeit] (Spin: JWA 1,1, 163; MPW 344) that does not arise from the mediated totality of reactions, and whose *"possibility"* we also cannot comprehend, insofar as we are only capable of understanding mediated relations (Spin: JWA 1,1, 163; MPW 345). Even before turning to the topic of freedom in his next step, then, Jacobi already draws attention here to an explanatory gap that reveals the inherent limitations of even the most advanced naturalistic worldview. The status of the striving for self-preservation as an "a priori desire," which was established in the first section, cannot be maintained in this form, but neither is there any way to move beyond it theoretically.

The assumption of an "absolute self-activity," however, is not plucked out of thin air here. If not its possibility, then certainly its *"actuality"* has long been known to us, in the sense that "it is immediately displayed in consciousness, and is demonstrated by the deed" (Spin: JWA 1,1, 163f.; MPW 345). Self-activity is not the same as freedom. Freedom is a uniquely human privilege, insofar as "among living beings" only man possesses that "degree of consciousness of his self-activity" that manifests in free action, namely in the fact and the act of being able to and wanting to distance ourselves from the interest in self-preservation (Spin: JWA 1,1, 164; MPW 345). The evidence adduced by Jacobi to show that we have the ability and the desire to do this—and not only an obligation—in other words, to show that our self-understanding as persons is intrinsically linked to the desire to be people who can distinguish between the useful and the good with regard to both our own actions and those of others, is the "feeling of honor" (Spin: JWA 1,1, 165; MPW 346). It is a feeling that cannot be equated with either respect for the law or sensual inclination. A person who acts out of a sense of honor is engaged with his entire being; in acting thus, he freely commits himself to a life lived according to more than merely instrumental calculations, a way of living in which he can place his trust and in which others can trust as well.

Jacobi does not assert that this effort is always or entirely successful, just as no one would ever claim that we can only bear to look in the mirror if we have transformed ourselves into flawless paragons of virtue. That fact that we do not always fully realize our potential to orient ourselves toward the good does not diminish the actuality of freedom. We are, after all, conditioned natural beings. The crucial point is that these failures do not mean that we have failed to live up to an imperative of reason, but that we have failed to live up to our own aspirations, which are revealed not only in the feeling of honor but in an entire array of moral feelings (esteem, love, gratitude, admiration).[17]

---

[17] On this point see the text added by Jacobi to his *Letter to Fichte:* "It is impossible that everything be nature and that there be no freedom, for it is impossible that what alone ennobles and elevates man *(truth, goodness, beauty)* be only delusion, deception, lie. So it would be, if there were no freedom. Impossible would be *true* respect, impossible *true* wonder, *true* gratitude and love, if it were impossible for freedom and nature to dwell in a single being, and the one to spin where the other weaves." (JF: JWA 2,1, 236; MPW 531f.) In this reference to the triad of the true, the good, and the beautiful, the good is explicitly named, whereas in the *Treatise on Freedom* it is defined indirectly, so to speak, as that which is neither useful nor pleasant, and it is positively designated in references to the "principle of honor."

Conversely, a multi-stage argument against Spinoza arises out of the irreducibility of such feelings to instrumental attitudes, one that still needs to be addressed in some detail here. According to Jacobi, Spinoza's claim that a free person would not resort to lying even if facing mortal danger[18] shows, on the one hand, that Spinoza has in fact identified a dimension of freedom that is independent of any utilitarian considerations. And it also shows at the same time that Spinoza, once the motivation provided by self-preservation has been removed from the equation, has no choice but to describe the free life as one so entirely governed by reason that it hardly has anything to do any more with our concrete experience. *In abstracto*, Jacobi writes in response to this state of affairs,

> Spinoza is right. It is just as impossible for a man of *pure reason* to lie or to cheat, as for the three angles of a triangle not to equal two right angles. But will a real being endowed with reason be so driven into a corner by the *abstractum of his reason*? Will he let himself be made such a total prisoner through a mere play of words? Not for a moment! If honour is to be *trusted,* and if a man can *keep his word,* then quite another spirit must dwell in him than the spirit of syllogism. XL. I hold this other spirit to be the breath of God in the work of clay. (Spin: JWA 1,1, 166; MPW 347)

With the reference to "this other spirit," Jacobi's fundamental objection to Spinoza's metaphysics comes into view. Starting from the question of the motivation for our actions, which Spinoza is even less able to answer than Kant without recourse to instrumental explanations, Jacobi insists on the existence of a *genuine striving for the good*. In addition to the natural drive to self-preservation, a second, "intellectual impulse" (Spin: JWA 1,1, 168; MPW 348) is also active within us, a desire for freedom which, whenever it is successfully realized, fills us with joy. In Spinoza's metaphysics, however, stretched as it is between the potency of substance and its expression in a finite conatus, such a desire has no place. For this reason, the order of elements in the relation of expression must be reformulated in a structurally analogous manner: The impetus to free action that is active within us is in itself a testament, not to the power of substance, but rather to "*a God who is a Spirit*" (Spin: JWA 1,1, 167; MPW 347).

---

[18] E IV, prop. 72, scholium. The fact that Jacobi takes aim at precisely this proposition becomes all the more relevant in light of Walther's use of this same proposition to very convincingly argue that Spinoza here anticipates Kant's "universalization theory in its pure form." (Manfred Walther, "Konsistenz der Maximen. Universalisierbarkeit und Moralität nach Spinoza und Kant," in *Motivationen für das Selbst. Kant und Spinoza im Vergleich*, ed. Anne Tillkorn (Wiesbaden: Harrassowitz Verlag, 2012), 113). He thereby confirms Jacobi's insight into the structural correspondences between Spinoza and Kant, though we should note that in splitting his text into two sections, Jacobi also shows that such correspondences can be read in two ways: in terms of an instrumental ethics of unfreedom on the one hand, and in terms of a non-instrumental ethics of freedom on the other. Jacobi's objection to Spinoza in the second section can thus also be applied to Kant by way of analogy. Countering the abstraction of pure reason that informs the work of both thinkers, he insists that the good, if it is in fact to provide a motivation for action in concrete persons, must already be concretely understood and intended prior to any rational universalization.

VI.

This brings me to my conclusion. Jacobi's position on freedom cannot be sustained without this metaphysics of action as its ultimate horizon; as I said previously, however, his position has nothing to do with the restoration of a theonomous morality. Supplanting Kant's ethical law with a divine codex is the last thing that he would have intended. In contrast to Kant, however, in Jacobi's case the metaphysical dimension does not come into play as a postulate of the highest good, in which duty and happiness allegedly correlate with one another—a correlation, we should note, that cannot help but call to mind the promise of divine rewards. The actuality of freedom here is not decoupled from the experience of happiness; it is accompanied by an incomparable joy, although we might wish we could have still more of it. Jacobi is not gesturing toward something that awaits us in another life, provided that we behave in accordance with the law and are therefore worthy of happiness. It is something that, as it were, lies behind this life—just as we are destined to strive for *self-preservation*, we are also destined to strive for *self-determination*. Jacobi refers explicitly to a "law" in this context, but a law which, in contrast to Kant's universal ethical law, is active within us as an always individual "expression" of a divine will (Spin: JWA 1,1, 167; MPW 348).

I find absolutely nothing scandalous in this claim; on the contrary, it frees us from the notion that self-determination requires us to supply ourselves with the determination of self-determination by our own efforts. Such a requirement already leads in Kant's *Religion within the Boundaries of Mere Reason* (1793) to the assumption of an indeterminate free power of choice that is prior to freedom, and which inexplicably and extratemporally commits itself in an intelligible act to choosing either the good or the evil as established by the hierarchical relation between the moral law and inclination. Well before this idea occurs to Kant, Jacobi has already established in the *Treatise on Freedom* that we can never fully grasp the relations that determine our "double" structure of impulses—a conception he posits in order to challenge the notion of a single basic drive—regardless of whether we consider it as a whole or from the more granular perspective of our own actions, because that would involve "a theory of creation," whose object "is to state the conditions of the unconditioned" (Spin: JWA 1,1, 168; MPW 348).[19] We can never get behind ourselves—but this in no way releases us from responsibility for what we do in accordance with the two drives.

It might seem more problematic that Jacobi, because he does not codify the orientation toward the good, places it entirely within the realm of desire and the consummation of free action. This is Hegel's objection. His enduring admiration for Jacobi's depiction of actual freedom was always tempered by his reservations regarding the fact that it lacked the stable objectivity allegedly guaranteed by ethical institutions. Considering, however, that in making this criticism, Hegel adduces the "beautiful

---

[19] It does Schelling no injustice to note that his *Philosophical Inquiries into the Essence of Human Freedom* attempts, on the basis of Kant and of Jacobi's *Treatise on Freedom* and despite Jacobi's warning, to express the "possibility and the theory of creation" in order to approach a concept of personal freedom. See Chapter 12 in this volume.

soul" Woldemar as evidence of the inadequacy of an appeal to moral feelings, two observations present themselves.

The first is that Jacobi himself uses this figure to analyze the dangers of a perverted striving for the good. In such a case an individual appears to strive after the good but is actually pursuing instrumental aims, without intending to do so or even realizing his true motivation. And second, notwithstanding the possibility of such unintentional misconduct, the fact remains that the good can only ever reveal itself in good acts. Here Jacobi aligns himself with Aristotelian virtue ethics. Being free requires practice on the basis of moral intuitions (the moral feelings of honor, gratitude, and admiration named by Jacobi), which provide both a source of orientation and a court of appeal. And just as with Aristotle, Jacobi designates *friendship* as providing the best form of practice. No ethical institution can bring forth friendship. On the other hand—and this is my objection to Hegel—a political community can count itself lucky if the free practice of friendship has already enabled its members to cultivate a set of basic moral intuitions.[20]

---

[20] Of course, Hegel knows this very well. While he explicitly points out the potentially anarchist danger of Jacobi's concept of freedom and nowhere refers to the foundational relevance of friendship, the chapter on "Conscience; the Beautiful Soul, Evil, and its Forgiveness" in the *Phenomenology* is clearly indebted to Jacobi's *Woldemar*. There Hegel uses the friendship between Woldemar and Henriette (albeit in an anonymized version) as a model for nothing less than "a reciprocal recognition which is *absolute* spirit" (GW 9, 361; G. W. F. Hegel, *The Phenomenology of Spirit*, ed. and trans. Terry Pinkard (Cambridge: Cambridge University Press, 2018), 388). On this point see Chapter 7 in this volume.

6

That, What, or Who? Jacobi and the Discourse on Persons

I.

On February 4, 1795, Schelling composes an exuberant letter to his good friend Hegel. Sequestered in far-away Bern and thus ignorant of the latest intellectual developments, Hegel needs to hear what the world is talking about. Schelling wants him to share in his excitement for the luminous prospects of a philosophy that marches under the banner of freedom as its "alpha and omega," and is therefore grounded in the "absolute I" as the completely "unconditioned." The letter ends abruptly, almost breathlessly, with a conclusion that deserves our careful attention. Schelling notes that "*God* is nothing but the absolute I" and then adds in a series of staccato pronouncements:

> Personality arises from the unity of consciousness. Consciousness, however, is not possible without an object; but for God, that is, for the absolute I, there can be *no* object, because this would mean that the absolute I had ceased to be absolute.— Hence there is *no* personal God, and our highest endeavor is the destruction of our personality, a transition to the absolute sphere of being, which, however, will never be *possible* in all of eternity;—thus only *practical* approximation to the absolute, and thus—*Immortality*. I must close now. Farewell. Answer your Sch[elling] soon.[1]

Modern philosophy is a *philosophy of subjectivity*—not a *philosophy of the person*. Schelling's sentences make this paradigmatically clear. To be sure, as finite beings we are all persons, but nothing about this status gives us cause to ascribe to ourselves something like "dignity." Rather, according to Schelling, to be a person is to be bound to objects, that is, to be entangled in dependencies, in a state of unfreedom. Only in this manner is the consciousness developed that a person characteristically has of himself. If this is indeed the case, however, then one has to accept the consequences that follow.

---

[1] Manfred Frank and Gerhard Kurz, eds., *Materialien zu Schellings philosophischen Anfängen* (Frankfurt a.M.: Suhrkamp, 1975), 125ff. G. W. F. Hegel, *The Letters*, trans. Clark Butler and Christiane Seiler (Bloomington: Indiana University Press, 1984), 33, translation amended.
In order to underline the distinctiveness of Jacobi's approach to the question of persons, the German terms "Personalität" and "Persönlichkeit" have been consistently translated as "personhood" and "personality."

First, it would be patently absurd to apply the concept of person to the absolute. What Schelling appeals to here as the principle of all orientation is an "absolute I" that posits itself as "I am I," as Schelling says following Fichte. But this I is certainly not a person, precisely because it is not defined by its dependence on the world of objects, but is rather understood as an "absolute sphere of being." The absoluteness of this sphere not only allows but actually requires one to identify that which was previously referred to as "God" with the being-an-I. However, for the reasons mentioned, there can be no "personal God" who would be self-aware. The second consequence relates to ourselves. If Schelling is right, it would be equally absurd to want to cultivate our own existence as persons. On the contrary, our goal must be to destroy this existence or at least to work toward its destruction. This is the only attitude toward ourselves that does justice to the principle of orientation provided by the "absolute I," and this attitude alone realizes the vision of freedom comprehensively guaranteed by this I that has taken over the place of God.

Schelling's letter is well known and widely cited. Until recently, however, it would have seemed rather strange to draw particular attention to its conclusion. Why bother to take an interest in the person, when it has been established that it represents nothing more than a deficient determination, one that fails to provide a productive starting point for any meaningful reflection on either transcendental or metaphysical principles or for an understanding of ourselves. Not the person but the paradigm of subjectivity has been the focus of countless studies and debates. Much has been said about this absolute distinction of an "I" first called into existence by Descartes, the so-called "father" of modern philosophy whose famous "cogito ergo sum" later metamorphosed into Kant's "I think" and from there made its way into the center of classical German philosophy, into the systems of Fichte, Schelling, and Hegel, where it finally, while undergoing numerous further transformations, conquered the realm of the absolute itself. The goal has been to clarify this genealogy and its pretensions, to defend it as an essential part of our intellectual legacy, or simply to condemn it as a misguided preoccupation of modernity.

I would not presume to claim that the fierce debate over whether the subject is truly dead or can still be resuscitated has been decided one way or the other. It should be noted, however, that the focus of discussion has recently undergone a decisive shift. Suddenly, the "person," a figure who had long been languishing in the background, has moved onto the main stage and is playing a central role.[2] The reasons for this shift are manifold. Most significant are no doubt the growing ethical concerns surrounding contemporary developments in science and technology, which have given a new

---

[2] Among the initiators see Theo Kobusch, *Die Entdeckung der Person. Metaphysik der Freiheit und modernes Menschenbild* (Freiburg/Basel/Wien: Herder, 1993), Robert Spaemann, *Personen. Versuche über den Unterschied zwischen "etwas" und "jemand"* (Stuttgart: Klett-Cotta, 1996), Dieter Sturma, *Philosophie der Person. Die Selbstverhältnisse von Subjektivität und Moralität* (Paderborn/Munich/Wien/Zürich: Schöningh, 1997). Dieter Sturma, ed., *Person. Philosophiegeschichte—Theoretische Philosophie—Praktische Philosophie* (Paderborn: Mentis, 2001). Since then, a flood of publications on the concept of person has appeared. For a recent interpretation of Jacobi, see Oliver Koch, *Individualität als Fundamentalgefühl. Zur Metaphysik der Person bei Jacobi und Jean Paul* (Hamburg: Meiner, 2013).

urgency and relevance to questions of personhood. But recent work in the philosophy of language is also significant here, especially work in the analytical tradition such as Strawson's *Individuals*.[3] This may have to do with the particular genealogy of the anglophone philosophical tradition, in which, thanks to Locke, a strong concept of the person has always been available. In any case, it should be clear from what has been said that the growing interest in persons stems from systematic changes in our approach to philosophical problems rather than from a specific engagement with classical German philosophy. In the latter context as well, however, a notable shift can be discerned. Due to the evolution of the broader discussion, it no longer seems irrelevant to ask what the canonical texts of this tradition have to say about the person. Most conspicuously, Kant's practical philosophy has now become the center of attention, taking the place of his "I think," but the transcendental philosophy and metaphysics of Fichte and Schelling are also the focus of renewed interest. The reflections that follow will engage with these thinkers to a degree, but their main focus is on someone else. After all, in light of the circumstances outlined above, one can hardly imagine a more appropriate occasion for bringing Jacobi into the discussion.

II.

In this case as well, a letter will help us to set the scene. On November 14, 1787, Jacobi writes the following lines to Lavater from Düsseldorf:

> Kleuker shared with me the contents of a letter you sent him that dealt primarily with Herder's *God* [, *Some Conversations*]. You say in this letter that the personal human being must personify, that this is part and parcel of the *childish* state and the *childish* mind of humanity. This I do not understand. To me, personhood is the alpha and omega, and a living being without personhood seems to me to be the most nonsensical thing one could conceive of. Being, reality, I have no idea what it is if it is not a person. To say nothing of God! What kind of a God would it be who cannot say to himself: I am who I am. The I-hood of finite beings is only on loan to us, borrowed from others, a refracted ray of the transcendental light, of the only *living God*. (JBW I,7, 10f.)

The contrast with Schelling could hardly be greater. The paradigm of a philosophy of subjectivity is countered here with the outline of a philosophy of "personhood." It is astonishing that Jacobi's declaration, despite having been written some eight years prior to Schelling's letter, reads as if it had been composed as a direct response to it. In order to underscore this anachronistic impression of proximity, which, as we will see, exists for good reason despite the major differences between the two thinkers, I have taken the liberty of reformulating their positions from the perspective of Jacobi. And I believe his comments would sound something like the following:

---

[3] Peter Strawson, *Individuals: An Essay in Descriptive Metaphysics* (London: Methuen, 1959).

Where you, Schelling, speak of the "alpha and omega" of freedom so as to trace that freedom back to a pure, absolute, and freely posited "I am I," I, Jacobi, as you can see, speak of the "alpha and omega" of "personhood." In the context of your own approach, this concept is intended to indicate a deficiency of being. For me, on the contrary, it is the concept on which all else depends, because without it I cannot understand what "being" or "reality" actually is—at least insofar as we are speaking here of living being and not of the lifeless material world. You, too, speak of being, even of the "absolute sphere of being," by which you surely do not mean material being. Your invocation of the I, which you value so highly, rules out such a meaning from the start. Allow me to return at a later point to the question of what I am to think of this absolute being-an-I. For now, I take as my starting point your assertion that being, on the one hand, and the consciousness of "personality" on the other can have nothing to do with one another. But is this true? Does it not rather depend on what we mean by consciousness here?

This I am prepared to grant: I share the conviction that being a person does indeed involve consciousness. But what you, Schelling, think of as an objectively mediated, *theoretical* consciousness, I take to be, in its primary and original sense, something entirely different, namely an *existential* consciousness—the living consciousness that I am myself and not this or that other person. If I were to destroy this consciousness of myself as a person or even merely demand its destruction, I would not destroy my entanglement in the world of objects, as you claim. I would destroy myself. Freedom, by the way, is just as important to me as it is to you. But precisely for this reason I insist on *personhood*, because I believe that it grounds that freedom to which I can lay claim even in my finitude. The real issue here is thus not the mere use of the word "person" or "personality," but what we mean by those terms. I can see that your approach to the topic does not get us very far. But who says that this is the one and only correct approach? On my conception of a primary, existential consciousness of myself, it is at any rate anything but absurd to insist emphatically on our status as persons.

Nor is it in any way absurd to attribute such a status to God. Because as you can see, this is not a matter of transferring a finite determination to the absolute. This would only be the case if consciousness were, as you assert, exclusively theoretical consciousness mediated through objects. But how could we ever be persuaded to deny to divine being the consciousness that I have in mind? "What kind of a God would it be who cannot say to himself: I am who I am"? In truth this God would not be absolute, he would be able to do even less than we can. Rather than an inappropriate projection of the finite onto the absolute, the situation here is reversed. Insofar as we are not God but are rather entangled in dependencies and constraints and still, as finite beings, can say "I" to ourselves, then we have to accept that this "I-hood" we attribute to ourselves is only "on loan to us." Just as a ray of light is refracted through a prism, so our being as persons, inasmuch as it is a finite being, is always only refracted. A refracted being, however, is nevertheless something completely different than the destruction of the person that you present as your goal.

It seems that everything hinges on the fact that we come within a hair's breadth of converging and yet ultimately fail to connect. We agree that there is far more at stake here than conceptual hair-splitting. That is why we both speak of being. And because we also agree, if I understand your enthusiasm correctly, that when we say being we mean being-free, we both also speak of an I, of the identity of being-an-I: I am. But what is the nature of this I named God who in your opinion can posit himself as "I am I" but cannot say to himself: I am who I am? Is that really an I—or is it not rather just a "mere IS"? (GD: JWA 3, 75). And who are we, if everything that constitutes our concrete being as persons is mediated through objects, while whatever is not captured by this mediation is always only to be identical to the absolute I?

III.

Who or what is a person? I will return in the course of my reflections to each of the points mentioned above. For now, however, I hope that my imagined dialogue has made clear that the (actual rather than fictional) controversy in which Jacobi involved the protagonists of classical German philosophy would be trivial if it were only a case of the one affirming what the other one disputes. If this were the case, then one could just as well look up the meaning of the expression "person" in a dictionary and take note of its positive or negative usage. In truth, however, even today there is still no such thing as a generally applicable definition of the person. What we have instead are only various applications of the term, in which its specific meaning derives from the particular epistemological, ontological, linguistic-philosophical, or ethical context in which it appears. Fortunately, we are able to gloss over this extraordinarily complicated situation in everyday speech. It is easy enough to distinguish, in the context of such communication, between persons and things, or "people" and animals. But everyday speech tells us nothing about *the specific way* persons differ.

This "specific way" however, is precisely the focus of philosophical debates, and in this context one can only agree with Kaplow's recent assertion that there is "hardly a concept in philosophy more difficult to explicate" than that of the person.[4] And it is even understandable that in the current discussion of ethics just mentioned, some have begun wonder whether granting the person such a prominent position was really such a wise decision. After all, rather than being able to take the meaning of this concept for granted and simply apply it to situations of ethical conflict, we now find ourselves faced with the need for a basic clarification of just which understanding of the person is under consideration in a given case. At the same time, however, one can also see why the current interest in the topic goes hand in hand with a reassessment of the history of philosophy. It is not because one hopes thereby to resolve the issue once and for all—the infinitely complex history of the concept of the person hardly gives us any reason to expect such a result—but because it is highly instructive to see under what circumstances and with which implications and consequences the discussion of persons has taken place in the past.

Who or what is a person? The explanations provided by Schelling and Jacobi in response to this question are radically divergent. And, consequently, the assessments they offer as well as the conclusions they draw are equally distinct. If "personality" is

---

[4] Ian Kaplow, *Analytik und Ethik der Namen* (Würzburg: Königshausen & Neumann, 2002), 230f.

an instance of theoretical consciousness, then its application to the absolute is out of the question. If, however, "personhood" is an instance of existential selfhood then one can also, with due regard for metaphysical relations of refraction, speak of a personal God. Might Schelling have pursued this option if he had encountered it early on? One can in fact discern a fundamental process of rethinking that begins with Schelling's *Freedom Essay*, as a result of which he both changes his view and also fails to change it, as we will see.[5] His early letter to Hegel is thus all the more important in the current context. It spells out what can be considered a typical verdict of the age. With his commitment to a personalist philosophy, Jacobi remains hopelessly isolated. The fact that he develops a completely new understanding of the person in his time, one that in its basic conception anticipates (among other things) some of the insights of twentieth-century French phenomenology, never comes to light. Why is this the case?

It seems plausible to claim that the dominance of the paradigm of subjectivity is responsible. And it is indeed no coincidence that throughout his life, Jacobi presented his own position as an explicit criticism of this paradigm. Already in 1789, he distances himself from assertions of a genealogy pointing back to Descartes by insisting "I am not a *Cartesian*." One "simply must not put the *sum* after the *cogito*" (Spin: JWA 1,1, 157). The famous debates with Kant, Fichte and Schelling provide ongoing evidence of this opposition. Nevertheless, here as well the situation is more complicated than the straightforward juxtaposition of subjectivity and personhood might seem to indicate.

First of all, one must take into account the fact that Kant's practical philosophy, as I have already suggested, is perfectly capable of integrating a perspective on persons despite being established on the basis of a philosophy of the subject. The relevant formulation of the categorical imperative makes this clear: "*So act that you use humanity, whether in your own person or in the person of any other, always at the same time as an end, never merely as a means.*"[6] Rather than positing a simple opposition, then, we must instead pose a more precise question, namely, whether the person that Jacobi has in mind actually has any relation at all to the "humanity" in the person invoked in Kant's moral law.

The second point to be considered is one that proves pertinent to post-Kantian philosophy and renders the situation even more confusing. My imagined dialogue already alluded to the proximity between Jacobi and Schelling, notwithstanding their obvious differences; we see it in the way they both fundamentally privilege being: "I am." This commonality reveals, however, that the paradigm of subjectivity clearly underwent a shift in post-Kantian philosophy, and that this shift occurred thanks to the influence of Jacobi. Jacobi's anti-Cartesian reordering of the *cogito* and the *sum*, his placement of the "I am" before the "I think," has found its way into the subject

---

[5] Schelling, *Philosophische Untersuchungen über das Wesen der menschlichen Freiheit und die damit zusammenhängenden Gegenstände* [1809], SW VII. F. W. J. Schelling, *Philosophical Investigations into the Essence of Human Freedom*, trans. Jeff Love and Johannes Schmidt (Albany: State University of New York Press, 2006). See also Chapter 12 in this volume.

[6] Kant, *Grundlegung zur Metaphysik der Sitten*, AA IV, 429. Immanuel Kant, "Groundwork of the Metaphysics of Morals (1785)," in *Immanuel Kant: Practical Philosophy*, ed. and trans. Mary J. Gregor (Cambridge: Cambridge University Press, 1996), 80.

itself and has, as it were, changed its complexion.[7] We must therefore ask a somewhat more precise question: How is it that the protagonists of classical German philosophy, Schelling as well as Fichte and Hegel, although they do indeed take the *sum* into account, nonetheless do not conceive of it as the personal *sum* referred to by Jacobi?

The third point to be considered is the position of Herder, who, as we have seen, was already mentioned in Jacobi's letter. It is noteworthy in this context that Herder likewise wants no truck with the subject, as will be explicitly underscored in his subsequent critique of Kant, and yet nonetheless does not opt for Jacobi's personalism. As he writes to Jacobi on February 6, 1784, "My dearest extramundane personalist ... restricted personhood is not suitable for the infinite being, since with us person only emerges through restriction, as a kind of mode or as an aggregate of being acting under the illusion of unity" (JBW I,3, 280f.). One can see that his objection closely parallels Schelling's line of argument. *Because* personhood constitutes a deficient determination, a finite "restriction," it is not suitable for the absolute. Herder, however, goes further, not only describing the unity of the person as mediated through objects but referring to it as an "illusion."

All this makes for a very strange situation indeed. It seems that Kant, of all people, is the only one with whom Jacobi could engage in serious discussion of personhood, while those who are much closer to Jacobi in their emphatic privileging of being want nothing to do with the person. I will come back to Kant later. In regard to the final two points previously mentioned, however, it is necessary to consider a circumstance here that dramatically demonstrates the strong context-dependency of the discourse on persons and also reveals a set of context-specific preferences that cannot be fully explained in terms of fundamental philosophical assumptions, pointing instead to dispositions best understood in the broader context of a history of mentalities.

IV.

The circumstance that I am referring to is the sensation caused by Spinoza's metaphysics in the period, a metaphysics in which the subject, to say nothing of the person, plays no part, which instead harnesses the concept of substance in order to elevate the divine *One-and-All* to the status of lodestar for all thinking and living. The first thing to note is that it was Jacobi himself who reminded his contemporaries of this monism "of *being* in everything existent," of "Sein in allem Dasein" (Spin: JWA 1,1, 39;

---

[7] See Fichtes *Grundlage der gesamten Wissenschaftslehre*, § 1: "man denkt nicht nothwendig, wenn man ist, aber man ist nothwendig, wenn man denkt. Das Denken ist gar nicht das Wesen, sondern nur eine besondere Bestimmung des Seyns" (FW I, 100). "it is not the case that if one exists then one necessarily thinks, but rather that one necessarily exists if one thinks. Thinking by no means constitutes the essence [of the I's being], but is only a specific determination of its being." J. G. Fichte, "Foundation of the Entire Wissenschaftslehre," in Fichte, *Foundation of the Entire Wissenschaftslehre and Related Writings (1794–95)*, ed. and trans. Daniel Breazeale (Oxford: Oxford University Press, 2021), 206.

MPW 199). The fact that he originally developed his own philosophy of the person in staunch opposition to Spinoza is the second. And the third point, finally, is that the famous "*Hen kai pan*" (Spin: JWA 1,1, 16; MPW 187), which Herder even uses as the heading for the previously mentioned letter, did not appear to Jacobi's contemporaries as it did to him, namely as the anonymous specter of radical self-loss, but rather as a magic formula that revealed the possibility of a new attitude toward life. It is clear that Schelling, Fichte, and Hegel immediately embraced Spinoza's metaphysics as the epitome of philosophy as a system of science, whereby they are once again following the path marked out by Jacobi. The question is why all of them, even those with no interest whatsoever in systems, embrace the *hen kai pan*-ideal with such enthusiasm and, foregoing any consideration of the personal character of Jacobi's *sum*, ignore everything in his position except the bare *sum* itself, in whose guise they seek to integrate freedom into Spinoza's metaphysics of substance as being-free. In order to understand this situation, we must turn to a deeper stratum of the protagonists' self-understanding.

The authoritative formulation comes from Lessing: "The orthodox concepts of the Divinity are no longer for me; I cannot stomach them" (Spin: JWA 1,1,16; MPW 187). This is exactly what Schelling affirms in his letter to Hegel: "For us as well, the orthodox concepts of God are no more. [...] Our reach extends *beyond* personal being."[8] In other words, the one single thing that is guiding Jacobi's readers when they turn away from the whole topic of the person, which indeed they reject as downright scandalous, is his talk of a personal God. From today's perspective, this criticism is easily misunderstood—after all, we live in post-metaphysical times. Its target might appear to be a style of thought that grasps in vain for a metaphysical realm, one whose mention can serve at best only as a reminder, to paraphrase Lavater, of the "childhood of humanity." But this is not what is meant here. The matter at hand is not *whether* one speaks of the absolute at all; it is rather exclusively a question of *how* one speaks of it. The problem is not that Jacobi speaks of *God* but that he speaks of God *as a person*, because in doing so he appears to restore the orthodox God, the God of the theologians and the church, "the personal, individual being who sits in Heaven above" as Schelling writes to Hegel,[9] when the point is that the idea of the One-and-All finally frees humanity from *this* God.

We would not need to consider these intellectual-historical contexts if they had remained philosophically inconsequential. In fact, however, the opposite is the case. This is not the place to address the philosophical distortions, not least in regard to Spinoza's own thought, that resulted from this religiously and theologically motivated program of emancipation. The crucial point here is that the fixation of the debate on the question of a personal God quite literally blocks the discourse on persons. *To what extent* and *under what premise* Jacobi engages in such talk, how and why

---

[8] Frank/Kurz, *Materialien zu Schelling*, 126.
[9] Letter from Schelling to Hegel of January 6, 1795 (Frank/Kurz, *Materialien zu Schelling*, 119; Hegel, *The Letters*, 29). The confrontation with the so-called Tübingen orthodoxy plays a crucial role here; see Birgit Sandkaulen, *Ausgang vom Unbedingten. Über den Anfang in der Philosophie Schellings* (Göttingen: Vandenhoeck & Ruprecht, 1990), 28–37.

he speaks *of us* at the most basic level as persons, in a word, the entire conception of his philosophy of the person—this all disappears behind the curtain of a scene staged between the One-and-All and Lutheran orthodoxy. Meanwhile, in a parallel performance, a concept of the person that has always already been conceived as deficient enters the stage and is easily cast as the villain. This is particularly clear in the case of Herder.

With the sole purpose of demonstrating the metaphysical irrelevance of the person, Herder took the trouble in the second edition of *God, Some Conversations* (1800) to compile an entire catalog of what he terms the "established usage" of this term. After eliminating the theological reference to the trinity of divine persons as not pertinent to the discussion, Herder's examination of philosophical and everyday usage yields the conclusion that person has retained its original meaning in all its various incarnations, namely that of *"mask"* or *"theatrical character."* The situation is no different in the case of Locke and Leibniz, as Herder's quotations make clear. According to Locke, for example, person is a "forensick," which is to say a juridical term, which qualifies someone to be recognized in a court of law and considered responsible for his actions. Following in Locke's footsteps, Leibniz refers to personal identity as an "apparence du soi," an appearance of the self that is to be distinguished from real identity. In short, as Herder concludes, "open what dictionaries one will," in all of them the words person and personality "indicate a 'peculiar character' or 'particular' under a certain appearance." Obviously, however, none of this has anything to do with the infinite.[10]

Indeed it does not, one can imagine Jacobi replying. Nonetheless, Herder's remarks, which refer to persons only in order to exclude them from the discussion, are extremely interesting. They not only shed light on the conventional understanding of the person in the period, that is, the "established" usage one would have found in the dictionaries of the era. They also illuminate the background to Jacobi's own reflections, revealing the assumptions from which he must distinguish his own position in order to make his intentions clear. If, with this in mind, one wants to relate Herder's list to Jacobi's efforts, then this relation can only be formulated ex negativo: what Jacobi is aiming at with the alpha and omega of personhood does not follow conventional usage; it cannot be traced back etymologically to the theatrical language of antiquity, to the persona as mask; and above all, it cannot be explicated by way of recourse to the philosophical authority of Locke. All of the individual orthodoxies Herder lines up next to the great scandal of the orthodox God in order to clear a path for the One-and-All—none of this is germane here. But then what is really at issue?

---

[10] Johann G. Herder, *God. Some Conversations*, trans. Frederick H. Burkhardt (New York: Veritas Press, 1940), 199ff. For Jacobi's confrontation with Herder see especially the Supplements IV and V of the 1789 edition of the *Spinoza Letters* together with Jacobi's later assertion that the second revised edition of Herder's *God*, published in 1800, also contains nothing "that might have required me to take back anything I said …" (Spin: JWA 1,1, 219). Jacobi did, however, introduce additional clarifications to Supplement IV in the third edition of the *Spinoza Letters* he prepared for the publication of his collected works (1819). I take these additions into account in the subsequent discussion. Note that Jacobi's above statement does not appear in di Giovanni's translation, which includes only excerpts from the Supplements added to the second edition.

V.

The answer to this question is by no means straightforward. A complicated pattern emerges from the various strands spun out thus far. The person is a complicated topic in its own right; Jacobi plays a complicated role in his contemporary context; and his philosophy of the person, which is our focus here, is also correspondingly complex. Also significant in this regard is the fact that his position involves a double differentiation. On the one hand, the meaning of the person takes shape in contrast to the philosophy of the One-and-All, whose monism Jacobi finds rationally compelling but also condemns for its practical consequence—the anonymous annihilation of the self. On the other hand, for the person to actually be able to take on the role that he ascribes to it, Jacobi must also develop an alternative to the concept of the person that Herder believes to have been "established" by Locke. Both perspectives culminate in what I previously referred to as the existential consciousness of selfhood.

In view of the complexity of the situation, however, it will likely come as no surprise that Jacobi never produced a special treatise on the *concept* of the person in general or of personal selfhood in particular. Personhood serves here as the point of convergence, requiring illumination from multiple perspectives, for a thinking that aims not merely to explicate concepts but rather to *disclose experiences*. According to Jacobi, our most foundational experience is the *experience of action*: only insofar as we are causal agents do we have an understanding of ourselves and of the world.[11] It is in this context of action that talk of the person finds its proper place. And it is within this framework as well that Jacobi's double differentiation is to be understood, because the problem posed in the specific form of the person is a problem that comes to a head in reference to both the philosophy of the One-and-All as well with Locke's theory of the person. I am referring to the problem of *identity*.

"Every being," Jacobi writes, "that has consciousness of its identity—of an I that *is permanent, existing in itself, and having knowledge of itself*—is a person" (Spin: JWA 1,1, 220; MPW 363).[12] The question is to what extent this statement can be understood as offering an alternative to the identity of the One-and-All, and, by the same token, to what extent this concept of identity goes beyond what Locke's "forensick term" offers in regard to the identification of a person? I will start with the second question, as this will clear a path that also enables access to the first.

First of all, it is noteworthy that Jacobi, departing in this case from his approach to Kant and the philosophy of the One-and-All, does not engage in an *explicit* discussion of Locke. He conducts this discussion implicitly, and in such a way that the understanding of the person is not drawn from a "dictionary" but becomes clear through the unfolding

---

[11] On this crucial foundation of Jacobi's thinking in the philosophy of action, expressed in his distinction between ground and cause, see Chapter 2 in this volume.
[12] Ein "jedes Wesen, welches das Bewußtseyn seiner Identität hat: *eines bleibenden, in sich seyenden und von sich wissenden Ich*, ist eine Person." Note: The italicized insertion (an addition in the third edition of the *Spinoza Letters* as mentioned above) can be found in the variants to the text listed in JWA; it is not included in MPW.

of Jacobi's argumentation, which, in keeping with his fundamental orientation toward action, poses the question of "Man's freedom" (Spin: JWA 1,1, 158ff.; MPW 341ff.).[13]

If we assume—this is the argument of the first part of this text—that as finite beings we are not autonomous but rather inevitably entangled in relations of dependency with our natural and social environment; if we further assume that, in accordance with this situation, our most urgent vital interest is not to perish in this web of inescapable dependencies; and if, finally, we assume that as rational beings we are in the position to give conscious shape to our survival interests—then it makes good sense to speak of the person. In this case, to be a person means to be in possession of the stabilizing consciousness of an identity that we, as finite but rational beings, *develop* in the context of our respective environments and experiences and on the basis of which we then also orient our future actions.

I leave aside the further steps that Jacobi follows here. Three things are important in the present context. The first is that over the course of just a few paragraphs of highly condensed argumentation, Jacobi develops a concept of personhood which, being based on an analysis of the finite but rationally surmountable conditions of our lives, is very much in step with contemporary thought. One can find variants of such reflections in a wide range of relevant contemporary debates, here under the label of naturalism. The fruitfulness of Jacobi's line of thinking results in particular from his implicit combination of two theories. He joins the striving for self-preservation, which Spinoza had declared to be the foundational impulse driving all action, with Locke's key statement regarding personal identity, namely, that it rests, as Jacobi puts it in this context "on memory and reflection" (Spin: JWA 1,1, 159; MPW 342). Indeed, this is in fact the essence of Locke's theory: the identity of the person extends as far as "consciousness can be extended backwards to any past Action or Thought."[14] The key assertion here, in other words, is that personal identity is an achievement of consciousness. Embedded in the context of experience, it is created through a retrospective performance of conscious *identification*. Following a distinction Jacobi makes use of elsewhere, but which is also increasingly widespread in current discussions of the person,[15] I will subsequently refer to this identity as *what*-identity.

The second point is that Jacobi's analysis of this *what*-identity clearly corresponds to the understanding of the person considered deficient by Schelling and Herder. Both Schelling's object-mediated unity of personal consciousness and Herder's "aggregate of being" acting under the "illusion" of unity presume this identity only ever arises through a confrontation with and integration of that which is alien to us. What I am, what I identify myself as, results from an ultimately inscrutable chain of spatio-temporal circumstances. Jacobi reinforces this point by placing this set of reflections under the heading of unfreedom.

---

[13] The complete heading of the text, which appeared as part of the 1789 edition of the *Spinoza Letters*, is "Concerning Man's Freedom" (JWA 1,1, 158; MPW 341). See also Chapter 5 in this volume.

[14] John Locke, *An Essay Concerning Human Understanding*, ed. Peter H. Nidditch (London: Oxford University Press, 1975), Chap. XXVII, 335.

[15] See Kaplow, *Analytik und Ethik der Namen*, 185ff. *and passim*.

The third point relates to the conclusion that he draws from his analysis of the *what*-identity of the person. He shares the conviction that this form of identity is deficient. But it in no way follows from this conviction that it should immediately be abandoned so that we can cross over into the "absolute sphere of being." Rather, as Jacobi emphasizes repeatedly, this *what*-aspect of our selves retains its significance on the most fundamental level, inasmuch as it takes into account our finitude and the temporal character of our existence. After all, what would we be without it? "Just return into yourself; divest your thinking of all sensuous representations for a moment, of all the experiences, sensations, judgments and inclinations that relate to those representations:—What remains to you after such an emptying out of your being?" ("Zufällige Ergießungen eines einsamen Denkers" [Occasional Outpourings of a lonely Thinker]: JWA 5,1, 204). Jacobi's well-known assertion that "without the *Thou* [...] the *I* is impossible" (Spin: JWA 1,1, 116; MPW 231), which Martin Buber erroneously tried to read as the first incarnation of his own dialogical philosophy,[16] is also best understood in this context.

This is not the end of the story, however, because upon closer investigation, the crucial shortcoming of this *what*-identity becomes apparent. And Jacobi's objection here is of the utmost interest. Despite initial appearances to the contrary, the identity achieved on the basis of "memory and reflection" is not capable of grounding itself but is rather caught in a circular loop. If my consciousness of personal identity is supposed to arise through a process of identification, then I must always already be in possession of this consciousness, because otherwise there would be no what as which I could identify myself. As Jacobi explains at the beginning of the second part of his reflections, entitled "Man has freedom," "Anything that is not already something cannot simply be *determined* to be something; in what has no property, none can be generated simply through relations; indeed, not even a relation is possible with respect to it" (Spin: JWA 1,1, 163; MPW 344).

The critique of the circularity of the reflection-model of consciousness has come to be associated with Fichte, but there is strong reason to believe that Fichte adopted it from Jacobi.[17] In keeping with Jacobi's "original insight," however, his solution to this problem looks quite different from that of Fichte. The point is not to break free of the circularity by transcending consciousness and entering into the impersonal identity of the absolute "I am I." Instead, Jacobi aims to reveal in precisely this context the essence of his own understanding of the person—the existential consciousness of personal identity, the consciousness of the particular concrete selfhood, which does not arise through identification but instead, as "permanent and existing in itself" represents the essential precondition for being able to reflexively develop a *what*-identity in the first place.

---

[16] Martin Buber, *Das dialogische Prinzip*, 6th ed. (Gerlingen: Lambert Schneider, 1992), 301ff.

[17] See Henrich, who attributed the break with the reflection-model of self-consciousness to Fichte, memorably describing it as "Fichte's original insight." (Dieter Henrich, "Fichte's Original Insight" [1967], in *Contemporary German Philosophy*, ed. Darrel E. Christensen et al., trans. David R. Lachterman, vol. 1 (Pennsylvania: Pennsylvania State University Press, 1982), 15–53. I take up this issue in Chapter 8 in this volume.

Rather than a what, to be a person in this sense means, crucially, to possess the free identity of a *who*. *Who* someone is—this is not fully captured by the answer to the question of *what* someone is—and at the same time it is also something other than simply the indication of a naked *that*, of sheer indeterminate being assumed to relate to the determinations of the *what* as a kind of substrate. We can now fully understand why, according to the previously cited remark, there is "hardly a concept in philosophy more difficult to explicate" than that of the person. Not only is the crucial aspect of this "who someone is" ungraspable with the means of a modern reflection theory of consciousness, the shortcomings of which it is, on the contrary, intended to overcome. It is just as resistant to the traditional instruments of a substance ontology, according to which one can distinguish between a thing on the one hand and its properties on the other.

Jacobi himself is fully cognizant of this situation. In referring to the existential selfhood of the person as the *"unique"* "spirit" of a human being, which "constitutes him as the *One* who he is, *this very One and none Other,*" Jacobi emphasizes the fact that the *who*-identity aims at an essentially singular, entirely individual existence and is to be recognized in this singularity of the utterly "incomparable" (WL: JWA 3, 26).[18] It is thus entirely appropriate to speak here of the dignity of the person. At the same time, we can now see that Jacobi's personalism not only differs from Kant's categorical imperative but contradicts it. For if, following Kant, the "humanity" in every person is to be respected, then this implies that an empirical person determined in space and time is being separated here from the universal aspect of *"personality."*[19] The moral law requires that only this universal dimension be taken into account, and for this reason it is strictly formal. Kant, however, fails to consider the individual and, as such, not spatio-temporally determined *who*-ness of every particular person for the reason that he is entirely unaware of it.

Furthermore, to return to the previous train of thought, we should note that this *who*-identity does not arise "only by way of a self comparison after the fact." As Jacobi's criticism of the reflection-theoretical circularity reads here:

> wherein would the comparing and imagining occur; wherein would the self become like to the self? And what would the self that had not yet been equated with itself be, the self without its own being and *permanence*, which only becomes a self *with* its own being and permanence, with *selfhood*, through identification, differentiation, and combination, through connection? And what, finally, enacted all this? (WL: JWA 3, 26)[20]

---

[18] Note, that Jacobi's text *Ueber eine Weissagung Lichtenbergs* [WL], first published in 1801, reprinted as part of the later work *On Divine Things and Their Revelation* (1811), is not included in MPW.
[19] Compare Kant's remark that the "person as belonging to the sensible world is subject to his own personality." Kant, *Kritik der praktischen Vernunft*, AA V, 87; Kant, *Practical Philosophy*, 210.
[20] "worin geschähe die Vergleichung und Einbildung; worin würde das Selbst dem Selbste gleich? und was wäre das noch nicht gleichgesetzte Selbst, das Selbst noch ohne eigenes Seyn und *Bleiben*, das durch gleich- ungleich- und zusammensetzen, durch verknüpfen erst zu einem Selbste *mit* eigenem Seyn und Bleiben, mit *Selbstseyn* würde? Was endlich verübte alles dieses?" (WL: JWA 3, 26).

It follows from this failure of reflection, however, that the free identity of the *who*, which is a precondition of the *what*, cannot be disclosed through "*cognition*." The consciousness of being this one and no other is consequently only a feeling, "an *immediate feeling of existence* [*Wesenheitsgefühl*] that is independent of the memory of previous states" (WL: JWA 3, 26).[21]

One final point remains to be considered. As previously indicated, Jacobi insists that it would be absurd to extinguish our memories, in other words, to attempt to free ourselves from the always mediated dimension of the *what*. That still stands. Thus, transcending this dimension does not mean approaching a state where the personal "feeling of existence" would prevail exclusively. Had Jacobi asserted such a thing, one could rightly ask him how one is supposed to conceive of such a state. But this is not the issue here. Rather, the point is that under the conditions of our finitude there can be no *what* without the *who* as its precondition, nor, conversely, can there be a *who* without a relation to the *what*. According to Jacobi, among our original experiences is the experience that both our "*independence*" and our "*dependence*" are limited. It thus follows for each of us "that he can just as necessarily be *only* One *among Others*, and never a *first* and *only One*; as he can necessarily only be One among Others to the extent that he is One and *none* Other; an independent, an *actual*, a *personal* being" (WL: JWA 3, 27f.).[22] The personal aspect of *who*-ness does not exist in isolation but only as one that presents itself under the conditions of otherness. And it follows from this situation that one must refer to the "*interior*" consciousness of the person, in contrast to the "*exterior*" consciousness of our temporal existence, as "*outside of time*," but also that one must not mistake this for a gesture toward a timeless eternity (WL: JWA 3, 27 Anm.). What is meant is rather an "identity over time," an identity that "permanently" comprehends in itself the past, present, and future and thereby also makes it possible in the first place for me to identify myself as *the one* looking back on my life, engaging with others, and planning for the future (GD: JWA 3, 113).

Moreover, while this reciprocal entanglement of the aspects of the *what* and the *who* of the person necessarily affects our existence, it only and exclusively affects *our* existence. In other words, should we refer, under the "name of *God*" (WL: JWA 3, 26), to a being whom we do not encounter in our world as one among others, who is not a part of this world, who is rather absolutely distinct from it, then it makes no sense to project upon this "*perfection* of being" (WL: JWA 3, 26) the perspective of our *what*-consciousness. To the extent, however, that here the aspect of otherness, which necessarily restricts our own personal "independence," falls away entirely and divine existence is for this very reason to be understood as an "unconditionally independent

---

[21] Corresponding to this is the transformation of the concept of substance into "substantivity" and its equation with "spirit" and "selfhood" (WL: JWA 3, 27). Jacobi expresses this matter with greater clarity in a letter to Jean Paul from March 16, 1800, in which individuality receives the distinction of being a foundational determination: "Identity is therefore simply based on substantiality, substantiality on individuality" (JBW I,12, 208). With regard to content, one can compare Jacobi here to Richard of St. Victor, whose interest highlighting the individual and immediate "quis" of the person over the "quid" led him to replace the concept of substance with that of existence.

[22] "daß er eben so nothwendig Einer *nur* seyn kann *unter Anderen*, unmöglich ein *Erster* und *Einziger*; als er, um zu seyn Einer unter Anderen, *nothwendig* seyn muß Einer und *kein* Anderer; ein selbständiges, ein *wirkliches*, ein *persönliches* Wesen" (WL: JWA 3, 27f.).

and completely self-sufficient" being (WL: JWA 3, 28), to this extent one is justified in attributing the status of person to this existence—the consciousness of the absolute *who*-identity, the "I am who I am." Of this absolute person, however, who is not, as we are, an "individual only *as part of* and *subordinate* to a species" (WL: JWA 3, 28), we necessarily can have no concept. In fact, we are ourselves in our own personal *who*-identity inaccessible to reflection from both within and without and therefore designate persons, not with a concept, but with a *name*.[23] Thus the one and only metaphysical reference to God that Jacobi is willing to allow is that of the absolute proper name (Spin: JWA 1,1, 261; MPW 376). *What* we designate with this name is simply the inexplicable precondition of a causally acting *who*, but a precondition that does not, as is the case with Kant, have merely the status of a regulative idea. Rather, we encounter it in our personhood as a constitutive precondition, because, in the case of the personal *who*-identity, in contrast to that of the *what*, we cannot retrospectively generate it ourselves and, inasmuch as it is the precondition of the *what*, we certainly cannot derive it from the spatio-temporal relations of the world.

VI.

These remarks on Jacobi's metaphysics, which, in the name of personhood, replaces a metaphysics of grounding [Begründungsmetaphysik] with a metaphysics of action, will have to suffice for the time being and should allow us to turn now to the second question posed previously. To what extent can one oppose this philosophy of the person, as it has been explicated above, to the philosophy of the One-and-All? Or to put it another way: just how persuasive is Jacobi's insistence on conceiving distinction between the absolute and the world in the form a personal transcendence? Is it not more plausible and also more productive to grasp this absolute distinction as a distinction *immanent* in the world? In this case as well the absolute is not a part of the world and certainly not the sum of its parts either; it is rather that totality underlying the interconnectedness of the finite as its inner structure, which, as a consequence, manifests itself at every point where selfhood stands in relation to otherness. The decades of effort that Jacobi invests into his Spinoza studies suggest that this question constitutes the punctum saliens of his own thought. And just as one can understand the genesis of Jacobi's personalism as a whole only in terms of his meticulous examination of Spinoza's work—rather than as an attempt to differentiate himself from Locke—it is also evident that Jacobi developed his own alternative position in the closest proximity to Spinoza's views.

What is so compelling about this philosophy? As Jacobi was the first to comprehend, it is precisely the fact that the structure of the One-and-All demolishes the conceptual framework of reflexive identification. The identity proposed here is not an *ens rationis*, a *what* identifiable only in concepts, but rather a *that*, an unprethinkable being and as such a whole, "whose parts can only be thought within it and according to it" (Spin: JWA 1,1 96; MPW 218). And if we now recall that Jacobi himself, in order to secure our

---

[23] See Chapter 7 in this volume.

status as persons, aims at the disclosure of an original identity that precedes the post hoc synthesis in "memory and reflection," then it is not so surprising that he invokes the same statement on both the side of Spinoza and the side of his "Antispinoza": "totum parte prius necesse est."[24] The whole necessarily precedes its parts.

And yet these two structurally related identities are nonetheless separated by an abyss that can only be crossed by way of a "salto mortale." The all-important difference lies in the personal *who*. It is this identity that disappears precisely to the degree that the absolute is conceived—as is entirely plausible from the perspective of rationality—as the internal structure of the world. Wherever this absolute then manifests itself, it deprives selfhood of its "independent" status as a person and reduces it instead to a mere determination of its own *that*. In other words, the *who* of the person here becomes a *what*—a property, in which the absolute *that* only internally modifies the "idem est idem" of its being. I cannot elaborate here on the "fatalism" that Jacobi describes as the consequence of this, the fact that in the horizon of the One-and-All time also disappears along with the freedom of the person and thus in truth everything belonging to the experience of action disappears. For now it is only important to recognize that the logic of the One-and-All, as it is paradigmatically analyzed by Jacobi in Spinoza, does indeed not have its foundation in the reflexive identification of the *what*. However, insofar as it neither can nor wants to think the *who*, all of its statements derive from the *that* al(l)one, which now generates its own *what* and brings it to mind in an anonymous intellect.

VII.

I will conclude with one final consideration. Is Jacobi wrong to also see this same logic, a logic concerned only with the relation of *that* and *what* but nowhere with the *who*, in operation in the systems of classical German philosophy? This may initially appear to be the case. After all, the goal in these systems is not simply a recapitulation of Spinoza but a philosophy that also internalizes Jacobi's insistence on freedom. As a consequence of such efforts, the problem of individuality becomes increasingly prominent over time—Schelling's rather brash claim that personality should be more or less destroyed is not the final word on the matter. And it is a further consequence of such efforts that eventually even the taboo of referring to the absolute as a personal God is abandoned. Schelling comes to call his own philosophy a "scientific theism," because he commits himself to just this point of view. Even Hegel, against whose logic the late Schelling positions his positive philosophy, later attests that Jacobi rightly sought to defend the "personhood" of God vis-à-vis Spinoza.[25]

---

[24] See Spin: JWA 1,1, 111, 115; MPW 227, 230; DH: JWA 2, 50, 82; MPW 288, 315; Jacobi's letter to Herder from June 30, 1784: JBW I,3, 329; as well as the "Addition. To Erhard O**" to *Allwill*: JWA 6,1, 231; MPW 490.

[25] Hegel, *Friedrich Heinrich Jacobi's Werke*, GW 15, 11. G. W. F. Hegel, "Review, Friedrich Heinrich Jacobi's Works, Volume III," in *Heidelberg Writings. Journal Publications*, ed. and trans. Brady Bowman and Allen Speight (Cambridge: Cambridge University Press, 2009), 9.

To be sure, I have insisted throughout these deliberations that this is far more than a debate about terminology. If Jacobi had merely limited himself to the use of the term "person" and had not reflected on the *structure* of personal identity, then he would hardly have been able to develop his personalist philosophy. But if one examines the structure of the later philosophies with this in mind, then one cannot avoid the conclusion that they stand in opposition to Jacobi from start to finish. Instead of the personal *who*, here one repeatedly confronts the determination of the *that* through its own *what*. What begins with Fichte's absolute F/Act [Tathandlung], according to which "*I exist purely and simply*, i.e., *I am purely and simply* **because** *I am, and I am purely and simply* **what** *I am—and I am both only **for the I**,*"[26] continues through Hegel's later criticism that Jacobi only knows "that God exists, not what God is."[27] And it is ultimately also still discernible in Schelling's theistic philosophy when it relocates the distinction between infinite and finite into God himself and maintains in this context that the move away from a "pure *that*" to the "concept, the *what*" occurs in order to ascribe to the "existing" the status of the "personal, actual God."[28]

It is true, however, that the perspective of the *what* provides a basis for explanations, even if these end up being—as the late Schelling would put it—only instances of evidencing [*Erweisen*], not of demonstration [*Beweisen*] in the full and proper sense. And so it is ultimately understandable that Jacobi's position remains a stumbling block despite its enormous impact, something he himself was well aware of as he conducted all of his debates. Because if selfhood is to be respected in the name of the person, then a *science* is ruled out from the beginning. "That is why my philosophy asks *who* is God, not *what* is he?" (Spin: JWA 1,1, 342). It is no coincidence that this is one of the last sentences Jacobi ever wrote.

---

[26] Fichte, *Grundlage der gesamten Wissenschaftslehre*, FW I, 98. Fichte, "Foundation of the Entire Wissenschaftslehre," 205.

[27] Hegel, *Enzyklopädie*, GW 20, § 73, 113. G. W. F. Hegel, *Encyclopedia of the Philosophical Sciences in Basic Outline. Part I: Science of Logic*, ed. and trans. Klaus Brinkmann and Daniel O. Dahlstrom (Cambridge: Cambridge University Press, 2010), 121.

[28] Schelling, *Philosophische Einleitung in die Philosophie der Mythologie oder Darstellung der reinrationalen Philosophie*, SW XI, 564, 565.

7

Brother Henriette? Deconstructions of Friendship in Derrida and Jacobi

Friedrich Schlegel found *Woldemar* tasteless. The future author of *Lucinde* was simply unable to make sense of a novel which, rather than recounting a tale of true love and eventual marital bliss, instead tells the story of a problematic friendship.[1] Other readers, however, saw things differently. A "most devoted Fichte," for example, wrote to Jacobi immediately upon reading *Woldemar* to tell him how "powerfully" the novel appealed to him, following this up with an announcement of his "complete agreement" with Jacobi, which "proves to me more than anything else that I am on the right track."[2] And we must not forget Hegel, whose reading of *Woldemar* provided the inspiration for his chapter on "Conscience; the Beautiful Soul, Evil, and its Forgiveness," which occupies such a prominent place in the *Phenomenology of Spirit*.[3]

Certainly nothing to scoff at. In contrast to Schlegel's utter bewilderment, one may infer from these reactions that Jacobi was not entirely mistaken in hoping, as he states in the preface of his novel, for the understanding of the philosopher—provided he is "something *more* than just a *philosopher by profession*" (JWA 7, 1, 208). If we look more closely at their responses, however, they, too, turn out to be somewhat peculiar. What are we to make of Fichte's insistence in the same letter that, in keeping with his task as a philosopher, he relates "in the form of a system" the same thing that Jacobi manages to express "insofar as human speech allows"?[4] If this is indeed the case, then shouldn't we have volumes of scholarship describing how in the *Wissenschaftslehre*, not only the "individual" (as we all know) but also the relation of *friendship* is successfully

---

[1] Friedrich Schlegel, "Jacobis Woldemar" (1796), in *Kritische Schriften und Fragmente*, vol. 1, ed. Ernst Behler and Hans Eichner (Paderborn: Schöningh, 1988), 177–91. It is worth noting that both the review and especially *Lucinde* reveal that Schlegel's views on love and marriage go hand in hand with a commitment to the precisely the ideal of "brotherly friendship" that Jacobi's novel criticizes. The misunderstandings and distortions contained in Schlegel's *Woldemar* review were rightly criticized years ago by Reinhard Lauth (Reinhard Lauth, "Fichtes Verhältnis zu Jacobi unter besonderer Berücksichtigung der Rolle Friedrich Schlegels in dieser Sache," in *Friedrich Heinrich Jacobi. Philosoph und Literat der Goethezeit*, ed. Klaus Hammacher (Frankfurt a.M.: Vittorio Klostermann, 1971), 165–208).
[2] Letter from April 26, 1796 (JBW I,11, 102). J. G. Fichte, *Fichte: Early Philosophical Writings*, ed. and trans. Daniel Breazeale (Ithaca: Cornell University Press, 1988), 413f.
[3] See Gustav Falke, "Hegel und Jacobi. Ein methodisches Beispiel zur Interpretation der Phänomenologie des Geistes," *Hegel-Studien* 22 (1987): 129–42.
[4] JBW I, 11, 102. Fichte, *Early Philosophical Writings*, 413.

deduced from the absolute I?[5] And with regard to Hegel, has anyone ever argued that the aforementioned chapter from the *Phenomenology* numbers among the most significant discussions of friendship in the philosophical canon? Is it not rather the case that Hegel's phenomenological reversal of Fichte here reveals the structure of a relationship that no longer depends at all on the participants themselves but ultimately only on the structure, which "is *absolute spirit*"?[6]

Having thus set the stage, I now want to take a leap that will lead me away from early romantic invocations of love and marriage as well as idealist reflections on the absolute and into the present. *Politiques de l'amitié* is the name given to the reflections that Derrida devoted to the subject of friendship.[7] It is both astonishing and, in light of the scenario just described, not so astonishing after all that in this book we finally learn what Jacobi's *Woldemar* is really about.

I.

At first glance, the two texts might seem completely dissimilar. Derrida's *The Politics of Friendship* is after all not a novel, in which the literary "presentation of an event" (JWA 7,1, 207) occupies center stage, in this case the fictional story of a friendship between Woldemar and Henriette.[8] It focuses instead on the canonical texts on friendship from the history of philosophy, from Aristotle through Montaigne up to Carl Schmitt and Blanchot, all of which are subjected to a deconstructive reading. I mention only in passing that Jacobi plays no role in Derrida's retrospective—only in passing, because my aim here is not to reconstruct any sort of direct historical influence.

At issue is rather a shared systematic context which, upon closer inspection, allows us to establish a substantive connection between these seemingly disparate texts. And a second glance enables us to see that their modes of presentation are part of this context. To be sure, with the exception of a few scattered remarks, Jacobi refrained from offering any theoretical reflections on friendship. But this does not mean that his novel is lacking in reflection. On the contrary, the philosophy of friendship presented here in literary form is not only already anticipated in the design of the "event" itself; the figures who participate in this "event" also engage in long conversations in which this philosophy finds expression. The situation is vice versa in the case of Derrida. What he presents here as the counterpart to a novel is not a theoretical treatise but rather what he explicitly refers to as an "essay," a genre designation that not only calls

---

[5] See Fichte's letter to Jacobi dated August 30, 1795 (JBW I,11, 55). Fichte, *Early Philosophical Writings*, 411f.
[6] Hegel, *Phänomenologie des Geistes*, GW 9, 361. G. W. F. Hegel, *The Phenomenology of Spirit*, ed. and trans. Terry Pinkard (Cambridge: Cambridge University Press, 2018), 388.
[7] Jacques Derrida, *The Politics of Friendship* [French 1994] (London/New York: Verso, 1997).
[8] As in the case of *Allwill*, the first version of *Woldemar* dates from the 1770s (1779). The reflections that follow, however, refer to the third edition of 1796, which includes substantial revisions not just in comparison to the first publication but also in regard to the second edition of 1794. *Woldemar* is not included in MPW and has not been translated into English.

to mind Montaigne's paradigmatic text on friendship but also gives the reader a sense of the evocative license that will characterize Derrida's own presentation.[9]

Philosophical novel versus essay—there is of course still a difference. Nonetheless, the choice of these forms reveals a shared sense of the general problematic motivating their reflections. The friend, as both authors explain in identical terms, is in essence not a *concept*.[10] Rather, as Jacobi states explicitly and Derrida clearly implies, he is an irreducibly concrete, singular "man with a name."[11] If this is essentially and not merely accidentally the case, however, then it follows that any effort to grasp the friend and friendship in the language of concepts will miss the mark. This reflective potential already embedded in the form of presentation was undoubtedly on Jacobi's mind when he expressed his hope of being understood by the philosopher who "is something more than just a philosopher by profession."

Having established the *substantive* rather than merely *formal* relevance of the mode of presentation in both cases, we are now in position to take a crucial further step. The shared sense of the general problematic mentioned previously can be cast into sharper relief by considering it in relation to one specific problem. Cast in the form of a question, which, by the way, because it is posed in the name of friendship, very deliberately asks about a "who" and not about a "what," this problem can be formulated as follows: *Who* is the friend, then, if he is definitively not a "concept"? For now, I simply want to gesture toward the difficulties that come into view here by quoting two passages from Jacobi's text. "Truly! Biderthal exclaimed in his delight" over the imminent arrival of his brother Woldemar: *"there is no friendship that can compare to the one between two such brothers!"* (JWA 7,1,217). Is this "truly" the case? That is indeed the question, but there is no question that Woldemar shares this view, albeit in a remarkable variation. "You know," he says later, as he finds himself compelled to point out the absurdity of his family's runaway expectations regarding a happy marriage (Schlegel was not the first): "you know that I often call Henriette *Brother Heinrich*—this is how I feel about her. It is incomprehensible to me how you could fail to see this, how all of you could be so grossly mistaken with regard to my intentions" (JWA 7,1, 325). Brother Henriette or "Brother Heinrich"—with the mention of this name, Woldemar clearly considers the

---

[9] Derrida, *Friendship*, p. vii.
[10] See Jacobi (GD: JWA 3, 51): "I ask, in order to move closer and penetrate more deeply: Who has ever possessed a friend and would want to say that he only loves his concept and not the man with the name; that the man with the concept is not the real thing; rather, that he is detrimental to it as a result of his defects?—Were such a person to exist, then it would necessarily be a matter of indifference to him, all the more so the more truly and selflessly he loved him, to see his friend laid in the grave. He would still have the concept, after all; he could even conceive of another who could take the place of his deceased friend, someone with still greater perfections, and without any defects at all: and this one would be immortal as well!" See Derrida: "A friend is always the friend. This friend is always the friend. As will be seen, a certain singularity remains required; this friend is not the concept *friend*, nor the friend in general." (Jacques Derrida, "Heidegger's Ear. Philopolemology (Geschlecht IV)," in *Reading Heidegger. Commemorations*, ed. John Sallis, trans. John P. Leavey Jr. (Bloomington: Indiana University Press, 1993), 165. This text "Heidegger's Ear" is included in the French and German editions of Derrida's *Politiques de l'amitié* but is missing from the English edition.)
[11] Jacobi (GD: JWA 3, 51). See Derrida: "The question of the proper name is obviously at the heart of the friendship problematic." "We have a real problem thinking friendship without the proper name." Derrida, *Friendship*, 251.

matter of his friendship with Henriette to be resolved. This is not even remotely the case. Because the question remains, and here I quote Derrida: "Why would the friend be *like* a brother?"[12] And furthermore, to follow this up with another question, who would the friend Henriette be, if she were not like a brother?

The second question points beyond a mere diagnosis of the problem to a possible solution. And it is only at this point that the paths of Derrida and Jacobi diverge in a manner, which, as I see it, can no longer be bridged. In anticipation of the conclusions of their respective stories, allow me to at least mention here the key indicator of this split. Derrida's reflections end with a supplemental text entitled "Heidegger's Ear." Jacobi's text, on the other hand, ends at the point where Derrida's deconstruction begins, with a lengthy discussion of "what *Aristotle* already knew 2,000 years ago" (JWA 7,1, 435).

II.

There is no need to pursue the individual twists and turns of either Jacobi's or Derrida's story in detail here. Instead, I want to retrace a line of argument that runs through both. To this end, and in order to define the constellation of problems with the greatest possible clarity, allow me to return again to the previously mentioned resistance to the "concept" of friendship. It is clear and by no means coincidental that both authors address this particular topic as part of a more fundamental analysis, one for which the "critique of subjectivity" can serve as shorthand, and which is related to a critique of the logic of identification. "Pure selfhood," as Jacobi formulates his fundamental objection to Fichte, "is pure *one-and-the-same* [Derselbigkeit] without the *one* [Der]."[13]

Assuming that one adopts the point of view of such a critique, then what could be more natural than to turn to the phenomenon of friendship in order to insist in precisely this context on the "one" who has been lost as a result of the "pure one-and-the-same"? From this perspective, the friend appears to be heaven-sent, the absolutely paradigmatic case, in view of which a theory of subjectivity runs up against its definitive limits—definitive because here the differential between the necessarily "pure" and the contingently "empirical" has lost its explanatory force once and for all. The critical option of the "one," what Derrida refers to as the "irreducible singularity or alterity,"[14]— this option is manifested by the friend *in persona* and, so to speak, in principle. Otherwise he would not be a friend, and otherwise there would be no friendship.

Doesn't this already sound like a promising conclusion? We now understand why Jacobi's and Derrida's preoccupation with friendship is anything but accidental, and we also see why certain other theoretical frameworks have generated little to no sustained interest in this phenomenon. Perhaps, as a finishing touch, we should also add to the juxtaposition of subject and friend that of concept and feeling, perhaps even the contrast between recognition regulated by the moral law or legal-institutional factors and the

---

[12] Derrida, *Friendship*, viii.
[13] "Reine Selbstheit ist reine *Derselbigkeit* ohne *Der*." Jacobi's letter to Jean Paul from March 16, 1800 (JBW I,12, 208). See Derrida, *Friendship*, 68ff. and 216.
[14] Derrida, *Friendship*, 22.

genuine and primordial relation of an I to a thou that manifests itself in friendship—or however one wants to phrase it. We could take these additional steps and then be done with the matter. And why would anyone object? Perhaps because it seems highly suspicious that Woldemar of all people, the novel's ambiguous protagonist, is himself very well aware of the situation just described. There is, for example, absolutely no need for a crisis in order to teach him that "man [...] feels himself more in another than in himself" (JWA 7,1, 234). Already in the first pages, we can see that he has taken this lesson to heart.

In other words, what might appear to be a conclusion is really only a starting point. And it is also this specific twist that reveals the theoretical sophistication of both Derrida's and Jacobi's reflections and thus differentiates them from conventional approaches to the topic. An outcome that would satisfy the latter serves for the former to mark the point at which deconstruction begins. To the extent that this is true, however, then we can formulate the crux of the matter as follows: the deconstruction of the subject does indeed lead us to the friend. But the goal that it pursues in this figure can in fact only be reached through a deconstruction of friendship itself. And this brings me to Brother Henriette.

III.

The figure of the brother under consideration here has nothing to do with familial relations. This is obvious in the case of the relationship between Woldemar and Henriette, but Derrida as well foregrounds this distinction repeatedly,[15] not least with an eye toward Montaigne, whose efforts to distance friendship from biological brotherhood could not be more pronounced. Precisely in Montaigne, however, one also comes across the statement, uttered in the same breath, that "the name of brother is truly a fair one and full of love: that is why La Boëtie and I made a brotherhood of our alliance."[16]

However, clearly the relation of friendship is distinguished from a natural relation, then, it is at the same time just as clearly invoked in the "name" of the brother. What are we to make of this? And furthermore, what does it mean against the backdrop of the political resonances of friendship that have always informed reflections on the topic, especially if we allow ourselves to be reminded by Derrida of that crucial expression of democratic consciousness which he never explicitly names but ceaselessly invokes: "Liberté, Egalité, Fraternité."[17] At first one might be tempted, if not to overlook the passage in Montaigne, then at least to relativize it away as harmless. After all, as one could object to Derrida, at issue here is obviously "only" a "fair" name and nothing more. On closer inspection, however, doing so only makes the question more urgent: why, if it is "only" a name, friendship is referred to by this name at all?

---

[15] Derrida, *Friendship*, 180, 202.
[16] Michel de Montaigne, *The Complete Essays.*, ed. and trans. Michael A. Screech (London: Penguin Books, 1991), 208.
[17] Derrida, *Friendship*, 21f.

This question cannot simply be waved away, and the answer is far from pleasant, though I should note that it has one facet I will only be able to touch upon here, leaving a more in-depth engagement to scholars in feminist theory. It is true that Derrida, in invoking the figure of the brother, thereby also highlights the masculine exclusion of the female friend from the canon of friendship, an exclusion that Woldemar expresses in extreme form with his reference to "Brother Heinrich."[18] Ultimately, however, this facet is best seen as an indication of a larger issue. Something else is much more important here, because it is more fundamental and substantial—the fact that the "fair name" of the brother absorbs that very "irreducible singularity and alterity" which the friend actually and essentially represents. In other words, we find ourselves in a rather dire situation: what had appeared to be an unambiguous choice between the subject and the friend has collapsed, insofar as the logic of identification is engaged in fraternal mischief-making at the level of friendship itself.

In his novel, Jacobi presents his diagnosis of this dilemma in remarkably vivid detail. Woldemar writes anthemic letters, sings the praises of "creation" (JWA 7,1, 348), and, before he knows it, the name Pygmalion flows from his pen (JWA 7,1, 348)—after all, in Henriette he finds his "old dream of friendship" fulfilled: "*to become and remain one*" (JWA 7,1, 355f.). And then, confronted with circumstances that cause his friend's behavior to appear less than fully transparent, he falls off the precipice. Not the dream, but the actuality of the "*one in all*" was an "illusion": "I have to leave my own self behind, as if I were a stranger, and put myself in her position! *Put myself?—Henriette* is an *other* to me; Henriette is *against* me" (JWA 7,1, 358). Whatever Woldemar might have initially intended with his reference to the other, the realization that brother Henriette could be "an other" turns his friendship into enmity.

Derrida offers a structurally identical diagnosis with regard to texts on friendship from the history of philosophy. According to Derrida, they all reflect the same ambivalence. On the one hand, any discussion of friendship presupposes that the friend, as the one who he is in his "certain singularity"[19] will be loved, cherished and mourned after his death. And on the other hand, as he is encoded in the figure of the brother, he is situated in the same moment in the context of intimacy, familiarity, identity or similarity, presence—and identified in this context. Notably, Aristotle proceeds in the same manner, a point to which I will return at the end of the chapter.

IV.

The "truth of friendship," as Derrida puts it, is to be found in "obscurity,"[20] insofar as it provides an exemplary demonstration of that which it initially seems to contradict: "the logic of the same."[21] This is the problem around which both texts revolve—but where and how are we to find its solution?

---

[18] As an alternate example Derrida notes: "that letter of the great and good Saint Francis of Assisi, who could not help but to write to a nun: 'Dear Brother Jacqueline.'" Derrida, *Friendship*, 156.
[19] Derrida, "Heidegger's Ear," 165.
[20] Derrida, *Friendship*, 16.
[21] Derrida, *Friendship*, 4.

When I asserted at the beginning of the chapter that the systematic kinship between Jacobi's two-hundred-year-old novel and Derrida's contemporary essay was astonishing, I also had something else in mind, something more than a shared diagnosis of the problem. More specifically, both authors invoke a figure whose appearance in such texts is hardly a common occurrence: the figure of *Echo*. As Jacobi writes in the preface to his novel, he would have "much preferred" to dispense with a preface entirely and simply "left behind a fable": the fable of Harmonia, whose request leads Jupiter, upon the completion of creation, to transform her into Echo so that even if she cannot remain among her creatures she can at least answer them in "broken tones" (JWA 7,1, 209f.).[22] This brokenness that characterizes Echo in contrast to Harmonia finds a direct correspondence in Derrida, who opposes Echo—"she who speaks from, and steals, the words of the other [*celle qui prend la parole aux mots de l'autre*]"—to any form of "ipseity" whatsoever.[23]

Echo, then. The fact that the way out of a friendship identified with brotherhood is underwritten by this figure in both texts is perhaps the best indication of their structural affinity. And on a first reading it also appears that the end of the novel serves to reinforce this affinity. Speaking in "broken tones," Echo is a figuration of distance, and it is precisely into this condition of distance that the friendship between Woldemar and Henriette liberates itself after a series of crises. Schlegel's disgruntled characterization of this conclusion as reflecting an "unresolved dissonance"[24] is no doubt to be attributed to his disappointed expectation of a love story. But his own description nonetheless comes substantially closer to capturing the truth than Hegel's version, which turns Jacobi's intended purpose on its head in concluding with a celebration of reconciliation, of the "*existence* of the *I* extended into two-ness."[25]

Neither "extended" into a state of reconciliation nor characterized by "unresolved" dissonance, the conclusion to the novel instead offers, in the truest sense of the word, an *Echo* of the "fable" from the preface. This, as I said, aligns Jacobi's intentions with those of Derrida and thus seems to confirm once and for all their complete agreement. In fact, however, we have now reached the point at which their paths diverge. As I already alluded to previously, with Echo, Derrida ultimately disappears (to use an expression inspired by the text) into "Heidegger's ear." Jacobi cannot accompany him there, and not only for historical reasons. It is because he has, for substantive reasons, long since turned to Aristotle, a turn that occurs directly prior to the novel's conclusion as sketched out above. It is worth pointing out in this context that in a letter to Wilhelm v. Humboldt from September 2, 1794, he describes his "presentation of Aristotelian moral philosophy" as the "greatest achievement" of the entire text. "These few pages have required more work, effort, and reflection than anything that I have contributed to the field of philosophy" (JBW I,10, 396). We should remember that this assertion

---

[22] Jacobi takes this fable from Herder, and its profound significance to him is evident from the dedication to Goethe, in which he expressly asks that his greetings be sent to "the poet of Echo." JWA 7,1, 207; see Jacobi's letter to Goethe from January 12, 1794 (JBW I,10, 302).
[23] Derrida, *Friendship*, 24, cf. 166f.
[24] Schlegel, "Jacobis Woldemar," 180.
[25] Hegel, *Phänomenologie des Geistes*, GW 9, 362. Hegel, *Phenomenology of Spirit*, 389.

comes from someone whose contributions to the "field of philosophy" include a brilliant reconstruction of Spinoza and a sweeping critique of Kant.

Jacobi's remarks in the letter to Humboldt render even more explicit what is already clear from the novel, namely, that the invocation of Aristotle constitutes anything but a gratuitous historical reference. This holds for Derrida as well, however, who also devotes significant attention to Aristotle, albeit not at the end of his essay but at the beginning. And as soon as one recognizes this, the situation becomes rather difficult, because strictly speaking, the paths of Jacobi and Derrida do not *diverge* in the sense that we can choose one of them while simultaneously keeping the other option available as well. Long before Heidegger ever enters into the picture, their reflections part ways in the sense that they *collide* in their respective readings of Aristotle. In the one case, Aristotle offers the solution to the problem and, in the other, he *is* the problem. According to Jacobi, he provides an alternative to the pernicious understanding of friendship for which, according to Derrida, he is taken to be largely responsible.

What is to be done here? This difficulty can certainly not be resolved *ex cathedra*. I will attempt to chart a path out of the dilemma by concluding with brief outline of the implications and consequences of their respective interpretations.

V.

First, it seems evident to me that Derrida's diagnosis of the problem is originally derived, not from Aristotle's but rather from Montaigne's model of friendship. Assuming this impression is correct, it can shed additional light on the specific affinity between his text and Jacobi's novel. From a structural (i.e., not a philological) point of view, it is not difficult to discern in the "old dream of friendship" that Woldemar dreams (only to awaken to an all the more painful reality) a reaction to Montaigne's paean to intimate and exclusive fraternity. Against the backdrop of Montaigne, moreover, one can also cast the decisive difference between the two texts into sharper relief. Jacobi's novel, it could be said, tests the integrity of this model of friendship and shows it to be lacking. In other words, he does not merely depict the transformation of friendship into enmity sketched out above but also reveals, through the utter devastation of his protagonist, how this model finally implodes, in order to then invoke Aristotle as a guide who can lead us out of the ruins. The logic of Derridian deconstruction is entirely different, implying on the basis of a historical retrospective that the texts of Montaigne and Aristotle were composed and should be read as representatives of a single canonical tradition rather than as indicative of a rupture.

There is, in principle, nothing wrong with such an interpretive strategy, but what does it mean in concrete terms? How does one establish that Aristotle's standpoint constitutes one of the first and most paradigmatic cases of friendship being cast into the "obscurity," in other words, that he renounces the "singularity" of the friend at the very moment of its identification? Inasmuch as Aristotle's so-called first or perfect friendship is the point of reference for all other forms of *philia*, Derrida rightly gives it primacy in his discussion. Rather than facilitating the exchange of pleasure or benefit, this form, to the extent that it is based on the virtue of the friends, contributes reciprocally to the well-being of the friend for the friend's sake. This is the only form of friendship, according to Aristotle, on which we can rely. Such friendship takes time, however, time to emerge and time to prove itself, and in light of our limited supply of time, attention, and strength, the implication is that it would be impossible to have *many* friends of this sort.[26]

This is exactly the point at which Derrida levels his objection. Because, according to Derrida, the specific constitution of perfect friendship goes hand in hand with the idea of its limited scope, the "incalculable singularities" of the friend are subjected to the "terrible necessity" of an identifying calculation or "reckoning" as the precondition of closeness and belonging.[27] The objection is as subtle as it is radical. There is a certain satisfaction to be found in seeing this perfect friendship, which, according to its own self-understanding, is located beyond all calculation, collapse into an "endurance of arithmetic."[28] Not even the reassurance that Aristotle does not provide a tally but leaves the question of how many friends one can have entirely open—even this cannot prevent the collapse, because Derrida has already anticipated this circumstance in his discussion of a "tragedy of number without number."[29]

Nonetheless, I do not find his objection convincing. In suspecting Aristotle's obviously *qualitative* (i.e., oriented toward the specific quality of perfect friendship) claim of a tragic quantification, he thereby casts suspicion on any intimacy or familiarity arising through friendship. This absolute rejection of intimacy under the heading of so-called "presence" is certainly radical, but perhaps for this very reason it is also counter-intuitive. It is difficult to see who the friend would actually be if his relationship to his counterpart, precisely because he has been named as this friend, was not characterized by a degree of familiarity that distinguished it from other relationships. From this perspective, Aristotle's decision not to put a figure on this unique intimacy is anything but incidental. It shows that the specific intimacy of friendship is characterized by a degree of latitude which, in contrast, is not to be found in Montaigne or Woldemar. Both explicitly quantify their "dream of friendship" as a relationship that involves one single friend.

This notion of latitude also leads to a second, even more important point. According to Derrida, the intimacy of the friend betrays *eo ipso* his egological identification. It was Aristotle himself, however, who raised the question of whether the very intimacy of friendship does not in fact incorporate distance rather than excluding it. Precisely this possibility is under consideration in his reflections on *virtue*. Whereas relationships based on pleasure or utility are in fact not concerned with the respective other, but rather primarily with the reciprocal satisfaction of specific interests, friendship grounded in the virtue of the friends is able to accomplish something qualitatively different. It makes possible a prudent distance in the midst of intimacy, the distance

---

[26] See Aristotle, *Nicomachean Ethics*, IX 10, in *The Complete Works of Aristotle*, ed. Jonathan Barnes, vol. 2 (Princeton: Princeton University Press, 1984).
[27] Derrida, *Friendship*, 20.
[28] Derrida, *Friendship*, 21.
[29] Derrida, *Friendship*, 22.

required in order for the other to be perceived as other at all.[30] Derrida did not simply overlook the dimension of virtue, of course. But he did not pursue the idea of an *intimacy in distance* to which it gives rise. Along with perfect friendship, then, Derrida also casts virtue into the abyss of identifying calculation.

Jacobi's reading of Aristotle, however, compels us to retrieve it from the depths. To open up a perspective on virtue as the decisive condition of a friendship in which the friend Henriette is not, or would no longer be absorbed into the figure of the brother—this is the focus of interest here. To be sure, Jacobi's staging of the encounter with Aristotle is extremely subtle. The question of virtue and the reliable behavior of the friend to which it gives rise becomes significant here because it also allows us to grasp Woldemar's previous self-understanding in Aristotelian categories. Woldemar, just like Montaigne, no doubt believed that his "dream of friendship" was a dream of *perfect friendship*. Its true content, however, is revealed through the unstable behavior that transformed friendship into enmity and ultimately led to his own self-destruction—he dreamt of friendship as a subtle form of pure, egotistical pleasure.

VI.

Brother Henriette: Jacobi's and Derrida's texts not only reveal structural similarities in terms of theoretical background, diagnosis of the problem, and perceived possibilities for therapy. By focusing on their readings of Aristotle, we can also see that both use the figure of the brother to deconstruct the presumably perfect friendship. Here, however, is where the crucial difference lies. Deciphering the subtle calculation of pleasure in this form in order to counter it with a friendship grounded in virtue is one thing, and pronouncing virtuous friendship itself guilty of identifying calculation is another.

In accordance with this difference, the "broken tones" of Echo also reverberate in very different ways in the two texts. Derrida hears these tones in "Heidegger's ear" and thereby arrives at the ultimate conclusion of his deconstruction of Aristotelian friendship. But it is telling that in his reference to § 34 of *Being and Time*, he points not to a main clause but only to an incidental comment in one of the subordinate clauses. In fact, Heidegger is not concerned with friendship at all here, but rather with seeing and hearing, and for this reason alone mentions "hearing the voice of the friend whom every Dasein carries with it."[31] The arbitrariness and complete indeterminacy of this sequence are, according to Derrida, its most distinguishing characteristic—so as to avoid the contemptible rhetoric of "presence," the friend in "Heidegger's ear" can only be delineated *via negationis*. "The friend has no face, no figure [*figure*]. No sex. No name. The friend is not a man, nor a woman; it is not I, nor a 'self,' not a subject, nor a person."[32] It is clear that the friend is not and cannot be a subject. I began my reflections

---

[30] The idea of a "friendship between a man and himself" is essentially related to this. See Aristotle, *Nicomachean Ethics*, IX 4, 1166a, and IX, 8, 1168b.
[31] Martin Heidegger, *Being and Time*, trans. John Macquarrie and Edward S. Robinson (Oxford: Basil Blackwell, 1962), 206.
[32] Derrida, "Heidegger's Ear," 165.

with this premise. But then who is the friend, if, in the very same breath, he is also deprived of his name? What ultimately remains is only the sheer anonymity of the other, and I cannot see how this outcome can be defended against the accusation that in its radical decontextualization of friendship, it appears not as an echo but merely as a mirror that reflects the stigmatized concept of the subject in the other.

Those who are not willing to pay this price will find an alternative in Jacobi's novel. His understanding of friendship, however, also comes at a cost. His return to Aristotle not only reminds us that friendship in the name of the friend must be grasped as a virtue that allows for the maintenance of distance in intimacy. This return also compels us to take note of a seemingly insignificant but in fact substantial adjustment to the Aristotelian text, which, reading against the grain, clarifies a certain ambiguity in the *Nicomachean Ethics* itself.

In order to establish the friendship of virtue, Aristotle refers to the *nous* as "the man himself."[33] The nous, however, as is then explained in Book X, is "something divine" in us as mortal beings.[34] In offering this reflection, Aristotle opens up the perspective of a metaphysics with which he in the same moment abandons the practical in favor of the theoretical life. Jacobi responds to this conceptual ambiguity with an unorthodox correction: with regard to the nous, he pulls the metaphysical perspective back out of the theoretical realm and inserts it into the practice of friendship (JWA 7,1, 449–51). And in order to give this covert repositioning the necessary performative punch, the relevant lines are spoken by—who else—the friends Henriette and Woldemar.

In order for the echo to remain an echo and not turn into a mirror, the "broken tones" of friendship must have the backing of a similarly broken metaphysics. Considered from the perspective of Derridean deconstruction, such a thought may be charged with the unforgivable crime of "onto-theology."[35] In the end, however, it is likely to survive the challenge.

---

[33] Aristotle, *Nicomachean Ethics*, IX 8, 1168b.
[34] Aristotle, *Nicomachean Ethics*, X 7, 1177b.
[35] Derrida, *Friendship*, 287 and "Heidegger's Ear," 215.

8

"I am and there are things outside me": Overcoming the Consciousness Paradigm with Jacobi's Realism

Introduction: Jacobi's Original Insight

In *Fichtes ursprüngliche Einsicht* (1967), Dieter Henrich advanced the influential claim that Fichte inaugurates a new era in the history of the theory of self-consciousness. Whereas philosophers from Descartes to Kant had considered the I as the foundational principle of knowledge but not in its own constitution, Fichte was the first to focus on the I itself, thereby establishing the untenability of the "reflection theory of self-consciousness." If self-consciousness arises as a result of the subject turning itself into an object, then some degree of self-knowledge must pre-exist this relation, because otherwise there could be no subject-I to identify with the object-I in the first place. This circularity, moreover, cannot be resolved by claiming that the pre-existing subject is not yet an I, that the I only emerges through the process of reflection, because in this case the identity of subject and object posited in self-consciousness becomes completely incomprehensible.[1]

There can be no doubt that Henrich's analysis identifies a fundamental challenge with which any theory of subjectivity must contend. As the exchange of names in the heading to my introduction makes clear, however, we disagree on a crucial point. It is not *Fichte,* but rather *Jacobi* who holds the copyright to the "original insight," which not only shattered the reflection model of self-consciousness but also invalidated the entire underlying *consciousness paradigm*. In other words, the overcoming of the consciousness paradigm and the introduction of a new *realist conception* of consciousness go hand in hand here. In this regard, my reattribution of the "original insight" to Jacobi is intended to indicate both a historical and a systematic primacy. Unless we take into account the prior work of Jacobi and its immense influence, the stakes of the debates among classical German philosophers during the epochal shift around 1800 simply cannot be fully understood. Discussing Jacobi, however, also allows me to advocate for a position whose potential has *not yet* been fully realized despite the many post-Kantian attempts to appropriate his work. Such is

---

[1] Dieter Henrich, "Fichte's Original Insight" [1967], in *Contemporary German Philosophy,* ed. Darrel E. Christensen et al., trans. David R. Lachterman, vol. 1 (Pennsylvania: Pennsylvania State University Press, 1982), 15–53.

the systematic aspect of my interest, which I consider to be the most important. It should be stated at the outset that an exhaustive treatment of either the two aspects mentioned would be impossible in the current context and is not the aim of the reflections that follow.

Two Paths to the Problem

Jacobi's Anti-Cartesian Privileging of the *Sum*

Jacobi's key texts, his book *Concerning the Doctrine of Spinoza in Letters to Herr Moses Mendelssohn* (1785/89) and the fictional dialogue *David Hume on Faith, or Idealism and Realism* (1787), both precede the post-Kantian discussion. This observation would be trivial were it not closely linked to more substantial matters. As a first step toward illuminating these matters, it will be helpful to consider a passage from Jacobi's later text. With regard to the unity of the I, as Jacobi explains here in the role of the first-person speaker:

> I cannot make a representation of it at all, for the peculiarity of its being is that *it remains distinct from every sensation and representation*. It is what I properly call "myself," and I have the most perfect conviction of its reality, the most intimate consciousness of it, since it is the very source of my consciousness and the subject of all its alterations. The soul would have to be able to distinguish itself from itself, *become external to itself*, in order to have a *representation* of itself. Certainly we have the most intimate consciousness of what we call our "life." But who can grasp it in a representation? (DH: JWA 2,1, 83f.; MPW 316)[2]

Jacobi's makes his critique of the reflection theory clear here. But he also engages the topic at a far more fundamental level than in our initial characterization above, attributing the failure of reflection to more than just formally circular reasoning. In fact, he is already several steps ahead of Fichte in formulating the problem. First, he has already identified the way out of the circularity of reflection, often characterized in contemporary theories of self-consciousness as an immediate, pre-reflexive familiarity with oneself. Insofar as the I always already has a "most intimate consciousness" of itself, self-consciousness cannot be seen as a consequence of reflection. And secondly, he then uses this insight as the basis for an even more incisive rejection of reflection. His approach has profound implications on both counts.

---

[2] Von der Einheit des Ich "kann ich mir gar keine Vorstellung [...] machen, denn das Eigenthümliche ihres Wesens ist, *sich von allen Empfindungen und Vorstellungen zu unterscheiden*. Sie ist dasjenige, was ich im eigentlichsten Verstande *mich selbst* nenne, und von dessen Realität ich die vollkommenste Ueberzeugung, das innigste Bewustseyn habe, weil es die Quelle selbst meines Bewustseyns, und das Subject aller seiner Veränderungen ist. Die Seele, um eine Vorstellung von sich zu haben, müßte sich von sich selbst unterscheiden, *sich selbst äusserlich werden können*. Von dem, was Leben ist, haben wir gewiß das innigste Bewustseyn; aber wer kann sich vom Leben eine Vorstellung machen?" (DH: JWA 2,1, 83f.)

With regard to this pre-reflexive self-consciousness, rather than restricting his focus to exclusively *mental* states, Jacobi explicitly brings an *existential* dimension into play. The I has a "most intimate consciousness" of its reality, of its life. In other contexts Jacobi speaks of the "I am" (DH: JWA 2,1, 37; MPW 277) or of *"existence"* (Spin: JWA 1,1, 29; 258; MPW 194; 373), with which he clearly intends to indicate something more than mere materiality. At stake here is in fact nothing less than a fundamental turning point in the conception of subjectivity, programmatically announced by Jacobi in the preface to the second, 1789 edition of the *Spinoza Letters* with his assertion "that I am not a *Cartesian*." "I [...] believe, one simply must not put the *sum* after the *cogito*" (Spin: JWA 1,1, 157). The continuous thread that runs from Descartes's *cogito* to Kant's *I think* (albeit with significant modifications) is thereby cut, and the first era of the theory of self-consciousness ends here, not with Fichte. In the aftermath, the problems with reflection come into even sharper focus.

Any attempt (necessarily misguided) to form a representation of the I must now be understood in relation to the fundamental awareness of the *sum*, of existence that is immediately conscious of itself. And this in turn necessitates a redescription of the aporia of reflection theory. The problem stems not from the retroactive identification of subject and object as the two poles of self-consciousness, but from the fact that these poles are differentiated in the first place. It is impossible for the I to return to itself in the process of reflection, because the modality of representation is always accompanied by a *splitting caused by the shift in perspective*. The *internal perspective* of the I, which essentially constitutes its "most intimate consciousness," is exchanged for the *external perspective* of a supposed self-observation, but this inevitably leads to a neglect of the fundamental awareness of the "most intimate consciousness." Taking up Jacobi's formulation here, this means that what we refer to as ourselves in the proper sense *defies any form of objectification in principle*. The I that Jacobi seeks to designate can never be an object, not even for itself.

In making this distinction between two modalities of knowledge—mediated and immediate—Jacobi also clarifies and specifies the epistemic implications of his "original insight." The I is present to itself exclusively as an immediate certainty, epistemically expressed in the mode of feeling: "We have no concept of qualities as such, but only intuitions," just as "of our own existence, we have only a feeling and no concept" (Spin: JWA 1,1, 258; MPW 374).

There can be no doubt that Jacobi's intervention has a profound impact on the formation of post-Kantian philosophy as a whole, including that of early German romanticism. In the absence of his "original insight" into the existential dimension of selfhood and the question of its epistemic representability, Kant's successors would never have been able to move beyond his transcendental philosophy to establish entirely new conceptions and logics of subjectivity. This is not the place to discuss the many examples of Jacobi's influence, including, in a case that is particularly noteworthy for its late date, on Hegel's treatment of "immediate knowing" in the "preliminary conception" of his *Encyclopedia Logic*. Nor will I consider here the significant ways in which this dimension of his thought becomes interwoven with his reconstruction of Spinoza's *Ethics*, whose primary distinction between substance and mode is reformulated by Jacobi as the "*being* in everything existent" (JWA 1,1, 39; MPW 199).

Instead, I will simply note that it seems odd to exempt Fichte from this influence,[3] especially since, among all of the protagonists of the early phase of post-Kantian philosophy, he and Schelling were Jacobi's most fervent and forceful advocates.[4] It can hardly be seen as anything other than a response to Jacobi, for example, when Fichte names not consciousness or self-consciousness but the F/Act [Tathandlung] of the "I am" as the foundational principle of his Wissenschaftslehre and also contradicts Descartes, claiming "the addition of *cogitans* is quite superfluous." As he goes on to explain, "it is not the case that if one exists then one necessarily thinks, but rather that one necessarily exists if one thinks. Thinking by no means constitutes the essence [of I's being], but is only a specific determination of its being."[5] With this statement, however, we have also reached the precise point where it becomes necessary to turn down the second path.

The Equiprimordial Certainty of Our Experience of Self and World

Some have tried to refute the views on self-consciousness to which Henrich's study has given rise, arguing that Fichte is ultimately not concerned with the psychological fact of the I but rather—as was the case with Descartes and Kant—with the project of grounding knowledge. From this it is said to follow that as a "philosophical construct," the "absolute I" has nothing to do with the constitution of our subjectivity.[6] Whether or not such a radical bifurcation in the usage of the term "I" accords with Fichte's intentions is not something we need to consider here. On the basis of Fichte's own assertions, we can establish that there is at least a dramatic difference with regard to primacy. He makes this point with particular clarity in a letter to Jacobi, where, after repeated assurances of the "striking conformity of our philosophical convictions," he insists that "My *absolute I* is obviously not the *individual* [...]. But the *individual must be deduced from the absolute* I, and the *Wissenschaftslehre* will immediately proceed to such a deduction in conjunction with its treatment of natural rights."[7]

---

[3] This can be seen both in the later works of Henrich and in Manfred Frank's analyses of early German romanticism, which are indebted to the former. In both cases, Jacobi's significance is acknowledged but always in the context of a post-Fichtean constellation. See Dieter Henrich, "Die Anfänge der Theorie des Subjekts (1789)," in *Zwischenbetrachtungen. Im Prozess der Aufklärung*, ed. Axel Honneth et al. (Frankfurt a.M.: Suhrkamp, 1989), 106–70; Dieter Henrich, *Der Grund im Bewußtsein. Untersuchungen zu Hölderlins Denken (1794–1795)* (Stuttgart: Klett-Cotta, 2004); Manfred Frank, *"Unendliche Annäherung." Die Anfänge der philosophischen Frühromantik* (Frankfurt a.M.: Suhrkamp, 1997).

[4] See Fichte's letters to Jacobi dated September 29, 1794, and August 30, 1795 (JBW I,11, 3, and 55ff.; J. G. Fichte, *Early Philosophical Writings*, ed. and trans. Daniel Breazeale (Ithaca: Cornell University Press, 1988), 411f.).

[5] Fichte, *Grundlage der gesamten Wissenschaftslehre*, FW I, 100. J. G. Fichte, "Foundation of the Entire Wissenschaftslehre," in *J. G. Fichte: Foundation of the Entire Wissenschaftslehre and Related Writings (1794–95)*, ed. and trans. Daniel Breazeale (Oxford: Oxford University Press, 2021), 206.

[6] Rolf-Peter Horstmann, "Gibt es ein philosophisches Problem des Selbstbewußtseins?," in *Theorie der Subjektivität*, ed. Konrad Cramer et al. (Frankfurt a.M.: Suhrkamp, 1987), 235ff. See also Rolf-Peter Horstmann, *Die Grenzen der Vernunft. Eine Untersuchung zu Zielen und Motiven des Deutschen Idealismus* (Frankfurt a.M.: Anton Hain, 1991), 280.

[7] Fichte's letter to Jacobi from August 30, 1795 (JBW I,11, 55. Fichte, *Early Philosophical Writings*, 411).

Against this backdrop, then, the aforementioned objection must be seen as valid. It is, however, both interesting as well as decisive for what follows that *Jacobi* had long since anticipated this very criticism. In the *Letter to Fichte* of 1799, he categorically rejects Fichte's I as an example of an intellectual construction taken to extremes, referring to it as "that *impersonal personality*, that naked I-hood of the I without any self" (JF: JWA 2,1, 212; MPW 516f.). And he likewise dismisses entirely the possibility that the "self" which the "I-hood" is lacking could ever be made comprehensible by way of a scientific deduction. The implications of this criticism can be unpacked in three steps.

First of all, we should note that Jacobi is clearly addressing himself *to our concrete first-person I*. Any confusion with an "I" conceived as the basis for a systematic grounding of knowledge is out of the question here, as can be gleaned from the entire range of Jacobi's critical objections to the course of post-Kantian philosophy, including those leveled against attempts to appropriate or co-opt his thought. Second, it is important to forestall another, related confusion, namely the confusion of the first-person I as conceived by Jacobi with Kant's "empirical consciousness," which serves in his philosophy as the presumed alternative to the transcendental (or otherwise named) I-principle. By decisively renouncing this transcendental-philosophical heritage, Jacobi simultaneously ensures that he does not participate in the widespread *circumscription of the problem of subjectivity*, in which subjectivity is understood in one of two ways. Either it consists in pure self-reference independent of all worldly conditions (an option that seems to confirm the rightly criticized failure to differentiate between the I-function and our first-person self-consciousness), or it is seen as an empirical phenomenon, exhibiting particular states and the attributes that correlate with its representation of objects.

Jacobi renders this alternative untenable. And this means, thirdly, that precisely insofar as the "intimate consciousness" the I has of its existence is not an empirical but very much a first-person consciousness, to this extent the *relation of the I to the world* comes to the fore and must be conceived completely anew. An isolated consideration of the I on its own is simply not possible. At the heart of Jacobi's "original insight," then, is the claim that any adequate understanding of ourselves must account for *an equiprimordial* and for this very reason *irreducible double certainty*. In the *Letter to Fichte* this appears as the quintessence of our fundamental conviction as beings in the world, as "the equal certainty that these two propositions have for the natural man: 'I am' and 'There are things outside me.'" (JF: JWA 2,1, 194; MPW 501). Experience of ourselves and experience of the world are originally and inextricably connected. Even in the awareness that I live *in the world*, I remain attentive to my own self, and, by the same token, the awareness that *I* am the one experiencing never leads me to disregard the world. With the defense of this double certainty, Jacobi disrupts the paradigm of consciousness, including the reflection model of self-consciousness, at the most fundamental level. Moreover, not only in foregrounding the first-person "I am," but also in his insistence on the inseverable connection between "*I*" and "*Thou*," which cannot be resolved into the one side or the other (Spin: JWA 1,1, 116; DH: JWA 2,1, 38; MPW 277; 231), he simultaneously becomes the thinker who poses the greatest challenge to post-Kantian philosophy.

The Representation Model of Consciousness

I am and there are things outside me. In our everyday experience, we are so familiar with this double certainty that we hardly see its assertion as a provocation; indeed, we are unlikely to think about it at all. Approaching it philosophically, one might be inclined to sidestep the provocation by way of a reformulation, referring to subject and object or to consciousness and object [Gegenstand] in order to indicate thereby a cognitive relation, according to which consciousness is always *consciousness of something and thus has representations of* objects. Perhaps one might even believe such a reformulation captures the existential certainty described previously, simply rephrasing it in somewhat more technical terms. Some of the statements of *Christian Wolff*, to whom we owe the German term for "consciousness" [Bewusstsein], suggest that this was in fact his opinion on the matter, and his own formulation of the consciousness paradigm will help cast the conceptual backdrop to Jacobi's position into sharper relief. The following three central passages from his German Metaphysics can serve as a summary:

> We are conscious of ourselves and of other things. No one can doubt this who has not been fully robbed of his senses, and should anyone seek to deny it, he would be making an assertion that stands in contradiction to his own experience, and he could readily be convinced that his assertion is illogical. How, after all, could he deny something or cast it into doubt if he were not conscious of himself and of other things? But whoever is conscious of that which he denies or casts into doubt, he is. And so it is clear that we are. (§ 1)
>
> The first thing we noted about ourselves was that we are aware of ourselves and of other things outside of us (§.1.), that is, that we know we now represent many things to ourselves as outside of ourselves (§.194). (§ 728).
>
> Because, according to this, the soul has the power to make representations of the world (§.753.), so these representations too must have a resemblance to the things that are in the world. Because if they had no such resemblance, then the soul would not be representing the world to itself, but rather something else. An image that does not resemble the thing [Sache] it is supposed to represent is not an image of that thing, but of another object (§ 17.18). (§ 769).[8]

Wolff does not seem to see the abyss toward which his statements lead him. From the fact that we are *conscious* of ourselves and other things, we are allegedly able to conclude that we *are*. Offering a variant of the Cartesian argument that is significantly more resolute than that of Descartes himself, Wolff deduces the being of the one who possesses consciousness from the mere mental apprehension of consciousness. To be

---

[8] Christian Wolff, *Vernünfftige Gedanken von Gott, der Welt und der Seele des Menschen, auch allen Dingen überhaupt*, in *Gesammelte Werke*, ed. Charles A. Corr, vol. I,2 (Hildesheim/Zürich/New York: Georg Olms Verlag, 1983). A partial translation of Wolff can be found in Christian Wolff, "Rational Thoughts Concerning God, the World, and the Human Soul, and Also All Things in General (1720)," in *Early Modern German Philosophy (1690–1750)*, ed. and trans. Corey W. Dyck (Oxford: Oxford University Press, 2019), 95–134. This translation has been amended and extended here.

conscious of other things means to *represent* them to ourselves *as* outside of us. From the central position of consciousness it follows that we do not engage with things, but only with our representations of things, which we relate in consciousness to something seemingly external to consciousness. The *correspondence* between representation and real things is *mediated through resemblance*—there must be a "model" for the image in our head in order to ensure that our representations refer to something truly external and in accordance with the representation.

But how can we become conscious of a relation of similarity that mediates cognition *in* consciousness, one whose assumption and validation presume that we do not operate solely in terms of representations, and how can we be certain of our own existence, if the basis of this certainty is merely an inference drawn from the mental apprehension of consciousness? This model of thought, which seeks to infer a real referent from the immanent representations of consciousness, never provides an answer to these questions. In the following I will refer to it as the *representation model* of *consciousness*, although I should note that the Latin term "representation" is semantically ambiguous and does not adequately capture the crucial difference that Jacobi seeks to articulate with his distinction between *Vorstellung* and *Darstellung*, or representation and presentation (DH: JWA 2,1, 69; MPW 305).

Clearly, the development of the representation model is an act of remarkable naiveté. And the reflection theory of *self-consciousness* builds on the representation model of consciousness with equal naiveté. If one assumes that consciousness *qua* consciousness has representations of objects, then it is but a small step to conclude that self-consciousness is that representation in which consciousness relates to itself as the intended object. This claim falls apart, however, once a non-naive, problem-oriented analysis has shown that the underlying representation model is, from the outset, threatened by *the abyss of skepticism*. It is anything but coincidental that *Reinhold*, who, with his "principle of consciousness," is the last post-Kantian to advocate for a rigorous conception of this model, also triggers a far-reaching debate about skepticism, which Fichte, Schelling and Hegel all attempt to overcome through recourse to Jacobi.

One wonders how Reinhold could have even considered this approach to be a viable option, given that Jacobi's analysis had long been ready to hand. Only the most superficial reception could give rise to the notion that the existential double-certainty that *I am and there are things outside me* has anything to do with a reformulation of the consciousness paradigm, to say nothing of being adequately captured by it. On the contrary, the insight into the skeptical abyss that haunts the consciousness paradigm means that a fundamentally new approach is required, one that gives full consideration to the double certainty. Jacobi performs this analysis and elucidates the necessary paradigm shift in the dialogue *David Hume*.

Idealism and Realism

Jacobi addresses the consciousness paradigm in this text under the heading of *idealism*, which, as my synopsis of the Wolffian model indicates, in this case also includes *empiricist* approaches, at least insofar as the presumed security provided by an uncritical ontology is abandoned. Hume's own conclusions about the skeptical implications of empiricism underscore this point from an insider's perspective.[9] And it is above all clear that Kant's *transcendental idealism* belongs here, toward which Jacobi's critique is directed in particular. It is no accident that Jacobi supplements the dialogue with a text entitled "On transcendental Idealism," which sets off a discussion of the meaning and significance of Kant's things in themselves that has continued into the present.

Under the heading of *realism*, Jacobi presents the paradigm shift initiated by his own position. In the *dialogue* itself he refers to this position as "*genuine*" or "committed" realism, in order to avoid any confusion with Kant's "empirical realism" (DH: JWA 2,1, 20, 32; MPW 264, 272). Moreover, having already challenged the conceptions and categories conventionally associated with idealism, he now makes use of none other than *Spinoza and Leibniz*—selectively, to be sure—in his explication of realism. His approach is not unproblematic, but not because these philosophers cannot be considered realists. Rather, the difficulties arise for reasons related to the execution of Jacobi's argument. But the end result is fruitful nonetheless, as I will show presently.

Although I cannot address all of the dimensions of this text and its complex interconnections with the first and second editions of the *Spinoza Letters,* it should already be clear from the preceding remarks it contains a sophisticated theoretical analysis, even if the double proposition *I am and there are things outside me* seems to suggest otherwise. In fact, the double proposition is really best understood only as kind of shorthand. To defend the lifeworldly certainty it expresses not only requires us to exchange a "natural" for a philosophical point of view, whereby we engage in a philosophical *discussion* of something about which "in everyday life, there is never any question" (DH: JWA 2,1, 21; MPW 265). Even more importantly, in the double proposition we find only the implication of an argument that must be elucidated before we can grasp how his attack on the consciousness paradigm actually unfolds.

As is apparent in all of its "idealist" variants, the consciousness paradigm is a paradigm of *theoretical* philosophy—consciousness becomes a topic insofar as it is the subject of cognitive operations in the modality of representation. Jacobi certainly does not deny that we relate to the world in a cognitive manner, but he does deny that our representations correspond in even the slightest way to that experience of reality of which we are certain as soon as we open our eyes. This objection, however, only speaks to one facet of his exhortation to realism. The other facet finds expression in the reminder that we are "beings" who are not "*only capable of intuition and judgment.*" As the I in *David Hume* exclaims, "*Surely,* my dear fellow, we can *also act!*" (DH: JWA 2,1, 53; MPW 290).

In the final analysis, overcoming the consciousness paradigm means grasping the connection between our experience of ourselves and the world as *practically* grounded, that is, *in the experience of action.* The "most intimate consciousness" of

---

[9] It is too seldom noted that neither the title of Jacobi's text nor his references in the text to the "*authority*" David Hume (DH: JWA 2,1, 24; MPW 267) is entirely free of ironic and provocative intent.

my existence in the certainty that "I am" is revealed in this context as the certainty that "I act," whereby another, equally primordial certainty also presents itself to me—that I live within a *web of worldly interactions*. Perhaps the representation model of consciousness holds a special appeal for philosophers, who do after all spend an inordinate amount of time sitting at their desks. The fact is, however, that we are *actors in the world*. We do not adopt the *observer* perspective of the theory of consciousness in order to work out which view of things is or is not available to us according to our cognitive capacities.

The Epistemic Realism of Intuition

In order to elucidate Jacobi's position, then, we must distinguish between epistemic and practical realism. In contrast to Jacobi's contemporaries (Fichte again immediately comes to mind), more recent interpreters have tended to neglect Jacobi's practical grounding of realism in favor of efforts to situate him within more familiar epistemological frameworks—a tendency that has not been conducive to a fruitful discussion of the key issues. Jacobi himself, however, clearly states the criterion for the differentiation and assessment of the two variants (DH: JWA 2,1, 38ff.; MPW 277ff.).

In the modality of intuition or perception (Jacobi uses these terms synonymously), the intuited object is *immediately present*. What obtains here is, as Hegel comes to refer to it in his own adaptation under the heading of "*sensuous certainty*," the "*now*."[10] In this modality, in other words, *temporal succession* plays no role in the sense that the object could be considered to be there prior to our intuition of it or the intuition prior to its becoming aware of the object. Nor, for this reason, is any conception of *cause and effect* involved. If we were beings who are only capable of intuition, then, according to Jacobi, we would not have access to the foundational concepts of temporality and causality at all, because they originate in the experience of action. I will return to this central thesis later. Strictly speaking, it is also the case, and I will return to this point as well, that my "most intimate consciousness" of myself, the certainty that I am really "myself" and not someone else, the feeling of unmistakably individual mine-ness, is only fully present to us in the modality of action.

From this perspective, Hegel's presentation of sensuous certainty can provide us with a productive starting point for an initial orientation. As he writes, sensuous certainty "expresses what it knows as this: It *is*; and its truth only contains the *being* of the item. For its part, consciousness only is in this certainty as the pure *I*, or, within that certainty, the *I* is only as a pure *This*, and the object likewise is only as a pure *This*."[11] We should refrain from adopting Hegel's disdainful tone, however. The disparity he insists on between the richness allegedly claimed by sensuous certainty and its actual poverty is not our concern. What proves crucial instead is something never mentioned explicitly but which informs Hegel's entire presentation—that the concept of consciousness in

---

[10] Hegel, *Phänomenologie des Geistes*, GW 9, 64. G. W. F. Hegel, *Phenomenology of Spirit*, ed. and trans. Terry Pinkard (Cambridge: Cambridge University Press), 61.
[11] GW 9, 63. Hegel, *Phenomenology of Spirit*, 60.

the *Phenomenology of Spirit* relies on Jacobi's earlier insights in order to initiate its own break with the philosophy of consciousness and thereby provide a new foundation for the entire experiential history of consciousness. Not only the foregrounding of the *Being* of the object is an indication of this but also the *immediacy* of the relation between *object and I* as it reveals itself in sensuous certainty.[12]

Even though Hegel goes on to show (as does Jacobi) how this relation is "in truth" mediated on both sides, the fundamental determination with which he begins accords with Jacobi's epistemic realism. In the original intuition that assures us of our being and of the being of the object, the intuiting I and the intuited object are involved equiprimordially. It would be misguided, however, to identify Jacobi's position with what has come to be known as external world realism, as if it were essentially a matter of asserting the independence of reality from the subject, a reality on which the subject then allegedly depends in all of its experiences. On this interpretation, "idealism" would be the opposing view that our understanding of reality derives exclusively from the operations of subjectivity.[13] But Jacobi is precisely *not* concerned here with contrasting the primacy of objective-realist and subjective-idealist perspectives.

In order to clarify the crux of the debate between idealism and epistemic realism, it helps to consider the way the argument in the dialogue unfolds and to take note of the clear division of roles between the characters of "He" and "I." It is, after all, the character of "He" who first articulates the essentials of epistemic realism; he only arrives at this point, however, after having been "maieutically" convinced of the untenability of his initial position. This position is untenable because it contains a mixture of *common-sense* convictions on the one hand and the representation model of consciousness on the other, and for this reason initially overlooks the basic convictions of the lifeworld completely.

At issue is the reference of representations to external reality of which "He" is actually certain. But then doubts again begin to creep in regarding the basis for this conviction. One possible clarification, he thinks, could be that I have two different types of representations: one I can generate at will and connect as I see fit, whereas with regard to the others "I feel passive." From this comparison, I can conclude that the involuntary representations "must have a cause outside me" (DH: JWA, 2,1, 36; MPW 275f.). I quote the subsequent objection of the "I" in its entirety, because it presents with particular intensity Jacobi's critique of the consciousness paradigm along with an unmistakable allusion to its Wolffian variant:

> I: But is that how it happens in fact? So, here is this table, there that chessboard with its pieces in place, and your humble servant speaking to you. Do we become *things in themselves* for you, *from representations*, only through an

---

[12] On the subtext of "Sensuous Certainty," see Brady Bowman, *Sinnliche Gewißheit. Zur systematischen Vorgeschichte eines Problems des deutschen Idealismus* (Berlin: Akademie Verlag, 2003).

[13] See Valentin Pluder, *Die Vermittlung von Idealismus und Realismus in der Klassischen Deutschen Philosophie. Eine Studie zu Jacobi, Kant, Fichte, Schelling und Hegel* (Stuttgart-Bad Cannstatt: Frommann-Holzboog, 2013). Oliver Koch, *Individualität als Fundamentalgefühl. Zur Metaphysik der Person bei Jacobi und Jean Paul* (Hamburg: Meiner, 2013) offers a different interpretation.

inference? Is it only in retrospect, through a concept that you add to us, that we manage to be something external to you, and not as mere determinations of your own self?—Why not? Representation, *as mere representation*, can and *must* indeed come ahead! It is everywhere the first. Actuality, or being, is added as predicate only later. Since our soul is a power of representation, it must start by producing a representation just as representation. Things first proceed from the Orphic ovum of intelligibility (i.e. from the *principium contradictionis*) without the dispensable circumstance of reality. (DH: JWA 2,1, 36; MPW 276)

Inferences about *being* are drawn from the immanent consciousness of *thinking*—this is the quintessence of the representation model in its *rationalist* variant. "He" rejects this variant. And yet he nonetheless returns again to the possibility that "we derive our conviction about the actual existence of the objects outside us because their representations are given to us without any doings of ours" (DH: JWA 2,1, 37; MPW 276). Without realizing that he remains de facto trapped in the representation model, he thereby invokes so-called external world realism, which he bases on the *empirical* variant of idealism. Subjective states serve as the starting point for inferences regarding their external sources, which are said to be given by sensation. In this case, however, not only does our immediate certainty of the actual existence of objects outside us disappear behind the passivity of a subject restricted to drawing causal inferences about the external world. This construction eliminates the "I" as well, without whose participation there can be no intuition at all.

Jacobi's most interesting contribution here consists in more than merely presenting this participation, this being-present of the "I," as a form of activity in rather than a passive response. To be sure, intuition is an activity which, as such, does not originate in the intuited object (DH: JWA 2,1, 77; MPW 311). And Jacobi's practical realism is entirely oriented toward an I that acts. The basic fact, however, which in no way contradicts this orientation, is that our consciousness as well is "given to us without any doings of ours," that "we are incapable of shutting it out too; and we feel no less passive with respect to it than we feel in respect of the representations that we call 'representations of external things'" (DH: JWA 2,1, 37; MPW 276f.). This argument completely transforms the stakes of the conversation. Now, rather than presuming that a distinction between actively generated and passively received representations provides the criterion for attributing a real reference to the latter representations, the representation model *as a whole* is superseded. Here Jacobi gives expression to the realism which also appears later in his exchange with Fichte in the form of the double certainty *I am and there are things outside me:*

> The object contributes just as much to the perception of the consciousness as the consciousness does to the perception of the object. I experience that I am, and that there is something outside me, in one and the same indivisible moment; and at that moment my soul is no more passive with respect to the object than it is towards itself. There is no representation, no inference, that mediates this twofold revelation. There is nothing *in the soul* that *enters* between the perception of the

actuality outside it and the actuality in it. There are no representations yet; they make their appearance only later on in reflection, as shadows of the things that were formerly *present*. (DH: JWA 2,1, 37; MPW 277)[14]

The course of the argument shows unambiguously that the realism Jacobi has in mind reveals itself in a flash of recognition, the recognition that "*I am.*" Insofar as an existential certainty is invoked at this moment, the "I" no longer appears in the function of a subject who produces representations and must ask about the grounds for his conviction that the external world is real. The certainty that "I am" is always already connected to the certainty of this world. But an additional point is also crucial in this context. It is clearly untenable to reduce the I to an effect of external stimuli as per the representation model, because it then becomes impossible to explain how the experiences I have are *my own*. The alternative, however, is not to credit me with the capability (or the burden) of being the author of my own existence, let alone to dissolve the I into a transcendental or logical-metaphysical meta-function.

This is the reason that Jacobi speaks of a "twofold revelation," pertaining simultaneously to the experience of the world *and* the I, and it takes no great effort to see that precisely this point will be the source of conflict in debates with post-Kantian philosophy. In the current context, this "twofold revelation," to which Jacobi also adds another key term—"belief"—provides a detailed blueprint for *both* the realist overcoming of the consciousness paradigm *and* the demarcation of the boundary with Kant. In other words, Jacobi's argument proceeds in a series of interrelated stages that will need to be unpacked.

On the one hand, one can follow Kant in attributing an "immediate certainty" to "sensible evidence," "like the certainty of my own existence" (DH: JWA 2,1, 20; MPW 264). This is Kant's *empirical realism,* which he does in fact conceive in terms of the *immediate* perception of external objects. The logical consequence is that Kant himself rejects the representation model on the basis of its inevitably skeptical implications.

> For in fact if one regards outer appearances as representations that are effected in us by their objects, as things in themselves found outside us, then it is hard to see how their existence could be cognized in any way other than by an inference from effect to cause, in which case it must always remain doubtful whether the cause is in us or outside us.[15]

---

[14] "Der Gegenstand trägt eben so viel zur Wahrnehmung des Bewußtseyns bey, als das Bewußtseyn zur Wahrnehmung des Gegenstandes. Ich erfahre, daß ich bin, und daß etwas ausser mir ist, in demselben untheilbaren Augenblick; und in diesem Augenblicke leidet meine Seele vom Gegenstande nicht mehr als sie von sich selbst leidet. Keine Vorstellung, kein Schluß vermittelt diese zwiefache Offenbarung. Nichts tritt *in der Seele* zwischen die Wahrnehmung des Würklichen ausser ihr und des Würklichen in ihr. Vorstellungen sind noch nicht; sie erscheinen erst hinten nach, als Schatten der Dinge, welche *gegenwärtig* waren." (DH: JWA 2,1, 37)

[15] Kant, CPR A 372.

On the other hand, we must recognize that what appears to be a structural concordance between Kant's and Jacobi's realism is really a concordance in name only. Kant, after all, justifies his empirical realism by insisting that it pertains exclusively to the "appearances" apprehended in space as a form of subjective intuition, while the things in themselves remain completely unknown to us. I have already analyzed at length how Jacobi critiques this position in his Supplement to *David Hume*.[16] Here I simply want to underscore that Jacobi's objection does *not*—as has often been claimed—target Kant's allegedly erroneous assumption of a causal relationship between the things in themselves and their effect on us. How could it, when Kant clearly limits the validity of the category of causality to the realm of appearance? This by now all-too-familiar objection can be traced back to Aenesidemus-Schulze. Jacobi actually takes the opposite tack. He argues that Kant, in denying the possibility of any causal relation that extends beyond the realm of appearance, also restricts the surety of our realist convictions to empirical realism. From this it follows that he must abandon the "resolutely" realist conviction to which he lays claim at the start of the *Critique of Pure Reason* with his appeal to the things in themselves. It falls into an extra-theoretical void that lacks any connection to the inner space of the transcendental philosophy.

According to Jacobi's analysis, then, Kant's transcendental idealism confronts us with a paradox. Kant neutralizes the problem of skepticism inherent to the consciousness paradigm by way of empirical realism, but only at the cost of making his entire theoretical framework more radically dependent than ever on the idealistic representation model.

> I am all there is, and outside me there is, *strictly* speaking, nothing. Yet the "I," this all that I am, is in the end also nothing but the *empty illusion* of something. It is *the form of a form,* just as much of a ghost as the other appearances that I call things, a ghost like the whole of nature, its order and its laws. (DH: JWA 2,1, 61, MPW 297)

The Supplement concludes with a challenge: "the transcendental idealist must have the courage, therefore, to assert the strongest idealism that was ever professed, and not to be afraid of the objection of speculative egoism" (DH: JWA 2,1, 112; MPW 338). And Jacobi sees this project realized in paradigmatic form in the "*Nihilism*" of Fichte's Wissenschaftslehre (JF: JWA 2,1, 215; MPW 519), inasmuch as Fichte, influenced by Jacobi's own insights, dismisses any reference to things in themselves as nonsensical. To put it another way: If Jacobi's antidote to idealism had been a realism claiming that our representations refer to an external reality (to things in themselves rather than only appearances), basing this claim either on an inference from thinking to being (Wolff) or an inference from sense data (Locke, Reinhold and, with some reservations regarding skepticism, Aenesidemus-Schulze), then he would have simultaneously been engaged in philosophical self-sabotage and failed to contribute anything substantial to the ongoing discussions of Kant. Neither of these is the case.

---

[16] See Chapter 9 in this volume.

Jacobi most certainly does not counter Kant by seeking to reinstate an epistemic causal relation between things in themselves and our representations. Precisely this claim constitutes the operating principle of the idealistic representation model in all its possible variants, which he criticizes as fundamentally flawed. With his insistence on a "twofold revelation," on the equiprimordial certainty that "the *I* and the *Thou*, the internal consciousness and the external object, must be present both at once in the soul even in the most primordial and simple of perceptions" (DH: JWA 2,1, 38; MPW 277), Jacobi's epistemic realism as a whole reaches back behind the representation model to access "the presentation of the actual itself" [Darstellung des Würklichen selbst] (DH: JWA 2,1, 68; MPW 304). There is no other evidence of this presentation than the presentation itself. Along the same lines, Jacobi also speaks of "groundless belief," knowing full well that no one in their everyday life says that he *believes* his experience of the world and himself to be real. Rather, we say that we *know* this. We cannot, however, provide a rational justification for the certainty that we lay claim to with this knowledge. As soon as we begin to ask after the grounds of our certainty, we end up back at the beginning of the dialogue in *David Hume* and the discussion goes in circles. It makes no sense to subject our experience of reality to the demands of evidentiary proof, skeptically asking whether we might only have access to appearances and even to ourselves only as an appearance, because the very act of doing so presupposes what can never be captured in the modality of representation.[17] As Schelling later comments in regard to this circumstance,

> I do not expect anyone to readily dispute that the reliability of all our knowledge is grounded in the *immediacy* of intuition. Profound philosophers have spoken about the knowledge of external things as a revelation that befalls us; it is not that [in saying this] they presume to have explained anything, but that they wish to intimate the general impossibility of communicating the connection between the object and the representation in discursive concepts; they also refer to our conviction of external things as a *belief*, either because the soul holds the most immediate commerce with that which it believes or to express concisely that this conviction is a blind certainty properly speaking, one that is grounded neither in inferences (from cause to effect) nor in any proof whatsoever.[18]

Schelling has clearly acknowledged and understood Jacobi's paradigm shift, although it is striking that he concentrates entirely on belief in the external world and fails to mention the equiprimordial certainty of the "I am" upon which Jacobi insists. He has

---

[17] See Chapter 3 in this volume. Correspondingly, Jacobi does not respond positively to Kant's comment in the preface to the B-edition of the *Critique of Pure Reason* regarding the "scandal of philosophy and universal human reason, that the existence of things outside us [...] should have to be assumed merely on *faith*, and that if it occurs to anyone to doubt it, we should be unable to answer him with a satisfactory proof" (CPR B XXXIX) (JWA 2,1, 393f.; MPW 554f.). Here as elsewhere, it goes without saying that Jacobi's recourse to belief has absolutely nothing to do with a so-called irrationalism.

[18] Schelling, *Abhandlungen zur Erläuterung des Idealismus der Wissenschaftslehre*, SW I, 376. F. W. J. Schelling, "Treatise Explicatory of the Idealism in the 'Science of Knowledge,'" in *Idealism and the Endgame of Theory*, ed. and trans. Thomas Pfau (Albany: State University of New York Press, 1994), 85.

not simply overlooked it. Shortly thereafter Schelling refers explicitly to the "identity" of "the two propositions, *I* am, and *There are things outside me*,"—but he does so "in order to prove their identity, and so that it can really exhibit the immediate connection which is otherwise merely felt."[19] It is a typical move—Jacobi's paradigm shift is to be subjected to a new set of proof procedures, not through a return to earlier positions, but rather by way of an extension of his own insights.

One final remark relates to current discussions: There is some basis for describing Jacobi's position as *direct realism,* including his thoroughgoing anticipation of direct realism's critique of the representation model. In light of this critique, it would be completely implausible to assign him to the opposing camp of "naive realism." Nonetheless, there are two reasons why I would hesitate to cast Jacobi as the progenitor of direct realism and have thus not presented my reflections under this heading. First, Jacobi's position, as I have repeatedly emphasized, is characterized by the claim of a "twofold revelation." Without giving full consideration to the dignity of our first-person certainty, a certainty that is non-empirical, our experience of the world cannot be adequately grasped. Jacobi's realism therefore necessarily implies recourse to a pre-reflective certainty of my selfhood, and it is unclear whether this is among the standard assumptions held by the advocates of direct realism. Second, in Jacobi's case, the epistemic realism of intuition is substantially expanded by his practical realism. Insofar as direct realism is conceived as a means to answer a theoretical question, on this point, at least— that is, the transition to practical realism—it falls short of Jacobi's "original insight."

The Practical Realism of Causality

As I said earlier, with this step Jacobi leaves the consciousness paradigm unambiguously and conclusively behind. There are, in other words, no residual elements from the philosophy of consciousness here that still remain to be processed. To adopt the latter perspective is to enter into an entirely different philosophical constellation, that of the transition *from theoretical idealism to practical realism,* as is later undertaken by Fichte and, in the *Vocation of Man,* takes the form of an explicit response to Jacobi's critique of nihilism. With that text, the loss of reality that the Wissenschaftslehre brings about theoretically is to be compensated on a practical level.[20] This, too, must be seen as an attempt to evade the provocation of Jacobi's "original insight," using the very means that he himself had only recently made available. Jacobi's own position, however, gives rise to no such dilemma, because he conceives the transition as occurring *within realism itself.*

The occasion for this transition is the question of how we acquire our conception of cause and effect, given that, first, it plays no role in the simultaneity of intuition and,

---

[19] Schelling, *System des transzendentalen Idealismus,* SW III, 344f. F. W. J. Schelling, *System of Transcendental Idealism (1800),* trans. Peter Heath (Charlottesville: University Press of Virginia, 1978), 9, translation amended.

[20] A similar idea, likely adopted from Fichte, also underlies Schopenhauer's *World as Will and Representation.* In fact, however, Schopenhauer's renewed fixation on "representation" represents a step backwards vis-à-vis the insights of his predecessors.

second, that the causal projections of the representation model of consciousness must all be rejected as inadequate. The answer is that we are beings who act:

> We know for instance, that ancient peoples, or the uncivilized tribes of today, did not, or do not now have, such concepts of cause and effect as those that arose among more cultured peoples before or since. They see living beings everywhere, and they know of no power that is not self-determining. For them every cause is a living, self-manifesting, freely acting, personal power of this kind; and every effect is an *act*. And without the living experience of such a power in us, a power of which we are continuously conscious, which we use in so many arbitrary ways, and which we can even let go of, without diminishing it—without this basic experience we should not have the slightest idea of cause and effect. (DH: JWA 2,1, 54; MPW 291)

Before addressing this statement in more detail, I would first like to approach the central issue it raises from a different angle. One might have the impression that Jacobi has left out something essential in his analysis of intuition. Our own experience makes clear that the certainty of reality in the relation between I and object presents itself to us instantaneously (or directly), which is to say free from any mediating operations. There is no temporal succession here, no earlier or later between the object and the perceiving self. We do, however, perceive such a succession in the objects themselves. The pure now of the intuition does not present the same unchanging phenomenon but rather the alternation and change of phenomena. The reorientation that Jacobi is calling for has its origins in precisely this observation.

For Jacobi, the perception that things change their appearances is not a purely epistemic matter, in the sense that I register these changes either in the role of an unaffected observer or as an "empirical consciousness" that is itself altered in conjunction with the perception of change. In the latter case, as Kant explains, I would have "as multicolored, diverse a self as I have representations of which I am conscious."[21] To perceive changes is to interpret them as occurrences of real interdependencies, which I do not simply *confront*, whether from a distance or in a state of affected receptivity, but with which I am *involved* due to the fact that I myself bring about changes in the world. To put it pointedly (although still completely in the spirit of Jacobi), a change in perspective takes place here, and one that does not only trace the representational schema of *subject and object* back to the fundamental relation of the "twofold revelation" of I and Thou. In practical terms, the schema of subject and object is also converted into an *intersubjective* connection, an interaction of *active subjects*, in which "I" am included. The "things outside me" are not stones. Nor are they stones for intuition. But whereas intuition as such behaves neutrally, as it were, with regard to objects, from the perspective of action, the perception of living relations of interaction is inscribed *into intuition itself*.

Everything that follows depends on this perspectival shift toward a practically interpreted relation of cause and effect, with which Jacobi once again (and from yet

---

[21] Kant, CPR B 134.

another direction) counters Kant's transcendental idealism. It will be helpful by way of orientation to first consider two possibilities for the implementation of an action-oriented semantics of causality. The first pertains to the self- and world-understanding of the "ancient peoples and uncivilized tribes of today." In this archaic world, everything appears as an act initiated by a person, all changes in nature (which is not even conceived as the other of spirit at this point) are understood as effects emanating from actors.[22] In adducing this insight both here and in later texts as evidence for the practical origins of our concept of causality, Jacobi reveals the deep historical and socio-cultural roots of our concept use. In terms of the realism he advocates, it also makes clear that he is fully attentive to the historical dimensions of the lifeworld. One could speak here with Hegel of a particular *form of consciousness* or with Cassirer of a *symbolic form,* meaning that "world" is only ever available to us as interpreted world. To assume that one "first" confronts the raw material of experience, upon which the archaic schema of a universally operative and perceivable actor causality is "then" impressed, would be to misconstrue the situation entirely.

The other possibility operates at the complete opposite end of the spectrum, attributing the action-oriented semantics of causality exclusively to the interactions of *human* subjects. And I mention it not as some abstract hypothesis presented with the aim of clarifying Jacobi's position. It is in fact exactly how Jacobi's practical realism is understood by Fichte, who bases the *Foundations of Natural Right* on this model (a book he announces in a letter to Jacobi, as we have seen). Both explicit and implicit references to Jacobi are discernible everywhere, including in Fichte's invocation of the "primitive peoples," who made the "objects in the sensible world […] into free, first causes, such as they themselves were," and in the assertion that Jacobi's *David Hume* "convincingly shows that representations of time, which in themselves contradict the pure concept of causality, are applied to that concept only from the representation of our own efficacy upon things."[23]

I have no intention of entering into a detailed discussion of the *Foundations of Natural Right* here. I simply mention Fichte's appropriation of Jacobi to show that one can read some of the latter's basic propositions through the aforementioned lens of an exclusively human interaction, as in the following:

> If, besides the immanent activity by which each preserves itself in being, the *individuals* also have the faculty for external action, then, in order for an effect to follow, they must come into contact (either immediate or mediate) with other beings. An absolutely penetrable being is a non-entity. […] The immediate

---

[22] A very similar idea of "animism" and "causality" can be found in the first chapter "The Concept of Enlightenment" of Horkheimer's and Adorno's *Dialectic of Enlightenment.* And more generally, although unconventional from a Kantian perspective, there is nothing unreasonable about the substance of Jacobi's action philosophical interpretation of causes, and he is by no means alone in advocating it. On this point and on the practical approach in Jacobi's works more generally, see Birgit Sandkaulen, *Grund und Ursache. Die Vernunftkritik Jacobis* (Munich: Wilhelm Fink Verlag, 2000), esp. 77–91, 103–32, 171–228.

[23] Fichte, *Grundlage des Naturrechts nach Principien der Wissenschaftslehre,* FW III, 25, 29. J. G. Fichte, *Foundations of Natural Right: According to the Principles of the Wissenschaftslehre,* ed. Frederick Neuhouser, trans. Michael Baur (Cambridge: Cambridge University Press, 2000), 25, 26, 28.

consequence of impenetrability at contact we call "resistance." So wherever there is contact there is mutual impenetrability; and hence there is resistance also—action and reaction. Resistance in space, *action and reaction*, is the source of *succession* and of time (which is the *representation* of succession). (DH: JWA 2,1, 59; MPW 295f.)

Actions, in other words, require someone who acts. Only individuals act. The internal dimension of action pertains to that which sustains the individual as individual. With regard to the external dimension of action, the individual aims to have an effect in the world, which can only occur if there is more than one individual. Actions that are directed toward the external world realize an effect only in the encounter with an embodied resistance, which is experienced as a reaction. And it is only in this fundamental interaction of embodied individuals that the representation of space and time takes shape.

One can see that here as well, Jacobi remains committed to his basic conception that the I always stands in relation to a Thou but at the same time can never be reduced to a mere effect of this relation. Here this means that an acting I necessarily relates to a world outside of itself, in which it intervenes to produce changes and also experiences the consequences of these interventions on its own person. Otherwise it would not be *acting*. At the same time, however, it cannot be a mere product of such interactions, because then there would be no individual who was functioning as the *author* of these actions.

> However much the individual may be determined from the outside, he can still be determined only as the result of the laws of his own nature, and to this extent he determines himself. He must be something absolutely on its own, for otherwise he could never be something for another, and receive this or that accidental determination. He must be able to be effective on his own, since otherwise no effect could occur or be sustained through him—nor, for that matter, could it even make its appearance in him. (DH: JWA 2,1, 56; MPW 293)

Having reached this point in the discussion, we must now consider Jacobi's fundamental difference from Kant, because it will allow us to move beyond the two previously described possibilities and reveal how Jacobi himself understands his conception. With his action-oriented semantics of causality, whose origin is to found in our own experience, Jacobi not only strikes a blow to the heart of Kant's approach to causality as an a priori category of the understanding; at the same time he also challenges the doctrine of space and time as a priori forms of intuition. Moreover, in the same moment, the transcendental distinction between the "I think" and the empirical I is eliminated, and this in turn has substantial repercussions for Kant's argument, including his presentation and resolution of the third antinomy. The idea of a causality of freedom, which Kant there ascribes to an "intelligible character" in the sense of an absolutely spontaneous beginning, outside of time and set apart from an "empirically" determined character, is no longer plausible from our action-oriented perspective, nor is the internal division of the self on which it depends. Such objections continue to inform contemporary debates; the fact that they are rarely traced back to Jacobi is not something we need to pursue here. It is crucial, on the other hand, that we address one additional key point in regard to Kant.

As mentioned previously, Jacobi has no intention of countering Kant's idealism by rehabilitating an alleged epistemic causal relation between things in themselves and appearances. His insight into the impossibility of such a relation as it is presented in Kant's theory, and especially his own alternative conception regarding the immediacy of intuition, preclude such an attempt. In formulating his practical realism, however, he most certainly does intend to rehabilitate causality as a relation that concerns the connections among things in themselves and not merely the lawfulness of appearances as governed a priori through the understanding. In the case of Kant, Jacobi asserts, it is a question of "*mere prejudgements of the understanding*" that apply "only for men and for the sensibility that is proper to humans" and thus have no "*truly* objective meaning" (DH: JWA 2,1, 60f.; MPW 296f.). In contrast, establishing such a "truly objective" meaning is precisely Jacobi's aim when he seeks to present, in the form of a "deduction" (DH: JWA 2,1, 60; MPW 296), "the absolute universality or necessity" (DH: JWA 2,1, 56ff.; MPW 293ff.) that characterizes our conception of cause and effect as well as associated concepts, notwithstanding the fact that they originate in experience.

The key point, then, is that in mobilizing his own action-oriented semantics of causality against Kant's category of causality, Jacobi expressly avoids restricting its application to human beings. It applies to the interrelations of *nature* as well, which now also appear in an entirely new light. This new perspective arises because the effort to secure "truly objective" validity for the concept of causality does not require the Kantian concept of a *causal mechanism* observable in its application to sensibility, in order to then transfer this idea to the "things in themselves." On the contrary, the action-oriented semantics of causality enables us to apprehend a nature whose uniqueness resides in the specific constitution and interconnectivity of *living organisms*. It is Jacobi's realism, not Kant's *Critique of Judgment,* that first brings biological nature to our attention, thereby touching, in the most literal sense, a vital nerve.[24] It goes without saying that *David Hume*—in a manner complementary to Fichte's *Natural Right*—was a source of inspiration for Schelling's nature philosophy precisely because of this claim to objectivity.

To be sure, Jacobi's deduction is not without its problems. Before I address these problems, however, we should note that they have nothing to do with the problems Hegel claims to have identified in his strident critique. Jacobi certainly did not formulate his propositions on the basis of unverified presuppositions;[25] indeed, he avoids this

---

[24] See Horstmann, *Grenzen der Vernunft*, 133f., 281f. Interestingly, Jacobi was among the first to receive a copy of the *Critique of Judgement* from Kant himself.

[25] According to *Faith and Knowledge,* one finds here a "remarkable piece of empiricism à la Locke and Hume" "with an equally glaring piece of German dogmatism of the analyzing kind kneaded into it" (GW 4, 348; G. W. F. Hegel, *Faith and Knowledge*, ed. and trans. Walter Cerf and Henry S. Harris (Albany: State University of New York Press, 1977), 99. Hegel's completely misguided assessment stems directly and primarily from the fact that in 1802 he thoroughly rejects Jacobi's interest in the alleged "nothingness of finitude" and for this reason also misunderstands Spinoza. It is clear from the sequence of the stages of consciousness in the *Phenomenology of Spirit* that he later revised his view. See Chapter 13 in this volume.

problem precisely because of the crucial role played by the *participant perspective* in his deduction. His starting point is a consideration of our constitution as selves, the fact that we are not a "transcendental I" but rather finite "I's," and as finite beings also self-evidently natural and embodied beings. To the extent that we are such beings, however, it is also the case that our interactions do not occur in a space exclusively defined by human intersubjectivity. Rather, we interact as the organisms that we are in the realm of nature, which reveals its biological constitution to us in the process. And this insight also reveals why Jacobi's invocation of *Spinoza and Leibniz* as supporters of a realist epistemology not only makes sense with regard to his position but also deserves to be taken seriously on its own terms.

It is evident that the approaches of both are diametrically opposed to the idealistic representation model of consciousness. A consciousness that does not relate directly to the world would be unthinkable for both, including Leibniz, whose monads do not draw inferences about an external world on the basis of representations but rather present the world directly in their perceptions. Accordingly, there can be no grounds here for distinguishing a realm of "appearances" in the Kantian sense from the "things in themselves" that remain unknown to us. Insofar as there are gradations of cognition, it is only a question of a more or less adequate presentation of reality, never of the basic relation to reality itself. Against this backdrop, it is clear that Jacobi knows exactly what he is doing when he orients his deduction of fundamental concepts toward Spinoza's conception of the *notiones communes* (DH: JWA 2,1, 61; MPW 297). According to Spinoza, these are also determined through experience. In contrast to the experience-based *notiones universales*, however, they are not generalizations from contingent standpoints but rather provide the general structure of all experience.[26] In addition, and most significantly, Jacobi's recourse to Spinoza and Leibniz makes sense because he recognizes that both approaches are grounded in a conception of the individual who, on the basis of his own unique *conatus*, his striving for self-preservation, interacts continuously with his environment.

In other words, the discovery of nature as an interactive space for living individuals gifted with an inner power, individuals who, without being mere effects of their environment, nonetheless live in relations of reciprocity with that environment and just as necessarily have a body as well as a consciousness, however rudimentary—this discovery can be traced back to the realism of Spinoza and Leibniz. Jacobi, we should note, does not present this discovery simply as a way to challenge Kant with a forgotten lesson from the history of philosophy. As we have seen, in the course of presenting his practical realism, he instead argues from the participant perspective of our own experience, a perspective that does not result from Spinoza's and Leibniz's conceptions but is rather confirmed by them.

---

[26] On this point see Brady Bowman ("Notiones Communes und Common Sense. Zu den Spinozanischen Voraussetzungen von Jacobis Rezeption der Philosophie Thomas Reids," in *Friedrich Heinrich Jacobi*, ed. Walter Jaeschke and Birgit Sandkaulen (Hamburg: Meiner, 2004), 159–78), who persuasively shows that Jacobi's realism is Spinozan. I do not, however, share the view that Jacobi thereby commits himself to the premises of Spinoza's metaphysics in a manner that contradicts his own critique of Spinoza.

Here, however, the problem with Jacobi's deduction also becomes evident. For if it is the case that Spinoza and Leibniz can provide a confirmation of realism and can thus be used vis-à-vis Kant to show how causality pertains to "things in themselves," then it appears that the realist project ultimately and necessarily culminates in a *dynamic naturalism*—a conception that can render nature and our own natural lives comprehensible but that eliminates any structural distinction between self-determined action on the one hand and the interdependencies of organically constituted individuals on the other. In the *Spinoza Letters*, however, this very same outcome is presented not in positive terms but as the basis for his criticisms of Spinoza and Leibniz.

The Irreducible Individuality of the Self

It can hardly be the case that Jacobi, in the heat of the battle against idealism, simply forgot his own objections. This does not mitigate the shortcomings of the deduction undertaken in *David Hume*, however, which can only be resolved through further reflection on the constitution of our reason, including reflection on the historical genesis of our rationality. Jacobi promptly provides both in the second edition of the *Spinoza Letters*, especially in *Supplement VII*. It is unnecessary to address these arguments here, however, because the roots of the resolution are already to be found in *David Hume* itself. These will also return us to the concerns of our initial discussion and ultimately allow me to clarify fully the provocation inherent in Jacobi's "original insight."

Interestingly, the resolution in question initially appears in the form of the *Leibnizian monad*. In light of what has been said previously, this means first of all that Jacobi does not retract or minimize, either here or in later texts, one of the key consequences of his practical realism, namely that it entails a naturalistic view of ourselves and the world. This point is critical. What he objects to is the grounding of this view in a naturalistic metaphysics. Thus he also rejects Schelling's conception of a philosophy of nature, which he actually criticizes even more vehemently than Fichte's approach. His reasons for doing so point us in the direction of our solution. But in order to arrive there, we must first acknowledge that we are finite and therefore natural beings. As such, we are *conditioned beings* (as Jacobi expresses it from 1789 onwards), who are *mediated* through the interconnectivity of nature. The immediate certainty of intuition and this mediated existence in the interconnectivity of nature do not contradict one another—the perspectives of epistemic and practical realism must be distinguished.

As Jacobi has shown in regard to the naturalism in question here, however, only those beings who are also and in an essential way "for themselves" can participate in relations of interaction. And in now returning to this point, he designates this being-for-itself with Leibniz (but not with Spinoza, whose substance metaphysics offers no basis for this idea) as the monad's structural form of being "a *unum per se*" (DH: JWA, 2,1, 78ff.; MPW 315). Every organic individual is *qua* individual a unum per se, a unity that includes plural determinations within itself but remains a simple substance. No organic individual draws its unity from the sum of its determinations, nor does its unity result from the addition of a further determination. Although one cannot separate being-for-itself from the determinations that it includes while remaining "without parts," it "precedes" them in a certain sense, because otherwise they would not be *its* determinations.

One key implication of this consideration relates to the point I alluded to previously. The context of interaction is an *intersubjective* context, because, according to the structural determination of being-for-itself, all organic beings are fundamentally *subjects*. And precisely because Jacobi aligns himself so closely with Leibniz here, he sees no reason to deny basic forms of life a consciousness, however rudimentary it may be. However, whereas Leibniz focuses in this context on the consciousness of an external world, Jacobi is clearly also concerned with the consciousness that the monad has of its *being-for-itself*. Thus, in taking leave of the philosophy of consciousness by way of the realistic paradigm shift, Jacobi also overcomes the view that consciousness is a privilege of human life. A basic form of awareness and even a basic form of self-awareness can be attributed to all organisms, otherwise they would be stones, which, obviously, they are not. "Life and consciousness are one" (DH: JWA 2,1, 86; MPW 318).

A second and even more critical implication follows from this. *Human consciousness* can be distinguished from that of plants and animals only by degrees, not absolutely. With regard to its organization as a whole, it is more complex. Already at the most basic level, however, the *consciousness of being-for-itself* cannot be explained in terms of the ensemble of a greater or lesser number of determinations or the type of these determinations. It goes hand in hand with these without being reducible to them. According to the structural logic of the being-for-itself, which *is not determined by content but rather modally*, as the immediate referral of all determinations back to "itself," the distinct quality of human consciousness resides in the capacity to achieve explicit awareness of the being-for-itself of its existence. It achieves this awareness through an *act of distinction*. "It is clear that we attain to the consciousness of our consciousness, to the feeling of ourselves, in no other way except by distinguishing ourselves from something outside us" (DH: JWA 2,1, 85f.; MPW 318).

The connection between this statement and the passage quoted at the beginning of the chapter should be immediately apparent. The "most intimate consciousness" of myself is pre-reflective in its self-reference, because I do not become aware of my determinations and attributes in the modality of an observing representation. It does not follow from a set of determinations that I am *I*, but rather from the realization of my being-for-myself that I am *I* and *no other*. In correspondence with their more complex organization, but not derivable from it, human beings have the ability to realize this distinction for themselves and thereby to experience themselves as individual persons who cause *themselves* to act.

With this idea of self-determination grounded in the act of distinguishing myself from others, a horizon opens onto the field of free action, that field in which a causality of the actor in the strict sense is to be located.[27] This causality does not lead us out of the realm of nature and into the sphere of the "supernatural," as if we had been

---

[27] See also the discussion of Jacobi's *Treatise on Freedom* from the second edition of the *Spinoza Letters* in Chapter 5.

transformed into completely different beings. Nonetheless, in the act of distinguishing we acquire a *relation to nature,* with the consequence that human life and human action bear witness to something that is not completely conditioned by natural relationships and can thus be understood as "unconditioned." But regardless of how Jacobi later spells out his understanding of freedom, it remains decisive—and this is the only point I will elaborate in this context—that his conception is inseparably bound to the performatively given certainty of *individual mine-ness* and thus to the *nonsubstitutability of this perspective*, and bound not by a structural connection to a Leibnizian monadic metaphysics but rather to the subjectivity of modal being-for-itself.[28] There is no other standpoint from which I can adopt this perspective; no standpoint, including that of my own self, from which I can explain it, which would mean that it could be traced back to something else. Determinations and attributes are amenable to an explanation, but how it is that these determinations are *for me* defies all explanation. Nor can one solve the problem by neutralizing the perspective of mine-ness in order to side-step its inexplicable irreducibility, because the consequence is a dissolution of the very meaning of that which we call "I."

Even without turning to Jacobi's metaphysics, we can see that the "logic" of this idea entails, firstly, another reversal of the sight lines of realism. Because being-for-itself is nonsubstitutable and thus precludes any explanation in principle, we do not achieve a better or worse understanding of ourselves if we grasp human life as proceeding from nature by way of a gradual development. From the perspective our being-for-itself, however, we do acquire a more qualitatively appropriate understanding of nature, to the extent that we come to understand nature as living and in every case focused in its own inner being-for-itself, but not—as least far as we can perceive—having progressed to the point of drawing the distinction through which we realize how it is to be a self-determining, individualized individual. The objection to Spinoza, then, which is raised from the beginning and continually reformulated, is that his approach to metaphysical naturalism both represses this premise of practical realism and is simultaneously contingent upon it, because it provides the only possible basis for his transition from a causal-mechanical to a dynamically organized understanding of the world.

Secondly, it follows from the "logic" of Jacobi's approach that the "original insight" reflected in his paradigm shift from the philosophy of consciousness to a doubly extended realism serves at nearly every step, as I have repeatedly suggested, as an inspiration to post-Kantian philosophy. Jacobian motifs appear in a range of interpretations and constellations in the work of Fichte, Schelling, and Hegel. In the wake of Jacobi, what has come to be known as "German idealism" proves to be much more of a *realism*, which adopts, along with the interest in understanding in the lifeworld, the always "twofold" relation of I and world and its intersubjective character. But one can see just as clearly, and without it being necessary at this point to further elaborate on the

---

[28] See Birgit Sandkaulen, "'Individuum est ineffabile.' Zum Problem der Konzeptualisierung von Individualität im Ausgang von Leibniz," in *Individualität. Genese und Konzeption einer Leitkategorie humaner Selbstdeutung*, ed. Wilhelm Gräb and Lars Charbonnier (Berlin: Berlin University Press, 2012), 153–79 and Charles E. Larmore, *The Practices of the Self*, trans. Sharon Bowman (Chicago/London: University of Chicago Press, 2010), where a very similar line of argument is pursued.

substantial indebtedness to Jacobi, why his "original insight" constitutes an ongoing provocation. Everywhere and in ever changing variants, attempts have been made to render it accessible to explanation, attempts which seek to avoid falling back into the observer perspective of the representation model and thereby acquire their typically "speculative" character, but which nonetheless fail to meet the challenge posed by Jacobi's approach.

From the point of view of the post-Kantian philosophical systems, the irreducibility and the nonsubstitutability of first-person being-for-itself in its relation to otherness prove intolerable—a relation, we should note, that must also be seen as the foundation for any experience of recognition rather than as its consequence. I am still uncertain whether the various efforts to master this challenge posed by the self arise solely from the interests of science or whether they also reflect some more primal, unexamined suspicion of the individual in his individuality. Be that as it may, one can always speak of something other than the I, but to the extent that one wishes to speak of consciousness, self-consciousness, subjectivity, the person, the I, or spirit in all possible variations, and if these expressions are to have substantial meaning "for me" (which is after all the claim of all post-Kantian approaches), then Jacobi's realism remains a permanent and, for structural reasons, insuperable provocation.

9

The "Tiresome Thing in Itself": Kant – Jacobi – Fichte

I.

In his *Crystal Clear Report* of 1801, Fichte describes Jacobi as "a reformer in philosophy simultaneously with Kant."[1] His assessment sheds valuable light on the nature of Jacobi's role in the formation of post-Kantian systematic philosophy, a role that was anything but a bit part. Indeed, it would be entirely incorrect to view Jacobi merely as the originator of one or two philosophical insights that are subsequently taken up and incorporated into philosophical systems developed primarily in dialogue with Kant. On the contrary, Jacobi helps create the very conditions of possibility for the formation of this philosophy. Nowhere is this more true than in regard to its guiding interest in the *system of reason*.

To be sure, the general affinity for philosophical system-building owes much to Kant. The post-Kantian situation, however, which is often framed in terms of the contrast between spirit and letter, is characterized by more than the mere conviction that Kant himself failed to construct a viable system and that this goal thus remains unfulfilled. Even more significant is how closely this conviction is intertwined with Jacobi's own philosophy, insofar as it would be unthinkable in the absence of his critique of Kant or of the furor surrounding Spinoza's *Ethics*. The furor, that is to say, caused by the authoritative model of a philosophical system that Jacobi had recently reconstructed as the only rigorously consistent one, in order to then also use it to exemplify the theoretically insoluble "contradiction" between a systematically unavoidable "fatalism," on the one hand, and the existential interests of freedom on the other. In incorporating this problem into their reception of Kant, the systems of post-Kantian philosophy self-consciously present themselves as valid alternatives to Spinoza's metaphysics and thus also lay claim to having resolved once and for all the contradiction between systematic and practical interests. We find a similar situation with regard to the keyword "reason." Here as well, there can be no denying Kant's significance. When we consider the efforts of the post-Kantian systems to transcend his approach, however, we can also

---

[1] Fichte, *Sonnenklarer Bericht*, GA I,7, 194. J. G. Fichte, "A Crystal Clear Report to the General Public Concerning the Actual Essence of the Newest Philosophy: An Attempt to Force the Reader to Understand," trans. John Bottermann and William Rasch, in *Philosophy of German Idealism: Fichte, Jacobi and Schelling*, ed. Ernst Behler (New York: Continuum, 1987), 47 (translation amended).

discern Jacobi's influence in the insistence on a specifically meta-rational dimension of reason conceived as prior to the designation criteria of the understanding. More specifically, we can discern the resonance of his reflections on the relation between mediation and immediacy. But there is also another aspect of Jacobi's influence to consider here, one that reveals its full complexity and only comes into full view over the course of time. Jacobi, rather than responding with satisfaction upon seeing his original intentions fulfilled, rejects the post-Kantian "philosophy of *one piece*" as a "veritable *system* of reason" (JF: JWA 2,1, 200; MPW 507). He rejects it with the same conviction that characterized his previous rejection of Spinoza, thereby also driving the system builders forward on their increasingly divergent intellectual paths. Jacobi's original influence on the formation of these systems and the impact of his subsequent criticisms on their further development are inseparable from one another.

In order to avoid the risk of oversimplification, in the discussion that follows I will separate out one particular strand from this complex web of influence—the strand that connects up to the problem of the *thing in itself*. In light of the historical context sketched out above, I want to emphasize that this represents only one of several strands that give shape to Jacobi's Kant critique and its reception. Nonetheless, it is a major one, and it is closely interwoven with the broader systematic pursuits of his contemporaries.

II.

"This thing in itself was therefore the point of departure beyond which Kant's *Critique of Pure Reason* could never move, and because of which it *had to* fail as an independent science."[2] Even in this late reminiscence from his Berlin lectures, Schelling's interest in the systematic implications of Kant's failure leads him to mention one text in particular where material pertinent to the matter at hand could be found: "I refer you to a synopsis which you can find in Jacobi's *David Hume, or A Discussion about Idealism and Realism*."[3] With his 1787 *Dialogue David Hume* and the Supplement "On Transcendental Idealism" contained therein, Jacobi had in fact positioned himself once again in the intellectual vanguard. By incorporating into the discussion of Spinoza an investigation of the theoretical problems of Kant's transcendental philosophy, he *expanded* its scope and thereby also inaugurated the twofold "sublation" of Kant *and* Spinoza that becomes a structural feature in the systems of German idealism. In addition, the same hermeneutics that comes to figure so prominently in the later philosophy also already appears here. Jacobi refers explicitly to "the spirit of Kantian philosophy" (DH: JWA 2,1,108f.; MPW 336f.) and presents as evidence of this spirit a series of long, verbatim excerpts from the first edition of the *Critique of Pure Reason*, in order to cast into particularly sharp relief their incompatibility with certain other statements and to indicate the measures necessary to establish clarity and consistency.

---

[2] Schelling, *Einleitung in die Philosophie der Offenbarung* [1842/43], SW XIII, 50. F. W. J. Schelling, *The Grounding of Positive Philosophy: The Berlin Lectures*, trans. Bruce Matthews (Albany: State University of New York Press, 2007), 123.
[3] Schelling, *Grounding of Positive Philosophy*, 124.

This diagnosis clearly struck a nerve. In addition to Schelling's remark, one can point to the still ongoing and sometimes bitter debates about the meaning or meaninglessness of the thing in itself, in which even today no contribution seems able to avoid repeating Jacobi's now canonical assertion that "I had to start from the beginning over and over again with the *Critique of Pure Reason*, because I was incessantly going astray on this point, viz. that *without* that presupposition I could not enter into the system, but *with* it I could not stay within it" (DH: JWA 2,1, 109; MPW 336). It is probably safe to say that this is the only sentence ever written by Jacobi that has really survived through the centuries.

Jacobi's astute assessment, however, is no less significant for revealing the true stakes of the debate. It is Fichte who, in his *Second Introduction to the Wissenschaftslehre* of 1797, highly recommends "all of Jacobi's philosophical writings" but especially the Kant-Supplement, in which he claims, "for ten years now the most thorough and complete proof [...] has been available for anyone to read."[4] But the proof of what, exactly? The proof, of course, that the concept of system in the Wissenschaftslehre offers the only legitimate and convincing formulation of the Kantian "spirit" rightly understood—that spirit which Jacobi, as the "clearest thinker of our era" had presented under the heading of a "properly conceived transcendental idealism."[5] Before Fichte even enters onto the scene, then, Jacobi's encounter with Kant had already led him to grasp what was to become the primary concern of the *Wissenschaftslehre*. If that isn't evidence of a powerful influence, then I don't know what is.

But just how is this concern to be understood? Wherein lies the unresolved problem that leads from Kant to Fichte by way of Jacobi, and for which the phrase "thing in itself" can only provide an initial orientation? Or perhaps the question is superfluous, given the scope and intensity of the previously mentioned discussion? At first glance, this does indeed appear to be the case. Admittedly, one cannot claim that all responses to Jacobi's diagnosis have been as unequivocally positive as the one offered up by Fichte in its immediate aftermath. Rather, evaluations of his views depend (not surprisingly) on the commentator's own position vis-à-vis the problem of the thing in itself, whether it is deemed to be theoretically sound or marred by irresolvable contradictions. As a consequence, the appraisals range from Vaihinger's fervently enthusiastic assertion that Jacobi's Kant-Supplement contains "perhaps the best and most important thinking on Kant that has ever been expressed,"[6] to severe rebukes, such as the claim that "the actual subject matter of the critique of pure reason and thus also the problem of transcendental idealism, were hardly even recognized by Jacobi."[7] A considerable

---

[4] GA I,4, 235. J. G. Fichte, *Introductions to the* Wissenschaftslehre *and Other Writings (1797–1800)*, ed. and trans. Daniel Breazeale (Indianapolis: Hackett, 1994), 66.
[5] GA I,4, 236 note. Fichte, *Introductions*, 68.
[6] Hans Vaihinger, *Kommentar zu Kant's Kritik der reinen Vernunft*, vol. 2 (Stuttgart/Berlin/Leipzig: Union Deutsche Verlagsgesellschaft, 1892), 36. See Hans Vaihinger, *The Philosophy of "As If": A System of the Theoretical, Practical and Religious Fictions of Mankind* [1913; *Die Philosophie des Als Ob*], trans. Charles K. Ogden (Petoskey, MI: Random Shack, 2015), 151f.
[7] Herbert Herring, *Das Problem der Affektion bei Kant*, Kant-Studien Ergänzungsheft 67 (Cologne: Kölner Universitäts-Verlag, 1953), 14: "Even less comprehensible is therefore the enormous influence that his critique of the Kantian philosophy exerted on his contemporaries, above all on Beck, G.E. Schulze, and Fichte."

range of opinion to be sure, but the very possibility of such variety also presupposes a degree of consensus regarding at least the basic elements of Jacobi's critique. And such is the case.

There has been a textbook account of this consensus since Windelband, one that gained additional traction in the wake of Vaihinger's commentary to the *Critique of Pure Reason* and continues to be repeated up to the present day. In Windelband's version the claim reads as follows: "*Jacobi* was the first to have seen" that "the concept of sensibility initially introduced [by Kant] involves a causal relation of being affected by things-in-themselves. Based on the doctrine of the analytic, however, according to which the categories must not be applied to things-in-themselves, such thoughts are impermissible."[8] In other words, Kant disregards his own restriction of the categories to the realm of appearance, such that in introducing his theory of affection he becomes entangled *ab ovo* in an *inappropriate use of the categories*. This, then, is the argument that allegedly encapsulates Jacobi's position and serves as the crux of the debate, though in light of the circumstances one should also add that the standard version of this argument—as presented by Windelband, for example—refers first and foremost to the *category of causality*.[9] The basic structure of the argument, however, remains unchanged in other versions of Jacobi's critique, where one can find it extended to applications of the categories of substantiality, reality or actuality that are allegedly just as untenable.

Clearly, whatever one's opinion on the validity of these pronouncements regarding Kant's alleged category error, there can be no denying the considerable success of the argument, to which even Adorno's *Negative Dialectics* attests.[10] Perhaps Jacobi also deserves credit for inspiring Adorno? It is, to be sure, an intriguing possibility, but one that is ultimately no more plausible as Windelband's continuously and unquestioningly repeated account. In fact, this account has nothing at all to do with Jacobi, but so much the more to do with the careless backward projection of an argument that actually originates with *Aenesidemus-Schulze*. It was the latter who, in 1792, in the course of his encounter with Reinhold's Elementary Philosophy, speaks of just such a "contradiction" between Kant's "premises" on the one hand, and his "results" on the other. For if it is the case, Schulze explains, that the "transcendental deduction of the categories" is "correct" and consequently "neither the concept of the *cause* nor the concept of *actuality*" can be applied to an "object outside of our representations," "then one of the most excellent principles of the critique of reason, namely that all cognition begins with the effectivity of independent objects upon our minds, is incorrect and false."[11] Schopenhauer, as we know, was also convinced by Schulze's clear and precise formulation of this argument,

---

[8] Wilhelm Windelband, *Lehrbuch der Geschichte der Philosophie* (1912) (Reprint, Tübingen: Mohr Siebeck, 1993), 481f.

[9] See among many others Erich Adickes, *Kant und das Ding an sich* (Berlin: Pan Verlag Rolf Heise, 1924), 49; Marcus Willaschek, "Phaenomena/ Noumena und die Amphibolie der Reflexionsbegriffe," in *Immanuel Kant. Kritik der reinen Vernunft*, ed. Marcus Willaschek and Georg Mohr, Klassiker Auslegen 17/18 (Berlin: Akademie Verlag, 1998), 339.

[10] Theodor W. Adorno, *Negative Dialectics*, trans. E. B. Ashton (New York: The Continuum Publishing Company, 1992), 183ff.

[11] Gottlob E. Schulze, *Aenesidemus oder über die Fundamente der von dem Herrn Professor Reinhold in Jena gelieferten Elementarphilosophie*, ed. Manfred Frank (Hamburg: Meiner, 1996), 184.

and perhaps his work served as the channel through which it found its way into the textbooks and, finally, to Adorno.

Be that as it may, I want to emphasize once again that none of this has anything to do with Jacobi's original analysis. To be sure, there are some striking parallels between the two texts, which, incidentally, supports the hypothesis that Schulze had Jacobi's text at hand, even if he never cites it. Both identify a contradiction between the opening of the *Critique of Pure Reason* and the reflections that unfold as it progresses, one that both discern in the tension between certain *realist* presuppositions and their *idealistically* grounded exclusion. But Jacobi never accuses Kant of inappropriately applying either the categories in general or the category of causality in particular. No such argument appears in either the Kant-Supplement itself or in the early note to Goethe where he first points out the problem.[12] Nor does it play any role at all in the later texts that at various points return to the question of the thing in itself. Not even the possibility that his oft-remarked authorial "esprit" might mean that he only alluded to the causality argument—leaving it to Schulze to provide a more systematic rendering—advances the discussion here. After all, Jacobi was hardly someone who needed a philosophical education in matters of causality, and he includes the Kant-Supplement as an appendix to a text in which questions regarding causes, grounds, and causality constitute the main focus of his own reflections.

Acknowledging this state of affairs has profound implications. If it is indeed the case, firstly, that the critique of the thing in itself served as a key motivation for the systematic transition to post-Kantian idealism, and if it also true, secondly, that the validity or at least the force of this critique in its Windelbandian version depends on claims of an inappropriate application of the category of causality, but that, thirdly, this claim was never made by Jacobi himself—how does this change our understanding of his influence on post-Kantian philosophy? Could it mean that Fichte attributed to the "clearest thinker" of the era an insight for which in truth Schulze alone should have been given credit? Or is the opposite the case—that Jacobi's decisive influence manifests itself most powerfully in the fact that Fichte himself was still in a position to distinguish between the versions of Jacobi and Schulze?

It is certainly noteworthy that Fichte's *Second Introduction* contains nothing associating the causality argument with Jacobi; he clearly attributes it to Schulze. The latter, Fichte explains, "has denounced loudly enough" the "utter inconsistency" demonstrated by Kant in forgetting "his own system's fundamental claim concerning the overall validity of the categories," and "employing a bold inference from the world of appearances in order to arrive at things that exist in themselves outside of us."[13] Considering Fichte's distinctly ironic tone here, one could be forgiven for presuming that he is not particularly impressed by this denunciation—a circumstance that would seem to give the advantage to Jacobi's alternative approach. But these considerations do

---

[12] According to Kant, as Jacobi explains in a letter to Goethe from December 13 and 14, 1785, we have "only *appearances* [...] of – *Nothing, which he calls something*. – and thus I present you with the key to the entire system, and reveal its essential core, which Kant himself has not yet tasted" (JBW I,4, 277).

[13] GA I,4, 235f.; Fichte, *Introductions*, 67f.

not get us very far; after all, Jacobi also takes issue with a contradiction in Kant. Fichte, however, seems simply to ignore this contradiction when he unequivocally praises Jacobi for demonstrating that "Kant has no knowledge of any 'something' distinct from the I."[14] Does this mean that Jacobi's influence, although different than previously understood, boils down to nothing more than a superficial misunderstanding cultivated by Fichte for strategic purposes?

I have presented the situation in rather stark terms here, not as a way to minimize Jacobi's impact, but rather to make clear that the complexity of the topic demands a more thorough investigation, and also to cast the key concerns of such an investigation into sharper relief. First, by way of a contrast with Schulze's argumentation, it will be necessary to reconstruct the specific features of Jacobi's interpretation of the problem of the thing in itself. Secondly, and against this backdrop, it will be necessary to show the extent to which the programmatic self-understanding of the *Wissenschaftslehre* takes shape precisely on the basis of this interpretation.

III.

"I trust, […] that the Kantian philosopher goes right against the spirit of his system whenever he says that the objects produce *impressions* on the senses through which they *arouse* sensations, and that in this way they *bring about* representations" (DH: JWA 2,1, 108; MPW 335). This is the problem that runs through Jacobi's text like a red thread or an oft-repeated refrain (DH: JWA 2,1, 109, 110f.; MPW 336, 337f.). The "spirit of the system" is incompatible with the claim that objects affect us in an originary way. Just how we are to understand this will be examined shortly. First, however, it is essential to grasp the complex *strategy* that Jacobi employs in the text, in which his theoretical sophistication as an author is on full display. To put it in the form of a question: Is the "Kantian philosopher" whose affection theory is under consideration here actually Kant himself? As confusing as this question sounds when we first hear it, the answer, according to Jacobi, is just as confusing. He is and he isn't.

The opening pages of the Supplement shed light on the reasons why he is not and cannot be Kant. As the very first sentence already indicates, "the Transcendental or Critical Idealism on which Kant's *Critique of Pure Reason* is constructed is not treated with sufficient care by some of the supporters of Kantian philosophy" (DH: JWA, 2,1, 103; MPW 331f.). The problem, in other words, is not Kant's own philosophy, but rather how it is presented by its interpreters. Precisely because they are interested in the widest possible dissemination, they end up promoting their own misunderstanding of that philosophy rather than its actual content, and in the very same measure as they seek to avoid the disturbing "charge of idealism" (DH: JWA 2,1, 103; MPW 332). It is thus all the more important to note the discrepancy between these timid interpreters and the intention of the text itself. The latter, Jacobi writes, "declares itself decidedly enough" (DH: JWA 2,1, 104; MPW 332) in the critique of the fourth paralogism, from which he then quotes repeatedly over the course of several pages.

[14] GA I,4, 235; Fichte, *Introductions*, 66.

One can speculate about which of the aforementioned "promoters" of Kant Jacobi might have had in mind in referring to the "Kantian philosopher."[15] What is essential here is that he intervenes in these early stages of the Kant discussion with the same incisiveness as in the ongoing Spinoza debate, which is similarly characterized by a trivialization of the actual problem and the theoretical stakes. As indicated by his reference to the dreaded label of "idealism," the appropriate response in Kant's case is to defend his text against all facile interpretations. And with regard to the attendant question of what constitutes an adequate reading, Jacobi's answer is clear. The "spirit" of transcendental idealism will not be revealed by replicating the sequence of arguments in the *Critique of Pure Reason* and therefore beginning with affection. Instead, one must take the opposite approach, reading the text "backward" from the point of view of its conclusion. But doesn't the argument that Kant is guilty of an inappropriate use of the categories also insist that we read the "premises" in light of the "results"? Indeed it does, and for this reason it is crucial to note that Jacobi does not begin with the "results" of the analytic, as this argument would suggest. As already mentioned, he starts instead with the critique of the fourth paralogism, the section in which Kant himself elucidates his conception of transcendental idealism and also expressly indicates that this is how he intended it to be understood from the beginning.

The fact that Jacobi allows Kant to speak in his own voice aligns perfectly with his aforementioned recommendation for how to read the text. It thus comes as no surprise that Fichte, in his analogous dispute with the "Kantianism to which these Kantians subscribe,"[16] expresses his admiration for this strategy in particular. Jacobi has "collected and cited" the "most decisive and striking assertions on this point [...] in Kant's own words." And he goes on to say that he has "no desire to redo what has already been done and cannot very well be improved upon."[17] Indeed, Jacobi's Kant presentation is as suggestive as it is loyal to the text itself. On closer inspection, however, it becomes clear that Jacobi does not simply cite from the text but also foregrounds certain words and phrases in a manner that has a signaling effect for the progress of the argument.[18]

---

[15] One plausible candidate is the Königberg court chaplain Johann Schultz. Jacobi had the first edition of his *Erläuterungen über des Herrn Professor Kant Critik der reinen Vernunft* [Explanatory Notes on Herr Professor Kant's *Critique of Pure Reason*] (Königsberg 1784; 2th. ed. Frankfurt/Leipzig 1791) in his library. Schultz's name also appears frequently in Jacobi's correspondence with Hamann. Two letters in particular from Jacobi to Hamann point to the original background of the debate (September 4, 1786 and November 14, 1786). The letters make clear that his plan to highlight the idealistic profile of Kantian philosophy constitutes a reaction to the contemporary reviews of the *Spinoza Letters*, in which Jacobi had been informed by the Kantians that his version of "belief" was at best a recapitulation of what can already be found in Kant, and a complete dead end if it is not. "What annoys me about his interpreters is the deliberate concealment of the idealism, which is, after all, the soul of the system" (Letter to Hamann, 14.11.1786, JBW I,5, 411).

[16] GA I,4, 237. Fichte, *Introductions*, 69.

[17] GA I,4, 235. Fichte, *Introductions*, 66.

[18] Note: In the original manuscript of 1787 he does this by using a larger script, spaced letters, and boldface. In the critical edition of Jacobi's works these emphases are reproduced by way of spaced letters, boldface, and small caps. In MPW only Kant's markings from the *Critique of Pure Reason* are included, and thus one is unfortunately unable to see how they differ from Jacobi's own markings. What follows should therefore be understood as referring to the German edition.

I will return to this point shortly. For now I simply want to note that Jacobi draws attention to the connection Kant conceives of here between transcendental idealism and empirical realism, and that it is this same connection which, for reasons that will be spelled out later, compels us to conclude that the "spirit" of Kant's philosophy is incompatible with the "Kantian philosopher's" claim that there are objects which "make impressions on the senses."

This, however, is not the end of the story. Merely critiquing a misguided Kant interpretation in order to prepare for the appearance of the true Kant does not solve the problem. On the contrary, according to Jacobi, the problem that arises with the positing of affecting objects is actually inscribed into the conception of Kant's own theory, inasmuch as "it is not possible to see how even the Kantian philosophy could find entry into itself without this presupposition and manage some statement of its hypothesis" (DH: JWA 2,1, 109; MPW 336). At this point, and only at this point, the dispute crystallizes into an *immanent* critique of Kant. By considering how Jacobi arrives at his own Kant critique against the backdrop of an emerging Kantianism, we can also see more clearly what distinguishes his reading from the variants that later gain currency in the context of early idealism. Prompted by Jacobi's verdict that the theory of affection is a foreign element in the body of transcendental philosophy, Fichte, for example, does not hesitate to post the full charge for this error to the account of Kantianism, which exhibits "a fantastic combination of the crudest sort of dogmatism (according to which the thing in itself is supposed to produce an impression within us) with the most resolute idealism."[19] His own system, on the other hand, appears as the one that Kant himself actually "entertained the *thought of*."[20] In comparison, Jacobi takes Kant at his word. However "contrary" (DH: JWA 2,1, 109; MPW 336) the positing of affecting objects might be to the "spirit" of Kantian philosophy, it is nonetheless a fundamental presupposition in the text whose centrality means that it cannot simply be interpreted away. Thus, in contrast with the claims made by the idealists, for Jacobi there is no way that Kant can lead us beyond "Kant's conflict with himself" (see GD: JWA 3, 88).[21] And only in this context does the strategic positioning of his text become fully visible. First, in addressing the "promoters of Kantian philosophy," his concern is to demonstrate their obliviousness to a problem, which also reveals a blind spot in Kant's own conception. And, secondly, as a consequence of this first step, he is able to issue a concluding challenge. Whoever, in light of the circumstances described, still wishes to "profess" (JWA 2,1, 112; MPW 338) transcendental idealism simply cannot remain a Kantian. Instead he must adopt an unprecedented new form of theory, namely, the "the strongest idealism that was ever proffered" (DH: JWA 2,1, 112; MPW 338).

---

[19] GA I,4, 237. Fichte, *Introductions*, 69.
[20] GA I,4, 230. Fichte, *Introductions*, 63.
[21] It is symptomatic that now, with idealistic philosophy having clearly occupied the field, the "disparity between the *spirit* of his doctrine and its *letter*" (ibid.) comes to mark, in an inversion of the topos, both the inevitable starting point of post-Kantian philosophy and also the irresolvable difference in spirit between Kant and his successors.

IV.

To contrast the internal logic of transcendental philosophy with the standpoint of the "Kantian philosopher" is the first task; the second is to establish what prevents Kant himself from successfully realizing the aims of this logic. Jacobi identifies *sensibility* as the source of the trouble, inasmuch as it becomes evident precisely in regard to this concept that one cannot "get into the system" without the presupposition of affecting objects:

> For even the word 'sensibility' is without any meaning, unless we understand by it a distinct real intermediary between one real thing and another, an actual means *from* something *to* something else; and it would be meaningless, too, if the concepts of 'outside one another' and 'being combined,' of 'action' and 'passion,' of 'causality' and 'dependence,' were not already contained in the concept of it *as real and objective determinations*. In fact, they are contained in such a way that the absolute universality and necessity of these concepts must equally be given as a prior presupposition. (DH: JWA 2,1, 109f.; MPW 336)

The central term in this passage is clear. If we are to take Kant's talk of *sensibility* seriously and attribute real significance to it, this also means taking seriously the assertion that "there are two stems of human cognition,"[22] and that sensibility, as one of these stems, is the "capacity (receptivity) to acquire representations through the way in which we are affected by objects," and that, finally, "sensation" is "the effect of an object on the capacity for representation, insofar as we are affected by it."[23] And from this it then follows that sensibility itself as well as the dyad of object and affected subject that relate to one another via this medium, and also the causality that is contained in this relation, must be deemed *real* in an emphatic sense. I will address the structural peculiarities of this state of affairs in more detail subsequently. First, however, it should be noted that Jacobi's understanding of affection as an original confrontation with the real underlies his conviction that this presupposition is incompatible with the requirements of transcendental idealism.

To phrase it the other way around: if there were some indication that this understanding misrepresents Kant's initial determinations, then and only then could the validity of his diagnosis of a contradiction be called into question. However, I consider such an objection to be purely hypothetical. Because even if we concede that more than 200 years of Kant exegesis have so far failed to clarify the situation,[24] this very failure only attests to Jacobi's innovative approach to the problem. Moreover, and in connection with this, one can also note that even today Jacobi's interpretation places

---

[22] Kant, CPR A 15.
[23] CPR A 19f. See also the beginning of the introduction to CPR B 1.
[24] See Thomas Pogge, "Erscheinung und Dinge an sich," *Zeitschrift für philosophische Forschung* 45 (1991): 489f.

him in the distinguished company of all those who, while they dispute the plausibility of his alleged argument regarding an inappropriate use of the categories, nonetheless never deny that Kant's initial assertion of affecting objects is equivalent to the assertion of real affection through real things in themselves. Truly, it is difficult to see how else to make rhyme or reason out of the numerous passages in the *Critique of Pure Reason*, or of the relevant passages in the *Prolegomena*, where the "existence" of the things that we can only know according to their "appearance" is simply assumed as a matter of course.[25]

As we have seen, this same interpretation also forms the basis of Schulze's argument. And so, on a superficial reading, it might seem as if the passage just quoted alludes to this argument in particular.[26] We can already offer an initial characterization of the essential difference between these two analyses, however. To accuse Kant of inappropriately extending the categories beyond the realm of appearances means both presupposing the theoretical framework of transcendental reflection and simultaneously asserting that Kant, by way of an objectification of this same framework, has opened up a dimension which the restrictions of his theory had declared off limits. Jacobi, on the other hand, has a completely different concern. The presupposition of affecting objects is indeed both indispensable and untenable, but not because it entails an inappropriate overextension of the theoretical framework. Rather, the problem is that it disappears into an extra-theoretical void from which there is simply no way for Kant to retrieve it with the means of transcendental idealism. The point is not that Kant has inadmissibly introduced affecting objects as the cause of the world of appearance, but rather that in pursuing the inner logic of his project to completion, a fundamental premise of that project is revealed as *utterly* inexplicable. Once one recognizes this, then it also becomes apparent that Jacobi's analysis is far more radical than that of Schulze, who ultimately does nothing more than confront Kant with a familiar skeptical trope.[27]

As the basis for a more precise explication, we can again turn to the beginning of the Supplement, more specifically, to the excerpts from the critique of the fourth paralogism. I have already mentioned that Jacobi cites this text verbatim while at the same time adding his own editorial markings, and we are now in a position to consider the significance of this gesture. Taking note of how Kant grounds the compatibility of transcendental idealism and empirical realism, Jacobi focuses his attention on the conditions under which this alliance, one that strongly affirms belief in the existence of an external world, comes about: it is then "only" a question of "representations (intuition)," "which are called external, **not as if they related to objects that are external in themselves** but because they relate perceptions to space where all things are external

---

[25] Kant, *Prolegomena*, AA IV, § 13, Anmerkung III. Immanuel Kant, "Prolegomena to Any Future Metaphysics that will be able to Come Forward as Science (1783)," trans. Gary Hatfield, in *Theoretical Philosophy after 1781*, ed. Henry Allison and Peter Heath (Cambridge: Cambridge University Press, 2002), 85.

[26] It is after all the real structures presupposed along with sensibility "which cannot in any way be reconciled with Kantian philosophy, since the whole intention of the latter is to prove that the objects (as well as their relations) are merely subjective beings, mere determinations of our own self, with absolutely no existence outside us" (DH: JWA 2,1, 109f.; MPW 336). See CPR A 129 and 378.

[27] Schulze, *Aenesidemus*, 183ff.

to one another, **but that space itself is in us**" (DH: JWA 2,1, 104; MPW 332).[28] As Kant further explains, this distinction coincides with the effort to resolve the ambiguity surrounding "the expression 'outside us,'" "since it sometimes signifies something that, as a thing in itself, exists distinct from us and sometimes merely something that belongs to outer appearance" (DH: JWA 2,1, 105; MPW 333).[29] Because only the latter option is under consideration here, then, in keeping with the conventions of transcendental speech, one should distinguish "empirically external objects from those that **might** be called 'external' in the transcendental sense," "by directly calling them 'things that are to be encountered in space'" (DH: JWA 2,1, 105; MPW 333).[30] It thus becomes clear what Jacobi seeks to indicate with his first set of editorial marks. Harking back to the separation between things in themselves and appearance, the compatibility between transcendental idealism and empirical realism maps directly onto a transformation whereby the reference to a subject-independent external world becomes the reference to a world conceived as external in space as a form of intuition.[31] With regard to the objective constitution of this world, the question of whether and how it relates to that which, "as a thing in itself, exists distinct from us," plays no role whatsoever.

Can anything at all be said about this relation? As indicated by the previously mentioned reference to objects "which **might** be called 'external' in the transcendental sense," Jacobi undertakes a second, even more important round of highlighting at this point. "**Now one can indeed admit**," Kant explains in the pertinent statement,

> that something that **may** be outside us in the transcendental sense is the cause of our outer intuitions, but this is not the object we understand by the representation of matter and corporeal things; for these are merely appearances, i.e., mere modes of representation, which are always found only in us [...]. The transcendental object is equally unknown in regard to inner and to outer sense. (DH: JWA 2,1, 104f.; MPW 332f.)[32]

That the thing in itself, here termed the "transcendental object," is entirely unknown to us, "an unknown ground of appearances" (JWA 2,1, 106; MPW 333),[33] is something of which Kant had assured us at the beginning of the Transcendental Aesthetic. Jacobi, however, in highlighting Kant's reservation that *it-may-be*, points to the crucial question of whether and how, given the presupposition that it is unknowable, the cause of external appearances can be addressed as external to the subject at all. His

---

[28] See CPR A 370. Note: In contrast to MPW, which uses Smith's 1929 translation of the *Critique of Pure Reason*, Jacobi's Kant quotations here and in what follows are taken from the newer and much improved translation of Guyer and Wood. I have reprinted Jacobi's markings in the text in boldface italics, in order to distinguish them from Kant's own emphases (in simple boldface). This represents a bit of a simplification in comparison to the practice of the critical edition, but it will suffice here to draw attention to the key points under consideration.
[29] See CPR A 373.
[30] See CPR A 373.
[31] Correspondingly, Jacobi also marks all passages that refer to "representation."
[32] See CPR A 372.
[33] See CPR A 380.

reasons for highlighting this reservation are clear, inasmuch as it follows therefrom that for the alliance of transcendental idealism and empirical realism, together with the restriction of the "outside us" to the external form of intuition, no genuine certainty of real subject-independent being can be achieved, whether by empirical or transcendental means. Thus it is certainly no accident (but neither is it an attempt to mislead the reader) that Jacobi's excerpt omits the passages dedicated to perception, where Kant scrutinizes the other side of the coin, that is to say the *material substrate*. His attempt to capture this "something real in space" according to the conditions of empirical realism can be seen in the characteristic proposition that follows upon his discussion of the modal categories, where he asserts that external perception is "itself the real."[34]

But if this is the profile of the transcendental idealism for which, as Kant insists, "we have already declared ourselves from the outset,"[35] then what is the status of the claim that objects affect us? In light of what was previously stated in regard to sensibility, such objects would have to present a reality that cannot be accounted for in terms of the constitutive powers of the subject. The "theory" (DH: JWA 2,1, 108; MPW 335; translation amended) offered up by Kant himself, however, offers no vantage point whatsoever from which to address such a reality. This impossibility, that is to say, the impossibility of retroactively justifying Kant's presupposition using his own means, is evaluated by Jacobi in four steps.

The first point is that the allegedly affecting objects cannot be identical to the "empirical object," insofar as the empirical objects already belong to the world of appearance (JWA 2,1, 108; MPW 335). By the same token, however, neither the second possibility—the *"transcendental object,"* nor the third—the *"representation of the object = x"* are viable candidates either (DH: JWA 2,1, 108f.; MPW 335). Given Kant's own terminological inconsistencies, this assessment might seem a bit confusing initially, but in the context presented by Jacobi, the relevant coordinates can be precisely established. It is clear that the *"representation of the object = x"* refers to the circumstance Kant addresses in the A-deduction using here the designation of a *"transcendental object"* and thereby indicating the thought of a general unity of objectivity that corresponds to the unity of apperception, with the former grounding the constitution of an empirical object.[36] This usage, however, must be distinguished from what Jacobi himself, on the basis of Kant's terminology in the critique of the fourth paralogism, consistently terms the "transcendental object." In light of his assertion that this is "at best" a "problematic" concept, "one *based* on the *entirely subjective form of our thought which pertains only to the sensibility proper to us*" (DH: JWA 2,1, 108; MPW 335), it is clear that his usage is intended to refer to the noumenon described in the concluding chapters of the Analytic. This highly subtle distinction, which Kant seeks to capture throughout his

---

[34] CPR A 375. Jacobi did not in fact ignore this issue. At a later point in his text he clearly notes that "all the objects of our experience are mere appearances, the matter and real content of which is nothing but our own sensation through and through" (JWA 2,1, 110; MPW 336f.).

[35] CPR A 370.

[36] CPR A 104ff. On this point see the direct citation from Jacobi DH: JWA 2,1, 108; MPW 333.

reflections in one and the same term, is thus not lost on Jacobi.³⁷ As for the related diagnosis that neither of these conceptions of the transcendental object is any better suited than the empirical object to ground the presupposition of an affecting object, in the case of the X as the "entirely undetermined thought of something in general,"³⁸ this point can be considered self-evident. With regard to the noumenon, however, the situation turns out to be explosive.

It is explosive because Kant himself raises the possibility of such a presupposition here and explicitly describes it as a *thought* that the understanding, in keeping with the "limitation of our sensibility," thinks. The understanding, according to this view,

> thinks of an object in itself, but only as a transcendental object, which is the cause of appearance (thus not itself appearance), and that cannot be thought of either as magnitude or as reality or as substance, etc.[…]; it therefore remains completely unknown whether such an object is to be encountered within or without us, whether it would be canceled out along with sensibility or whether it would remain even if we took sensibility away.³⁹

In other words, in drawing attention to the fact that the "transcendental object" *qua* noumenon must by Kant's own account be seen as a "problematic concept of an object,"⁴⁰ *based on the entirely subjective form of our thought*, Jacobi simultaneously underlines, with an eye toward the amphiboly chapter,⁴¹ the very structure to which he had already ascribed the reservation of *it-may-be* in his excerpt from the critique of the fourth paralogism (see DH: JWA 2,1, 109f; MPW 336). Moreover, as has again become apparent and is now all the more clear, this reservation not only implies that the understanding cannot account for the how-ness of the object it thinks as the "cause of appearances." Rather, insofar as the logic of a "problematic concept" implies only that it is free of internal contradiction and thus merely the logical possibility of

---

³⁷ See the entire passage: "On the contrary, according to this same hypothesis we know not the least of the *transcendental object*. Whenever objects are being considered, that is not what we are discussing. At best this concept is a problematic one *based* on the *entirely subjective form of our thought which pertains only to the sensibility proper to us*. Experience does not yield it, nor can experience yield it in any way—for whatever is not an *appearance* can never be an object of experience, and appearance, or the fact that some affection of the sense or other is in me, does not establish any reference on the part of representations of this sort to an object of any kind. It is the understanding that *adds* the object to the appearance by combining the manifold of the latter into one consciousness. *We say that we cognize the object only when we have produced a synthetic unity in the manifold of intuition, and the concept of this unity is the representation of the object=x*. This= x, however, is not the *transcendental object*. For about the latter we never know anything. And it is only assumed as intelligible cause of appearance in general simply in order that we may have something corresponding to sensibility understood as receptivity." (JWA 2,1, 108; MPW 335f.) See also the passages CPR A 250ff. in particular. Making reference to the same passages adduced by Jacobi, Allison elucidated these different aspects in 1968 (Henry E. Allison, "Kant's Concept of the Transcendental Object," *Kant-Studien* 59 (1968): 165–86). In his case, however, the transcendental object conceived as a cause is categorized in terms of an "existential claim," a move which, according to Jacobi, is superfluous.
³⁸ CPR A 253.
³⁹ CPR A 288.
⁴⁰ CPR A 254, 287.
⁴¹ See the direct quotation of the aforementioned Kant passage, again with revealing markings, in JWA 2,1,276, note.

thinking it, it follows from the stipulation *it-may-be* that the very reality of the object thought as the subject-external cause is impossible to verify. Whether "inside us or outside us," then—in the horizon of thinking, the point "where this cause is, and what kind of connection it has with its effect," necessarily "remains hidden in the deepest obscurity" (DH: JWA 2,1, 110; MPW 336). And, we should add, it cannot be otherwise in the case of a "mere analytic of the pure understanding" that must renounce "the proud name of an ontology."[42]

There is, however, still a further point to be made in regard to Jacobi's focus on this conflict between the external reality presupposed by the theory of affection and the mere logical possibility of a causally operative reality associated by transcendental theory with a thought of the understanding.[43] It relates back to the matter of Kant's allegedly inappropriate use of the categories. More specifically, insofar as the standard version of this accusation as expressed by Windelband has been both attributed to Jacobi and at the same time dismissed as inapplicable to Kant, commentators have consistently based their claims on Kant's own distinction between cognition and thinking.[44] Kant, so the argument goes, certainly cannot be accused of applying the category of the cause in particular to things in themselves, since he himself declares in view of the noumenon that only a "transcendental use" is permissible with categories abstracted from the conditions of sensible intuition and thus designated as "pure."[45] This is indeed the case, and the only comment that needs to be added is that the critical mobilization of this point against Jacobi completely ignores the textual evidence. Not only does his reference to the "form of our thinking" indicate his keen awareness of precisely the difference that he has allegedly overlooked. Even more, he shows that it is actually the legitimate, *unschematized* use of the categories, the use that is fully in keeping with the "spirit" of transcendental idealism, that not only fails to achieve anything in regard to the problem of affection, but actually subverts the attempt to do so.

The fourth and final step illuminates the profound pitfalls of attributing a position to Jacobi that one then attempts to refute with arguments that reproduce, almost verbatim, the critical core of his own theory. If it has thus far been shown that neither the empirical object, nor the indeterminate something = x, nor the noumenon can provide a legitimate basis for Kant's presupposition of affecting objects, now the failure of the final possibility becomes clear, a possibility that was in any case only ever considered hypothetically, namely, that we might arrive at "any such thing" through the insight that "in the representations that we call appearances we feel passive" (DH: JWA 2,1, 111; MPW 338). This possibility is no less doomed to fail, because it implies the assumption of a sensation of "cause and effect understood transcendentally," that

---

[42] CPR A 247. On this point, see the particularly informative sequence in the preface to the second edition CPR B XXVIf. with the associated footnote.
[43] See Jacobi, *Über das Unternehmen des Kritizismus, die Vernunft zu Verstande zu bringen* (1802) [On the Efforts of Critical Philosophy to Bring Reason to its Senses]: JWA 2,1, 276 note, where a series of excerpts on this point reinforces the idea that this forms the center of his analysis.
[44] See among many others Adickes, *Kant und das Ding an sich*, 49ff.; Willaschek, "Phaenomena/Noumena," 339.
[45] CPR A 247f.

is, in a sense that involves applying the category of causality beyond the limits of appearances, so as to "infer [the existence of] things outside us in a transcendental sense in virtue of it, as well as their necessary connections with one another" (DH: JWA 2,1, 112; MPW 338). This would truly be a case of inferring a real cause from an effect, an inference that Jacobi does not claim has actually been made by Kant but whose absurdity he instead foregrounds through his use of the subjunctive, insisting that "the whole of transcendental idealism would collapse as a result, and would be left with no application or reason for being" (DH: JWA 2,1, 112; MPW 338).

The broader consequence of Jacobi's argumentation is that the presupposition of affecting objects must be unequivocally abandoned to maintain the consistency of the theory. And what exactly does this mean? Returning to the faculty of sensibility, there is one more point to address in the reconstruction of the text. I referred previously to Jacobi's use of the crucial term "the real." Now we must consider the structure that becomes visible along with it, according to which sensibility constitutes an instance of a *medial in-between* and in this way forms the "medium" between world and subject by relating them to one another. The pivotal thesis advanced by Jacobi in this context is that only this medial structure can guarantee the original presupposition of the real.

In making this assertion, he shows, first of all, the extent to which sensibility does indeed form a point of resistance that cannot be integrated into the theoretical framework of transcendental idealism. Any attempt to do so will inevitably result in a sublimation of the "medium" into subjective perception and the real into a mere datum in space as a form of intuition. His thesis, moreover, is also significant because it reveals the inverse approach to be *ab ovo* futile, that is, an approach which proceeds from perception in order to discover something like the source of the datum. To do this would entail an inference from effect to cause. That Jacobi never accuses Kant of such an error can be seen, as previously noted, in his insistence that the logic of transcendental philosophy "would collapse" in such a case. But it is no less clear from his claim that such a move would contradict the unique medial logic of the presupposition itself. Third, we should note that the identification of sensibility with its "medial" character also eliminates the option, both as a counter to and in correspondence with the reductive concentration on the subject, of now suddenly shifting to the side of objects in order to secure the reality of the presupposition from that vantage point. The conclusion to be drawn from all of this is the fourth and final point. It follows namely from the structural features described that Kant's affection theory ends up sequestered in a space entirely foreign to the "spirit" of transcendental idealism, but whose coordinates align precisely with those that demarcate Jacobi's *own position*, that of a "genuine" or "committed" realism (DH: JWA 2,1, 20, 32; MPW 264, 272).

The hallmark of this realism, as Jacobi makes unmistakably clear in the relevant passage from the Supplement as well as in the main text *David Hume* itself is its "commitment" to transcending the Kantian alliance between transcendental idealism and empirical realism (DH: JWA 2,1, 106f., 20f.; MPW 333f, 264.f.). More specifically, it grounds the certainty of reality in a structure that simultaneously accommodates, as Jacobi demonstrates on the basis of the in-between of sensibility, "internal consciousness and the external object" in "the same indivisible instant" and "without any operation of the understanding—indeed, without the remotest beginning of the generation of the concept of cause and effect in the understanding" (DH: JWA 2,1, 38; MPW 277). With this equiprimordiality of both moments, whereby neither can arise without the other nor be reduced to the other, the certainty in question here is transformed into the *immediate* certainty that Jacobi refers to as belief, even as a "*truly miraculous*" "revelation" (DH: JWA 2,1, 33; MPW 272). The seemingly religious and irrational character of these terms has always been a source of suspicion. Just how misguided the perpetuation of this misunderstanding has been becomes clear, however, if we again turn our attention to Kant, who deploys the *very same structure* when he foregrounds an "immediate perception" of the real prior to any inferential operations as the essential moment of empirical realism.[46]

What needs to be kept in mind in what follows is, first, that there is in fact a structural kinship between Jacobi's "committed" and Kant's empirical realism, with the difference between the two positions consisting exclusively—but also pivotally— in their respective conceptions of what is given, in immediate certainty, "outside of us." And, secondly, this in turn allows us to identify a further commonality at the heart of this very difference. Insofar as Jacobi aims to transcend the scope of a merely empirical realism to arrive at the equiprimordial "revelation" of a subject-independent reality, he is also able to make sense of Kant's unexamined and seemingly incongruous affection-theoretical presupposition, which, as we have seen, cannot be justified within a transcendental-philosophical framework.[47] This possibility, which Jacobi explicitly addresses later, would seem to suggest that the center around which his analysis crystallizes into an *immanent* critique of Kant is identical to the one that lends his *own* position its potency (JWA 2,1, 391f.; MPW 552f.). To say this, however, is in no way tantamount to asserting that Kant *explicitly* advocated for something like Jacobi's realism. Rather, the opposite is the case, as becomes clear at the latest with the specific determination of a real causality "contained," as Jacobi puts it, in the medial in-between of sensibility. The fact that the character of this containment cannot be illuminated by way of the category of causality has meanwhile been repeatedly shown. The strategy that Jacobi pursues in the further course of the dialogue *David Hume* is thus to locate the origin of the concept of the cause in the practical circumstances of our action rather than in any theoretical operation, and with this he consciously places himself in the starkest possible opposition to Kant.[48]

In other words, it is not a category error attributable to theory-internal contradictions that is the issue here, but neither is it a case of conflicting external motivations. Rather, the failure to see that his affection-theoretical premises are in need of their *own* clarification is, according to Jacobi's diagnosis, responsible for the confusingly inconsistent impression made by Kant's philosophy. The whole appears, as we can now see, as a noncommittal combination of elements from a "committed" realism and a "committed" transcendental idealism, the focus of which is not coincidentally

[46] CPR A 371; see also DH: JWA 2,1, 20; MPW 264.
[47] See Günter Zöller, "Das Element aller Gewißheit. Jacobi, Kant und Fichte über den Glauben," *Fichte-Studien* 14 (1998): 1–41.
[48] See Chapter 8 in this volume.

provided by the repeated assurance that it would after all be "absurd" if there could "be an appearance without anything that appears."[49] The fact that a noumenal "nothing" is designated as a real "something" here, without Kant himself having tasted this "essential core" of his own philosophy—this is the point made by Jacobi in his early letter to Goethe mentioned above.[50]

V.

On the basis of this highly differentiated and perceptive analysis, Jacobi concludes that the only credible option available to the transcendental idealist is to postulate a "speculative egoism," "the strongest idealism that was ever professed" (DH: JWA 2,1, 112; MPW 338) which, in keeping with the "spirit" of the theory, dispenses entirely with the presupposition of things that are "outside us in a transcendental sense" and "have connections with us *which we would be in a position of perceiving in any way at all*" (DH: JWA 2,1, 112; MPW 338). At the same time, as the reconstruction of his text has made clear, Jacobi insists on the need to make a *choice* between alternative options, the parameters of which are not explicitly articulated at this point but are nonetheless clearly recognizable. Those who wish to escape the Kantian dilemma and are not interested in the option of a speculative egoism can always defect to the other side and adopt the standpoint of a "committed realism." This possibility, however, also comes at a significant cost—that of consciously renouncing the quest for an *epistemological explanation* of our instantaneous certainty of reality and of relegating any understanding of the determinations "contained" therein to an investigation bound to the practical circumstances of action.

We know how Fichte responded when faced with this constellation. With his previously mentioned claim (formulated in reference to Jacobi's "proof") that "Kant has no knowledge of any 'something' distinct from the I," he clearly casts his vote for the "speculative egoism" to which the *Wissenschaftslehre*, with its categorical exclusion of any and all reality that might exist independently of subjectivity, gives definitive expression. And here we can see that bypassing the misleading standard interpretation of Jacobi's text in order to submit it to a thorough investigation pays off in very concrete terms.

After all, what was it that led Fichte to conclude that Jacobi had "so correctly" grasped transcendental idealism, whereas all the other interpretations offered only grotesque distortions of their own "dogmatism" masquerading as the "astonishing discovery" of the "great genius" Kant?[51] As is evident even at the level of the quotations Fichte takes from Jacobi's text,[52] his enthusiasm stems from the fact that Jacobi's Kant interpretation does not rely, either in an affirmative or critical sense, on linking Kant's assertions on

---

[49] CPR A 251f.; CPR B XXVIf.
[50] See also his *Introduction to the Author's Collected Philosophical Works* (1815): JWA 2,1, 390f.; MPW 551f.
[51] GA I,4, 237. Fichte, *Introductions*, 69.
[52] See GA I,4, 235. Fichte, *Introductions*, 66.

affecting objects back to the (mis)application of the categories, which is to say that it derives instead from Jacobi's interest in directing attention to the "transcendental object" as a *construct of thought*. This aligns with Fichte's own aim: to show that the thing in itself, correctly understood as "*noumenon*" is nothing but "a mere thought."[53] And as absurd as it is for some "interpreters" to try "to ascribe efficacy, a predicate that belongs only to reality, to a mere thought," to allow, in other words, a mere thought to "*have an effect* upon the I,"[54] by the same token, it is equally reasonable for Jacobi to refrain from attributing such operations to Kant. In other words, in invoking the difference between a schematized and a transcendental use of the categories, critics of Jacobi's supposed argument employ the exact same reasoning that Fichte uses in objecting to his "Kantian" contemporaries—albeit with one essential difference. Fichte is no less resolute than Jacobi in his insistence on the consequences that follow from the notional status of the noumenon.

To this point, then, the situation is clear. But it is equally clear that the impetus for distinguishing a "mere thought" produced by the understanding is drawn from a different source in each case. What Fichte so unequivocally and seamlessly ascribes to the perspective of "the most resolute idealism," "according to which all being is produced only by the thinking of the intellect and which knows nothing whatsoever of any other type of being,"[55] must, according to Jacobi's diagnosis, be revised based on the insight that no such resolution is to be found in Kant himself. On the contrary, it is (irresolutely) called into question by the assumption of affecting objects. Does this mean, as was proposed previously, that Fichte simply failed to recognize both issues, that is to say, both the contradiction noted by Jacobi in the structure of the *Critique of Pure Reason* itself as well as Jacobi's own appeal to realism, which is formulated on the basis of this very same contradiction? A closer inspection leads us to a rather different finding. And by way of conclusion, I would like to sketch out how Fichte seeks to realize his programmatic objective in this context—albeit at the cost of considerable shifts with regard to both Kant's and Jacobi's positions.

The starting point is provided by his claim that the noumenon "is something that, in obedience to certain laws of thinking (which themselves have to be established and have been established by Kant), we merely *think of* in addition to the appearances, and something that, in conformity with these same laws, we *must* think of and add to the appearances."[56] If what Fichte meant here were the same as what Jacobi was aiming at with his stipulation of the *it-may-be* as the logic of a "problematic concept," then the claim would be unobjectionable. In fact, however, Fichte has something very different in mind. This becomes clear at the moment where he, too, addresses Kant's talk of affecting objects, a discussion in which he again reveals his indebtedness to Jacobi's text. What is telling here, however, is not only that Fichte confidently ignores Jacobi's analysis, according to which none of Kant's determinations of the object formulated within the transcendental reflection matches up with the opening affection theory. He

---

[53] GA I,4, 237. Fichte, *Introductions*, 69.
[54] GA I,4, 237. Fichte, *Introductions*, 69.
[55] GA I,4, 237. Fichte, *Introductions*, 69.
[56] GA I,4, 236. Fichte, *Introductions*, 68.

does indeed replace this with a diametrically opposed assertion, but even more striking is the particular way in which he attempts to prove this opposing view. Leaving aside for the moment the question of whether he is simply being careless or intentionally pursuing strategic interests, it is in any case clear that he tacitly identifies the noumenon with the "representation of object = X."[57] In concrete terms, this means that what Fichte cites, that is to say the explicit basis for his argumentation, is Jacobi's observation cited above that "the understanding [...] *adds* the object to the appearance" (DH: JWA 2,1, 108; MPW 335).[58] It is not difficult to see that this sentence provides the model for the previously mentioned remark about the logical necessity of thinking the noumenon. But Fichte has ignored the difference to which Jacobi carefully draws attention in his own text. As a result, he not only manages to equate Jacobi's observation, which corresponds exactly to Kant's text in its focus on the indeterminate X as relating to the unity of apperception, with the noumenon. In doing so, Fichte also simultaneously posits the concept of the unity of objectivity in general as the constitutive ground of affection. The object that the understanding "*adds* [...] to appearance" is thereby transformed into the affecting object itself, with regard to which it can now of course be unequivocally claimed that it "*is only thought of as exercising an effect.*"[59]

With the support of Jacobi's Supplement "On Transcendental Idealism," then, Fichte has managed to introduce a set of reflections for which neither Jacobi nor Kant can legitimately be seen to offer any basis whatsoever.[60] In doing so, however, he does manage to resolve the problem of affection, which is now no longer sequestered in an extra-theoretical void—providing an occasion for the "crude dogmatism" of the "promoters of the Kantian philosophy"—but is instead absorbed without remainder into the constitutive conditions of the "intelligence." Fichte's approach thus complies with Jacobi's injunction to renounce absolutely the presupposition of a subject-independent reality, but it complies in such a way that this renunciation no longer results in the complete elimination of this presupposition. Rather, the point is to declare it to be the result of a logically necessary production of subjective acts of cognition, whereby it is *posited as* a presupposition.

However, we have still not considered the complete series of shifts or fully explicated Fichte's programmatic objective. The second shift consists in the claim that the "cornerstone of Kantian realism" can also be found at the point of convergence of the reflections sketched out here.[61] Fichte thus does not hesitate to map the alliance

---

[57] On this point, although presented in a different context and without reference to Jacobi's Kant Supplement, see Gerold Prauss, *Kant und das Problem der Dinge an sich*, 3rd ed. (Bonn: Bouvier, 1989), 130f., note.

[58] See GA I,4, 240f.; Fichte, *Introductions*, 71f.

[59] GA I,4, 241. Fichte, *Introductions*, 72f.

[60] In contrast to his texts, in one of his letters to Jacobi Fichte clearly acknowledges his actual distance from Kant: "Everyone knows you are a realist and I am, after all, a transcendental idealist and an even stricter one than Kant. Kant clings to the view that the manifold of experience is something given – God knows how and why. But I straightforwardly maintain that even this manifold is produced by us through our creative faculty." Letter to Jacobi of August 30, 1795 (JBW I,11, 55; J. G. Fichte, *Early Philosophical Writings*, ed. and trans. Daniel Breazeale (Ithaca: Cornell University Press, 1988), 411).

[61] GA I,4, 236 Note. See I,4, 243. Fichte, *Introductions*, 68, 75f.

described by Kant and recapitulated by Jacobi—that between transcendental idealism and empirical realism—onto his own position. His reason for doing so is clear. Beyond his unwavering interest in establishing the system of the *Wissenschaftslehre* as the only valid reconstruction of Kant, Fichte is just as concerned as Kant himself was not to disregard the conviction that the outside world is real. There can be no denying, however, that his approach entails a shift in relation to Kant. Restricted by definition to the realm of appearance, in Kant's empirical realism the ground of appearance, however problematic it may be, is still to be located beyond the limits of this realm. But precisely this separation loses all meaning in Fichte. It is dissolved to the exact extent that the constitution of the empirical object is now entirely conflated with the presupposed object *thought of as exercising an effect*.[62]

What are the implications of such a complete unfettering of so-called empirical realism? This is, to be sure, a constitutive feature of what Fichte terms "committed idealism." At this point, however, we cannot read this label without simultaneously thinking of the complementary concept that Fichte clearly has in mind here. Indeed, as is evident from the comments on Jacobi that follow immediately after his reference to "Kantian realism," what appears here under the guise of empirical realism is none other than the "committed" realism of Jacobi.[63] Again, it remains an open question whether Fichte unconsciously conflates these two structurally related but intrinsically distinct realisms, or whether this is an intended consequence of performing the operation just described. There can be no question, however, that this obfuscation brings a third shift into focus, one which relates to Jacobi himself and also brings the programmatic objective of Fichte's efforts into full view. On the basis of what has been shown to be a rather bold interpretation of both Jacobi and Kant, Fichte aims in the course of *one and the same operation* to present the system of the *Wissenschaftslehre*, precisely in so far as it disposes of the "tiresome thing in itself"[64] as described and thereby provides a *rigorously idealistic* version of Kant, as the system which is able to integrate Jacobi's *alternatively realist* position into itself from the start.

For Fichte, then, deciding in favor of "speculative egoism" means not having to decide at all. It suffices to downgrade what Jacobi presents as a strict alternative between two options to a mere "distinction"—the difference between the "philosophical viewpoint" and that of "life," which are realized within the system on entirely different levels. Simultaneously suggesting the distinction between speculation and praxis, and thus again mirroring one of Jacobi's own motifs, it is this difference—and not simply the adaptation of a Kantian framework—that forms the specific background for the profile formulated in the *Foundation of the Entire Wissenschaftslehre* according to which the

---

[62] See GA I,2, 62; J. G. Fichte, "Review of Aenesidemus," in *Early Philosophical Writings*, 74.
[63] GA I,4, 236 note. Fichte, *Introductions*, 68. See especially the previously mentioned letter from Fichte to Jacobi from August 30, 1795. JBW I,11, 56f.; Fichte, *Early Philosophical Writings*, 412: "If I were to go even further, and were I, from within the supposedly hostile territory [of idealism], to guarantee the security of realism's domain, then by rights I should be able to count upon – not merely an alliance of a sort – but upon an alliance in every respect."
[64] GA I,4, 243. Fichte, *Introductions*, 75.

"Critical Idealism" of the Wissenschaftslehre could also be called "a real-idealism or ideal-realism."[65]

The details of this program cannot be elaborated here, but this much is certain: It is one thing to strive, in a hoped-for "alliance" with Jacobi[66] for nothing less than a full integration of "life" into the system. It is another thing to succeed in this effort. As is shown by his continuous and evolving attempts to determine the appropriate relationship between these elements, Fichte spent his entire life wrestling with this challenge.

---

[65] GA I,2, 412; J. G. Fichte, "Foundation of the Entire Wissenschaftslehre," in J. G. Fichte, *Foundation of the Entire* Wissenschaftslehre *and Related Writings (1794-95)*, ed. and trans. Daniel Breazeale (Oxford: Oxford University Press, 2021), 343.

[66] See the cited letter to Jacobi, JBW I,11, 56f.

Part Two

Critical Relations

10

I-hood and Person: The Fichtean Aporia and the Debate with Jacobi

Introductory Considerations

For any scholar interested in the history of German idealism after Kant, the topic of "System and the critique of systems around 1800" has an undeniable appeal.[1] The phrase captures a constellation of problems that shape post-Kantian German philosophy on every level. Indeed, one can say without exaggeration that here, at the true onset of modernity, a set of concerns emerges that are continuously debated (not discovered) in the nineteenth and twentieth centuries, and that continue to shape the contemporary philosophical landscape.[2] In addressing these concerns, less comprehensive reviews of the epoch tend to neglect thinkers such as Jacobi, Friedrich Schlegel, Friedrich von Hardenberg (Novalis), and Jean Paul, giving preference instead to the main philosophical protagonists: Fichte, Schelling, and Hegel. A consequence of this restricted focus, however, is that we can easily lose sight of the extent to which the systems developed by these protagonists, both with regard to their genesis and their specific form, are indebted to their incorporation of system-critical motifs. Moreover, and even more importantly, in the course of this incorporation, they themselves engage in the critique of systems, attacking one another not simply for specific, allegedly dubious claims but in foundational terms, while, on the other hand, not only Kant but also Spinoza serves in all cases as indispensable foils for their own system-building endeavors.

From this perspective, assuming that we are also ready to abandon once and for all the obsolete, Kroner-inspired trajectory that charts a path "from Kant to Hegel,"[3] the origins of the critique of systems turn out to be extraordinarily complex. Common to all participants is the conviction, inscribed into the very structural logic of their

---

[1] This chapter was originally delivered as a contribution to the Vienna conference series on "The System of Reason: Kant and German Idealism."
[2] See Birgit Sandkaulen, "System und Systemkritik. Überlegungen zur gegenwärtigen Bedeutung eines fundamentalen Problemzusammenhangs," in *System und Systemkritik. Beiträge zu einem Grundproblem der klassischen deutschen Philosophie*, ed. Birgit Sandkaulen, Kritisches Jahrbuch der Philosophie 11 (Würzburg: Königshausen & Neumann, 2006 c), 11–34.
[3] Jaeschke and Arndt have recently offered a comprehensive overview of the post-Kantian epoch in which they attribute a decisive role to Jacobi (Walter Jaeschke and Andreas Arndt, *Die Klassische Deutsche Philosophie nach Kant. Systeme der reinen Vernunft und ihre Kritik 1785–1845* (Munich: Beck, 2012).

argumentation, that systems thinking cannot be dismissed as a mere manifestation of philosophical overreach, simply to be cast aside without consequence. On the contrary, the systematic impulse is perceived as an urgent and serious challenge and thus constitutes the focus of interest. How best to address this challenge, however, how, exactly, systems and the critique of systems are related—this has not been decided in advance. Rather, attempts to address these questions give rise to fierce debates, in which a range of different models of critique become visible.

Three models can be distinguished on the basis of their key structural elements. The most radical variant comes from Jacobi, who was also the first to introduce the problems related to system and the critique of systems into the debate. Originally developed on the basis of his engagement with Spinoza's *Ethics* and therefore first presented in the specific context of his "*Spinoza and Antispinoza*" (Spin: JWA 1,1, 274), the counter model he develops *via negationis* aims to pierce the heart of all systems thinking, to contradict it at its very core. This *act of contradiction* finds expression in what Jacobi refers to as his "salto mortale," the daring leap that would later make such an impression on Kierkegaard.

A second variant is characteristic of early German romanticism. Writing primarily with reference to Fichte's system of the Wissenschaftslehre, both Schlegel and Hardenberg are also unwilling to simply abandon all systematic ambitions. Unlike, Jacobi, however, they do not insist on the anti-systematic contradiction of the leap. Rather, in keeping with Schlegel's famous dictum that it is "equally fatal for the mind to have a system and to have none," they seek in their counter models to "combine" the two options.[4] The early romantic project thus aims to be both simultaneously: *system and non-system;* or as Hardenberg puts it in his *Fichte Studies*, to "systematize systemlessness."[5]

The third variant is again completely different. Taking their cue from Jacobi, Fichte, Schelling, and Hegel all share the conviction that Spinoza's metaphysics provides the paradigmatic model of a philosophical system.[6] This model, however, serves here as the foil for a critique of systems that aims to offer "a counterpart to Spinoza's *Ethics*,"[7] one that is motivated neither by an interest in anti-systematic contradiction nor in a simultaneous combination of system and non-system, but rather by the desire to construct an *alternative system*. This desire is fueled by the expectation that their

---

[4] Friedrich Schlegel, *Philosophical Fragments*, trans. Peter Firchow (Minneapolis: University of Minnesota Press, 1991), 24.
[5] Novalis, *Fichte Studies*, ed. Jane Kneller (Cambridge: Cambridge University Press, 2003), 187.
[6] An example is Hegel's striking assertion "that Spinoza is made a testing point in modern philosophy, so that it may really be said: You are either a Spinozist or not a philosopher at all." Hegel, *Vorlesungen über die Geschichte der Philosophie*, TWA 20, 163f.; G. W. F. Hegel, *Lectures on the History of Philosophy*, vol. 3, trans. Elisabeth S. Haldane and Frances H. Simson (Lincoln: University of Nebraska Press, 1995), 283. See also, among others, Peter Rohs, "Der Pantheismus bei Spinoza und im Deutschen Idealismus," in *Subjektivität und Anerkennung*, ed. Barbara Merker, Georg Mohr, and Michael Quante (Paderborn: Mentis, 2004), 102–21.
[7] Schelling, *Vom Ich als Princip der Philosophie oder über das Unbedingte im menschlichen Wissen*, SW I,1, 159. F. W. J. Schelling, "Of the I as the Principle of Philosophy or On the Unconditional in Human Knowledge," in *The Unconditional in Human Knowledge. Four Early Essays (1794–1796)*, trans. Marti Fritz (Lewisburg: Bucknell University Press, 1980), 69.

approaches can successfully neutralize the threat of system-destroying critiques, a goal which can only be achieved if one takes the threat seriously and manages to respond to the objections that constitute it within the alternative system.

It is only against this backdrop that the specific contours of the well-known dispute between Fichte and Jacobi become fully visible. The dispute is characterized by a certain asymmetry, not only with regard to chronology but also in substantive terms, and it will be important to keep this in mind as we proceed. From Jacobi's point of view, the debate appears as a structural recapitulation of the debate with Spinoza, in which the previous antithesis of "my Spinoza and Antispinoza" is transformed in the context of the Fichtean Wissenschaftslehre into the antithesis of "quintessential philosophy" [Alleinphilosophie] and "my non-philosophy" [Unphilosophie] (JF: JWA 2,1, 198; MPW 505).[8] This notion of a recapitulation both grounds and permeates the *Letter to Fichte* (1799) in which Jacobi, building on his pioneering Kant critique of 1787, intervenes in developments in post-Kantian philosophy and decisively shapes their further course. In contrast, Fichte's aim from the beginning is to accommodate Jacobi's system-critical objections into his own program. The problems that have occasioned Jacobi's system-contradicting leap are to be resolved by addressing his concerns vis-à-vis Spinoza within the system of the Wissenschaftslehre, where all understanding of self and world is grounded in a structure of absolute subjectivity.

In connection with a no doubt sincere expectation that his systematic ambitions will meet with Jacobi's recognition and approval,[9] Fichte draws a distinction early on that will guide his thinking to the end: between *idealism* and *realism* or *speculation* and *life*. While, for Fichte, these categories do pertain to two essentially different perspectives, they do not lead to the disintegration of the system but should (and can) instead be grounded, differentiated, and mediated within framework of the Wissenschaftslehre.[10] In terms of the analysis undertaken later in the chapter, it is crucial to note here that from the outset, Fichte also merges the distinction between and systematic integration of these two perspectives with his view of the difference between the idea of the *absolute I* and the phenomenon of the individual. "My absolute I," as he writes in a letter to Jacobi from August 30, 1795, "is obviously not the *individual,* though this is how offended courtiers and irate philosophers have interpreted me, in order that they may falsely attribute to me the disgraceful theory

---

[8] In the *Letter to Fichte,* Jacobi also gives his compelling definition of the self-contained, integrated structure of a system as "a philosophy of *one* piece" (JF: JWA, 2,1, 200; MPW 507). Fichte was so impressed by this formulation that he repeatedly makes use of it himself over the course of the successive versions of the Wissenschaftslehre. The phrase also continues to appear even in Schelling's final works.

[9] See also Fichte's letter to Jacobi of September 29, 1794: "if there is any thinker in Germany with whom I wish and hope to agree in my particular convictions, then it is you, most venerable sir" (JBW I,11, 3).

[10] Significantly, Fichte first formulates this plan in his letter to Jacobi of August 30, 1795 (JBW I,11, 55–7). The prospect raised here in regard to the standpoints mentioned of an "alliance in every respect" (JBW I,11, 57; J. G. Fichte, *Early Philosophical Writings,* ed. and trans. Daniel Breazeale (Ithaca: Cornell University Press, 1988), 412) is then made public, as it were, in the Second Introduction to the Wissenschaftslehre. See Chapter 9 in this volume.

of practical egoism. Instead, *the individual must be deduced from the absolute I*, and the *Wissenschaftslehre* will immediately proceed to such a deduction in conjunction with its treatment of natural rights."[11]

Whatever we are ultimately to understand as comprising the categories of "life" and "realism," with his reference to the centrality of the concrete individual, the person in his or her specific individuality, Fichte has indeed grasped a crucial feature of Jacobi's system-critical aims. But just how plausible is Fichte's assertion that he fully complies with the demand for an account of personal subjectivity? To the extent that one takes his claim seriously, then the question has a significance that transcends the historical context of his dispute with Jacobi; indeed, it is crucial for an adequate understanding of the entire range of post-Kantian efforts at philosophical system building.

The discussion that follows will proceed in three stages. In a first step, and with a view toward Fichte's *Second Introduction to the Wissenschaftslehre* of 1797, I will analyze the immediate circumstances to which Jacobi is responding in his *Letter to Fichte* and in related comments he makes to Jean Paul. In a second step, I will consider Fichte's reply as articulated in his letter to Jacobi from April 22, 1799, which also includes a fragmentary clarification of his project, as well as in the *Crystal Clear Report* of 1801. Here the focus will be on the new strategy employed by Fichte as he attempts to resolve the reemergent conflict between speculation and life. And finally, in a third step, I will examine the *Crystal Clear Report* with an eye toward whether Fichte's defense provides a convincing response to the challenge of concrete subjectivity and can adequately account for the self-understanding of persons.

I-hood and Person: An Overview of the Problem

Fichte's Visit to the Tailor

What do we mean when we say "I," that is, when we use the linguistic expression "I"? In the *Second Introduction to the Wissenschaftslehre* Fichte answers this question with two examples from "everyday life":

> Suppose you call out to someone in the dark, "Who is there?" And suppose too that, acting on the assumption that you will recognize his voice, he replies, "It is I." In this case it is clear that he is referring to himself as this specific person and that this is the manner in which what he says is meant to be understood: "I am the person who goes by such and such a name, and I am not some other person with a different name." He replied in this way because when you asked "*Who* is there?" you already assumed the presence of some rational being or another and merely wished to know which, of all the rational beings that might possibly be present, was actually there.

---

[11] JBW I,11, 55. Fichte, *Early Philosophical Writings*, 411.

Thus the first example. The second reads as follows:

> But let us imagine (if you will forgive me for using this example, which I find to be particularly apt) that you are sewing or altering someone's garment while she is still wearing it and that you accidentally manage to cut her. In this case she will cry out, "Stop, that is *I*! You are cutting *me*!" What is she trying to say in this case? She is not announcing to you that she is this or that specific person and no other, for this is something you already know quite well. Instead, what she wishes to tell you is that what you have just cut is not her dead and insensate garment, but her living and feeling self—which is something you did not know. In this case, she employs the word "I" in order to distinguish herself, not from other people, but rather from things.[12]

To my knowledge, this passage has generally received little attention in the scholarship. It is worth taking a closer look at Fichte's examples, however, because they provide a starting point from which just four moves will take us to the crux of the dispute between Fichte and Jacobi in regard to systems and the critique thereof. First, it should be noted that for Fichte, the use of the expression "I" always appears in the context of a differentiation. Whoever says "I" speaks of himself and immediately distinguishes himself from an other. However, depending on whether the other in question is a someone or a something, the distinction bound up with the use of "I" can refer to either persons or things. Reformulated in grammatical terms, this means that in the use the first person singular "I," a distinction is made between "I" and "you" in one case, and between "I" and "it" in the other. While we can readily agree that this is indeed how we speak, we are still a long way from grasping what Fichte has in mind here.

To do so, we must also recognize (the second move) that the particular use context affects the meaning of the expression "I." Depending on whether I am distinguishing myself from persons or things, I also relate to myself in one of two different ways. But how does this become apparent? We are now getting closer to the heart of the matter, because Fichte is insinuating here that distinguishing among persons involves an external demarcation, whereas drawing a distinction between persons and things involves an internal one. The fact that I am "I," that is to say, this particular person, becomes apparent relative to other persons who have already been referred to in order to identify me as the one who I am. In contrast, the distinction between myself and an object does not depend on a detour through external relations. Even more significantly, moreover, the latter distinction is not even accessible to an external perspective, but rather evokes the inner perspective of my "living and feeling self." Thus we can already see that Fichte privileges this second relation over the first one.

---

[12] Fichte, *Zweite Einleitung in die Wissenschaftslehre*, FW I, 503f. J. G. Fichte, *Introductions to the Wissenschaftslehre and Other Writings (1797–1800)*, ed. and trans. Daniel Breazeale (Indianapolis: Hackett, 1994), 89.

Third, and connected with this point, is the acknowledgement that the expression "I" is by no means always used in reference to a particular person, who, as such, stands in relation to other persons as well as to objects. In fact, the aspect of personal determinateness is not relevant at all for the inner perspective of the "living and feeling self." Instead of marking the distinction between an *individual person* and object, in this case the expression "I" refers to a self that is a *subject* as opposed to an object. And from here, the fourth move is self-evident. "In short," Fichte concludes, "I-hood and individuality are very different concepts […]. Through the former concept we oppose to ourselves everything outside of us, not merely persons other than ourselves; the concept of I-hood comprises not merely our own specific personality, but our entire mental or spiritual nature."[13]

Does this mean that "I-hood" cried out in pain from the prick of the needle? The inner perspective of the "living and feeling self" that provides the supra-individual, universal certainty of "our entire mental or spiritual nature"? Given that Fichte found his tailoring example "particularly apt," the dilemma that emerges here appears all the more striking. In fact, the problem that Fichte's visit brings to light has its origins in his basic theoretical framework, which, in proceeding from a conception of "I-hood," is structurally determined from the first to the last by a highly precarious relation to the concrete I.[14]

Synthesis and Abstraction

In the *Second Introduction to the Wissenschaftslehre*, Fichte seeks to defend his conception against the allegedly pernicious confusion of the supra-individual and the individual I. His polemic is thus directed toward the "incapacity" of those who imagine that the concept of "I" always only refers "to their own individual person," an incapacity that Fichte diagnoses not as a "weakness of the intellectual power" but as a "weakness of their entire character."[15] At the same time, his polemic also reveals the substantive difficulty that plagues the Wissenschaftslehre. This becomes clear in the course of two opposing movements that are paradigmatically presented in the context of the passage cited.

One movement is that of the deduction or the genetic construction, which is designated here as the "synthesis of the concept of the person."[16] This synthesis implies an original opposition between "I-hood" as a purely self-referential "subject-objectivity" on the one hand, and the "it" as the marker of sheer objectivity on the other, onto which the concept of "I-hood" is then transferred, resulting in the "you." "The concept of the 'you' arises from the union of the 'it' and the 'I.' The concept

---

[13] FW I, 504. Fichte, *Introductions*, 89.
[14] This temporal specification should be understood literally. Fichte's circles incessantly around the problem of how the hierarchical distinction between I-hood and the individual, concrete I can be resolved within a systematic philosophy. His concerns first appear in *Some Lectures Concerning the Scholar's Vocation* of 1794 and continue through the late reworkings of the Wissenschaftslehre.
[15] FW I, 504f. Fichte, *Introductions*, 90.
[16] FW I, 502. Fichte, *Introductions*, 87 (translation amended).

of the I within this opposition (i.e., the concept of the I as an individual) is the synthesis of the I with itself."[17] In regard to the first move described in the analysis of the examples, this means that Fichte transcends the first-person perspective in order to establish a meta-instance that is expressly characterized as "not synthetic, but thetic," and from which the concrete relations among "I," "you," and "it," must first be derived.

The opposing movement correlates directly with this claim of the synthetic construction of the person, insofar as, according to Fichte, anything that is the product of a synthesis can be abstracted from in turn. This procedure of arriving at "the I as such, i.e. the non-object," by way of an "abstraction" from all individual determinateness,[18] can be understood in two ways. From a systematic perspective, the principle of the genetic construction itself is revealed in this manner. In contrast, from a practical standpoint, the consequence is an ethical imperative directed toward the concrete person, who must renounce her own individuality in favor of an "I-hood" identical to reason. And this culminates, finally, in a description of the *Wissenschaftslehre* as a theory, for which "the only thing that exists in itself is reason, and individuality is something merely accidental. Reason is the end and personality is the means; the latter is merely a particular expression of reason, one that must increasingly be absorbed into the universal form of the same. For the *Wissenschaftslehre*, reason alone is eternal, whereas individuality must ceaselessly die off."[19] In other words, we are confronted here with "a system whose entire essence, from start to finish, is aimed at overlooking individuality within the theoretical realm and disavowing it within the realm of practice."[20]

Against this backdrop, the difficulty that plagues Fichte's model is clear. Quite apart from the fact that, from both a theoretical and a practical-moral perspective, the arguments tend decisively toward an annihilation of the individual person, and it therefore makes no sense to speak of its irreducible recognition, two key points must be highlighted here. It is, first of all, incomprehensible how and from what source a *principium individuationis* is to be drawn and how, given the hierarchy of I-hood and person, the extrinsic determinateness of the individual can be generated at all. Secondly, however, and in conjunction with this, it is even more important to recognize that both the synthesis and the abstraction end up transforming what really matters here—the *"living and feeling self"*—into a blind spot, whereby the *singular inner perspective*, the mine-ness of the person, disappears into a dead corner of the construction. Fichte, with good reason, had initially addressed his tailor's visit to this self, only to lose sight of it (not coincidentally) in an ill-advised functionalization of the example to illuminate our "entire mental or spiritual nature."[21]

---

[17] FW I, 502. Fichte, *Introductions*, 87.
[18] FW I, 502. Fichte, *Introductions*, 87f.
[19] FW I, 505. Fichte, *Introductions*, 90.
[20] FW I, 516f. Fichte, *Introductions*, 101.
[21] FW I, 503f. Fichte, *Introductions*, 89.

In Alliance with Jacobi? On the State of the Discussion around 1800

Individuality as Foundational Feeling: Jacobi's Reaction

I have deliberately formulated the foregoing critical reflections without any consideration of Jacobi's views. But the question of how Fichte's previously cited remarks were specifically intended to secure Jacobi's approval and establish an "alliance"[22] between them has in the meantime become unavoidable. How could he have expected Jacobi to respond to his insistence on the accidental relation of individuality to I-hood and reason, an insistence that called to mind Spinoza's relation of expression between substance and mode?[23] That is to say, what reaction did he expect from a philosopher who was firmly convinced, and who had made this conviction public as early as 1789, that Spinoza's monism "can only be successfully attacked from the side of his *individuations*" (Spin: JWA 1,1, 234),[24] and who had, in both philosophical and literary texts, given expression to his substantive interest in the irreducibility of personal subjectivity?

All of the many facets of Jacobi's *Letter to Fichte* cannot and need not be discussed here. With regard to our focus on the status of the person, it will suffice to consult the crucial passage in which Jacobi delivers his stern but, given the subject matter, unsurprising response to Fichte. Here, underlining both the attractive force of the system, the logic of "quintessential philosophy," as well as the opposing critique of systems contained in his own "non-philosophy," Jacobi concretizes his allegation of nihilism in practical terms:

> Don't teach me what I know and understand how to demonstrate perhaps better than you might like, namely that if a *universally valid and rigorously scientific system* of morality is to be established, one *must* necessarily lay at its foundation that *will that wills nothing*, that *impersonal personality*, that naked *I-hood* of the I without any *self*—in a word, *pure and bare inessentialities*. For love of the secure progress of science you *must*, yea you cannot but, subject conscience (*spirit most certain*) to a living-death of *rationality*, make it *blindly* legalistic, deaf, dumb, and unfeeling. (JF: JWA 2,1, 211f.; MPW 516f.)

---

[22] See the letter from Fichte to Jacobi cited in footnote 10. See also his subsequent letter to Jacobi of April 26, 1796: "Yes, dear noble man, we are in complete agreement, and this agreement with you proves to me more than anything else that I am on the right track. You too seek all truth where I seek it: in the innermost sanctuary of our own being. But whereas you promote the revelation of the spirit *as spirit*, insofar as human speech allows, my task is to construe this spirit in the form of a system, so that it may be introduced into the schools in place of pseudo-wisdom" (JBW I,11, 102f.; Fichte, *Early Philosophical Writings*, 413).

[23] See Peter Rohs, *Johann Gottlieb Fichte*, 2nd ed. (Munich: Beck, 2007), 75.

[24] The remark is found in Supplement VI to the second edition of the *Spinoza Letters*, which addresses the differences and similarities between Spinoza and Leibniz. With regard to Spinoza, Jacobi then goes on to say, "He gave no account, however, of the inner possibility of such individual things in the absolute continuo of his unique substance; no account of their subdivision, interaction, community, or of that uniqueness, which, because of a wonderful bello omnium contra omnes present due to a fleeting individuality, engulfs all unity with and into the infinite" (JWA 1,1, 234). Not translated in MPW. With this statement, Jacobi precisely anticipates Fichte's dilemma.

It is evident, especially insofar as the concern here is with an inner self-relation in the form of conscience, that Jacobi not only rejects the structuring principle of the mere "I-hood of the I without any self," which he sees as being in conformity with the system but for this very reason also an empty intellectual abstraction. In addition, in speaking up for the "self" Jacobi also distances himself from the extrinsic determination of the individual person to the very same degree that Fichte attempts to deduce it and thereby, as we have seen, relegates the "living and feeling self" to a dead corner. It is thus crucial for an understanding of their arguments to note the homonymy of the term "person," a term for which semantic clarity can only be achieved with regard to the specific contexts in which it is used.[25] In Jacobi's case, his statements to Jean Paul prove particularly informative in this regard. In a letter from March 16, 1800, reaffirming the views presented in his letter to Fichte and clearly referring to the text from *Second Introduction to the Wissenschaftslehre* mentioned above, he writes:

> Individuality is a foundational feeling; individuality is the root of the intellect and all cognition; without individuality no substantiality, without substantiality nothing at all. I-hood as a mere equating of—nothing, as nothing, in nothing, through nothing, is an utter non-thought [...]. Pure selfhood is pure *one-and-the-same* [Derselbigkeit] without the *one* [Der].– *He* or *that* is necessarily always an individual [...]. The personality of the human being is unthinkable as a mere hovering through synthesis.[26]

Traditionally, the debate between Fichte and Jacobi has been addressed under the heading of the "atheism controversy." If we add to this designation the so-called "pantheism controversy" of the 1780s and the subsequent "theism controversy" with Schelling, then it would appear that Jacobi's primary achievement was to have initiated the religious disputes associated with classical German philosophy. Such an interpretation, however, depends on a radical circumscription of Jacobi's concerns. This is already obvious in the case of the debate with Fichte, the focus of which has by now become clear. In terms of Jacobi's own contribution, the texts attached to the *Letter to Fichte* must for this reason be treated as essential to the formulation of his position. It is no coincidence that the overarching concern of these texts, a concern that has always been central to Jacobi's project, is the figure of the "*actual person*" (see JF: JWA 2,1, 253; MPW 488; taken from the novel *Allwill*) and the corresponding criticism of a concept of "personality *without person or distinction of persons*" (vgl. JF: JWA 2,1, 256; MPW 534, taken from the novel *Woldemar*). It is a concern that also goes hand in hand with Jacobi's claim that this personal individuality, which cannot be reduced to extrinsic determinations, is inaccessible to systematic approaches. In his immediate reaction to Jacobi, Fichte responds accordingly, touching only briefly on religious matters in his letter from April 22, 1799, and the fragmentary self-clarification he includes with it. For Fichte, the most significant and enduring

---

[25] See Chapter 6 in this volume.
[26] Jacobi's letter to Jean Paul from March 16, 1800 (JBW I,12, 207f). See Oliver Koch, *Individualität als Fundamentalgefühl. Zur Metaphysik der Person bei Jacobi und Jean Paul* (Hamburg: Meiner, 2013).

consequence of their exchange stems from his recognition that, as a result of Jacobi's objections, he must once again return to the relation between *speculation and life* that he had thought to have definitively clarified.

Speculation and Life: Fichte's Defense Strategies

Fichte's goal is to defend his position. Prior to elucidating the relevant arguments in this regard, however, we need to take note of a crucial circumstance. In keeping with his disappointed hopes for Jacobi's endorsement, Fichte responds with genuine indignation, but this does not lead, as it does later in Schelling's case, to the publication of a strident pamphlet. The consequence is rather a serious re-examination and re-evaluation of his project. And in the process, the so-called "standpoint of life" that Fichte identifies with Jacobi's position (albeit in disregard of his double philosophy) is not only spared from direct criticism or even any suspicion of constituting a deficient, to say nothing of a false perspective. Fichte actually goes so far as to insist that *life* constitutes both the starting point and the end goal of the Wissenschaftslehre.

> Consequently, I hereby publicly declare what is the innermost spirit and soul of my philosophy: Man has nothing at all other than experience, and all that he arrives at, he arrives at only through experience, through life itself. All of his thinking—whether unrestrained or scientific, common or transcendental—proceeds from experience, and, in return, intends experience. Nothing has unconditioned value and meaning other than life; all remaining thinking, musing, knowing, only have value insofar as they relate in some way to the living, proceed from it, and intend to return to it.[27]

It remains to be determined whether and to what degree this assertion holds up under scrutiny. Significant in this regard is the fact that Fichte at least claims to share the convictions associated with the standpoint of life. Speculation and life do not bifurcate into two separate and incompatible worlds; rather the task of science consists precisely in capturing and presenting life "in an exhaustive manner," as Fichte puts it.[28] As noted above, Fichte had already taken a similar tack in adopting Jacobi's realism, also incorporating the latter's critique of Kant's position on things in themselves, and he maintains his adherence to it under the now dominant heading of life. Taken as a whole, this means that in the Wissenschaftslehre, Fichte pursues a significantly more

---

[27] Fichte, *Sonnenklarer Bericht an das grössere Publicum, über das eigentliche Wesen der neuesten Philosophie*, FW II, 333f. J. G. Fichte, "A Crystal Clear Report to the General Public Concerning the Actual Essence of the Newest Philosophy: An Attempt to Force the Reader to Understand," trans. John Bottermann and William Rasch, in *Philosophy of German Idealism: Fichte, Jacobi and Schelling*, ed. Ernst Behler (New York: Continuum, 1987), 47. On Fichte's position, see Günter Zöller, "Das Element aller Gewißheit. Jacobi, Kant und Fichte über den Glauben," *Fichte-Studien* 14 (1998): 1–41, and Marco Ivaldo, "Wissen und Leben. Vergewisserungen Fichtes im Anschluß an Jacobi," in *Friedrich Heinrich Jacobi. Ein Wendepunkt der geistigen Bildung der Zeit*, ed. Walter Jaeschke and Birgit Sandkaulen (Hamburg: Meiner, 2004), 53–71.

[28] Fichte, *Fragment*. Appendix to Fichte's letters to Reinhold and Jacobi from April 22, 1799 (GA III,3, 331; JWA I,12, 58ff.). Fichte, *Early Philosophical Writings*, 433.

expansive concept of transcendental philosophy than Kant. The difficulties previously mentioned and to be discussed further below arise from this approach.

Having completed this preliminary clarification, let us turn now to the specific relation between speculation and life in Fichte. A review of his relevant statements on the matter allows us to distinguish a methodological and a substantive or thematic aim.[29] From a *methodological* point of view, Fichte's primary interest is—not coincidentally—to repudiate Jacobi's assertion of nihilism by claiming that it stems from a misunderstanding of the Wissenschaftslehre. Fichte argues that the Wissenschaftslehre could only be suspected of nihilism if it claimed to produce new and real objects in pure thought, the unreality of which, however, would be obvious in this case. In fact, there can be no question of such a claim. With regard to the "standpoint of speculation," the intent is not to pass off unreal thoughts as having reality, but only to pursue the *cognition* of life in the form of a "systematic deduction,"[30] which is to say by way of its copying, reinvention, or reconstruction. "Our philosophical *thinking* has no meaning [by itself] and has not the least content. All meaning and content is to be found only in that thinking which is *thought of* in our philosophical thinking."[31] As a mere means for the cognition of life, however, the transcendental system not only lacks any genuine content. In addition, it strives toward its own abolition, inasmuch as, following the completion of the work of cognition, "the instrument can be discarded as of no further use."[32]

Fichte has chosen a bold strategy to defend himself here. Whether it is well considered, however, or even plausible, is another matter. In asserting that his philosophical system is devoid of content or meaning in itself, he not only adapts the allegation of nihilism for his own purposes, as a result of which he is also obliged to develop the doctrine of appearance of knowledge that appears later in the work.[33] Even more significantly, it is as noteworthy as it is peculiar that Fichte hopes to solve his problem by adopting precisely those epistemological procedures of science to which Jacobi objects. "We comprehend a thing only in so far as we can construct it, i.e. let it arise before us in thoughts, let it *become*"—taking recourse to *Supplement VII* of his *Spinoza Letters*, this is how Jacobi had described the basic operating principle of scientific thought in the *Letter to Fichte*. And from this he had gone on to conclude that if "a being is to become for us *a fully* comprehended object," then "we must cancel it in thought as something *objective, as standing on its own* […] in order to let it become something thoroughly *subjective,* our own creation, *a mere schema*" (JF: JWA 2,1, 201f; MPW 508).

These reflections have nothing to do with the presumption that the schema created in thought falsely makes its own claim to reality. Rather, Jacobi's critique of nihilism

---

[29] One can also identify a functional aim, that of seeking to determine the role of the philosophy that presents life *for* life itself. In this context, Fichte oscillates between purely descriptive and revisionary determinations, and in doing so also reveals his fundamental uncertainty.
[30] FW II, 354. Fichte, *A Crystal Clear Report*, 64.
[31] GA III,3, 331. Fichte, *Early Philosophical Writings*, 433.
[32] GA III,3, 331. Fichte, *Early Philosophical Writings*, 433.
[33] See Birgit Sandkaulen, "Spinoza zur Einführung. Fichtes Wissenschaftslehre von 1812," *Fichte-Studien* 30 (2006 b): 71–84.

takes issue with the obliteration of the *original reality* upon which the construction is based. That which is to be grasped through construction is inevitably nullified in its "*standing on its own*" and replaced by the schema that we have produced. For Jacobi, the problem is failing to see the hiatus that arises here, ignoring the discontinuity between the original convictions of life and what remains of them *via constructionis*, and instead relying entirely on the unreal structuring principle of an "impersonal personality," a mere "I-*hood* of the I without any *self*." It is therefore also significant that Fichte—as though he had actually failed to see the target of the objection—attempts to clarify the operations of his scientific construction with metaphors of bodies and machines.[34] To be sure, this approach foregrounds the technical aspect of the process, but at the same time it also makes clear that any insight into what Fichte explicitly refers to as the "mechanism of life"[35] is only possible by way of the dissection of life itself.

"The living body which we are copying is *ordinary, real consciousness*. Our deductions, which can only proceed step by step, represent the gradual assembly of the parts of this body. Until the entire system stands completed before us, everything which we can present is no more than a part."[36] This comment underscores once again the *methodological* aim of the system-building project, illuminating with a dangerous plasticity its status as a technical construction project of precisely the sort that Jacobi opposes. And in doing so, it also illuminates the *substantive* aim that goes along with this. With regard to content, the intent is to pursue the systematic deduction of the Wissenschaftslehre up to the point (which is also its culmination) where "*completely real ordinary thinking*" is captured and rendered transparent by way of a genetic portrayal [*Abbildung*].[37] Fichte attaches the greatest importance to the completeness of this "portrayal": "Every deviation of it from actual consciousness would be the surest proof of the fallacy of its deduction."[38]

---

[34] See FW II, 346ff.; Fichte, *A Crystal Clear Report*, 57ff., where Fichte (long after his contemporaries had moved on to organic models of thought) adduces the "mechanical artifice" of a *clock* in order to project the interrelation between part and whole in this example, along with the constructive inference from the part to the whole, onto the "fundamental system of all consciousness," in which a "quasi-mechanical connection" can be identified and which should accordingly be treated in a constructive manner. This mechanistic interpretation of life is of course also highly problematic because it makes it impossible to see how the dimension of freedom could still be thematized from *within* life. In this respect, while Fichte is being consistent when he unexpectedly places speculation and life into a relation where "*The one is impossible without the other*," going on to say that "LIFE, understood as active surrender to the mechanism [*of nature*], is impossible WITHOUT THAT ACTIVITY AND FREEDOM (*i.e. speculation*) WHICH THUS SURRENDERS ITSELF," "SPECULATION *is impossible apart from* THAT LIFE FROM WHICH IT ABSTRACTS" (GA III,3, 333; *Early Philosophical Writings*, 435). With this dichotomy of mechanism/life and freedom/speculation, however, which follows necessarily from the logic of the system, he has at the same time completely detached himself from the task of integrating "life" as it is understood and promoted by Jacobi.

[35] GA III,3, 332; Fichte, *Early Philosophical Writings*, 434. vgl. FW II, 349; Fichte, *A Crystal Clear Report*, 59f.

[36] GA III,3, 332. Fichte, *Early Philosophical Writings*, 434.

[37] GA III,3, 332. Fichte, *Early Philosophical Writings*, 434.

[38] FW II, 394. Fichte, *A Crystal Clear Report*, 95.

However, one has the impression here that Fichte, at least initially, misunderstands Jacobi on this point as well. Apparently, he not only believes that Jacobi erroneously criticized his model for claiming to be a form of "real thinking" but also that his criticisms were leveled prematurely, at a moment when the assembly of the individual parts was still *in statu nascendi*. Instead, Jacobi should have waited until the system had been completed.[39] It is in this context that one also finds Fichte's sole reference to his "philosophy of religion," the completion of which he sees as his only remaining philosophical task and which, as he announces to Schelling at this same time, he is in the process of elaborating. If, however, one adopts the "standpoint of life" that Fichte himself attributes to Jacobi, then simply meeting the criterion of completeness in the hope that the diverse, "regionally" differentiated elements can be pieced together at some later point is not nearly enough. The orientation toward life raises questions on a much deeper level. Foundational in the truest sense of the word, at issue here is the claim to a comprehensive understanding of the *constitution* of consciousness itself. But how, in following the procedures of the construction laid out here, could this claim ever be redeemed?

Neither Cajus nor Sempronius: "Actual Consciousness" in the *Crystal Clear Report*

It is telling that around 1800, in both *The Vocation of Man* and in the *Crystal Clear Report*, Fichte opts for a dialogical form of presentation. This is no coincidence, nor is it insignificant in theoretical terms. In doing so, Fichte is responding to Jacobi's provocation. The form reflects his urgent need to convince himself that he has successfully established the relations between speculation and life and thus to defend the Wissenschaftslehre as a philosophical system free of distortion and false ambition, one that enables the cognition of life. Also relevant in this context is the fact that in both texts, the part played by the lifeworldly consciousness who is to be convinced by the Wissenschaftslehre repeatedly recites lines taken directly from Jacobi. We need not examine these borrowings in detail here.[40] Considering these features of the texts, however, we would certainly be justified in expecting them to provide a full and accurate account of the self-understanding of the person that Jacobi espouses as a basis for his claim that it is inaccessible to systematic thinking.[41]

---

[39] GA III,3, 332. Fichte, *Early Philosophical Writings*, 434.
[40] See with reference to *The Vocation of Man* Jaeschke and Arndt, *Klassische Deutsche Philosophie nach Kant*, 158–61. Especially noteworthy in the *Crystal Clear Report* is Fichte's emphasis on finding versus producing in comparison with Jacobi's point regarding Spinoza in his conversation with Lessing (JWA 1,1, 28; MPW 193): "certain things admit of no explication: one must not therefore keep one's eyes shut to them, but must take them as one finds them."
[41] This accords with the fact that Jacobi is even addressed by name in the introduction to the *Crystal Clear Report*. Subsequent to the previously cited passage describing the relevance of experience and the vital relation of the Wissenschaftslehre to life, Fichte goes on to assert that "This is the tendency of my philosophy. The same is true of the tendency of the Kantian philosophy, which, at least on this point, will not disavow me; the same for Jacobi, a reformer in philosophy simultaneously with Kant, who, if he wanted to understand me, if only on this point, would raise few complaints against my system." FW II, 334; Fichte, *A Crystal Clear Report*, 47 (translation amended).

It should hardly surprise us at this point that these expectations are disappointed. Rather than delivering on his promise of completeness, Fichte instead puts his theoretical predicament on full display in both texts. The *Crystal Clear Report*, in which Fichte's argumentation is anything but crystal clear, can serve as example here.[42] At no point is he able to clarify which "actual consciousness" the Wissenschaftslehre actually refers to in order to take what is *found* in life itself and *manufacture* it for cognition by way of a genetic portrayal.[43] This is certainly not the only obscure feature of the text, but it is an essential one.

In one version, "actual consciousness" appears as a universal "fundamental consciousness." In this case, both the starting point and the end goal of the Wissenschaftslehre are formulated in complete disregard of any individual or even species-based determinations of consciousness. Instead, the focus is on a priori "fundamental determinations," that hold "for all reason" and therefore exclude as irrelevant even the classification as human.[44] Clearly, for a presentation of the Wissenschaftslehre that intends to promote it as a reconstruction fully committed to capturing the experience of human life, this starting point is as internally consistent as it is counterintuitive. Indeed, Fichte seems to withdraw here into a transcendental program à la Kant, one that strictly separates a priori and a posteriori conditions but which here is also an expression of the aporetic situation into which he has maneuvered himself by insisting that he makes no claim whatsoever to "real thinking."

In a complementary move, "actual consciousness" is reduced to categorical determinations. And to this corresponds in turn the fact that in this consciousness the evidence of "self-consciousness" is then revealed in the form of "*I-hood*," the "subject-objectivity" of which "every child who has simply stopped speaking of himself in the third person and calls himself I,"[45] has already acquired. But in order to also establish "I-hood" as the starting point for the systematic derivation of consciousness, the partner in the dialogue is informed of a circumstance that brings to light the unresolved dilemma plaguing Fichte's efforts. Whenever I "think *my self*," I have "this determined individual, the Cajus or Sempronious" in mind. Thus one arrives at the "pure I" when one "disregard[s] the particular determinations of [ones] individuality [...] and simply reflect[s] on the *convergence* of the thinker and the thing thought."[46]

Here it is definitely unclear, for one, how in the course of a reflection that has removed even the species designation "human" from the "foundational consciousness" in question so as to "construe[] the entire common consciousness of all rational beings absolutely *a priori*,"[47] one suddenly becomes concerned with concrete, named individuals. This confusion then carries over into Fichte's subsequent deliberations, in which we encounter a second version of "actual consciousness." "Certainly the I of

---

[42] On Fichte's *The Vocation of Man*, see Chapter 11 in this volume.
[43] FW II, 357f., 397f.; Fichte, *A Crystal Clear Report*, 66f., 97f.
[44] FW II, 352f. Fichte, *A Crystal Clear Report*, 62f.
[45] FW II, 362f. Fichte, *A Crystal Clear Report*, 70f.
[46] FW II, 364f. Fichte, *A Crystal Clear Report*, 71f.
[47] FW II, 379. Fichte, *A Crystal Clear Report*, 83.

actual consciousness is also particular and separate; it is one person among several people, each of whom, for himself and in the same way, calls himself I; and it is precisely to the consciousness of this personality that the Wissenschaftslehre pursues its deduction."[48] With this assertion Fichte has again exploded the Kantian framework and expanded the intended complete portrayal of life to the assertion of having deduced the specific individual. But precisely in doing so, he also draws attention to a further, truly decisive point.

It is just as unclear, after all, and with regard to both of the passages cited, exactly what we gain from Fichte's formulaic characterization of the difference between the pure and the individual I. What is the nature of the so-called "special determinations" that individualize the "I," thereby giving rise to the particular person? And most significantly, how does Fichte intend to render the *self-identity of this particular person* comprehensible, given that identity is ascribed to the idea of a self-referential "I-hood" whose pure form comes to light precisely when one abstracts from the "individuality" with which it is "indivisibly united" in "common consciousness"?[49]

In other words, if we assume that the names of Cajus or Sempronius actually designate the someone who thinks *himself*—disregarding for the moment whether "thinking" appropriately describes the activity under consideration here—then abstracting from this perspective will not give us anything we can then simply incorporate back into it. Rather, it is a case of two categorically and substantively distinct forms of self-reference, whose allegedly common denominator precisely does *not* consist in the abstract subject-object identity that results from the implosion of the reflection model of self-consciousness. If, conversely, this process of abstraction is supposed to guarantee that the Wissenschaftslehre can anchor its principle of construction in the "I-hood," then the unique *mine-ness* of Cajus or Sempronius— even if we set aside the awkward question regarding individuating factors—was never of concern at all. And from this it follows further that the claim to portray life in its entirety can only be satisfied with regard to generic determinations of reason that are totally inadequate to our concrete life experiences.

Once again, we find that the construction process ends up forcing the "living and feeling self" into a dead corner. And for this reason we are no better off if, turning to Fichte's earlier texts for support, we limit ourselves to identifying the individuating factors and simply refrain from asking whether the deduction pursued in each case is successful or turns out to be completely unworkable theoretically. Because regardless of whether the *principium individuationis* is to be located in the spatiotemporal conditions of the corporeal interactions among "I"'s (as in *Foundations of Natural Right*) or in a quasi-Leibnizian world of reason, where "determinate points of individuality"

---

[48] FW II, 382; Fichte, *A Crystal Clear Report*, 86 (translation amended). Whereby he of course underlines the difference between this end goal of the concrete I and the instance from which it is derived: "The I from which the Wissenschaftslehre proceeds is something entirely different; it is absolutely nothing more than the identity of the conscious-being and the conscious; and for this distinction one must raise oneself by abstraction above all that remains in the personality."

[49] FW II, 382. Fichte, *A Crystal Clear Report*, 86.

influence one another in predetermined ways (as in the *System of Ethics*),⁵⁰ the perspective of I-hood is always, to quote Thomas Nagel, a "view from nowhere." At best, it reveals an extrinsic determinateness that superficially separates individuals from one another, an outcome that is anticipated in the author's predilection for the rhetoric of geometric quantification in both the *Wissenschaftslehre nova methodo* and the *Crystal Clear Report*. Such a perspective, however, cannot capture how it is *for* the particular person himself, the individual, to be this "living and feeling self." This aspect of the unique being-for-myself of the person has nothing to do with empirical spatiotemporal determinations nor with a priori distributed possibilities of action, and it certainly has nothing to do with the idea of a self-identical "I-hood" that constitutes "our entire mental and spiritual nature."

Jacobi based his critique of the Wissenschaftslehre on precisely this aspect of personal existence, which is also the locus of the concrete consciousness of moral responsibility. And in order to make this point sufficiently clear, in his *Letter to Fichte* he included (among other things) the following excerpt from the novel *Allwill*: "As little as infinite space can determine the particular nature of any one body, so little can the *pure* reason *of man* constitute with its will (which is evenly good everywhere since it is *one and the same* in all men) the foundation of a particular, *differentiated* life, or impart to the *actual person* its proper individual value." (JF: JWA 2,1, 253; Anhang 3; MPW 488) Under consideration here is the dimension of "*who* one is." For Jacobi, as for Fichte, this question in no way excludes the predicative dimension of "*what* one is." What is crucial, however, is that the dimension of the "who"—already referred to by Boethius as the *individual subsistence* of the person—cannot be reduced to the "what"-dimension.⁵¹ In Fichte, the fleeting figure of the "living and feeling self," who repeatedly appears and then disappears again, is intended to capture the "who," whereas the "what"-perspective clearly dominates in the construction of the system. Before Fichte even sets out to defend himself, then, Jacobi has already blocked off any and all attempts to arrive at the "actual person" by way of scientific quantification. Personhood, as a *qualitatively* determined phenomenon, simply cannot be constructed within a system, within a "philosophy of *one* piece." It requires other, "unphilosophical" means for its presentation. We should not be surprised that Fichte's defiant attempt to capture the fullness of life in the form of a system ends aporetically.

---

⁵⁰ FW IV, 227. J. G. Fichte, *The System of Ethics: According to the Principles of the* Wissenschaftslehre, ed. and trans. Daniel Breazeale and Günter Zöller (Cambridge: Cambridge University Press, 2005), 216. The question regarding the origin of such "points" is answered in the *Wissenschaftslehre nova methodo* with the logic of determinability and determination, according to which I as an individual and a person "am a portion of the {realm of} rational being, a portion that has selected itself therefrom" (J. G. Fichte, *Wissenschaftslehre Nova Methodo*, ed. Erich Fuchs (Hamburg: Meiner, 1994), 177; J. G. Fichte, *Foundations of Transcendental Philosophy (Wissenschaftslehre) Nova Methodo (1796/99)*, ed. and trans. Daniel Breazeale (Ithaca: Cornell University Press, 1992), 351). This answer not only reduces individuality to the representation of a determinate "quantum" of a "mass" (149, 233; 457, 302), but also proves fundamentally unable to explain even this idea itself. If the mass of rational beings is thought of as a general and thus determinable quantity of reason, then precisely in this case, there is no "one" who could "single himself out" and in this way manifest himself as a determinate individual. If, on the other hand, such a singling out involves externally distinguishing the one and the other, the latter of which would also be a determinate rational being, then one has already presupposed what one is in fact trying to understand, without having provided a qualitative criterion of distinction to ground the assertion that "what is spiritual is divisible" (149; 302).

⁵¹ See Chapter 6 in this volume.

11

Fichte's *Vocation of Man*—A Convincing Response to Jacobi?

A discussion of Fichte's best-known work, his essay of 1800 on *The Vocation of Man*, strikes me as an especially promising avenue through which to approach the topic of "transcendental philosophy between metaphysics and politics."[1] It is a topic that speaks to philosophers' engagement with fundamental questions of philosophy as well as their efforts to contribute to the concrete understanding of our own lives, and combining these two arenas is precisely the ambition of Fichte's text. In a sequence of three steps, he seeks to provide us with something like a basic introduction to the "vocation of man."

The question that concerns me in the following is whether Fichte's efforts are successful and convincing. And, as might be expected given the question, I do harbor certain critical reservations in this regard. These are in no way related to the project of the "vocation of man" as such, however, which I consider to be extremely important. Thus I have no problem whatsoever with the so-called "popular philosophical" approach of the text, which "is not intended for professional philosophers," but rather seeks to address the development of "recent philosophy so far as it is useful outside the schools."[2] Fichte's desire to reach a lay audience is unquestionably sincere, and the staging of his arguments—which will constitute the focus of my analysis—plays a crucial role in this context. My primary reservation regarding the success of his efforts pertains rather to the vision of the vocation of man that he presents. This reservation is one I share with Jacobi, who went so far as to claim that Fichte's text, especially the third part, was simply unreadable.[3] I mention this, however, not as a way to *historicize* the problem in question, but rather because Jacobi objections provide a key to understanding the problem in its *systematic* significance.

---

[1] This chapter was first presented in conjunction with a conference held in honor of the philosopher Marek Siemek.
[2] Fichte, *Die Bestimmung des Menschen*, FW II, 167. J. G. Fichte, *The Vocation of Man*, trans. Peter Preuss (Indianapolis: Hackett, 1987), 1.
[3] Letter to Jean Paul from February 13, 1800: "truly, I thought I was losing my mind, I lost my ability to see and hear, and by the time I had finished the book, I was nearly unconscious." (JBW I,12, 193)

Fichte Reacts to Jacobi

The reasons why Jacobi comes into play here at all and why he must be included in the discussion are clear from the context out of which Fichte's text emerged. The *Vocation of Man* cannot be understood simply as a response to Johann Joachim Spalding's famous book of the same name, nor should it be subsumed under the general rubric of the so-called "atheism controversy," in order to then claim that it marks a turn toward something like a philosophy of religion in Fichte's thought. In fact, the text was clearly written in response to Jacobi's *Letter to Fichte* of 1799, and grasping this immediate context is crucial to any effort to evaluate it. Not least, it is noteworthy in this context that Jacobi's letter mentions none of the remonstrances of the religious orthodoxy against Fichte (which had, after all, been the immediate cause of the atheism controversy). Reduced to its essence, Jacobi's position can be summarized as follows:

First of all, we must recognize that Jacobi's pioneering book, *Concerning the Doctrine of Spinoza in Letters to Herr Moses Mendelssohn* (1785/1789), provides a key backdrop to the debate, a book whose impact on the formation of post-Kantian philosophy is every bit as profound as that of Kant's *Critique of Pure Reason* itself. Jacobi's analysis centers around three interrelated claims: (1) Spinoza's substance monism deserves admiration as the paradigm of an entirely self-contained philosophical system. (2) As a consequence of achieving the highest possible degree of systematic rigor, it is necessarily fatalistic; it excludes the free will of concrete persons. (3) Because it has achieved the highest possible degree of systematic rigor, it is impossible to refute Spinoza's philosophy; it can only be contradicted—freedom can only be recovered by way of a voluntary leap out of the system. There cannot be a *system of freedom*.

On the basis of this analysis, we can summarize the challenge posed to the *Wissenschaftslehre* by Jacobi's critique in three points: (1) Fichte's *Wissenschaftslehre* presents us with an instance of a "veritable *system* of reason" (JF: JWA 2,1, 200; MPW 507). This distinguishes Fichte's philosophy from that of Kant and it leads Jacobi to express his great admiration for Fichte. (2) At the level of systematic philosophy, Fichte's philosophy appears as a competitor to that of Spinoza. It does not, however, *overcome* Spinoza's metaphysics; rather, his substance monism is transformed into a monism of the I, a constructivism leading to a "whole" that is "just a deed = deed" (JF: JWA 2,1, 201; MPW 507). (3) This simultaneously repeats and exacerbates the problem. Under the conditions of the transcendental-philosophical construction, not only the freedom of the concrete person disappears but also reality in its entirety, including that of the I himself. Fichte's idealism leads to nihilism.

Fichte was shocked by this assessment. He had expected his efforts to receive an unequivocal endorsement from Jacobi, whom he considered to be the "deepest thinker of our time," placing him "high above Kant."[4] Years later, he is still searching for a way to respond to Jacobi's *Letter*—*The Vocation of Man* represents only the first attempt to craft a response that will refute Jacobi's objections. Even if we leave aside

---

[4] See Fichte's letter to Reinhold from January 8, 1800 (in Walter Jaeschke, ed., *Transzendentalphilosophie und Spekulation. Der Streit um die Gestalt einer ersten Philosophie (1799–1807). Quellenband*, Philosophisch-literarische Streitsachen 2.1 (Hamburg: Meiner, 1993), 65).

for the moment the large number of literal borrowings from Jacobi's writings, this context explains, firstly, the nature and sequence of the first three sections of the text. Under the headings of "Doubt," "Knowledge," and "Belief,"[5] Fichte pursues a course of reflection that begins with Spinoza's metaphysical naturalism before proceeding to the idealism of the Wissenschaftslehre and concluding with the practical realism of the lifeworld.

Secondly, it provides the concrete point of reference for the rhetorical staging of the three sections. Fichte introduces a figure by the name of "I" as the representative of the reader, that is to say Jacobi, as a result of which the reflections unfold from a *first-person perspective*. From this perspective, the "I" considers the advantages and disadvantages of both *Spinozan naturalism and the Wissenschaftslehre* for the concrete conduct of life, in other words, in terms of whether or not they provide a convincing answer to questions about ourselves and the world. As the reader follows the progress of the argument, which of course culminates in a conclusive victory for the Wissenschaftslehre, she can and should use this "I" as a point of reference. If his questions are answered satisfactorily, then Fichte has achieved his goal.[6] As I have already suggested, I will take this staging of the argument very seriously in the following analysis.

Doubt—Spinoza's System and the Problem of Freedom

We come now to Fichte's first section. One should not, of course, expect an *ad verbum* debate with Spinoza, who is never even mentioned by name. In order to develop his own view of the "vocation of man" and thereby achieve clarity regarding himself and his place in the world and cease, the "I" does not retreat into the library to study the canon. Rather, on the basis of his own independent reflection, he arrives at an initial position, which, albeit with some differences in the details, is essentially Spinozan in nature. This is also part of the message. Following Jacobi's line of argument, Fichte seems to be saying that whenever we begin to think seriously, we will initially adopt a Spinozan point of view.

Let us thus consider the matter from this perspective of the "I." Here the aim is not to reconstruct Spinoza's *Ethics* down to the last detail, but to clarify, first, *how* and *why* one arrives at such a position, and, secondly, *what* it means for us to live in a universe conceived along Spinozan lines. From this perspective, the starting point of reflection is the inverse of that found in Spinoza. Instead of moving from principle to that which is grounded, from all-encompassing substance to the individual, the "I" begins with the

---

[5] Preuss translates this section of Fichte's work with "faith," but I have opted for "belief" because it better captures Fichte's own position and the influence of Jacobi. See also Daniel Breazeale's translation in J. G. Fichte, *Foundation of the Entire Wissenschaftslehre and Related Writings (1794-1795)*, ed. and trans. Daniel Breazeale (Oxford: Oxford University Press, 2021), 357.

[6] The general degree to which Fichte operates here with literal borrowings from Jacobi's texts, not least from his *Spinoza Letters*, is deserving of a detailed study in itself. See some of Fichte's borrowings in Walter Jaeschke and Andreas Arndt, *Die Klassische Deutsche Philosophie nach Kant. Systeme der reinen Vernunft und ihre Kritik 1785-1845* (Munich: Beck, 2012), 158–61.

concrete perception of the individual, in order to ascertain the principle that grounds it and then to consider the consequences thereof for his practical self-understanding. Fichte, in other words, inserts something like an epistemological section prior to presenting the Spinozan approach to ontology. Or, to put it still more precisely: Fichte makes explicit that the starting point of all philosophical worldviews is to be found in our deeply rooted *need for explanation*. We try to make sense of the particular phenomena of our experience and find that we have understood them when we can trace them back to a sufficient ground. In fact, it is this rational "explanation according to the principle of sufficient reason" that drives the "I" forward in his deliberations and that he becomes consciously aware of as constituting the maxim of his reflections.[7]

Whether such a reconstruction of Spinoza's position is actually "permissible" may be a matter of debate. For my part, I do not see any difficulties here. Jacobi had already proceeded in this fashion in his own reconstruction of Spinoza, notably placing the rational operations associated with the principle of sufficient reason at the center of the discussion. And as far as Fichte is concerned, he certainly does not intend to damage the opposing system with this exposition. After all, he lets the "I" operate according to the "principle of sufficient reason" in the second part of the text as well. This corresponds to the *Wissenschaftslehre nova methodo,* according to which the labor of philosophy arises precisely from the effort to connect the "idea of a ground or foundation" to a prior "fact" of experience.[8] The difference between the two systems is thus not to be found at the level of this reason-seeking approach as such, but rather in the question of which explanatory reason is sought for which facts.

Against this backdrop, it is significant that the "I" begins his reflections with a view toward the concrete environment—he turns to plants, trees, and animals and their respective characteristics.[9] Before directing his attention inward, in other words, before he himself as "factum," as concrete I, becomes an object of investigation, he directs his gaze *intentione recta* away from himself and onto the world. In previous descriptions, Fichte had always zealously referred to such an attitude as *dogmatic*. In its more harmless variant, dogmatism described for Fichte our everyday realist conviction that what we perceive most certainly exists. But Fichte also identified a more pernicious philosophical variant of "dogmatism," which in this case referred to a theory that materialistically derives our consciousness from the conditions of the world and thereby makes consciousness into something dependent, something entirely unfree. Fichte also cast the battle between systems in similar terms—at least *up until this point*—as a conflict between *dogmatism* and *idealism*. According to this model, Spinoza appeared as a dogmatist who takes being as his starting point rather than consciousness. And with this argument Fichte denied Spinoza's *Ethics* any conception of freedom whatsoever.

---

[7] FW II, 186. Fichte, *Vocation,* 16.
[8] J. G. Fichte, *Wissenschaftslehre Nova Methodo,* ed. Erich Fuchs (Hamburg: Meiner, 1994), 12ff. J. G. Fichte, *Foundations of Transcendental Philosophy (Wissenschaftslehre) Nova Methodo (1796/99),* ed. and trans. Daniel Breazeale (Ithaca: Cornell University Press, 1992), 88ff.
[9] FW II, 171. Fichte, *Vocation,* 5.

It seems to be more than a mere coincidence that the expression "dogmatism" is no longer used in *The Vocation of Man*. Fichte's earlier accounts of Spinoza, as found, for example, in the *First Introduction to the Wissenschaftslehre* of 1797, had presented a completely misguided caricature of Spinoza's philosophy, accusing it of turning consciousness into a determinate "product of things" without, however, having been able to explain how a consciousness could ever originate from matter.[10] Spinoza's actual position has of course nothing to do with this crude portrayal, and the idealist gesture with which Fichte believed he could triumph over a "consistent dogmatism, which simultaneously turns into materialism" was anything but convincing.[11] In other words, Fichte seems to have realized in the interim that things were more complicated than he had assumed, and that he would do well to strive for a level of sophistication in his argumentation that at least *approximates* that of his opponent.

The progress Fichte has made in conceptualizing the opposing system finds concrete embodiment in the figure of the "I." Considering first the phenomena of the external world, he establishes for himself that the things we perceive in nature are precisely determined by certain properties. We further observe that these properties change and that, taken together, this series of new states forms an ordered sequence: "I enter into the unbroken chain of appearances, since each link is determined by the one preceding it and determines the one following it."[12] Establishing that all of nature is subject to such strict sequentiality, however, is not yet an adequate explanation of phenomena. The question here is what brings about the change in states.[13] In a second step, the "I" therefore assumes the operation of an active principle that underlies the change of appearances. There must be a vital force in nature, a "particular, self-active, original force of nature,"[14] which is manifest in a unique way in all possible phenomena and expresses itself in accordance with the specific context in which it appears.

With this consideration, which interweaves the "horizontal" chain of phenomena with the "vertical" vector of a principle of force, the "I" does in fact illuminate an essential structural feature of Spinozan monism. I mention this point in order to underscore my opinion that the introduction of a concept of force here is not an extraneous addition. Spinoza, after all, defines divine substance as *natura naturans*, as

---

[10] FW I, 433ff. J. G. Fichte, *Introductions to the Wissenschaftslehre and Other Writings (1797–1800)*, ed. and trans. Daniel Breazeale (Indianapolis: Hackett, 1994), 18ff.

[11] FW I, 437. Fichte, *Introductions*, 23. In addition to causing one to wonder whether Fichte had really even read the *Ethics* carefully and in its entirety, passages such as these also raise the question of how intensively he had engaged by this point with the Spinoza interpretation of Jacobi, who certainly cannot be accused of such a "materialist" misreading. On the contrary, in the context of his fatalism allegation in the *Spinoza Letters*, Jacobi had created a fictitious dialogue in which the following lines are spoken by Spinoza himself: "As regards fatalism, I disavow it only to the extent that it has been made to rest on materialism, or on the absurd opinion that thought is only a modification of extension, like fire and light, etc.; whereas it is just as impossible for thought to derive from extension, as for extension, from thought." (Spin: JWA 1,1, 79; MPW 212)

[12] FW II, 174. Fichte, *Vocation*, 7.

[13] FW II, 175. Fichte, *Vocation*, 8.

[14] FW II, 177. Fichte, *Vocation*, 9.

an originally active principle, to precisely the same extent that he grasps the essence of substance as *potentia*, as an original vital energy that operates in an accordingly modified form in all individual things.[15]

The key implication of this *metaphysical naturalism*, however, becomes apparent when one integrates the human being into the force field of nature. It is clear that this human being can never fall out of nature. In contrast with the previously mentioned "dogmatic" primitive materialism, however, acknowledging this no longer means deriving human consciousness from matter and thereby robbing it of any independence whatsoever. Rather, the "I" considers the possibility that the one force of nature presents itself in the guise of many different forces. One must assume that there is a "thinking force" in nature that is just as original as vegetal and animal forces,[16] a force specific to humans as a species that comes together in an ensemble of "form, peculiar movement, and thought" to constitute an "anthropogenic force," which expresses itself individually in each individual.[17] From this it follows that one can plausibly explain the consciousness of each individual. Figuratively speaking, it functions as something like an energy source, one that operates in accordance with the conditions of its particular environment but by no means arises as a product of that environment.

From an epistemological perspective, the "I" has thus arrived at Spinoza's explosive claim that mind and body, consciousness and matter, do not stand in a causal relation to one another. But in addition, something crucial has also been achieved in practical terms. It has now been established, again by adopting Spinoza's theory, that we are entirely justified in assuming that we are not wholly determined by external circumstances. Starting from an awareness of the force operating within us, we form the idea of an ethics and, as a consequence, the faculty of conscience with its entire range of associated moral feelings, which provide the standards we use to evaluate our actions.[18] In making all this clear in his role as a proxy for the reader, the "I" also reveals that what Fichte had previously so triumphantly described as "dogmatism" and dismissed as absurd no longer plays any role here.

By the same token, however, we must now also take seriously what occurs in a dramatic turn at the culmination of this course of reflection. At the moment he steps back to assess the results of his efforts, the "I" is overcome with "anguish," "revulsion," and "horror"—his understanding has been intellectually satisfied but his heart

---

[15] The possibility cannot be ruled out that Fichte's new portrayal of Spinoza owes its inspiration to Herder, whose *God. Some Conversations* had first appeared in 1787 and had recently been republished in a revised second edition in 1800. Herder had initially introduced the concept of force in order to counter Spinoza, more specifically, to counter the alleged "Cartesian error" in his conception of matter, and then, following Jacobi's vehement protest (see his critique of Herder and the corresponding comments on Spinoza's concept of *potentia* in Supplements V and VI to the 1789 edition of the *Spinoza Letters*), had attributed it to Spinoza himself. Fichte's appropriation of this version shows, however, that he is no more convinced than Jacobi is by Herder's claim that a consideration of the concept of force can simultaneously lead to the resolution of the problem of freedom. It is thus all the more striking to see what ultimately transpires in the third book of *The Vocation of Man*.

[16] FW II, 180. Fichte, *Vocation*, 12.

[17] FW II, 181. Fichte, *Vocation*, 12.

[18] FW II, 188. Fichte, *Vocation*, 18.

bleeds.[19] Although everything appears to be in perfect order, he has no wish to live in this natural universe and thus finds himself torn between its opposing theoretical and practical interests. What the "I" is missing is *freedom*. And crucially, he is now in a position to state very precisely what is meant by the lack of freedom in this context. By this advanced stage in his reflections, he has already come to the conclusion that he is not a product of external things. At the same time, he has understood that he has at his disposal an independent power allowing him to align his actions with ethical maxims. Literally the only thing missing is the possibility of *ascribing its actions to himself personally*. The concepts of guilt and merit only retain their relevance with regard to "positive law."[20]

It is essential for the remaining discussion to consider this conclusion: A person is free if he can be held *personally responsible for his actions*, whether good or bad, and this presupposes an actor who can direct his will toward self-determined ends.[21] There is in fact no such subject of action in Spinozan monism, however, and precisely this shortcoming formed the basis of Jacobi's main objection to Spinoza's philosophy. For Spinoza, the agency of each individual is a modification of the divine potency. It can be heightened through insight into the interrelations of nature or weakened through ignorance thereof; there can be no question, however, of an authorial subject who intentionally takes the initiative in action. Spinoza literally describes the idea of acting according to a purpose, of a *causa finalis*, as the most serious illusion we can have regarding ourselves and our place in the world.

Knowledge—Theoretical Idealism and Nihilism

The exact nature of the challenge has now become clear. First, we can see that the straightforward juxtaposition of "dogmatism" and "idealism," of determinism and freedom, fails to do justice to the matter under consideration. In Spinoza's monism as well, there is a concept of freedom, the realization of which is the goal of the entire *Ethics*. Consequently, everything depends on the precise determination, that is, on the precise concept of freedom that is to be promoted. Second, it is at least as important to note that Fichte has introduced in the guise of the "I" a concrete authority whose judgment is of decisive significance. After all, who else would be qualified to make decisions that pertain to the arena of practice? Depersonalized arguments regarding the coherence and stringency of a theory are insufficient in such cases, as Jacobi had stressed from the beginning. We must take seriously the fact that the "I" reacts with "horror" to something which his understanding presents to him as rationally compelling. The heart, the innermost core of the person, must also receive its due. For the concept of freedom this means that it must account for the fundamental self-understanding of the "I"—the understanding that one is personally responsible for one's actions, something of which the "I" becomes truly aware in the moment

---

[19] FW II, 190. Fichte, *Vocation*, 19.
[20] FW II, 189. Fichte, *Vocation*, 18.
[21] FW II, 192ff. Fichte, *Vocation*, 21ff.

where—on the basis of a rational explication—he recognizes the loss of self entailed in conceiving it as a modified expression of the universal force field of nature.

From this we can see, thirdly, how the matter must be further developed. If the Wissenschaftslehre intends to emerge victorious, then Fichte will have to persuade the "I" that his philosophy can do justice to the self-understanding of concrete persons. And he must combine this with convincing evidence that he has resolved the conflict that has arisen between the heart and the understanding. Is he successful in this effort?

The answer to this question is to be found in the third section of the text. With regard to the second section, it is enough for now to note the purely negative result—the initial attempt to persuade the "I" to embrace the Wissenschaftslehre as a welcome solution has failed dramatically. Fichte of course knows this himself; after all, he staged the failure. The unfortunate "I" is confronted with an idealist theory that addresses exclusively epistemological questions and mistakes the productive dissolution of reality into processes of consciousness for the freedom being demanded.[22]

However, the "I" does not fall into the annihilatory idealist machinery of knowledge simply as a result of his own independent reflections. A nocturnal spirit comes to his "assistance," leading him, by way of deceitful counsel, to the conclusion that he is free when all of existence, both that of the world and that of the "I" himself, disappears into the empty image-world of knowledge. "True, you liberate me: you absolve me of all dependence by transforming me and everything around me on which I might be dependent into nothing. You do away with necessity by doing away with and annihilating all being."[23] Not only has the critical question originally posed by the "I" fallen out of view here. For the alleged "freedom" that results from this complete renunciation of his most heartfelt aspiration he must also pay the price of nihilism.

In presenting this extraordinarily dramatic scenario, Fichte clearly intends to address directly Jacobi's claim that idealism and nihilism amount to the same thing. In doing so, however, Fichte operates strategically. In the second section on "knowledge," he had presented only one half, namely the *theoretical* half of his Wissenschaftslehre. Fichte wants to convey the point here that only when one considers this half in isolation does the impression of nihilism arise, and he makes the same argument in a private reaction to Jacobi's *Letter*. According to Fichte, Jacobi failed to consider the practical part of the Wissenschaftslehre at all. The planned solution to the problem in the form of the practical section is thus still pending. At this point, however, Fichte's loses the thread of his argument, and in a manner that proves quite revealing, as will presently become clear.

Belief—Practical Realism and Reason's Blueprint for the World

Fichte certainly faces a formidable challenge. In the second section, he first de facto transformed the systems controversy back into the old opposition between "dogmatism" and "idealism" and then intensified it in the form of the opposition

---

[22] FW II, 240ff. Fichte, *Vocation*, 59ff.
[23] FW II, 240. Fichte, *Vocation*, 60.

between *dogmatism* and *nihilism*. Therefore, the primary and most pressing objective of the Wissenschaftslehre must now consist in repairing the loss of reality brought about by knowledge. With emphatic recourse to the "organ" of *belief*, with which Fichte again alludes to Jacobi, the *practical* section of the Wissenschaftslehre then in fact takes up this proof. To the extent that we act, the reality that has been dissolved in knowledge recovers its existence—this is the lesson that the "I" learns to his relief, now speaking without the assistance of the nocturnal spirit and thus entirely in the voice of Fichte.

This reality is not without its peculiarities, however. It is true that Fichte (in the guise of the "I") claims to leave the image-world of knowledge and return to the "standpoint of natural thought."[24] However, this is only a claim. In truth, Fichte effects a change in perspective here that completely transforms the "natural," which is to say the realist mindset of the "I." As we saw, the "I," in keeping with this mindset, began his deliberations with the observation of plants, trees, and animals and used this as the basis for his subsequent reflections. But there is no longer any talk of *this* world. It has disappeared for good, because in the meantime the "I" has taken the place of this world—its perspective on action now constitutes the starting point of reflection.

With this replacement of the world with the "I," undertaken in the name of "practical reason,"[25] Fichte recapitulates in the *Vocation of Man* a point that had already figured as a central lesson in the *Foundation of the Entire Wissenschaftslehre*. Practical idealism provides the guarantee of *realism*, insofar as both the certainty of our own existence and that of the world as well as the conviction that our actions are free arise from one and the same source. We are neither subjugated to nature nor, conversely, are we condemned to annihilate all reality in knowledge. Rather, we *create reality* in shaping the world according to the purposes of our will. Of course, in doing so we are bound to confront a certain physical resistance. What is crucial, however, is that it is only from the perspective of our practical interests that such obstacles can even come into view, and thus they have no relevance at all for the *idea* of freedom.

"My world is the object and sphere of my duties and absolutely nothing else."[26] By way of this idealist conception of a world that is to become actual through action, the "I" otherwise known as Fichte not only assures himself of its environment and the presence of other "I's."[27] He also elevates himself to the status of protagonist in a monumental historical-philosophical drama—featuring "the absolute demand for a better world,"[28] which involves tasks ranging from the technological transformation of nature to the moral and political emancipation of all humanity to the establishment of a "supernatural" world of reason where sensuous conditions no longer obtain.[29]

Allow me, however, to interrupt this virtuous flight of fancy to remind us of the "I" who had previously been seized by doubts regarding his vocation and torn between theoretical and practical interests. Have the problems of this "I" really been solved? Or has Fichte rather forgotten something essential when he has the "I"—in

---

[24] FW II, 253. Fichte, *Vocation*, 71.
[25] FW II, 263. Fichte, *Vocation*, 79.
[26] FW II, 261. Fichte, *Vocation*, 77.
[27] FW II, 259ff. Fichte, *Vocation*, 76f.
[28] FW II, 265. Fichte, *Vocation*, 81.
[29] FW 11, 281ff. Fichte, *Vocation*, 93ff.

symbiotic identification with Fichte himself—join in this upwelling of enthusiasm? He has indeed. Having foregrounded the problem of nihilism and then subsequently attempted to regain reality by conceiving the world in terms of action, Fichte now appears to have *completely lost sight of* the original problem facing the "I."

This point is crucial, and in order to characterize it with the greatest possible precision, it will be helpful to first reconsider it from a different angle. If the "I" had actually complained previously about losing all independence whatsoever in the naturalistic system, then it would have been an interesting experiment to reconfigure the problem in idealist terms and attempt to establish that we produce the world in knowledge according to the laws of knowledge. One could have then also considered whether, even after the nihilistic failure of this experiment, the solution of practical realism might prove persuasive, that is, the idea that we create the world not in knowledge but practically, according to the laws of action. In the process, one would very soon come across the kinds of problems that Schelling and Hegel identified in their criticisms of Fichte. Their attack on the subject-centeredness of Fichte's Wissenschaftslehre is after all partly grounded in the idea that there can be no talk of a successful recuperation of reality as long as that reality can only be considered secure with regard to the "sphere of my duties." And beyond that: in considering Fichte's transition to his late philosophy, we can see that he himself felt that his previous efforts to immunize himself against nihilism were clearly in need of revision.[30]

I will not pursue this line of argument any further here, because the real crux of the matter lies elsewhere. More specifically, as a consequence of outlining the constellation of problems described above, it also becomes clear that over the course of *The Vocation of Man* a theoretical stance has found its way into the discussion that was entirely absent from the "I's" original confrontation with Spinozan monism. Rather than maintaining his focus on Jacobi's objections, first to Spinoza and then to his own approach, Fichte retreats into a theoretical position in which—taking Kant's Copernican revolution as his inspiration—he turns to the question of the relative primacy of subject versus object. But the question whether an object stands opposite to the subject and which side of the dyad determines the other played no role whatsoever in the first part of *The Vocation of Man*. The question was a completely different one and had a completely different structure. There, in the name of his consciousness of freedom, the "I" objected to the loss of *himself, his personal, concrete responsibility for his actions,* which would be the consequence if it were indeed nothing more than a small part of the great whole of living nature, albeit one in possession of its own power.

In other words, regardless of the general theoretical and practical aims of the Wissenschaftslehre, if Fichte truly wanted to vanquish Spinoza's metaphysical naturalism and convince Jacobi, then he would have to respond to *this specific* objection. In his presentation of practical reason at the latest, Fichte would have to have shown

---

[30] Paradoxically, this ultimately even leads to an attempt to ground the Wissenschaftslehre in the thought of an absolute being, meaning that he takes his cue from Spinoza himself in the form of an indispensable minimal ontology. It is not surprising in this context that Fichte's late philosophy continues to be plagued by the structural problems that I discuss here with regard to the *Vocation of Man* and that pertain to the status of the *individual self*.

that in transforming Spinoza's nature into the world posited by the subject, he can also account for the *self-understanding of irreducibly concrete persons*. Fichte, however, does not simply neglect this problem. On the contrary, in a manner that is both unexpected and yet also not so surprising, his high-minded reflections develop a dynamic of their own, which ultimately leads to a conception of the world of reason that is essentially identical to that of Spinoza himself.

The "I" has apparently failed to notice what is happening here on a structural level and now of course voices no objections to the consequences. At this point, he is happy to repeat the deliberations that had previously led him to Spinoza's metaphysical naturalism under the new auspices of a practical Wissenschaftslehre. This means that what was previously assumed—based on the observation of natural phenomena—to be the metaphysicum of a *general force of nature* is now replaced—based on the experience of the finite will—by the *will of a universal reason*. This eternal will is even elevated to the status of a divine will, with the result that the "I's" effort to achieve self-understanding is literally transformed into a prayer addressed to the "creator of the world."[31] And yet, it is easy to see that in this conflation of "deed" and "product" we are presented with nothing other than a version of the *absolute F/Act* [Tathandlung], in other words, of the principle of absolute I-hood, which Fichte had placed at the forefront of the Wissenschaftslehre and thereby clearly indicated his indebtedness to Spinoza's model of efficacious substance.[32]

Once we have identified this monistic structural element, however, the consequences for the finite "I" very quickly become apparent. And in fact the "I" readily agrees that he must "adapt" to the "order of the spiritual world"; he is, after all, "only a link in its chain." Fittingly, he also refers shortly thereafter to a "higher world plan," in the realization of which he intends to participate as "one of the instruments of the purpose of reason." And of course this self-description is followed directly with the ardent insistence that "my breast is closed to annoyance over personal affronts and offenses and to the promotion of personal merit; for my whole personality has long gone and disappeared in the contemplation of the goal."[33] Rather than actually addressing Jacobi's objection, Fichte repeats what he has written elsewhere, in the *Second Introduction to the Wissenschaftslehre*, for example: "the only thing that exists in itself is reason, and individuality is something merely accidental. Reason is the end and personality is the means; the latter is merely a particular expression of reason, one that must increasingly be absorbed into the universal form of the same. For the *Wissenschaftslehre*, reason alone is eternal, whereas individuality must ceaselessly die off."[34]

---

[31] FW II, 303. Fichte, *Vocation*, 110.

[32] FW II, 297. Fichte, *Vocation*, 106. The religio-philosophical transcending of his position in these passages, which has typically been read as a response on the part of Fichte to the atheism controversy, is thus more accurately interpreted as a rhetorical gesture intended to disguise the intellectual scaffolding of the Wissenschaftslehre but which, in doing so, also brings its structural affinity to Spinoza's monism more clearly into view.

[33] FW II, 298–312. Fichte, *Vocation*, 107–18.

[34] FW I, 505. Fichte, *Introductions*, 90.

But didn't the "I" argue passionately at the end of the first section for the recognition of his *personal* interests and against the conception that he was nothing more than a link in the universal order? That may be so; by this point, however, the "heart" has long since been dismissed as irrelevant. All that matters now is the contemplative "eye," which remains "cold and untouched" as it observes the world, because it knows that "the plan of the eternal world" will ensure that everything is for the best.[35] But perhaps we can again come to Fichte's aid here? Doesn't it make a difference whether the "I" understands himself as a moment in an all-encompassing nature, or as a moment in the world plan of reason, in the sense that in the first case he justifiably reclaims his personal freedom of action but in the second is happy to serve as a mere "instrument"? It is significant with regard to the difficulty that has emerged that Fichte himself does not even bother to consider this possibility. On the contrary—by the end he has repressed both the complaints of the "I" and his own reconstruction of Spinozan monism so completely that one can only marvel at what he comes up with by way of a conclusion.

Far from using the plan of reason to mount an attack on metaphysical naturalism, the "I" instead brings things to a close with a paean to the universe—to "the eternal stream of life and power and deeds" that flows through all of living nature and unifying all living things.

> Here it flows through my veins and muscles as self-producing, self-forming matter, and outside of me deposits its bounty in trees, plants, and grass. Formative life flows as one continuous stream, drop by drop, in all forms and wherever my eye can follow it. And it looks at me differently from every point of the universe, as the same force through which in secret darkness it forms my own body …. Everything which moves follows this general trait, this single principle of all movement, which conducts the harmonious tremor from one end of the universe to the other: the animal without freedom; I, from whom movement originates in the visible world without thereby having its source in me, with freedom.[36]

This hymn to universal life presents itself here as if it were a completely new insight. And to be sure, when the "I" assures us at this point that "the dead inert mass, which was only stuffing of space, has disappeared,"[37] then we can only congratulate him on his discovery. However, we also cannot fail to notice the *literal repetitions* from the first section that appear here, even though they are not clearly identified as such. In referring to the "dead inert mass" of matter, Fichte not only de facto falls back on his earlier attack on Spinoza's dogmatism, thus negating the more sophisticated characterization documented in the first part of the text. At this point, he even goes so far as to credit *idealism* alone with having developed the conception of an inherently living and dynamic nature.

---

[35] FW II, 311f. Fichte, *Vocation*, 117.
[36] FW II, 315f. Fichte, *Vocation*, 120f.
[37] FW II, 315. Fichte, *Vocation*, 120.

A Brief Synopsis

I come now to my conclusion. Under consideration was the question whether Fichte's *Vocation of Man* offers a compelling account of the human lifeworld. I had indicated in advance that I have critical reservations in this regard, reservations which I share with Jacobi. Having now considered the text in some detail, it should be clear where the problem lies. I would like to close by highlighting three points. First, I find it utterly baffling that Fichte could have ever imagined Jacobi being persuaded by this text in particular. To be sure, at the beginning he appears to have understood that Jacobi objects to Spinoza's monism on the basis of the consciousness of freedom possessed by irreducibly concrete persons. But the more he becomes involved with the thematics of the Wissenschaftslehre and thereby struggles with the allegation of nihilism, the more his argumentation develops its own dynamic, ultimately leading him to a position identical to the one for which Jacobi had criticized the *Wissenschaftslehre* in the *Letter to Fichte*—that it does not resolve the problems that arise with Spinoza's metaphysics but instead structurally reproduces them and, as a result of the constructivist approach, actually ends up exacerbating them.

Second, the source that feeds Fichte's negative prejudice against the individual is equally mysterious to me. Clearly, the internal dynamic of the text (driven more unconsciously than consciously) develops out of this negative view, which ultimately leads to a situation in which the depersonalized "I" happily accepts his role as a mere instrument of universal reason, convinced that it is only in this role that he can be a morally and politically responsible being. The difficulties are intensified here by the fact that with such a conception, Fichte actually goes further than Spinoza, who, after all, was willing to grant to each individual mode a singular, eternally inalienable essence. We should note, moreover, that this problem is not limited to Fichte—it can be found in Hegel and Schelling as well. But whence and why the suspicion that the individual, to the extent that it is not assimilated and integrated into the whole (of nature, reason, the state, spirit) will be a source of egoism, anarchy, and amorality? Because it is a question that interests me on a substantive level, I have been thinking about this puzzle for some time, and I have begun to wonder whether the source is perhaps to be located outside of philosophy, in mental and cultural dispositions, for example in the core values of Protestantism.

My third point turns the diagnosis of this negative prejudice against the individual into a positive claim. What I share with Jacobi and would like to offer up for discussion is the systematically relevant conviction that this suspicion and consequent marginalization of the individual are ultimately unproductive. Whether our concern is metaphysics or politics, we simply cannot manage without the participant perspective manifest in the intentional consciousness of freedom possessed by concrete persons. It may be the case that one cannot simply presuppose this consciousness, that it must be discovered, or as Jacobi says, "disclosed." Insofar as Fichte's text inspires debate on this subject, it proves to be not only important but also extremely topical.[38]

---

[38] And in contributing to this debate, I hope I have argued at least partly in the spirit of Marek Siemek, who himself offered a series of extraordinarily interesting reflections on the "individual-mine-ness." See Marek J. Siemek, *Von Marx zu Hegel. Zum sozialpolitischen Verständnis der Moderne* (Würzburg: Königshausen & Neumann, 2002), 106.

12

This Individual and No Other? On the Individuality of the Person in Schelling's *Freedom Essay*

Schelling's Personalist Turn

Those philosophers engaged in contemporary debates about personhood have often struggled to find pertinent reflections on the topic in the texts of classical German philosophy. Schelling's work constitutes an exception in this regard, thus offering what seems to be yet another example of his unique feel for the significance of new philosophical problems. To be sure, neither the person nor "personality" (Schelling's preferred term) occupies a central position in his *Philosophical Investigations into the Essence of Human Freedom*. As the title indicates, that position is held by freedom. The concept of the person, however, is clearly of crucial importance in this context. After all, as Schelling explains on the basis of his differentiation between a "formal" and the "real and vital" concept of freedom, universal entities, principles, or laws do not act. Rather, the agents of any actions that are free and for which they thus can be held responsible are always persons; this applies just as much to God as it does to humans.[1]

With this insight, Schelling at least appears to leave his previous philosophy behind. He had, to be sure, been committed from the beginning to the "alpha and omega" of freedom but had only ever attributed a decidedly negative role to personhood.[2] Instead of serving as the prerequisite for freedom, it was cast instead as an impediment to it— the consciousness that persons have of themselves was an indication of their finitude, their empirical entanglement in the world of objects. According to this account, the concept of the person was a concept of theoretical philosophy which, in the context of the absolute freedom of the unconditioned, was simply meaningless and which, on a practical level, one must strive to overcome. The claim that we must actively work toward the "destruction of our personality," in other words, corresponded to the view

---

[1] Schelling, *Philosophische Untersuchungen über das Wesen der menschlichen Freiheit und die damit zusammenhängenden Gegenstände*, SW VII, 352, 394f. F. W. J. Schelling, *Philosophical Investigations into the Essence of Human Freedom*, trans. Jeff Love and Johannes Schmidt (Albany: State University of New York Press, 2006), 23, 58f.

[2] See esp. Schelling's letter to Hegel from February 4, 1795, written in the context of his essay *Of the I as Principle of Philosophy, or On the Unconditional in Human Knowledge*: G. W. F. Hegel, *The Letters*, trans. Clark Butler and Christiane Seiler (Bloomington: Indiana University Press, 1984), 32f.

that to understand absolute freedom as personal was simply to reveal one's attachment to obsolete orthodox prejudices.

By the time of the *Freedom Essay* however, things read very differently. Linking the concept of the person to the constellation of problems associated with freedom leads to a significant shift. What was previously described from a theoretical perspective as a deficiency now becomes the explicit condition of all practice, the conception of which has also changed, as can be seen not least in Schelling's transformation of the absolute into a personal God. Indeed, in his role as the "supreme personality," this God represents the very epitome of personhood. On the other hand, to speak of God as an "impersonal being" is now denounced as evidence of glaring philosophical defects and associated with the inadequacy of Fichte's and Spinoza's positions.[3] In making such assertions, however, Schelling is merely redirecting attention away from a problem that is just as relevant to his own new position as his previous conception was indebted to Spinoza and Fichte.

This is not the place to discuss the reasons for Schelling's change of heart. It should be noted, however, that his new approach would have been unthinkable without the influence of Jacobi. Not only had Jacobi developed his prominent critiques of Spinoza's and Fichte's systems from the start as a defense of personal freedom, characterizing both the activity of absolute substance and that of the absolute I as nothing more than a system-conforming "actuosity or agility" (JF: JWA 2,1 236; MPW 531), which unjustifiably usurps the expression of a free *act*—unjustifiably in the sense that there is not nor can there ever be a concrete actor, whether in the form of the absolute or its finite modifications, to whom original responsibility for an action could be attributed. His influence is also substantiated by Schelling's apparent familiarity with Jacobi's critical statements on his earlier nature and identity philosophy, which appear in *Drei Briefe an Friedrich Köppen* (1803) [Three Letters to Friedrich Köppen], and the gist of which is to confront systematic monism with an insistence on "dualism" (BK: JWA 2,1, 367).[4] Finally, we should bear in mind that while the *Freedom Essay* itself presents Jacobi's critical reservations regarding systems as an "old but in no way forgotten legend," Jacobi's fundamental objection that "the concept of freedom is [...] completely incompatible with system" nonetheless provides the basis for the framing of the problem.[5]

Schelling's revised position clearly acquires its specific contours against this Jacobian backdrop. It must be demonstrated that a *system of freedom* is indeed possible; a system, in other words, which—in line with previous claims—posits a universally valid nexus of rational explanation and which simultaneously—in a break with previous options—is able to account for freedom not in merely "formal"[6] terms but as the actual freedom

---

[3] SW VII, 395. Schelling, *Freedom Essay*, 59.
[4] See Chapter 13 in this volume.
[5] SW VII, 336. Schelling, *Freedom Essay*, 9. The translators of the English edition of the *Freedom Essay*, Jeff Love and Johannes Schmidt, quite rightly include a selection of excerpts from Jacobi's texts among the materials with which they supplement their edition (i.e. Jacobi's conversation with Lessing and his treatise on freedom in the second edition of the *Spinoza Letters*).
[6] SW VII, 347, 349. Schelling, *Freedom Essay*, 19f.

of individually acting agents. The determination of human freedom as the "capacity for good and evil" is related to this.[7]

The questions under consideration in what follows pertain directly to this project. Did Schelling actually revise his conception or simply his terminology? Did he really emancipate himself from the Spinozan understanding of system or is this merely how things appear on the surface? In other words, just what are we to make of Schelling's new emphasis on the person?

Unity and Individual Identity of the Person

"Personality," Schelling writes, is based "on the connection between a self-determining being and a basis independent of him."[8] The premise for this explanation is a previously posited difference, according to which an ontological distinction must be drawn between the ground of existence and that which exists as two aspects of a being. I will return to the particularities of this claim shortly. It is worth remarking already at this point, however, that Schelling attributes the original insight into this basic ontological situation to the program of his *Philosophy of Nature* and combines this with the assertion that, in developing this distinction, the philosophy of nature "most decisively [turned] from Spinoza's path."[9] Differentiating himself from Spinoza is one of Schelling's central aims, but insofar as (according to Schelling) this has already been accomplished through the philosophy of nature, the new conception of personality can allegedly be constructed upon this foundation without any difficulties. This assertion, however, is anything but clear.

Regardless of what, precisely, Schelling means by this statement, in anticipation of the determinations that he subsequently introduces into the primordial distinction between ground and that which exists, we can at this point already specify the following features of his concept of the person. First, the structure of personal existence is not simple but is rather differentiated within itself. The unity of the personality, in other words, is layered on top of an internal difference. And this in turn means, secondly, that it is characteristic of persons that they combine within themselves a "real" and an "ideal" principle. They are real inasmuch as they are natural and thus also embodied beings, and they are ideal in the sense that they are distinguished by a specific intellectual capacity, whose connection with the natural substrate constitutes what Schelling terms the "spirit" of a person.[10] What Schelling proposes is thus a structure of personality according to which the being of persons never consists solely in mental attributions of consciousness, but neither is it to be understood simply as a special kind of natural phenomenon. And it must further be recognized that the manner in which these natural and intellectual aspects are combined cannot be explained in terms of a progressive

---

[7] SW VII, 352. Schelling, *Freedom Essay*, 23.
[8] SW VII, 394. Schelling, *Freedom Essay*, 59.
[9] SW VII, 357. Schelling, *Freedom Essay*, 27.
[10] SW VII, 364, 407. Schelling, *Freedom Essay*, 33, 69.

development of the intellect from a starting point in the purely natural constitution of a living being. Rather, the real independence of the natural basis corresponds to the ideal self-determination of thought. In sum, this means that Schelling clearly seeks to guard against both idealistic and doubly naturalistic misunderstandings of the existence of persons and thereby secure for them a form of existence that is *sui generis*. There can be no denying that this program is highly promising in its basic outline, and it is certainly not without relevance for contemporary discussions.

As revealing as these observations may be, however, the truly decisive point, and the one that constitutes the focus of the deliberations that follow, has not yet been addressed. All that has been indicated so far is that the specific form of the existence of persons overlays the internal difference between their natural and intellectual aspects. This explanation, however, would only be sufficient if it could also show that the general structure of personality specific to every person is not simply repeated identically in all individual persons—since this would mean that no one could be distinguished from another—but rather that in the case of each individual person something uniquely particular is meant. The specific composition of the structure of personality must be something specific, in other words, what must be included in the concept of the person is the determination of a person's *individuality*. Indeed, in reviewing the complicated history of the concept, one sees that it was in fact through the identification of the "individua substantia" or, more precisely, the "individua subsistentia," that Boethius was able to bring a new understanding of the expression "persona" into circulation, one that stood in contrast to the earlier definition of persona as a mask.[11]

Whether or not Schelling had this history in mind is anyone's guess. More important here is the substantive question of whether and, if so, how he intends to address this requirement. After all, even in the context of the discussion occurring among his contemporaries, this much is already clear—if, in the course of his rehabilitation of the person, he failed to account for her individual existence, then his proclamation of a system of freedom would inevitably fall short of the position formulated by Jacobi, who had from the beginning insisted on the individuality of the person but had also anchored his claim regarding the epistemic inaccessibility of the person to this same individuality.[12] So where does stand Schelling on the matter?

It is noteworthy that the previously quoted statement gives no indication of an answer. Indeed, considering the predominance of references to "personality" here, one even might be tempted *prima facie* to offer a de-individualized interpretation, inasmuch as Schelling's usage seems to hearken back to that of Kant, who opposes *personality* to the empirically determined *person,* thereby invoking the universal category of "humanity" to which each individual person must subordinate herself.[13]

---

[11] Ancius M. S. Boethius, *The Theological Tractates; The Consolation of Philosophy*, ed. Eric H. Warmington, trans. Hugh F. Stewart, Edward K. Rand, and S. J. Tester (Cambridge: Harvard University Press, 1973), 85, 87.

[12] See Chapter 6 in this volume.

[13] Kant, *Kritik der praktischen Vernunft*, AA V, 87. Immanuel Kant, *Critique of Practical Reason (1788)*, in Immanuel Kant, *Practical Philosophy*, ed. and trans. Mary J. Gregor (Cambridge: Cambridge University Press, 1996), 210. See Kant, *Grundlegung zur Metaphysik der Sitten*, AA IV, 429. Kant, *Groundwork of the Metaphysics of Morals*, in *Practical Philosophy*, 79f.

Such a reading would make little sense, however. After all, Schelling's use of the term "personality" is precisely *not* intended to indicate a hiatus between the "sensible world" and the "intelligible world," but rather to reveal the integration of two worlds that remain separated in Kant. Acknowledging this fact does not render Schelling's usage any less irritating, but it does provide us with a clear indication that in developing a conception that diverges from Kant, he is obviously focused on the individuality of personality. In fact, his distinctive use of so-called "selfhood" [Selbstheit] is also crucial in this context. "Selfhood *as* such," Schelling writes, "is spirit."[14] If one applies this statement into the structure of personality, then it means that spirit denotes both the connection, the *overarching unity* of the internal difference, as well as the *unique individual identity* of this unity in each particular case.

Schelling's apparent equation of personal unity and identity, however, does not solve the problems of personality. On the contrary, this is precisely the point at which they actually begin. In contrast to the Boethius-inspired tradition that dates back to Richard of St. Victor, and also in contrast to Jacobi, it cannot be Schelling's intention to highlight the essential incommunicability of the individual person. Rather, his aim of explicating a systematic interrelationship requires him to illuminate the aforementioned equation in its emergence. But how does one do this? The difficulties that will be involved in such a task can already be anticipated by the fact that, strictly speaking, Schelling engages in two different operations, which goes hand in hand with his de facto postulation of two different conceptions of personal identity.

One of these, more specifically, the "selfhood" just mentioned, belongs to the context of the foundational metaphysical assumptions of ontology. On this account, it is not spirit which, by serving as a third (or a first) element with respect to the natural and the intellectual aspects of the person, can reliably guarantee her individuation. Rather, according to Schelling, a person owes her individual profile to just one of the two relata, and not, as one might expect, to the "ideal" aspect of the "self-determining being," but to the natural "basis." It is evidently this idea with which Schelling intends to bridge the gap between his earlier "philosophy of nature" and his current, personality-theoretically modified position, and accordingly, one can designate that which is articulated here as "spirit," the "selfhood raised to spirit,"[15] as the selfhood of a *natural self*. Juxtaposed with this self, however, one finds the identity of a *moral self*, which is traced back to an intelligible act that precedes the temporally conscious life of the person. It is allegedly because of such an "initial act" that a given human being must be understood, not as an "undetermined generality," but as "this individual and no other."[16] In retrospect, this casts the natural self of spirit in a rather peculiar light, as it means that this self does not guarantee the unique identity of the person. But then what does it guarantee?

---

[14] SW VII, 364. Schelling, *Freedom Essay*, 33.
[15] SW VII, 370. Schelling, *Freedom Essay*, 38.
[16] SW VII, 384 und 389. Schelling, *Freedom Essay*, 50, 54.

The Distinction between Ground and That Which Exists in Reference to Spinoza

Not the overarching unity but the individual identity of the person constitutes the weak spot in Schelling's program—this should be clear from the previous remarks. In order to delve more deeply into the matter, however, a particular approach is necessary, one which, following the direction suggested by Schelling himself, takes as its starting point the previously mentioned difference between ground and that which exists. This difference is articulated as a kind of ontological generalization, but one that is intended in two cases, that of God and of human beings, to be capable of grounding the personality of each, and in such a way that the constitution of God is prior to that of humans. Given the metaphysical orientation of the text, one might initially find this claim to be entirely reasonable. Upon closer inspection, however, it turns out to be untenable.

Admittedly, the internal constitution of the absolute does in fact contain the elements that then enter into the determination of human personality. Only later in the text, however, does one discover that a personal determinateness is actually under consideration here; more specifically, it becomes clear only after Schelling speaks, in connection with the divine creation, of the *human being*. At this point, in connection with a reference to the "selfhood" of this human being, the expression "personality" appears for the first time. It is then projected backwards onto the constitution of the absolute, onto a God who now—and only now—acquires the status of the "highest personality." It is clear that the argumentation goes in a circle here, a circle whose outline, as a consequence of the backward projection of human markers of personality onto God, also bears the traces of a rather blatant anthropomorphism, which is made all the more glaring by Schelling's effort to dress it up in the robes of theosophical speculation. Nonetheless, in the reflections that follow, neither the circular justification as such nor the anthropomorphizing approach to the absolute that accompanies it will be my primary focus. Rather, Schelling's belated characterization of the particular constitution of the absolute as person-specific is noteworthy for a different reason— it suggests that positing the difference between ground and that which exists as a way to characterize two aspects of a being provides neither an illuminating nor a persuasive basis for ascribing personhood to that being. But what, then, is at stake in the delineation of this difference?

If one takes seriously Schelling's claim in the *Freedom Essay* that, despite "narrating a myth,"[17] he intends to present reflections of a scientific nature, and if one consequently tries to look beyond the theosophical diction to discern the inner design that gives shape to the argument, then it becomes evident first and foremost that what lies behind the distinction between ground and that which exists is the determination of the *causa sui*. With the publication of the *Denkmal auf Jacobi* [1812; *Monument to Jacobi's Work*

---

[17] Walter Jaeschke, "Freiheit um Gottes willen," in *Schellings Weg zur Freiheitsschrift. Legende und Wirklichkeit*, ed. Hans Michael Baumgartner and Wilhelm G. Jacobs (Stuttgart-Bad Cannstatt: Frommann-Holzboog, 1996), 213.

on the Divine Things] at the latest, he makes this explicit: "God has to have something before him, namely *himself*—just as surely as he is *causa sui*."[18] This "ground of his existence," which forms his basis to the same extent that he is the *cause* of himself, is subsequently identified by Schelling as *"nature"* in God, in order to then immediately append to this definition a discussion of the will and desire of the ground.[19] Readers would be well advised, however, not to turn their attention immediately to these ascriptions, already formulated here in explicitly anthropomorphic terms, but rather to dwell for a bit longer on the initial determination. In considering Schelling's theoretical framework as presented here, one cannot help but be struck by the fact that the *causa sui* is the very first determination in Spinoza's *Ethics*: "Per causam sui intelligo id, cujus essentia involvit existentiam."[20] Schelling does not say explicitly that he has Spinoza's initiatory definition in mind here. It is clear, however, that it serves as his model for distinguishing between the ground, namely *essence*, and that which exists, namely *existence*. But perhaps we are doing Schelling a disservice in inserting this Spinozan backdrop into the constellation of the *Freedom Essay*? Didn't Schelling assure us already in the philosophy of nature that this distinction marked a "most decisive" deviation "from Spinoza's path"?

It is quite possible to acknowledge this backdrop and still make sense of Schelling's assertion of a divergence. What Spinoza presents as a difference that is posited and abolished simultaneously is separated by Schelling—or so it appears—into an actual difference, whereby the *being* of God turns into his *becoming* and the talk of God acquires an intentional ambiguity—a fissure runs through his constitution, insofar as the ground in God is not *"He Himself"* as *actu* existing.[21] However, it is no coincidence that Schelling immediately seeks to prevent this fissure in the divine from developing into an actual fracture, which would ultimately render the becoming of God completely incomprehensible as *causa sui*. Consequently, it is in truth a "circle, out of which everything becomes," which here means that ground and that which exists are reciprocal preconditions for one another.[22] The idea, however, that one cannot think essence without existence, any more than one can think existence without essence, was already part of Spinoza's definition, whose dualistic opening with regard to a real divine becoming Schelling brackets off with his approach. Has any real progress been made, then, in his theoretical foundations, progress that would provide one with a firm footing for a personalist interpretation?

Schelling himself seems to have suspected that the answer is no, that so far progress has only consisted in a symbolic—and precisely for that reason, theosophically tinged—augmentation of the Spinozan model. To be sure, one has to read quite a bit further before finding what Schelling presents as the conclusive revelation regarding

---

[18] Schelling, *Denkmal der Schrift von den göttlichen Dingen des Herrn Friedrich Heinrich Jacobi und der ihm in derselben gemachten Beschuldigung eines absichtlich täuschenden, Lüge redenden Atheismus*, SW VIII, 62. F. W. J. Schelling, *Monument to Jacobi's Work on the Divine Things* (1812), trans. Hadi Fakhoury, author manuscript, Kabiri, forthcoming.
[19] Schelling, *Freiheitsschrift*, SW VII, 358f. Schelling, *Freedom Essay*, 27f.
[20] Spinoza, *Ethics*, E I, Def. 1.
[21] SW VII, 360. Schelling, *Freedom Essay*, 28.
[22] SW VII, 358. Schelling, *Freedom Essay*, 28f.

the significance of this foundational initial distinction. In return for the effort, however, one is made privy to

> the highest point of the entire investigation. For a long time already we have heard the question: What end should serve this primary distinction between being in so far as it is ground and in so far as it exists? For there is either no common point of contact for both, in which case we must declare ourselves in favor of absolute dualism, or there is such a point; thus, both coincide once again in the final analysis.[23]

To assert an "absolute dualism" would lead to an absurd Manichaeism, while abolishing it would return us to Spinoza's path—this is the state of affairs that he finally presents to the reader. Schelling's attempt to find a way out of this dilemma is thus all the more remarkable. It involves the postulation of an original "being *before* all ground and before all that exists, thus generally before any duality," an "absolute *indifference*" that guarantees both the unity of the divine being and serves as the "*non-ground*" [Ungrund] out of which the duality, as he puts it, "breaks forth."[24]

It now sounds as if Schelling is no longer distancing himself from Spinoza's foundations by way of a symbolic dynamization of the *causa sui*, but rather by moving in the direction of a per se absolute that precedes even the Spinozan *causa sui*. In fact, however, this move ends up bringing him back to Spinoza in a different sense. The indifference to be disclosed in what Schelling refers to here (certainly not coincidentally) as a "dialectical discussion,"[25] is, structurally speaking, the very same point to which Schelling had already turned his attention from an identity-philosophical perspective, viewing Spinoza's divine *Substance* as the unity which, in the form of its attributes, that is, as *extensio* and as *cogitatio,* expresses itself in different ways as a whole. Reading the text carefully, one sees that Schelling now repeats the very structure that had previously prompted him to develop a realist philosophy of nature and an idealist philosophy of spirit in parallel to one another. The non-ground cannot be this "in any other way than in so far as it divides into two equally eternal beginnings, not that it can be both *at once*, but that it is in each *in the same way*, thus in each the whole, or its own being."[26]

---

[23] SW VII, 406. Schelling, *Freedom Essay,* 68.
[24] SW VII, 406f. Schelling, *Freedom Essay,* 68f.
[25] SW VII, 407. Schelling, *Freedom Essay,* 69.
[26] SW VII, 408. Schelling, *Freedom Essay,* 70. Compare this with the earlier formulation in *Philosophy and Religion* (1804): "The third form by which reflective cognition tends to choose to express the Absolute is the disjunctive. This is known primarily through Spinoza. It is only One [Eines], but in the same manner this One can be regarded now as all-ideal, now as all-real; it arises from the combination of the categorical and the hypothetical. This one and the same—not at once but in like manner—can be regarded now as the one, now as the other; it is therefore in itself neither the one nor the other (according to the first form). Rather, it can be considered the combined essence [Wesen] or identity of both (according to the second form) and, in its independence from both, likewise under this attribute, now under that attribute." SW VI, 24f. F. W. J. Schelling, *Philosophy and Religion (1804)*, trans. Klaus Ottmann (Putnam: Spring Publications, 2010), 14. The most recent investigation of Schelling's *Freedom Essay* as it relates to Heidegger and Jacobi is to be found in Konstanze Sommer, *Zwischen Metaphysik und Metaphysikkritik. Heidegger, Schelling und Jacobi* (Hamburg: Meiner, 2015).

It can therefore be clearly seen that substance—in the role of non-ground—is the point of convergence to which Schelling relates the internal difference between ground and that which exists that he has gleaned from the *causa sui*. And this also explains why the two "eternal beginnings" diverge to form the "real principle" of *nature* and the "ideal principle" of *the understanding*. It is evident that, together with the attributive position of these two principles, Schelling also incorporates the substantial features of Spinoza's model into his own conception, that is, the reference to *extensio* and *cogitatio*, with the result that both principles stand in the closest possible connection to one another but neither can be traced back to the other. The independent foundation of nature corresponds to the ideal autonomy of thought—this profoundly Spinozan insight has been reasserted. But what does all of this have to do with the question of personality? Why does it lead to a rehabilitation of theism if one introduces the dynamization of the *causa sui* into the differential manifestation that Spinoza had always seen to be operative in regard to substance and its attributes?

Now it might seem that despite all of my efforts, this description of the problem fails to consider two things. One could argue that in claiming that Schelling simply reproduces the same Spinozan structural pattern with which he had always been preoccupied in the guise of a personal God, we overlook two things: First, the attribute of *extensio* is by definition not identical to Schelling's concept of nature, and second, that the unifying principle of substance fails to capture fully what Schelling intends with the term "spirit." And in fact, Schelling adduces these very arguments in his *Stuttgart Seminars* in order to guard against any interpretation that would see "Spinoza's system […] as entirely identical with that of the more recent philosophy of identity."[27] Interestingly, in doing so, he not only confirms the plausibility of such a suspicion but also, in the effort to explain "my system" by way of an "outline of modern philosophy," also reveals the reason for this plausibility. By invoking as points of reference the Cartesian substance dualism of mind and matter and then the "absolute identity of the two principles" in Spinoza, Schelling shows that he is actually and not simply hypothetically orienting himself toward this constellation of attributes.[28] In the end, however, the difference is alleged to be all the greater, since "Spinoza's physics are completely mechanical," and substance here is only grasped as an "empty" identity of its attributes

> rather than making *it* the principal object of his philosophy. *Precisely* at this point, which Spinoza does not investigate any further, the concept of the living God can be found, namely, God as the supreme personality. Hence it is altogether true [to say] that Spinoza at the very least ignores the personality of the supreme Being, if he does not positively deny it.[29]

---

[27] Schelling, *Stuttgarter Privatvorlesungen*, SW VII, 443. F. W. J. Schelling, "Stuttgart Seminars," in *Idealism and the Endgame of Theory. Three Essays by F. W. J. Schelling*, ed. and trans. Thomas Pfau (Albany: State University of New York Press, 1994), 214. The reference to the "more recent philosophy of identity" is especially noteworthy in this context.
[28] SW VII, 443. Schelling, *Stuttgart Seminars*, 214.
[29] SW VII, 443f. Schelling, *Stuttgart Seminars*, 214.

Although the two arguments point in two different directions, they are clearly united in advocating for the interests of "life" and, by the same token, in imputing to Spinoza's metaphysics that lifeless rigidity of which the *Freedom Essay* also speaks: "The error of his system lies by no means in his placing things *in God* but in the fact that they are *things*—in the abstract concept of beings in the world, indeed of infinite substance itself, which for him is exactly also a thing."[30] And what if this truly were nothing but an imputation, one that has become no more compelling for having been stereotypically repeated by philosophers up to and including Heidegger. In fact, it seems extremely unlikely that Schelling would have forgotten what he was eager to emphasize in *The I as Principle of Philosophy* as "the most sublime idea in Spinoza's system,"[31] namely that here God's *essentia* is posited as *potentia*, as absolute power or force: "Dei potentia est ipsa ipsius essentia."[32] But if one assumes that such forgetfulness on the part of Schelling is impossible, then one must not only approach his critique of Spinoza's alleged thing-construct with extreme caution; one is also fully justified in suspecting that precisely the adoption of this divine potentiality of being from Spinoza is what makes the "ground" in Schellings conception so lively and nature—in its attributive identification with essence—so dynamic.

Against this backdrop, any claims regarding a "most decisive" departure from Spinoza lose all credibility, and it follows from this that the nature-philosophical foundation of God contributes nothing with regard to the question of his personality. God as person must, according to Schelling's own deliberations, have a natural foundation, an unconscious force within himself. Even more significantly, however, this force, again according to his own deliberations, would have to manifest an individual identity—the ground in God would have to be an individuated one. The *Stuttgart Seminars* do indeed point in this direction, referring to an "*individual essence*" as the basis of the ideal universal and identifying this "first primordial force" with an "egoism in God," toward which divine love reveals itself.[33] But what is the individuating principle here? It is telling that Schelling here, as is also the case in the *Freedom Essay,* answers this question only in anticipation of "human" circumstances[34] and is not really able to make clear how one should actually conceive of the divine "*selfhood*"[35] to which he refers. If it is the divine process of coming to consciousness which, as seems to be the case on the one hand, separates the two principles and thereby renders them recognizable *as such,* then it must be assumed that their respective ground has already been individuated without, however, any justification having been given for this. If, however, as also seems to be the case on the other hand, it is this process in which the separation of the principles first effectuates the "concentration" [Kontraktion] of

---

[30] SW VII, 349, 350. Schelling, *Freedom Essay,* 20.
[31] Schelling, *Ichschrift*, SW I, 195f. F. W. J. Schelling, "Of the I as the Principle of Philosophy or on the Unconditional in Human Knowledge," in *The Unconditional in Human Knowledge. Four Early Essays (1794–1796)*, trans. Marti Fritz (Lewisburg: Bucknell University Press, 1980), 95f.
[32] E I, prop. 34.
[33] Schelling, *Privatvorlesungen*, SW VII, 438. Schelling, *Stuttgart Seminars,* 210.
[34] SW VII, 432. Schelling, *Stuttgart Seminars,* 206.
[35] SW VII, 438. Schelling, *Stuttgart Seminars,* 210.

the ground itself,³⁶ then one is forced to confront the unanswerable question of what sort of being would be able to recognize and integrate *as his own* the identity that has been split off from him.³⁷ In other words, if one looks past the anthropomorphic language and focuses on the structures of this ontology, one finds that there is just as little reason here as there is in the case of Spinoza to think the living being of God as anything other than the unity of an anonymous and absolute potency that actualizes itself as such, whether instantaneously or in an eternal circle.

The same therefore also applies to the objection that Spinoza neglected to make "substance" his "principal object." Remedying this situation so as to defend God's living personality can hardly mean referring to the original indifference of the "non-ground," which, after all, presents in its "very lacking of a predicate"³⁸ the absolute opposite of a personal determinateness. Consequently, only the idea of "connection" remains, as was already mentioned on the occasion of the first set of reflections on the structure of personality—the connection of different principles that Schelling had designated as spirit. To the extent that the unity does not merely provide the foundation for the separation of the principles but also overlays them *in their separation,* to this extent, God is a person—thus Schelling's accompanying argument, which, however, in his dialectical presentation of an identity of identity and difference is not only incapable of specifying the individual signature of this person. In addition, the attempt to supersede Spinoza by way of personality theory once again comes at the cost of a dramatically truncated presentation of his position. One would certainly be justified in questioning whether the idea of a spiritual connection of the attributes is truly foreign to Spinoza— it is after all the *intellectus infinitus* that *objectively* overlays the *formal* separation of the attributes here, which also, in the form of the *amor Dei intellectualis* gives expression to the substantial unity as the *consummation of its love.* Spirit and love, in other words, are by no means missing; indeed, Spinoza's train of thought in the *Ethics* actually culminates in these determinations—and again one finds it hard to believe that Schelling simply failed to see this when he so obviously uses these Spinozan features— now cast in personalist terms—to ground his own conception.

With regard to both objections, one paradox finally remains to be considered. Even if one concedes that Schelling *would like* to call his proposed structure of overarching unity *personal,* and if one further concedes that the individual identity thereof can only ever be thought of anthropomorphically, then the question inevitably arises as to how these two points can be reconciled. What does it mean for the personality of God that his "true and proper self" is said to consist in the subordination of natural selfhood to universal love?³⁹ In this case, is this true "self" really anything other than the *highest selflessness*—and thus again something that is personality in name only?

---

³⁶ SW VII, 434. Schelling, *Stuttgart Seminars,* 207.

³⁷ Given these problems, it is also no longer possible to be persuaded by Schelling's third argument against Spinoza, namely, his claim that here the attributes are thought without reciprocal relation (*Privatvorlesungen,* SW VII, 443. *Stuttgart Seminars,* 214).

³⁸ Schelling, *Freiheitsschrift,* SW VII, 406. Schelling, *Freedom Essay,* 68f.

³⁹ Schelling, *Privatvorlesungen,* SW VII, 439. Schelling, *Stuttgart Seminars,* 211.

The Ontology of the Person: Natural Selfhood without Self

"God, or more exactly, the being that God is," as Schelling impresses upon his reader in the *Monument to Jacobi* is "the ground—and in a double sense." He *is* the ground of himself, but he "also *makes* himself into a ground, by making precisely that part of his being, with which he operated earlier, passive."[40] Thus "begins" the creation of a world said to be independent of God, independent because the difference within God is alleged to be the condition of possibility for difference outside God. That is to say, as the *cause* of himself, God is at the same time cause of the world, insofar as he relates creatively to his own *ground* as the ground of the world. Though it might seem unnecessary given all that has been said already, it is nonetheless essential to note that in presenting this central theorem, Schelling is of course only repurposing one of Spinoza's most important propositions for the "more recent philosophy of identity": "eo sensu, quo Deus dicitur causa sui, etiam omnium rerum causa dicendus est."[41] Schelling clearly wants to explicate this "eo sensu" and with the aim of establishing, in the course of this explication, a clear contrast between the idea of a free, personal "act" and the necessity that characterizes an anonymous "occurence."[42]

In conjunction with this effort, Schelling also introduces a new variant of the difference between ground and that which exists, which now appears as the difference between *ground and cause*.[43] And he accordingly goes on to claim that the absolute, as that which overlays the difference, is both—"ground *as well as* cause"[44]—this is the argument with which he confronts Jacobi, to whom he is clearly indebted for his formulation of the cause as a personal principle of action, but whose monitum against any conflation of ground and cause he indignantly repudiates. Schelling's move is peculiar in one particular respect: Jacobi's criticism of this conflation did not first appear in his later polemic against Schelling *Von den göttlichen Dingen und ihrer Offenbarung* [1811; On Divine Things and Their Revelation],[45] to which Schelling responded with the *Monument to Jacobi*. It had in fact already appeared in 1787, in the dialogue *David Hume on Faith, or Idealism and* Realism, and then again in the crucial *Supplement VII* to the 1789 edition of *Concerning the Doctrine of Spinoza in Letters to Herr Moses Mendelssohn*, meaning that it was originally directed at Spinoza himself. With regard to the latter, Jacobi argued that because his system conflates the logic of the ground with that of action—ratio sive causa—it goes beyond the purely rational relations of implication between ground and consequence. Precisely in doing so, however, it only manages to arrive at the conception of a "blindly acting being" (Spin: JWA 1,1, 265), which, in the absence of its own "individual actuality" (Spin: JWA 1,1, 23; MPW 190) is incapable of generating the real difference of a genuine otherness

---

[40] Schelling, *Denkmal auf Jacobi*, SW VIII, 71. Schelling, *Monument to Jacobi*, see footnote 18.
[41] E I, prop. 25, scholium.
[42] Schelling, *Freiheitsschrift*, SW VII, 396. Schelling, *Freedom Essay*, 59f.
[43] See SW VII, 365. Schelling, *Freedom Essay*, 34. See also Schelling, *Aphorismen zur Einleitung in die Naturphilosophie*, SW VII, 177.
[44] Schelling, *Denkmal auf Jacobi*, SW VIII, 71. Schelling, *Monument to Jacobi*, see footnote 18.
[45] See GD: JWA 3, 105ff.

(Spin: JWA 1,1, 255ff.; MPW 371ff.).[46] Against this backdrop, it becomes clear that Schelling's supposed innovation, the both-and of ground and cause, is not only not an innovation at all, but also runs the risk of becoming entangled in the same set of problems that Jacobi had already identified in the case of Spinoza.

In another respect, however, it is understandable that Schelling ignores this connection, whether knowingly or unknowingly. As is in the case of the ontology of the absolute, it is crucial in the case of its relation to the world as well that the explanatory power of the system is not sacrificed in the effort to integrate personhood and causal action. Both are supposed to obtain simultaneously, and I have no intention of denying that Schelling's desire to have both is genuine rather than mere pretense. With regard to the absolute, however, he fails in practice to realize this intention, as has been shown in the foregoing considerations. As elaborated systematically, the personality of God denominates little more than a structure characterized by the features of Spinozan identity philosophy, a structure that remains the same despite having been given a new name, whereas the invocation of individual "selfhood" in relation to God's "true self" would have made the problem clear. But where does this leave us as regards the constitution of human beings?

In terms of the ontological groundwork, there is initially no serious difficulty here. The question concerning the absolute that has remained open thus far, namely, the question as to what the principle of the individuation of the ground could be, here finds an answer in divine creation. On this account, our natural self, the individual determinateness of the ground, is always at hand—it is the "selfhood" that is "raised up from the ground of nature" by divine understanding.[47] By implication (this is how we are presumably to understand this raising up) the absolute being contains within itself all individual beings in *real* but undifferentiated form. To this extent they originate neither on the basis of "external representation,"[48] nor by way of a *creatio ex nihilo*; rather they have their origin in a "genuine *impression* [Ein-Bildung]," an incorporation of the "idea," which constitutes an "awakening"[49] and thus an actualization of the real, its actualizing elaboration into something "comprehensible and individuated."[50]

Schelling himself does not speak here in terms of a distinction between reality and actuality. This distinction, however, which comes from Spinoza, can nonetheless help to clarify how one should grasp the difference between what is implied in the (attributive) ground and what is expressed out of it, or, as Schelling's puts it, "proclaimed."[51] And as a result one can also see more clearly how Schelling attempts, now moving well beyond his previous position, to incorporate the dimension of actuality that had always been a concern of Spinoza's, albeit at the cost of entangling him in the previously alluded to aporias. In other words, Schelling now turns to the very dimension that he had

---

[46] For a more exhaustive discussion of this topic, see Birgit Sandkaulen, *Grund und Ursache. Die Vernunftkritik Jacobis* (Munich: Wilhelm Fink Verlag, 2000) and Chapter 2 in this volume.
[47] Schelling, *Freiheitsschrift*, SW VII, 364. Schelling, *Freedom Essay*, 33.
[48] SW VII, 361. Schelling, *Freedom Essay*, 31.
[49] SW VII, 362. Schelling, *Freedom Essay*, 31.
[50] SW VII, 361. Schelling, *Freedom Essay*, 31.
[51] SW VII, 363. Schelling, *Freedom Essay*, 32.

previously only ever referred to as arising from "external representation," and thus through "reflection," and which was therefore to be negated in true intuition.[52] In the context of this shift, moreover, yet another parallel becomes apparent.

Spinoza grasps the actualization of modal being in the form of the *conatus*, the *striving for self-preservation*, in which divine potency manifests itself in the particular. Schelling, in order to characterize "selfhood" in its living dynamism, speaks of the "self-will [Eigenwille] of creatures"[53]; he also refers explicitly, however, to "the drive to preserve oneself not in general but in this defined existence," and in this context he insists that this very drive shows "that it is not merely a geometric necessity that has been active here," but rather that the desire itself is "that which creates."[54] There can be little doubt that this assertion is once again directed against Spinoza's alleged object metaphysics, which Schelling seeks to supersede with his more animated alternative. In fact, however, the basic idea is the same in both cases, and it is thus evident that just as Schopenhauer's metaphysics of the will has its roots in Schelling's *Freedom Essay*, the latter has its roots in Spinoza's *Ethics*. Nonetheless, there is one essential and very consequential difference. With Spinoza, divine power precedes the attributes within the expressive structure of substance. It thus manifests itself in equal measure in both attributes and therefore constitutes, in the modified form of *conatus*, the "middle" of the finite individual being composed of body and spirit.[55] For his part, Schelling also ascribes a form of will to both principles. In the course of his attributive equation of essence with nature, however, he shifts the actual expression of the will onto the side of the real principle in the form of self will, and in doing so, this will—and therefore selfhood in general—takes on the characteristic of an egocentrism and, consequently, of "evil." This circumstance will have significant implications for his conception of personality.

These only become clear, however, at the point where he presents his model of the moral self. Remaining for the moment in the current context, how, precisely, are we to understand the natural self of the person, given that what has been said applies to all living things? All life strives for self-preservation, and insofar as it is expressed out of the divine ground through divine understanding, it also contains both principles—it pursues its self-will in a relation to the whole. According to Schelling, however, what gives the human being his unique constitution is that here the highest measure of individual distinction corresponds to the highest measure of conscious awareness in the truest sense of the phrase. There is "complete consonance" between the two, as Schelling asserts in regard to the aspects of the real and the ideal.[56] It is certainly tempting to understand this consonance, which is after all intended to characterize the specific existence of persons, as a *self-relation*. Persons do not simply execute the

---

[52] See, for example, Schelling, *System der gesammten Philosophie*, SW VI, 181ff. F. W. J. Schelling, "System of Philosophy in General and of the Philosophy of Nature in Particular," in *Idealism and the Endgame of Theory. Three Essays by F. W. J. Schelling*, ed. and trans. Thomas Pfau (Albany: State University of New York Press, 1994), 171.
[53] Schelling, *Freiheitsschrift*, SW VII, 363. Schelling, *Freedom Essay*, 32.
[54] SW VII, 376. Schelling, *Freedom Essay*, 43.
[55] E III, prop. 9, scholium.
[56] Schelling, *Freiheitsschrift*, SW VII, 363. Schelling, *Freedom Essay*, 32.

tasks imposed upon them by the laws of their species; rather, they enter into a relation with their natural interest in self-preservation, consciously doing what less complex beings do blindly. This could be read as a paraphrase of Schelling's insistence that selfhood, "through its unity with the ideal principle, becomes *spirit*,"[57] and in the form of personality thereby transcends the entanglement of all other beings in nature.

Precisely here, however, is where the problem with this conception lies. In order to be able to grasp the structure of consonance as a self-relation, individual identity would have to be such that the person is able to distinguish her interests from *herself* and relate them to *herself*. Where, however, in the current context, could one find such a "herself"? Schelling himself seems to have realized that the natural self-will of the person, although it certainly gives the person her physical vitality, is in no way sufficient to furnish the relation of consonance with the dimension of a spiritual self-reference. Adapting a passage from Jacobi, he indicates that the relation between ideal and real principles parallels that of "vowel and consonant" [Selbstlauter und Mitlauter].[58] The difference is striking, however. Whereas Jacobi invokes the image of the voiced "vowel" sound [Selbstlaut] in this passage to suggest the uniqueness and incomparability of the person—something his conception legitimately allows him to do (WL: JWA 3, 27)—Schelling's identification of vowel and ideal principle is a dead end, since this principle as such represents the opposite of all selfhood, namely, the general or universal. Thus the two principles may very well form a harmony within the person, but the chord that resounds is merely an event occurring in the course of the creative unfolding of the absolute. As an echo of the structure of the absolute, it resonates with the sound of unity, not of personal identity.[59]

Individuality as Primordial Position: The Moral Self-Creation of Personal Identity

The constitution of the human person, as it occurs (in the truest sense of the word) in the metaphysically grounded harmony of nature and intellect, possesses a "selfhood having become animated by spirit,"[60] but *it is not a self*. Relying on the adequacy of Schelling's conception of personality as developed thus far thus seems unlikely to lead to a successful outcome. And the further progress of his investigation shows this suspicion to be correct. In accordance with the overall theme, he is indeed primarily oriented toward the distinction between the possibility and the actuality of good or evil.

---

[57] SW VII, 364. Schelling, *Freedom Essay*, 33.
[58] SW VII, 363. Schelling, *Freedom Essay*, 32.
[59] Adolphi has also noted that, at best, Schelling's distinction between ground and that which exists is able to account for the particular, not for the individual. (Rainer Adolphi, "'Geschehen aber zu denken ist immer das Schwierigste.' Zu den Problemen des Prozeßansatzes in Schellings Freiheitsphilosophie," in *Schellings Weg zur Freiheitsschrift. Legende und Wirklichkeit*, ed. Hans Michael Baumgartner and Wilhelm G. Jacobs (Stuttgart-Bad Cannstatt: Frommann-Holzboog, 1996), 267.)
[60] Schelling, *Freiheitsschrift*, SW VII, 365. Schelling, *Freedom Essay*, 33.

But what Schelling presents under the heading of a mere possibility is a more or less exact description of the deficient status of the personality. The fact that both principles are potentially "severable"[61] in a human being (in contrast to the absolute) means, namely, that in this state of potentiality he still stands before a "threshold"; he has reached a point where he must "step out of his indecision."[62] And precisely this means that at this point, in this state of *indecision*, there is in fact still no one present, no one who would be *someone* and could place the real and ideal in relation to *himself*. This corresponds on the other hand to what Schelling grasps under the heading of actuality and connects with an intelligible act—the decision, not for this or that particular act, but rather, and prior to anything else, for "the intelligible being of *this* individual."[63] The missing self, the individual identity of the person, is thus addressed here for the very first time and in an entirely different manner than the natural self-interest which had thus far been treated in isolation. As Schelling explains, clearly paraphrasing Jacobi, this self appears in the guise of an "initial action whereby he is this individual and no other."[64] The fundamental difference between the two, however, is crucial. Far from attributing such "*being oneself*" to an act of self-creation, Jacobi speaks only of a "*feeling of existence*" [Wesenheitsgefühl], in which the person in question "finds" herself to be "this being" (WL: JWA 3, 26).

With his more modest conception of personal identity as a *discovery* that cannot be explicated further, Jacobi has perhaps arrived at the more plausible solution. After all, the act of self-creation is either simply a metaphor for the fact that this identity is in possession of an internal perspective that cannot be adequately captured by external attributions. Or this act must be understood as the absolute act of a *causa sui* and, as a consequence, be subject to the explications with which Schelling, beginning with the distinction between ground and that which exists, had previously occupied himself. Indeed, we are confronted here with an extremely peculiar theoretical situation. On the one hand, it is evident that Schelling really does conceive the intelligible act as something carried out by a *causa sui* and which, entirely in line with Spinoza, is not only to be understood as the identity of freedom and necessity[65] but also in "eo sensu" as *causa rerum*. It appears as *causa rerum* here in the sense of a *causa* for a series of actions that proceed from the self-created being with internal necessity and only appear as such in the temporal life of the person. In light of this evolution of an inner and therefore allegedly free necessity, one cannot help but be astonished to find that Schelling chooses, at this of all moments, when human *freedom* is ostensibly the issue, to negate any and all distinction between the actor and his act and give free reign to a fatalism that he had just sought to counter in the groundwork of his system.

---

[61] SW VII, 364. Schelling, *Freedom Essay*, 33.
[62] SW VII, 374. Schelling, *Freedom Essay*, 41.
[63] SW VII, 384. Schelling, *Freedom Essay*, 50. Emphasis in original.
[64] SW VII, 389. Schelling, *Freedom Essay*, 54. Compare the following passage from Jacobi: "Through his spirit man becomes something utterly incomparable, an individual for himself and without otherness, his *unique* spirit constitutes him as the One who he is, *this One and no Other*." (WL: JWA 3, 26)
[65] SW VII, 384. Schelling, *Freedom Essay*, 49.

It is therefore remarkable, on the other hand, that Schelling completely refrains from utilizing the resources of his ontology to shed light on the act of self-creation of the individual being. The very explanation that is called for by the act *self-creation* seems to be hindered by the fact that the process aims at the creation of *individuality*. Along these lines, and in an explicit departure from Spinoza, Schelling himself emphasizes that "the saying determinatio est negatio [determination is negation] holds in no way for such [individual] determinateness since the latter is itself one with the position and the concept of its being, therefore it really is the essence in its being [Wesen in dem Wesen]."[66] This formulation reveals what one does indeed encounter here for the first time—not the dialectical structure of an overarching unity that is itself rooted in an unpredicated "non-ground," but rather the *determinateness of a primordial position*. "This individual and no other"—precisely *this individual* falls entirely outside the scope of the considerations developed by Schelling thus far and to this extent, we should note, also lacks any ontological model whatsoever in the constitution of the "divine personality."

On the basis of this finding, one could draw the conclusion that Schelling, having arrived at the point of a primordial position, would now be obligated to subject his systematic intentions to a radical interrogation. He does not do so, however. And that in turn means that the position of individual identity is not only immediately thought of as one with the logic of Spinozan necessity just outlined.[67] Above all, it also means that the self-creation of being coincides with the creation of a moral self, which is inserted into the ontological groundwork to the extent that this self has to decide in favor of good or evil and therefore for a particular constellation of the two principles. The "evil individual" and the "good individual"[68] thereby become the figures with regard to which it can be shown what it means to superordinate either the real principle of self-will over the ideal principle of the universal will or vice versa.

Had Schelling given any serious consideration to the implications of invoking a primordial position of the self, then he would have also recognized the need to now provide yet another explanation clarifying how this self relates to the structure of the overarching unity of the two principles. Instead, in keeping with his earlier reflections, the figure of natural "selfhood" once again gains the upper hand, such that the self of "the evil individual" consists precisely in elevating the natural drive for self-preservation to the egoism of a "ruling and total will" [Allwillen], rather than "making it into the basis."[69] In contrast, the self of "the good individual" consists in overcoming selfhood, in bringing it "back from activity to potentiality."[70] The intrinsic logic of the primordial

---

[66] SW VII, 384. Schelling, *Freedom Essay*, 50.

[67] In making a case for Schelling's pre-reflexive concept of freedom, Sturma also highlights the relevance of this primordial position of the individual self. He has no problem, however, with the internal necessity of self-determination (Dieter Sturma, "Präreflexive Freiheit und menschliche Selbstbestimmung," in *F. W. J. Schelling. Über das Wesen der menschlichen Freiheit*, ed. Ottfried Höffe and Annemarie Pieper, Klassiker Auslegen 3 (Berlin: Akademie Verlag, 1995), 149–72.

[68] SW VII, 386. Schelling, *Freedom Essay*, 51.

[69] SW VII, 389. Schelling, *Freedom Essay*, 54. The allusion to Jacobi's novel *Allwill* is unmistakable here.

[70] SW VII, 400. Schelling, *Freedom Essay*, 63.

position, in other words, disappears either into the decidedly consonant order or in the decidedly dissonant inversion of the principles. In consequence, "the good individual" not only again finds his well-defined place in the ontology of the divine constitution, but also, in diminishing his natural selfhood to a power that operates entirely in accord with the universal, "this individual and no other" paradoxically decides not to be "this individual" but rather the one who contributes to "a distant future" when "God will be all in all things."[71]

The Impersonal Abolition of the Person

By way of summary and conclusion, then, one can (and should) say that in insisting on the primordial position of personal identity, Schelling has, on the one hand, undeniably put his finger on the key issue. He clearly owes this insight to the influence of Jacobi, whose name, unlike those of Schelling's other interlocutors, seems to have been intentionally left out the *Freedom Essay*. As a result, a valid objection to Spinoza has also come into view, one that is persuasive because it offers a genuine alternative to the latter's *determinatio as negatio*. The extent of its impact becomes immediately clear in relation to Hegel, who also dedicates the whole undertaking of his *Science of Logic* to the "sublation" of Spinozan metaphysics with the aim of remedying the "defect" of "*personality*" that prevails there. In the process, however, he subordinates the realization of this goal to the "absolute principle of Spinozan philosophy" in order to drive it forward to the point at which it becomes a "*self-negating negation*," a negation of the negation.[72]

At the very moment of discovery, however, Schelling pulls his finger away again. Moreover, he shows just how disinclined he is to truly acknowledge what he has uncovered when he goes on to attribute to every human being a "feeling [...] as if he had been what he is already from all eternity."[73] If it had truly been his intention to find an adequate expression for the position of individual identity, then he should not have said "*what*" but rather "*who.*" This is no mere oversight. Because if he had said *who* rather than *what*, he would have had no choice but to subject the conception of personality developed thus far to a thorough revision.

In fact, however, Schelling does the opposite, as becomes especially clear in the *Stuttgart Seminars*. In apparent contradiction to the *Freedom Essay*, here he goes so far as to place the soul above the spirit, which, as "that which is properly man's personality," is identified with "conscious desire" and, in its real aspect, is related to "the individuality in man" or, more precisely, "*the individual will* [Eigenwille]."[74] The soul, on the other hand, is "the properly divine in *man* [...] it is something *impersonal*, the proper Being,

---

[71] SW VII, 404. Schelling, *Freedom Essay*, 66.
[72] Hegel, *Wissenschaft der Logik* (Wesenslogik: GW 11, 376). G. W. F. Hegel, *The Science of Logic*, ed. and trans. George di Giovanni (Cambridge: Cambridge University Press, 2010), 472. See Chapter 15 in this volume.
[73] Schelling, *Freiheitsschrift*, SW VII, 386. Schelling, *Freedom Essay*, 51.
[74] Schelling, *Privatvorlesungen*, SW VII, 466. Schelling, *Stuttgart Seminars*, 231.

to which personality as an intrinsic nonbeing shall remain subordinate."⁷⁵ As I said, this initially sounds like a contradiction, like a further transformation of the entire model. A closer look, however, reveals that Schelling does not change his position at all; instead, he merely draws the conclusion that follows from the analysis presented in the *Freedom Essay*.

To the extent that the conception of individual personality is essentially based on the natural interest of a consciously pursued self-will, as was the case there, and decidedly *not* on the position of the "this individual and no other," then it is only logical to demand from such a person that she disregard her own self. But then it is just as logical that Schelling is thereby led expressis verbis back to Kant, whose moral philosophy he *seemed* to leave behind in favor of a personalist approach. The categorical imperative, of which Kant has "only the formal expression," is now transformed into an "'act according to your soul,'" which entails acting "not as a personal being [persönliches Wesen] but in an entirely impersonal manner, without allowing your personality to disrupt its influence on you."⁷⁶

And, finally, doesn't this also remind us of something else? Was it not the case that Schelling had years ago insisted that the only path to freedom leads through "the destruction of our personality"? In spite of all appearances to the contrary, then, it turns out that on a general level as well, Schelling has not changed his original conviction, only modified it. Apart from his brief but undeveloped moment of insight into the primordial position of individual identity, he merely exchanged the *theoretical* framing of his conception of personality for a *practical* one, without, however, changing the meaning of the expression in the least. What was and still is meant by this expression is—*determinatio negatio est*—the determinate negation of *finitude*, which, as a consequence of the distinction between ground and that which exists, has now emigrated from the external world into the inner nature of divine and human being, where it now and forever after stands ready to be *overcome*. Jacobi's insistence on the irreducibility of the individual person, which can only be acquired at the cost of its epistemic inaccessibility, has nothing to do with any of this.

---

⁷⁵ SW VII, 468. Schelling, *Stuttgart Seminars*, 232.
⁷⁶ SW VII, 473. Schelling, *Stuttgart Seminars*, 235 (translation amended).

13

System and Temporality: Jacobi Contra Hegel and Schelling

Hegel, Jacobi, and Spinoza

Much can be said about the confrontation with Kant, Jacobi, and Fichte that unfolds in Hegel's *Faith and Knowledge*. My focus in the following chapter, however, will be limited to the author's criticism of Jacobi, who figures as the literal center of this triad, and I want to address right at the outset what must be seen as the decisive issue. What Hegel finds most irritating in Jacobi's version of the so-called "metaphysic of subjectivity"[1] is, without a doubt, his insistence on the centrality of the question of time, a question that leads directly into a dispute over the correct interpretation of Spinoza. According to the claim Jacobi formulated in *Concerning the Doctrine of Spinoza in Letters to Herr Moses Mendelssohn,* Spinoza's ontology founders on the problem of time. Hegel, on the other hand, dismisses this assertion as completely nonsensical. For him, it simply reveals that Jacobi has made two crucial mistakes.

First, Hegel asserts, Jacobi's preoccupation with the phenomenon of time is misguided on a general level, because time, as an index of finitude, is a topic undeserving of the attention of a serious philosopher. In occupying himself with the "nothingness" of the concerns of our finite existence, Jacobi thus addresses a question that is per se entirely irrelevant.[2] Even worse for Hegel is Jacobi's second error, which is that he presents the problem of time as a challenge to Spinoza's ontology, even going so far as to discern an internal contradiction in the design of Spinoza's *Ethics*. As Hegel puts it, "the nature of Jacobi's polemical procedure is this then: he either complains about the absence of succession and finitude [in Spinoza] and simply demands their presence in speculation, or he reads them into Spinoza and then finds absurdities."[3] For Hegel, on the other hand, it is crystal clear that for Spinoza, the phenomenon of time is to be understood solely as an illusory product of the human "imagination."[4]

This fundamental disagreement constitutes the kernel of a fascinating debate. On the one hand, what is at stake is the question of what the text of Spinoza's *Ethics* actually

---

[1] Hegel, *Glauben und Wissen,* GW 4, 412. G. W. F. Hegel, *Faith and Knowledge,* ed. and trans. Walter Cerf and Henry S. Harris (Albany: State University of New York Press, 1977), 189.
[2] GW 4, 377. Hegel, *Faith and Knowledge,* 139. See Birgit Sandkaulen, "Das Nichtige in seiner ganzen Länge und Breite. Hegels Kritik der Reflexionsphilosophie," *Hegel-Jahrbuch* 2004 (2004): 165–73.
[3] GW 4, 359f. Hegel, *Faith and Knowledge,* 114.
[4] GW 4, 354f. Hegel, *Faith and Knowledge,* 107.

says. Jacobi insists that Spinoza's "sub specie aeternitatis" model of ontology does indeed require the dimension of time for its elaboration but is simultaneously unable to integrate time into its conceptual framework without internal contradictions. Hegel, in contrast, tries to neutralize this problem by declaring it nonexistent. On the other hand, and in direct connection to this narrower dispute, there is a fundamental disagreement as to whether time should be considered a philosophically relevant topic at all. I will return to this second point later in the chapter. First, however, I want to address the question of how one should read Spinoza. Is Jacobi correct in his diagnosis that the *Ethics* is plagued by unresolved problems with time? Or is Hegel right in claiming that Spinoza's theory consistently presents time as a mere product of the imagination, in other words, that Jacobi projects assumptions onto the *Ethics* that are entirely false? Before turning to Spinoza's own text in an attempt to find an answer to this question, it will be helpful to address the two aforementioned interpretations in greater detail.

With regard to Jacobi, I shall briefly recapitulate three decisive structural features of his discussion of Spinoza in order to contextualize the problem of time.[5] First, Jacobi is to be credited with the earliest rational reconstruction of the *Ethics*, in which he reveals Spinoza's model to be a self-contained system of a metaphysics of immanence. Second, and in connection with this, we should note that Jacobi admires this system for its exemplarity and also considers it to be irrefutable. This brings us to the third point, which is that the criticism Jacobi nonetheless levels against Spinoza's "fatalism" has the methodological character of a *practical contradiction*. Such a contradiction must be strictly distinguished from a *theoretical refutation*. The "doctrine of Spinoza," as Jacobi argues in his exchange with Mendelssohn, is "irrefutable" [unwiderleglich], not "*uncontradictable*" [unwidersprechlich] (Spin: JWA 1,1, 290). This distinction between refutation and contradiction marks the point where Jacobi's substantive critique of Spinoza begins. As this critique makes clear, to proceed according to the logic of the system is to unavoidably come into direct conflict with the convictions that guide our daily lives. In terms of the crucial question of our "freedom," this conflict pertains above all to the possibility of free action, which can simply no longer be adequately understood once the concept of *causa finalis* is eliminated. But it also has significant implications with regard to the dimension of time, because "an action which is not in time is a non-thing" (Spin: JWA 1,1, 257; MPW 373). Jacobi's fundamental interest in time is thus oriented toward the conditions of human existence, an orientation that goes hand in hand with his insistence that Spinoza's ontology fails, for systematic reasons, to account for this interest.

As already indicated, Jacobi does not claim that the dimension of time is completely absent in the *Ethics,* and presenting a simplistic contrast between eternity and time is far from his intention. The point of his objection is rather that while Spinoza has the temporality of the finite world very much in mind, the logic of the system means that he can only deal with it aporetically. This objection targets Spinoza's effort to provide a universal and rational explanation of the world, which, in renouncing traditional ideas

---

[5] On this point, see Birgit Sandkaulen, *Grund und Ursache. Die Vernunftkritik Jacobis* (Munich: Wilhelm Fink Verlag, 2000) both in general and, on the problem of time, esp. chapter VI, 133–69 as well as Chapters 2, 3, and 4 in this volume.

of creation, must supply a *"natural explanation of the existence [Daseyn] of finite and successive things"* (Spin: JWA 1,1, 251). In the process of developing this explanation, however, Spinoza ends up committing himself to the self-contradictory determination of an "eternal time."

Given Jacobi's admiration for the consistency and irrefutability of the *Ethics*, the diagnosis of an internal contradiction might seem surprising. Can a system really be both internally consistent and simultaneously self-contradicting? As Jacobi sees it, the two are not mutually exclusive. On the contrary, their combination here is directly connected to his core assertion—that a system which seeks to advance not just a *logical* but also an *ontological* claim must necessarily be based on an ambiguous foundation. It is ambiguous because, in the interest of providing a rational explanation of the world, it ends up "confusing the concept of *cause* with the concept of *ground*" (Spin: JWA 1,1, 255; MPW 371). The degree to which this *confusion of ground and cause*, which is as fundamental as it is problematic, bears upon the question of time, follows directly from Jacobi's explanation of these terms. The *logical* relationship between ground and consequence is defined by the exclusion of temporal succession. In contrast, the *real* relation between cause and effect, referred to as the *principium generationis* by Jacobi, can *only* be understood in the context of conditions characterized by temporal succession, in which it also becomes clear that we experience this real causality originally in our own action.[6] The difference between cause and consequence is logical, whereas the difference between cause and effect is temporal: The fact that a conflation of these two aspects is constitutive of Spinoza's approach means that the temporal reality of coming-to-be and ceasing-to-be, of becoming and change, is not simply ignored but is rather logically deformed in the theorem of immanence.

As a result of this deformation, it appears that the real succession of changing modes is integrated into the interior of substance without at the same time destroying the eternal connection between infinite substance and finite mode. Moreover, according to Jacobi's account, this corresponds perfectly to Spinoza's description of *"time, measure, and number"* as "beings of the imagination" in his 12th letter (JWA 1,1, 253; MPW 371).[7] The concept of time, which is produced by the *imaginatio*, implies a separation of modes from substance. It therefore has no significance for reason, which integrates change in its pure form, as it were (i.e., without any imaginatively generated remainder),

---

[6] Jacobi states explicitly that "as the concept of cause is distinguished from that of ground, it is a concept of experience which we owe to the consciousness of our own causality and passivity, and cannot be derived from the merely idealistic concept of ground any more than it can be resolved into it" (Spin: JWA 1,1, 256; MPW 371f.). In other words, the concept of cause and the corresponding concept of effect are in no way intended to refer to the causality of natural laws. Rather, according to Jacobi, this type of causality of natural laws emerges from a *union* of ground and cause that has its logical counterpart in the principle of sufficient reason [Grund], according to which "everything conditional must have a condition" (Spin: JWA 1,1, 256; MPW 372). This union [Vereinigung] of ground and cause is unproblematic as long as the "essential difference" between logical and real relations of conditionality remains transparent, but the mixing [Vermischung] of these two concepts entails the neutralization of this difference. In this case, "one takes the liberty of replacing one with the other, and using them in this way. The result is that things come to be without coming to be; that they change without changing; that they can precede or follow one another without being before or after one another" (Spin: JWA 1,1, 256; MPW 372).

[7] See Baruch de Spinoza, *The Letters*, in *Spinoza. Complete Works*, ed. Michael L. Morgan, trans. Samuel Shirley (Indianapolis: Hackett Publishing Company, 2002), 789.

into the logic of the ground.⁸ In truth, however, as Jacobi explains, this interpretation entails a self-deception of reason. In the paradoxical figure of an "*eternal time*," the supposed integration of modal change has always already been neutralized. This follows necessarily from the fact that a self-enclosed system of immanence cannot accommodate a forward progression of time, but must instead, figuratively speaking, bend time back into a circle. Precisely for this reason, moreover, the "mathematical analogies" adduced by Spinoza fail to strengthen his claims.⁹ Geometric figures as such have nothing to do with the phenomenon of real succession. Thus, to the extent that Spinoza (or anyone else) makes use of such figures to illustrate that the idea of immanence can be reconciled with a consideration of real changes in the realm of the finite modi, then he allows himself, in Jacobi's words, to be "deceived by the imagination." In fact it is the observer himself who subjectively projects a movement onto the geometric figure that is by no means objectively present in the thing itself¹⁰ (Spin: JWA 1,1, 251f.).

---

⁸ "From the proposition, Becoming cannot have become or have originated any more than *Being* or substance, Spinoza drew the correct consequence that matter must have an eternal and infinite actuosity [Actuosität] of its own, and that this actuosity must be an immediate mode of substance. This immediate, eternal mode, that he believed to be expressed by the relation of motion and rest in natura naturata, was for him the universal, *eternal, unalterable* form of individual things and of their unceasing change. If this *movement* did not have a beginning, *individual things* could not have begun either. Not only were these things eternal in origin, therefore; they also, according to reason, existed *simultaneously*, regardless of their succession: for in the *concept of reason itself*, there is no prior or posterior, but everything is necessary and simultaneous, and the one and only consequence permitted in thought is that of *dependence*. So the moment that Spinoza elevated the experiential concepts of movement, of individual things, of generation and succession, into concepts of reason, they were at once *purified* of everything empirical for him; and, with the firm conviction that everything had to be considered only secundum modum quo a rebus æternis fluit, he could regard the concepts of time, measure, and number, as one-sided representational views abstracted from this modus, and hence as beings of the imagination to which reason did not need to give any attention before it had first reformed them, and brought them back to the truth (vere consideratum)." (Spin: JWA 1,1, 253f.; MPW 370f.)

⁹ Jacobi refers primarily to the geometric figure in Spinoza's 12th letter. Also relevant is the figure included in the *Ethics* E II, prop. 8.

¹⁰ Just how intensively Jacobi concerned himself with this set of problems becomes especially clear in the revealing addendum he inserted into the third edition of his *Spinoza Letters,* which appeared in 1819 in the context of the publication of his collected works. Here he writes: "With regard to individual things, Spinoza does indeed deny the possibility of a *becoming that has become* [gewordenes Werden] but not of a becoming that has not become, that is without beginning or end, or a truly actual coming-to-be and ceasing-to-be thereof, albeit only in an eternal, self-circling flow. Individual things, Spinoza expressly teaches, do not arise directly from the infinite; rather each individual thing presupposes an infinite succession of other individual things. Hence individual things arise out of God only in an eternal and infinite sense, not in a temporary, finite, and transitory sense; *for they arise from one another only in the sense that they successively create and destroy each other,* but remain no less unchangeable in their eternal existence because of this (Eth. P.I, Prop XXVIII) [...]. It is thus undeniable that Spinoza asserted the actual existence of an *eternal temporality,* a beginningless but actual and true coming-to-be and ceasing-to-be of finite, actual and true individual beings in a necessary progression. However, he easily managed to dismiss the objection that it is absurd to think *an eternal time could ever arrive at the present day,* by showing how, in the face of reason, time disappears from temporality necessarily and of its own accord; with the result that temporality is immediately transfigured into something unchangeable and eternal, into the very Godhead itself [...] In truth, however, the system gains nothing from this, as I believe I have made sufficiently clear in the three places mentioned previously. Indeed, the twofold question to be posed to Spinoza only now comes to the fore; whether he proposes that there is only being in nature but no becoming; or conversely, that there is only becoming in her, but no being. In answer to the second question we receive a clear no; but to the first only a yes *with* no, and, by virtue of this *with*, a collection of conflicting elements that simply cannot be united to form a truly peaceful alliance." (Spin: JWA 1,1, 252f.)

Jacobi draws a radical conclusion from this analysis. Spinoza's entanglement in the contradiction of "eternal time" shows that his attempt to provide a universal explanation of the world by way of a philosophical system is doomed to fail. The phenomenon of temporal existence serves as a warning sign in this regard and indicates the limits of reason. If we fail to respect these limits, then the experiential foundation of our understanding of ourselves and the world is destroyed, with grave ethical consequences.

We can now better understand why Hegel, to whom I now turn, responds to this analysis with polemical indignation. If Jacobi is right, then not only is Spinoza's ontology called into question, but also Hegel's own systematic ambitions. As articulated in *Faith and Knowledge,* these ambitions are indebted to Spinoza's *Ethics* precisely insofar as that they mobilize the prospect of a holistic philosophy of identity in opposition to the "reflective philosophy of subjectivity" proposed by Kant, Jacobi, and Fichte. But what chance of success can Hegel hope to have if the problem of time subverts the persuasiveness of any and all claims to rigorous systematicity? I have already elucidated the general line of argument adopted by Hegel in this context. In his view, there is no problem at all, because "true philosophy" does not concern itself with the irrelevant "nothingness" of temporal existence. But this argument alone does not provide a sufficient defense against Jacobi's critique. Rather, to invalidate Jacobi's analysis, it must be shown that Spinoza's *Ethics* had already insisted on the "nothingness" of time.

As the amount of space devoted to the dispute alone makes clear, Hegel considers the establishment of this antecedent to be of the greatest importance.[11] In its basic outline, however, Hegel's argumentation is clearly structured and not overly complicated. To support his claim that Jacobi's diagnosis goes completely astray, that it is absurd to assert that Spinoza entangled himself in the aporia of "eternal time," Hegel provides a reading of Spinoza that, in contrast to that of Jacobi, is constituted by a fundamental separation of time and eternity. Only the dimension of eternity is ontologically significant. In contrast, the ontic phenomenon of time is based on an "abstraction" that obscures the true relation between substance and its modes. This corresponds to Hegel's insistence that Spinoza's approach can only be adequately understood to the extent that one strictly distinguishes between two kinds of infinity.

More specifically, a distinction must be made between the "*infinitum actu,*" on the one hand, and what Hegel calls "empirical infinity" on the other.[12] The absolutely infinite is characterized as "the absolute affirmation of the existence of any nature," and Hegel continues: "this simple definition makes the infinite into the absolute and true concept, equal to itself and indivisible, which of its essence includes the particular or finite in itself at the same time." According to Hegel, Spinoza designates this type of the infinite as the "infinity of the intellect [Verstandes]," which, in Hegel's interpretation, is directly connected to "intuitive cognition." In contrast, "empirical infinity" is a matter for the "imagination." In abstracting from affirmative infinity, the imagination is characterized by negation. It thereby splits the mode off from substance, breaks it

---

[11] Hegel, *Glauben und Wissen,* GW 4, 354–60. Hegel, *Faith and Knowledge,* 107–15.
[12] GW 4, 354f. Hegel, *Faith and Knowledge,* 108. All of the following quotations can be found on 354ff./108ff.

down into individual, quantifiable elements and only then ascribes to it an existence in time. "Duration," as Hegel explicitly remarks, is a "time moment, a finite," that is only posited "through the imagination." And "empirical infinity" likewise emerges in precisely this way, as the successive imagining of individual things that are fixed in time and distinct from one another.

Against this backdrop, Hegel seeks to advance two claims. Inasmuch as "imagination, or reflection, is only concerned with single things or with abstractions and the finite," then it is clear, first, that single things in their temporal existence "are nothing in themselves."[13] That they exist in this form only for the imagination (which is to say, not actually) is what Spinoza, according to Hegel's account, wants to prove through his geometric examples. Second, it is also clear to Hegel that Jacobi is entirely incapable of speculative thinking, being completely fixated instead on the "imagination." For this reason, Jacobi regards the "nothingness" of temporal existence as something actual in itself, although nothing could be further from the truth, and for this reason he also confronts Spinoza with an objection that is demonstrably absurd. Not only is Jacobi grasping at straws when he cavils at the alleged paradox of "eternal time." In addition to this, the very notion that Spinoza intends to provide a "natural explanation of the existence of finite and successive things," an intention that Jacobi attributes to the *Ethics*, already reveals his fundamental misunderstanding of Spinoza's philosophy. After all, how could it have ever occurred to Spinoza to attempt such an explanation, given that he aimed to achieve precisely the opposite, namely, to destroy abstract "singularity and finitude" in the "idea"?[14]

Now we have clarified the positions of the two thinkers and, at the same time, revealed the deeper motivations driving their confrontations with Spinoza. Both Hegel and Jacobi are engaged in more than mere doxography. On the contrary, there are substantive issues at stake—both seek to shed light on our understanding of ourselves and the world, and, for both, Spinoza's *Ethics* is seen to possess exemplary validity. Precisely for this reason, however, it is crucial not to view their interpretations as equally valid hermeneutic variations but instead to carefully consider the plausibility of each in terms of the source text. Did Jacobi get it right, or was Hegel correct to

---

[13] GW 4, 355f. Hegel, *Faith and Knowledge*, 108.

[14] Compare the passage in its entirety: "This transformation is of the simplest; [for] imagination, or reflection, is only concerned with single things or with abstractions and the finite—they have absolute validity for it. But in the Idea this singularity and finitude is brought to nought, because the opposite of reflection or of imagination, the mental or the empirical opposite is thought as one [with the Idea]. Reflection can comprehend this much: that things which it posits as particulars are posited as identical. What it cannot comprehend is that in the identity they are nullified; for since it is only reflection that is active, its products are absolute. So, to its delight, it detects an absurdity: it posits both the identity of what exists for it, only in separation, and the absolute standing of those same separate entities in this identity. This is Jacobi's case. He posits the abstract entity 'time' and the abstract entity 'single thing,' which are products of imagination or reflection, as existing in themselves; and then he finds that, if the absolute *simul* of the eternal substance is posited, the single thing and time, which only are in virtue of having been removed from it, are equally posited along with it. He fails to reflect on the fact that when the single thing and time are restored to the eternal substance from which they were taken, they cease to be what they only are if torn away from it. So he retains time and singularity and [finite] actuality within infinity and eternity itself." (GW 4, 356; Hegel, *Faith and Knowledge*, 109)

dismiss Jacobi's analysis as the product of faulty thinking incapable of moving beyond the mere imagination?

The evidence is not in Hegel's favor. According to his reading, Spinoza's conception of metaphysics is essentialist to the core. But how can this be the case, given that Spinoza distinguishes between two forms of modal existence: essential or real existence (which, like substance, is eternal) and the actual existence of modes in time?[15] This actual existence is already introduced in prop. 28 of the first part of the *Ethics* as the infinite interdependence of finite things, and it shapes the entire line of reasoning from the second part onward, including the *conatus* theory, which identifies the striving of a mode for self-preservation with its "*essentia actualis*." As an actualized essence, the striving for self-preservation therefore extends indefinitely in time.[16]

Hegel's essentialist interpretation of Spinoza does not even penetrate to the point of these concrete structures of temporal finitude. On the contrary, to declare the temporal being of things to be the product of "the imagination," and to support this claim with a misleading reference to prop. 28 of the first part of the *Ethics*,[17] is tantamount to the destruction—in the truest sense of the word—of the ontological ground that provides the indispensable support for an ethical theory oriented toward the actual conduct of everyday life. Hegel's erroneous conception of the *imaginatio* underscores this point. The *imaginatio* is by no means responsible for the alleged pseudo-existence of the temporal world, as Hegel claims. The problem, according to Spinoza, is that in relating to this world, it fails to adequately acknowledge its actual existence.[18] Hegel's strangely synonymizing reference to "imagination or reflection" is thus extremely revealing. Lacking any credible basis in Spinoza's own work, it shows the conceptual framework to which Hegel is actually indebted. In *Faith and Knowledge*, he has clearly projected the approach of *Schelling's* philosophy of identity onto Spinoza's *Ethics*. I will return to this matter shortly.

The point here is not simply that the projection which Hegel claims to discern in Jacobi actually applies to his own interpretation. In the case of Jacobi, the accusation is in fact completely misguided. Unlike Hegel, Jacobi offers a precise analysis of Spinoza's position. What should be noted in this context is, first, that Jacobi never loses sight of the difference between essential-real and temporal-actual existence. Moreover, and in connection with this, he recognizes that Spinoza's theory of human cognition and action is based on the presupposition of an actually existing human body (Spin: JWA 1,1, 105ff.; MPW 223ff.). Second, and even more crucially, Jacobi takes the additional step of questioning the *possibility of grounding* this difference under the conditions of a metaphysics of immanence, and he localizes the challenge of such a grounding in

---

[15] See Spinoza, *Ethics*, EV, prop. 29.
[16] E III, prop. 7 and 8.
[17] Hegel, *Glauben und Wissen*, GW 4, 355. Hegel, *Faith and Knowledge*, 107.
[18] Spinoza's statement in the 12th letter can also be related to this: as a consequence of its inadequate cognition, the *imaginatio* forms an abstract *concept of time*, which splits the modes off from substance. Spinoza's critique of this abstraction, however, does not mean that temporality as an ontic phenomenon is negated, as Hegel asserts. In doing so, he overlooks entirely Spinoza's distinction between essential and actual existence of modes, a distinction he treats extensively in the 12th letter.

Spinoza's claim that the temporal being of things does not follow immediately from the eternal substance, but only through a process of mediation.[19]

After all, even if one establishes temporal being as a factum that must be taken into account by any ontology that purports to be complete (especially in terms of providing ethical guidance for life), but one that cannot be directly derived from the eternal being of substance, then the question still remains as to how this factum is to be integrated into the unity of the system. What can it mean, in other words, when Spinoza assures us in this very context, that "all things that are, are in God, and so depend on God that they can neither be nor be conceived without him"?[20] According to the all-embracing unity required by the system, the dimension of temporal existence cannot be situated beyond immanence. Therefore it cannot be thought of as an open—*indefinite*—process either, but rather must be conceived as *infinite*, "as actually infinite," with the consequence that precisely the necessity of thinking this infiniteness of actual existence leads to the "absurd concept of an eternal time," a difficulty "which no mathematical construction can get rid of" (Spin: JWA 1,1, 257; MPW 373).[21] Jacobi does not, of course, assert that Spinoza himself made reference to the determination of an "eternal time." Rather, he argues that Spinoza was able to deceive himself about the paradox lurking at the center of his model through his use of geometric examples.

Hegel, Jacobi, and Schelling

Jacobi's response to Hegel's treatise is to be found in his text *Drei Briefe an Friedrich Köppen* [Three Letters to Friedrich Köppen], which appeared in 1803 as an accompaniment to Köppen's book on Schelling. If one considers these letters against the backdrop of the issues just discussed, then it might initially appear that the dispute over the status of time failed to generate a reaction. Jacobi does not mention Hegel's defense of Spinoza and to that extent he also refrains from arguing for the accuracy of his own analysis. What he does dispute as a mischaracterization of his position pertains to his concept of reason. More specifically, he rejects Hegel's claim "*that for me reason is something generally subjective*" (BK: JWA 2,1, 369), a claim that is entirely at odds with Jacobi's insistence on a distinction between substantive and adjective reason.

Rather than pursue this thread of the discussion here, however, I want to remain with the question of time, because, as we can see upon closer inspection, this topic is

---

[19] E I, prop. 28, scholium; See Jacobi, Spin: JWA 1,1, 109; MPW 226.
[20] E I, prop. 28, scholium.
[21] Thus, rather than adopting Hegel's erroneous distinction between infinite and "empirical," that is to say, indefinite infinity, this means that in the case of Spinoza one must in fact reckon with *two types of infinite infinity*: with an essential infinity and an actual infinity. And it is crucial in this context that the dilemma of actual infinity cannot be resolved by way of a distinction between duration and time. If one disregards the abstract and thus inadequate concept of time, which is formed by an *imaginatio* that is not relevant here anyway, Spinoza does not maintain any consistent distinction between duration and time in the *Ethics*, and this finding in particular points us back once again to the fundamental problem identified by Jacobi.

most certainly under consideration in the text. Indeed, it constitutes Jacobi's primary concern. And it becomes clear at the same time why Jacobi no longer has any need to refer to Spinoza's own treatment of the topic. Spinoza's successor turns out to be *Schelling's* philosophy of identity, which explicitly articulates the conclusion only implied in the work of Kant and Fichte and which is described by Jacobi as "obviously correct [...] as soon as one presumes the absolute necessity of a philosophy of one piece" (BK: JWA 2,1, 364). Long before the dispute over "divine things" then, Schelling appears here for the first time in Jacobi's crosshairs, because Jacobi, who correctly surmised that Hegel was the author of *Faith and Knowledge* based on its style, had at the same time also recognized that the conception of system underlying Hegel's critique originated with Schelling.[22] It is thus by no means false for him to assume that the attack, although published under Hegel's name, must be understood as a de facto joint undertaking on the part of Hegel and Schelling. A statement in one of Schelling's letters provides concrete evidence of this and simultaneously alerts us to the crucial issue. In a note sent along with a copy of *Faith and Knowledge* to Wilhelm Schlegel in August 1802, Schelling writes that "Jacobi's speculative side is very persuasively dealt with, including his most recent statements, with which you are familiar, and including the basic principle from which they all clearly derive, namely the fear of the annihilation of the finite" (JWA 2,2, 489).

This is precisely the topic that Jacobi then highlights, almost as if he had read Schelling's note, framing the entire line of attack in *Faith and Knowledge* as an attempt to defuse the provocation of his double philosophy. His willingness to confirm, for reasons of systematic logic, the need for a "philosophy of one piece" and at the same time to refuse to grant such a project his unequivocal approval, is perceived by Hegel and Schelling as a "contradiction," which they "are only able to explain in psychological and moral terms, as a form of intellectual cowardice ... that makes me afraid of losing my *finite* being and gives rise to my contemptible refusal to pass over from finitude into infinity" (BK: JWA 2,1, 365). But as if this were not enough, having allegedly ascertained that Jacobi knows full well what the logic of the system demands but fails to mobilize this insight for the purposes of any system-building project—"because, as I said, I shudder at the thought of losing my finitude and my temporality"—they have no choice but to infer from "the perfection of non-willing an imperfection in ability." In other words, Jacobi is not only accused of holding fast to a phenomenon that is in truth utterly insignificant, but also of being incapable of speculative thinking (BK: JWA 2,1, 365f.).

Jacobi himself remains unimpressed by this diagnosis. He neither defends his position on what Schelling terms his fear "the annihilation of the finite," nor does he reject this allegation as an unacceptable conflation of psychological and substantive motivations. He merely acknowledges that the critique of his position proceeds in this fashion, and no more than this is required, given that he has already subjected Schelling's philosophy to a thorough critique in the second letter to Köppen. This

---

[22] On this point see also Birgit Sandkaulen, "Die Ontologie der Substanz, der Begriff der Subjektivität und die Faktizität des Einzelnen. Hegels reflexionslogische 'Widerlegung' der Spinozanischen Metaphysik," *International Yearbook of German Idealism* 5 (2008): 235–75.

account, which addresses three of Schelling's texts published around 1800, is thus a matter of some importance.[23] But in what sense?

Based on Schelling's assertion that in conceptualizing his philosophy of nature and his transcendental philosophy as two different sciences, he had always had their absolute unity in mind, Jacobi takes the presentation of the system of identity as a starting point for an interpretation that situates all three texts within a *single* conceptual framework. It should be noted at the outset that this move is not entirely unproblematic. After all, irrespective of how one feels about Schelling's self-interpretation, there is no denying that Jacobi neutralizes certain indisputable differences between the philosophy of nature and the philosophy of identity by adopting an approach that interweaves text passages from both contexts. The passages he selects, however, are particularly compelling. Extending across multiple contexts, they indicate the fundamental dilemma with which Schelling is in fact struggling and which, according to Jacobi's account, can be traced back to his desire to solve "the mystery of the origin and the existence of things, the quintessence of which we call world, nature, or universe, by human means," that is to say, through an act of systematic construction (BK: JWA 2,1, 355).

As a result, not only does this world as an actually existing finite world disappear from view, insofar as it is always already resolved into a unity that transforms the difference between finite and infinite into a one that is merely internal. Even more disastrous for this approach is the consequence that follows therefrom: that references to nature lose all determinate meaning. "Its being," as Jacobi recapitulates Schelling's outline of a speculative physics,

> is thus identity and indifference of capability and incapability [Indifferenz des Könnens und Nichtkönnens]: *pure*, utterly indifferent *busyness* [Geschäftigkeit]. It aims neither at form nor deformity, but, in absolute terms, at a *neither the one nor the other*, it desires absolutely that which can never become, and is thus an eternal becoming and *only* this. An eternal, hermaphroditic copulation without procreation is the essential character of its working and weaving. It dualizes itself, to the extent that it dualizes itself, solely in order to bring forth this state of simulated procreation. (BK: JWA 2,1, 359f.)

It is obvious that in the figure of "eternal becoming," in which nothing actually ever becomes or is supposed to become, Jacobi discerns a return of the problem of "eternal time" previously identified in Spinoza. By the same token, however, Jacobi's presentation reveals that the severity of the problem in Schelling far surpasses that of Spinoza. Schelling is the heir of and successor to Kant and Fichte, who were the first to explicitly and consciously articulate the constructivist paradigm of systematic logic. In

---

[23] See *Erster Entwurf eines Systems der Naturphilosophie* [First Plan of a System of the Philosophy of Nature] and the *Einleitung zu dem Entwurf eines Systems der Naturphilosophie* [Introduction to the Outline of a System of the Philosophy of Nature], both published in 1799, as well as the *Darstellung meines Systems der Philosophie* [Presentation of my System of Philosophy] from 1801.

comparison with Spinoza, this means, first of all, that Schelling's philosophy of nature and philosophy of identity no longer provide any basis for distinguishing between the essential and actual-temporal existence of the finite, a distinction which Spinoza had been able to posit as ontologically meaningful. Indeed, Schelling actually espouses the view that Hegel, as we have seen, will falsely project onto Spinoza's ontology, and which Schelling himself apparently deems an adequate understanding of Spinoza—that the finite world, as a temporally constituted world, is "utterly and absolutely nothing" and originates solely "on the basis of laws of reflection."[24]

Second, as a consequence of this aggressive annihilation of the temporal world and the sublation of the finite into an absolute unity with the infinite, the allegation of having deceived oneself about the inner contradiction of the conception also loses its relevance—again in contrast to the case of Spinoza. The contradictory idea of an "eternal becoming," which is "in no way anti-*productive*, but which is completely anti-*product*" (BK: JWA 2,1, 359),[25] which combines within itself an "antiproductive productivity and productive antiproductivity" (BK: JWA 2,1, 361)—precisely this idea is systematically elaborated and postulated as the only accurate understanding of the circumstances. Schelling also pays a price for adopting this view, however, that of having to forfeit any and all determinate meaning as well as any possibility of making statements that disclose precise features of reality. As Jacobi remarks on this situation, "in order for reason to flourish, the understanding has to founder," and he then goes on to conclude in decidedly ironic terms that "the immersion into this state of universal insight is accompanied by such self-satisfied perceptual and observational bliss that anyone who has experienced it would burrow deep into the earth with shame at the thought of harboring a wish for anything more" (BK: JWA 2,1, 361). Did Hegel perhaps take note of Jacobi's critique of Schelling here? The fact that years later, in the preface to the *Phenomenology of Spirit*, Hegel distances himself from Schelling with remarkably similar arguments, certainly suggests as much.

Questions for Schelling and Hegel

Whether he was directly inspired by Jacobi or not, Hegel's break with Schelling offers an indisputable indication that the previously so fervently desired "annihilation of the finite," as well as the polemic against Jacobi, with its characterization of the temporality of finite existence as a mere "nothingness," was based on a fatal misconception. The misconception lies in failing to grasp what has to be achieved philosophically. Schelling, by the way, adopts the same view when he later categorizes the entire phase of his philosophies of nature and identity under the rubric of a "negative philosophy" (which he had presumably been pursuing all along), and in this same context pays particular attention to the phenomenon of time: "Time is the starting point of all

---

[24] Schelling, *Fernere Darstellungen aus dem System der Philosophie*, SW IV, 385f.
[25] Jacobi writes, "keineswegs antiproduk-*tiv*, doch ganz und gar anti-*produktisch*." The exact wordplay cannot be reproduced in English.

philosophical investigations, and one will never be able to provide an intelligible account of development without offering a precise explanation of time."[26]

In light of these substantial revisions, it is no exaggeration to claim that at the turn of the century, Jacobi is clearly well ahead of his time. But this insight also forces us to confront two questions. The first is what motivated Schelling and Hegel to adopt the view that they initially espoused. This view cannot be ignored, for the simple reason that without an analysis of the starting point, it remains unclear to what extent and why the systems end up "in motion." How is it possible, in other words, that the phenomenon of time comes to be adamantly rejected as unreal and any interest in this phenomenon dismissed as irrelevant, when the aim of post-Kantian philosophy is to found a new realism? One plausible motivation, it seems to me, is to be found in Kant's theory of time as an a priori form of sensible intuition. In his treatise of 1802, *Über das Unternehmen des Kritizismus, die Vernunft zu Verstande zu bringen* [On the Efforts of Critical Philosophy to Bring Reason to its Senses], Jacobi not only considered Kant's position on this matter in his discussion of the problematics of time but vehemently criticized it. Conversely, Kant's own ascription of time to the realm of appearance may have inspired his successors to categorize temporal phenomena as mere products of the imagination and to look elsewhere for the "true reality." Are Schelling and Hegel, then, still "Kantians" in this regard, whose interpretations of Spinoza's ontology and Jacobi's critique of Spinoza must be considered unequivocally false as a result?

The second question follows directly from this possibility. If my conjecture is correct (which is not to say that it already provides an explanation for the striking aversion to the finite), then the next step would be to assess the subsequent post-Kantian systems with an eye toward whether, when, and to what degree we can observe a distancing from Kant's theory of time. But this is not all, because, insofar as we are concerned with the ambitions of *system-building projects*, then what must be investigated is not merely the status of time as an ontologically significant phenomenon, but rather how this aspect is *integrated* into the system as a whole. It is therefore crucial to pursue the problem that Jacobi already identified in his first encounter with Spinoza—that, for reasons of systematic logic, the recurrence of the paradox of an "eternal time" must also be expected in post-Kantianism.

---

[26] F. W. J. Schelling, *System der Weltalter. Münchener Vorlesung 1827/28 in einer Nachschrift von Ernst von Lasaulx*, ed. Siegbert Peetz, 2nd ed. (Frankfurt a.M.: Vittorio Klostermann, 1998), 16. With regard to his own earlier conception, Schelling now expressly notes: "But an eternal happening is no happening at all" (SW X, 124; F. W. J. Schelling, *On the History of Modern Philosophy*, ed. and trans. Andrew Bowie (Cambridge: Cambridge University Press, 1994), 133).

14

Third Position of Thought toward Objectivity: Immediate Knowing

It should be noted at the outset: In order to reconstruct Hegel's "Third Position of Thought Toward Objectivity" in full detail and subject its critique of immediate knowing to an exhaustive examination, one would have to write an entire book. And to offer this qualification is simultaneously to reveal what Hegel's text is not. Notwithstanding the suggestive power it evinces on a surface level, an effect that is very much intentional, the text is neither easily accessible, nor does it actually provide the compelling assessment of immediate knowing for which its progression of stridently critical chords might initially be mistaken. Indeed, grounds for skepticism regarding its claims can already be found in the performative contradiction in which Hegel entangles himself here, one he certainly would have preferred to avoid—if it had been possible.

In contrast to a critical analysis of the text, this contradiction can be formulated quite succinctly: If the standpoint of immediate knowing were truly as philosophically marginal as Hegel's presentation suggests (on a surface level), then there would have been absolutely no reason to give it a second glance. However, not only is this standpoint taken up as the third and thus concluding position in the „preliminary conception," receiving, as opposed to Kant's critical philosophy, a section all to itself; it also becomes the subject of a debate which, in comparison with the topics covered in the first two positions—metaphysics, empiricism, and critical philosophy—gives rise to what is by far the most detailed investigation.

Insofar as it is possible within the limits of a single chapter, the aim of my subsequent reflections will be to elucidate this highly complex debate and make it accessible to a critical appraisal. After first explicating the fundamental conflict that organizes the text (1.), I will turn to Hegel's review of Jacobi's works (hereafter: *Jacobi-Review*) (2.), a consideration of which is indispensable to my argument, and which is especially helpful in unpacking the multiple semantic layers of the term "immediacy" (3.). Only then does it become possible to provide an adequate structural overview of Hegel's train of thought (4.), on the basis of which the substantive statements contained in the text can be interpreted relative to the function of the "Third Position" (5.). A concluding reflection will consider whether Hegel successfully realizes his objectives (6.).[1]

The Fundamental Conflict

As mentioned previously, the standpoint of immediate knowing has a significance for Hegel that stands in inverse proportion to his conspicuous efforts, as extensive as they are varied, to deny it any importance whatsoever. This contradiction is indicative of an implicit fundamental conflict, one that places every single sentence in the text into a state of polysemy, in some cases to the point that the actual meaning is rendered unrecognizable. The source of this conflict has a name—that of Jacobi—whose invocation also allows us to formulate the performative contradiction that inheres in the "Third Position" as follows: In forcefully insisting that Jacobi's position is utterly untenable and thus poses no challenge whatsoever to his own claims, Hegel ends up confirming precisely the opposite, namely, that it does indeed constitute a challenge for him, and in fact the central one.

If one continues on to see how the argument progresses, then the problems of the text appear with still greater clarity. It becomes evident that even a reader entirely ignorant of Jacobi's approach, and thus not in a position to evaluate it by way of a comparison with Hegel's own deliberations, would be unable to learn anything substantive about this approach from Hegel, whether positive or negative. Such an outcome is impossible for structural reasons, as is established by the fact that Hegel makes no reference whatsoever to the challenge with which Jacobi had been identified in contemporary debates since the publication of his *Concerning the Doctrine of Spinoza in Letters to Herr Moses Mendelssohn*. What Hegel does indicate at the beginning of the "Third Position" is merely the fact that Jacobi's insistence on the mode of an immediate certainty, one prior to any mediated knowledge and thus radically inaccessible to any attempts at rational justification, also entails a criticism of Kant, with regard to both the certainty of the unconditioned as well as the sensuous.

What Hegel fails to mention, however, or rather, what he conceals in making the completely misguided claim that Jacobi's "polemic" against cognition contained in

[1] In the following, the "preliminary conception" to the science of logic of the *Encyclopedia* of 1830 will be cited parenthetically in the text as VE with an indication of the paragraph and the page number in GW 20 as well as an indication of the corresponding page in the English translation: G. W. F. Hegel, *Encyclopedia of the Philosophical Sciences in Basic Outline. Part 1: Logic*, ed. and trans. Klaus Brinkmann and Daniel O. Dahlstrom (Cambridge: Cambridge University Press, 2010). To date there have been only a very few scholarly treatments of the "Third Position," and their selective concentration on specific theorems and paragraphs makes clear that we still lack an adequate understanding of Hegel's text, both with regard to its background as well as its conceptual architecture. See Kenneth Westphal, "Hegel's Attitude toward Jacobi in the 'Third Attitude of Thought toward Objectivity,'" *The Southern Journal of Philosophy* 27 (1989): 135–56; Pirmin Stekeler-Weithofer, *Hegels Analytische Philosophie. Die Wissenschaft der Logik als kritische Theorie der Bedeutung* (Paderborn: Schöningh, 1992); Christoph Halbig, *Objektives Denken. Erkenntnistheorie und Philosophy of Mind in Hegels System* (Stuttgart-Bad Cannstatt: Frommann-Holzboog, 2002); Christoph Halbig, "The Philosopher as Polyphemus? Philosophy and Common Sense in Jacobi and Hegel," *International Yearbook of German Idealism* 3 (2005): 261–82.

Supplement VII to the *Spinoza Letters* was "derived from Spinoza's philosophy itself" (VE: § 62, 101; 110), is the aspect of Jacobi's Spinoza critique that plays a far more constitutive role in his own project. This critique, in casting Spinoza's metaphysics as the exemplary case of a perfect and consequently irrefutable system of necessity, one that can only be contradicted by an equally resolute leap undertaken in the interests of freedom, not only inspires all contemporary efforts to develop an alternative system of freedom; it also insists that they are all doomed to fail. Jacobi's comments on immediate certainty thus do not simply indicate his opposition to the operation of mediating knowledge as "knowing to be of the finite only." This is how Hegel characterizes it (VE: § 62, 101; 111), an interpretation which also implies that Jacobi's sole concern is the distinction—viewed by Hegel as too hastily drawn and untenable—between the dimensions of the infinite (God) and the finite (the empirical world). Rather, it is in his claim of certainty that the aforementioned leap finds its decisive expression in the opposition between a systematic philosophy on the one hand, which transforms immediacy into universal mediation, and a "non-philosophy" [Unphilosophie] on the other, which "discloses" the limits of rational mediation in the name of freedom.[2]

In this regard, the "*either-or*" that Hegel denounces in § 65 (a paragraph that plays a pivotal role in the organization of the whole) as a "relapse into metaphysical understanding" is certainly relevant to the choice between two options presented by Jacobi. In substantial terms, however, this choice has an entirely different content than the one Hegel suggests with his critical reference to a mutual exclusivity of immediacy and mediation indebted to the traditional logic of identity (VE: § 65, 106; 115). This alone, however, that is to say, the undeniable difference between the actual alternative that Jacobi proposes and what becomes of it in Hegel's presentation of the standpoint of immediate knowing, is not the reason that the issue turns out to be so explosive and, as a consequence, enables us to read the text of the "Third Position" as the devilishly complicated documentation of a fundamental conflict. After all, perhaps Hegel simply misconstrued Jacobi's line of thought. If so, then an analysis of the "Third Position" would need to uncover any serious misunderstandings, a goal that would not be without consequences for Hegel's claim to have refuted the standpoint of immediate knowing as unsustainable.

But that is not the aim here. Misunderstandings are not the problem in this case, but rather something much more fundamental. Not only did Hegel correctly grasp the challenge posed by Jacobi's "either-or" as a fundamental objection to any and all systematic aspirations; in fact, his entire philosophical program since his arrival in Jena, from the polemics of *Faith and Knowledge* and the new conception of the *Phenomenology* all the way up through the *Science of Logic*, takes shape as an ongoing effort to neutralize this provocation. As with Fichte and Schelling, the aim throughout is to prove that the leap is a completely unnecessary exercise, one judged to be "unphilosophical" in the truest sense of the word, inasmuch as it is quite possible to rework Spinoza's system into a system of freedom, to transform substance into subject. So why does Hegel conceal this impetus for his critique of immediate knowing? The

---

[2] For a detailed account of Jacobi, see Birgit Sandkaulen, *Grund und Ursache. Die Vernunftkritik Jacobis* (Munich: Wilhelm Fink Verlag, 2000), on the confrontation with Hegel in particular see esp. 229ff., and Chapter 2 in this volume.

answer has already presented itself, thereby also establishing the direction that a further investigation of this text should take. If Hegel had in fact introduced Jacobi's systems-critical provocation and its structural implications into the equation, he would have had to offer a different account of Jacobi's position. And not only would this have precluded Hegel from criticizing immediate knowing in the stark terms that characterize his surface-level argumentation; even more significantly, it would have precluded him from addressing this standpoint in the context of a "preliminary conception" [Vorbegriff]—that is to say in the framework of a new introduction written in order to "explicate and bring about" [herbeiführen] the standpoint of logic and thereby offer a corrective to the *Phenomenology*, to which this function had previously been attributed (VE: § 25, 68f.; 66. Translation amended).

This brings us to the crux of the matter and the actual reason for the difficulties of the text. The fundamental conflict that tacitly organizes the "Third Position" can be traced back to Jacobi. But it also intensified as a result of the ultimately impossible task that Hegel subsequently sets himself with the "preliminary conception" and which, according to his aims, he must set himself. On the one hand, he seeks to provide, prior to the presentation of the logic itself, a foundation on the basis of which the logic itself can proceed and can demonstrate, by way of the essence-logical operation of the "essential, self-positing unity of immediacy and mediation," the overcoming of the alternative proposed by Jacobi (VE: § 65, 107; 116). On the other hand, however, he must ensure that the beginning of the logic is marked by "the complete *absence of any presupposition*" (VE: § 78, 118; 125).

Here one could object that this problem actually pertains to all the "positions of thought toward objectivity" and not only to the question of immediate knowing. In a certain sense, this is indeed the case, and it underscores the dilemma in which Hegel finds himself. However, the fact that this dilemma is not only directly and profoundly connected to the challenge posed by Jacobi, but that it also originates there (prefacing, so to speak, all of the specific positions Hegel addresses), follows from the reference to the logic of essence that Hegel himself makes (not coincidentally) in the context of "Third Position." That is to say: in the case of Jacobi, the determinations of immediacy and mediation most certainly do not pertain to "*simple* thought-determinations" (VE: § 25, 69; 67), as in the case of the other positions, but rather to the basic operators of the logic, and in such a way that precisely the establishment of their reflection-logical "unity" would not only neutralize the leap but would also simultaneously and definitively solve the problem of the presupposition—within the logic. But what if one has only progressed as far as the antechamber of the logic? On the basis of what presuppositions, which must not appear as presuppositions, is one able to gain entrance into the interior space of the self-sublating presupposition, of the mediation of immediacy?

The Programmatic Insights of the *Jacobi-Review*

How to eliminate the threat of Jacobi's provocation—this is the fundamental problem, and it becomes clear as early as in *Faith and Knowledge* that Hegel's efforts toward this end are associated with certain protocols related to its presentation. There, Hegel evades the challenge of the systems-critical leap by reframing Jacobi's position as a particularly misguided variant of the so-called "reflective philosophy of subjectivity," even going so far as to adopt a targeted strategy of "cauterization," or destructive excoriation and burning.[3] With regard to anything written subsequently, it is advisable as a matter of principle to differentiate between Hegel's presentation of Jacobi and the latter's actual position. This proves crucial not only in order to ensure an authentic reading of Jacobi himself but also a productive interpretation and discussion of Hegel. To be able to go a step further, however, and identify the sources of the specific difficulties presented by the "Third Position," we must also remind ourselves at every stage of the function performed by the treatment of immediate knowing in the "preliminary conception" of the logic—namely, to offer a solution to the aporia of the introduction of which it is in truth the expression.

We will turn our attention later to the sleight of hand by which Hegel, relying on a strategy of "external reflection" (VE: § 65, 107; 115), attempts to gain control of the situation, or more accurately, to conceal the dilemma sketched out above. For the moment it will suffice to indicate, by way of a question, a matter that will be of particular significance in this regard. We have seen that Hegel refrains from engaging in any substantive way with Spinoza—but why does Descartes play such a prominent role in the "Third Position" (and not, for example, in the previous section on metaphysics)? And how should we interpret the fact that he almost immediately resorts to the claim that Descartes is the "originator" of the standpoint of immediate knowing and Jacobi merely an epigone, whose "modern propositions […] can count only as superfluous iterations" of Descartes's pronouncements (VE: § 64, 106; 114f.)? There is, in other words, much that remains unresolved.

It is thus all the more important to preface the critical analysis of the text—which, as I hope to have already made clear, cannot simply proceed according to the linear sequence of the paragraphs—with a consideration of Hegel's Heidelberg *Jacobi-Review* of 1817, in order to cast what has been said into sharper relief and to render what follows as transparent as possible.[4] In this context, two observations can be made that may appear on the surface to be tangential to the issue under consideration but are in fact of substantial importance. In 1817, Hegel also composed the original version of the "preliminary conception" for the Heidelberg *Encyclopedia*, in which the investigation of immediate knowing is missing. At the same time, it is notable that in the *Jacobi-Review*—in contrast to *Faith and Knowledge* as well as

---

[3] The "weapons that the journal will wield are manifold; they will be called bludgeons, whips, and cudgels;—it is all done for a good cause and the gloriae Dei; there will no doubt be the occasional complaint; but the cauterization has indeed been necessary." Letter from Hegel to Hufnagel from December 30, 1801 (*Briefe von und an Hegel*, ed. Johannes Hoffmeister, vol. 1, 3rd ed. (Hamburg: Meiner, 1969), 65). On *Faith and Knowledge*, see my analysis in Birgit Sandkaulen, "Das Nichtige in seiner ganzen Länge und Breite. Hegels Kritik der Reflexionsphilosophie," *Hegel-Jahrbuch* 2004 (2004): 165–73 and in Chapter 13 in this volume.

[4] In the following, the *Jacobi-Review* will be cited parenthetically in the text as JR with an indication of the page number in GW 15 as well as of the corresponding page in the English translation G. W. F. Hegel, "Review, Friedrich Heinrich Jacobi's Works, Volume III," in *Heidelberg Writings. Journal Publications*, ed. and trans. Brady Bowman and Allen Speight (Cambridge: Cambridge University Press, 2009).

the "Third Position"—Hegel's tone is decidedly collegial. But that is not all. Hegel explicitly asserts in this context that "in terms of *philosophical insight*, it was of the utmost significance that Jacobi brought out the moment of *immediacy* in our knowledge of God so distinctly and emphatically" (JR 11; 9). Why does Hegel express his appreciation here for a position that he had completely ignored in 1802 and then accuses in 1827/30 of philosophical naivete and epigonality, describing it as a "sole and simple polemic" (VE: § 62, 100; 110) and denouncing it as a standpoint that "gives itself over to the wild arbitrariness of imaginings and assurances, to moral self-conceit and the arrogance of sentiments or to an opining and rationalizing lacking any measure" (VE: § 77, 117; 124)? Has he temporarily forgotten what he is trying to accomplish here? Is this why he defers the analysis of immediate knowing to the later version of the "preliminary conception"?

In fact, something entirely different is going on. In 1817 Hegel knows full well how he wants to deal with Jacobi, or to put it more precisely and with an eye toward the crucial point—how he wanted to deal with him in the *Science of Logic*, the final part of which had just appeared. Having completed his logic, Hegel is free to adopt a friendly tone and openly reveal what he owes to Jacobi as well as how he incorporated the latter's provocative challenge—which, as Hegel understands it, necessitates a "complete revision of logic" [Nothwendigkeit einer völlig veränderten Ansicht des Logischen] (JR 25; 26)—into the procedures of the logic and in this way transformed Spinoza's substance into absolute spirit. It depends, in other words, on the perspective. It makes an enormous difference whether one speaks from the perspective of a completed logic or, in the context of a "preliminary conception," is confronted anew with the question of how the standpoint of this logic is to be achieved in the first place.

To this extent, the highly illuminating insights into Hegel's thought process that are revealed in the *Jacobi-Review* stand in neither a contradictory nor a complementary relation to the "Third Position." Rather, the *Review* is incorporated into the "Third Position" as a subtext, and, in accordance with the change in perspective, the surface level of that text must enact a nearly complete inversion of the very same motifs so as to render them "preliminary" enough for a "preliminary conception." At the time of the *Review*, Hegel apparently did not trust himself to carry out this restructuring in a way that would serve his interests, to say nothing of presenting it in a manner that would appear plausible, while he later avoided giving an account of this process. In order to make the relation between these texts as clear as possible and thereby render the "preliminary conception" accessible to a critical reading and evaluation, the following elements in the *Review* must be at least briefly addressed:

On a general level, it is crucial to recognize that the insights Hegel provides here into the intellectual underpinnings of the *Science of Logic*, insights that he offers both *ex post* and in conjunction with an explicit reference to the Spinoza debate, are arranged in a manner that has significant implications. This includes, firstly, the doubly affirmative reference to Jacobi. Jacobi was, first of all, correct in his assertion that "every consistent system of philosophy must in the end lead to Spinozism," as well as in his antithetical claim that any affirmation of freedom understood in terms of "self-determination and personality" is incompatible with Spinoza's metaphysics, whereby this dimension of freedom encompasses both the aspect of "individuation" as well as of God as absolute "spirit" (JR 9ff.; 7ff.). Now that Hegel has identified these two points of agreement, however, the second step is to establish their relation in a way that differs from the contradiction of the leap, whose provocative force Hegel has already attempted to blunt by referring to it as a "transition" made by Jacobi "in his *innermost*" (JR 11; 9). More important, however, is the way in which Hegel shores up this assertion, namely, by locating the alleged "transition" from substance to spirit between two poles of immediacy. According to Hegel's account, not only Jacobi but also Spinoza was a philosopher of immediacy, indeed the original one, who for this reason was able to grasp "the truth" only in its "*initial immediacy*" [erste Unmittelbarkeit], therefore only in terms of substance, and more precisely, only in "*pure intuition* (which is the same as *abstract thinking*)" (JR 9f.; 7f.).

This equation of immediacy, intuition, and abstract thinking is adopted word for word in the "Third Position," where, however, it is no longer linked to Spinoza but rather, and in a highly intricate manner, to Jacobi—the crucial significance of this move should be kept in mind. What facilitates this process for Hegel and also subcutaneously drives the argumentation forward in the "preliminary conception" is a motif that he already unfolds in the *Jacobi-Review* following his assertions regarding Spinozan immediacy. If one arranges things the way that Hegel has, then it also becomes clear, thirdly, why Jacobi's critique of mediation ultimately fails to achieve its aims despite its admirable intentions. Instead of transcending mediation in an act of sublation, he simply dispenses with it in "an external rejection and dismissal" (JR 11; 10). The result is doubly unsatisfactory. Because "his consciousness of absolute spirit remains fixated in the form of *immediate*, merely *substantial knowledge*" (JR 13; 12), he de facto fails to overcome Spinoza's standpoint; in fact he actually ends up reinforcing it instead, while at the same time his "positive ideas have the value of *mere assurances* only […]" (JR 23; 24). Having framed things in this way, Hegel is then able to solve both problems in one fell swoop. Subjecting Spinoza's substantial immediacy to a reflexive process of mediation guarantees the overcoming of substance in subject and thus also simultaneously promises to ground, in the form of mediated immediacy, the certainty of a knowledge that Jacobi's "esprit" could only allude to but never establish "as *necessary*" (JR 23; 24). We will turn shortly to the question of exactly how this constellation enters into the "preliminary conception."

However, a fourth point must also be considered in this context, one that reveals the grave shortcomings of Hegel's seemingly elegant solution and, consequently, also saddles the change of perspective documented in the "preliminary conception" with the heavy burden that has already been mentioned. The figure of thought sketched out corresponds to the model of the logic of essence. This means, and Hegel actually pursues this approach in the *Jacobi-Review*, grasping the indicated mediation as the reflection-logical figure of a "*negation of negation*" (JR 11; 9), and at the same time assuming that the only negativity which is subject to self-clarification here is the one that had already, in the process of an absolute negation of the finite, been inscribed into the Spinozan "intuition" of substance. The fact that immediacy is in truth always already the product of a mediation, and that precisely this is what must be realized in the form of the double negation, is the argument Hegel advances against both Spinoza and Jacobi. But the consequence of this approach is not only a fundamental distortion of his opponent's actual conceptions.[5] An even more serious problem arises with regard to Hegel's own position. The essence-logical reflection, precisely to the extent that it performs the turning back to the ground in order to allegedly reveal every presupposition [Voraussetzung] as a positing [Setzung], discloses the indispensable presupposition at the beginning of the logic of being—the commitment to the "true" in its "initial immediacy," in other words, to Spinoza.

The Ambiguous Semantics of Immediacy

We are now in a position to characterize precisely not only the unspoken conflict of the "Third Position" but also of the "preliminary conception" as a whole. Given that Hegel considers the introduction to the *Phenomenology* to have been a failure, his task in the "preliminary conception" cannot be the provision of a solution to some sort of general problem with introductions and beginnings; rather, he must offer renewed assurance that the introduction is working toward a "Spinozistically" prepared beginning of the logic without explicitly introducing Spinoza into the debate. It is already evident that in the context of the standpoints whose "positions of thought toward objectivity" are to be criticized for their deficits, there is no meaningful place for a discussion of Spinoza. After all, the transformation of substance into subject is the central project, reserved for the logic itself as its integral task. But for this very reason, a different task proves to be all the more crucial. What must be avoided at all costs is the appearance of any explicit reference to Spinoza in the course of laying the groundwork for the start of this process. Because this would be tantamount to ascribing to the logic a starting point extrinsic to itself, one that no essence-logical reflection could ever reintegrate or sublate.

On the basis of this unspoken premise on Hegel's part, we can now also discern the particular significance of the "Third Position." There can be no serious confrontation with Jacobi here, because Hegel engages in this debate over immediate knowing exclusively as a means to the aforementioned end. In order to provide access to the desired beginning of the logic subcutaneously, that is to say, without any specific invocation of Spinoza as its precondition, and to be able to carry out the essence-logical sublation of the conflict revealed by Jacobi in the first place, the standpoint of immediate knowing is strategically instrumentalized. The basis for this instrumentalization is an approach in which the term "immediacy" is characterized at every moment by an ambiguous semantics. In pursuing this approach, Hegel takes advantage of something that our discussion of his *Jacobi-Review* has made apparent, namely, the arrangement

---

[5] For a detailed discussion, see Birgit Sandkaulen, "Die Ontologie der Substanz, der Begriff der Subjektivität und die Faktizität des Einzelnen. Hegels reflexionslogische 'Widerlegung' der Spinozanischen Metaphysik," *International Yearbook of German Idealism* 5 (2008): 235–75 and Chapter 15 in this volume. Only against the backdrop of Hegel's stylization of the proposition "*omnis determinatio est negatio*" into the fundamental theorem of Spinoza, to which Hegel himself attributes the "omnis" in the *Jacobi-Review* (JR 10; 9), can we understand his peculiar remark in the "Third Position," where he asserts that Jacobi is indebted to Spinoza himself for his critique of cognition. With this theorem, Hegel also obscures the distinction between Spinoza's three forms of cognition—his talk of "intuition" as identical to "abstract thinking" thus has nothing in common with Spinoza's *scientia intuitiva*.

that we can now see has been sub-textually incorporated into the "Third Position," according to which "immediacy" has never been a precise term but rather has always had multiple, or, more precisely, four distinct meanings.

As we have seen, he first introduces the figure of substantial immediacy as a designation for Spinoza's position, which is, second, to be equated with Jacobi's position, insofar as the latter, in failing (according to Hegel) to productively employ any form of mediation, is alleged to have de facto codified the Spinozan "intuition" of substance. A third and a fourth version, on the other hand, can be found in the immediacy that is proposed as a basis for the certainty of spirit, about which, however, Jacobi (according to Hegel) was only able to offer unsubstantiated assertions—again due to the lack of mediation—and which therefore could only be systematically generated and conceptually stabilized in the logical form of mediated immediacy.

The operation necessary to adapt this logical scenario to the change in perspective that characterizes the "preliminary conception," that is to say, to the introduction to the logic in question here, is a simple one, but it remains virtually undiscoverable in the text itself. It consists in maintaining the fourfold meaning of immediacy but intentionally allowing the differential attribution to their respective initial and concluding determinations to implode. In the case of the first and second versions, the consequences present themselves immediately. Even in the absence of any explicit reference to Spinoza, the figure of an "initial immediacy" remains present, in that it is officially identified with Jacobi's position of immediacy and at the same time always already surreptitiously aims at the "Spinozistically" infused opening to the logic of being. In order to recognize this semantics of immediacy in the text, it is necessary to focus throughout on the signaling expressions that refer to indeterminate abstractness, which, in terms of content, aim to ground the certainty of being in general. In the case of the third and fourth versions, the consequences with regard to the disavowal of the standpoint of immediate knowing are no less significant; in fact, they are even greater. Here the allegedly deficient "assurances" of immediate knowing are rendered even more contemptible as part of a polemical attempt to discredit the indeterminacy of Jacobi's "wild arbitrariness of imaginings and assurances," whereby the critique lays claim to the methodological standards of a philosophy which, insofar as it is not "a mere offering of assurances, nor imaginings, nor the arbitrary back-and-forth thinking of rationalization [Räsonnement]" (VE: § 77, 117; 124), is committed to a sufficient, that is, concrete knowledge of spirit.

It thereby becomes apparent why the text seems so easily decipherable on the surface and yet is in truth exceptionally difficult to parse. Against the backdrop of the arrangement presented in the *Jacobi-Review*, we can see that Hegel, in introducing the previously mentioned fourth type of immediacy, which is "mediation and immediate relation to itself in one" (VE: § 74, 114; 122), puts his own position into play (surreptitiously, of course), and in such a way that, when measured against it, both the abstractness of (the first) immediacy and the arbitrariness of (the second) immediacy become vulnerable to critique. Under the conditions of the change in perspective, which allows both the difference between these two immediacies as well as the one internal to the first immediacy to implode as planned, and also employs the generic proposition of the indeterminacy of immediate knowing to do so, this critique ends up targeting a standpoint of immediacy so broadly conceived that there can be no doubt regarding its untenability. It appears in this particular form, however, only because Hegel himself has constructed it to be this way in the process previously described. But precisely because the goal is to decode the interests that give rise to this construct in terms of the fundamental conflict sketched out previously, it is all the more important to distinguish carefully between these two dimensions—between (indeterminate) abstractness on the one hand and (indeterminate) arbitrariness on the other—because in each case Hegel is aiming at something different.

Our efforts in this regard are facilitated by a circumstance through which Hegel in a sense "betrays" the instrumental character of his approach, even though he spares no effort in attempting to then immediately cover up again the sleight of hand that he has employed. This gesture suggests that reshaping the arrangement found in the *Jacobi-Review* to suit the textual form and argumentative structure of the "Third Position" is not so simple after all. Rather, it can only succeed on one condition, one that has already been hinted at—not only must Cartesian philosophy be introduced into the debate, Descartes himself must be established as the "originator" of the standpoint of immediate knowing. It is astonishing that commentators have entirely ignored this point as well, despite its having a prominence in the text that borders on the obtrusive (in contrast to the concealment of Spinoza). It is especially surprising given that the interest in a substantive discussion and clarification of "immediate knowing" could in theory be well served by a structural comparison of the Cartesian certainty postulated in the "*Cogito, ergo sum*"—which certainly should not be read as a syllogism (VE: § 64, 105f.; 115)—with a position like that of Jacobi.

What is crucial here, however, is something else. That Hegel has no interest in such a comparison and that, on the contrary, the incorporation of Descartes into the deliberations of the "Third Position" offers the most telling expression of his instrumental appropriation of Jacobi, is revealed by the fact that if he had truly wanted to conduct a serious debate on the matter, he would have had to engage with the philosophy of Descartes and that of Jacobi in an entirely different manner. He fails on both counts; that is to say, Descartes is also dealt with here in exclusively instrumental terms. He is urgently needed (as a terminological placeholder for Spinoza) in order to represent the substantial (first) immediacy, whose conflation with the factual standpoint of Jacobi was never more than an assertion even in the arrangement of the *Jacobi-Review*, but which now, given that Spinoza must recede into the background, has become impossible to document. The entire dilemma of the enterprise thus becomes obvious to the extent that Hegel can only realize his aims with regard to the "Third Position" on the condition that, in drawing upon the "cogito ergo sum," he borrows the terms "thinking" and "being" directly from Descartes.[6]

Otherwise, that is to say without having recourse to this terminological deception, everything would remain in limbo—both the suggestion (intended to surreptitiously lay the groundwork for the logic of being) that the designation of abstract and indeterminate immediacy is in fact applicable to Jacobi's standpoint, as well as the possibility of criticizing this immediacy from the perspective of a mediated immediacy, the validity of which is entirely dependent on the logic but which at this point, in

---

[6] On this point, see the concluding section VI.

the run-up to the logic itself, cannot yet be argued in these terms. In other words, only the appropriation of Descartes's terminology enables Hegel to stage the change in perspective through which the logical arrangement of the *Jacobi-Review* is transformed into the "external reflection" of the "Third Position."

A Structural Sketch of the "Third Position"

It will come as no surprise that this final point, in directing our attention to the specific mode of presentation that characterizes the text, also brings us back again to § 65, which I have already described as the organizational center of Hegel's entire analysis. Taking this center as our starting point, our task now is to determine how the figures of thought uncovered thus far find application in Hegel's concrete investigation of the standpoint of immediate knowing. For the purposes of orientation, it will be essential to first familiarize ourselves with the outline of the text by way of a sketch of its structure, inasmuch as Hegel's own efforts to conceal the fundamental conflict that inheres in the "Third Position" (and thereby more effectively realize his aims) extend even to the formal aspects of the investigation.[7] A different, substantially more complex

[7] According to this schema, which mirrors the conventional form of a discussion as well as Hegel's typical reliance on a step-by-step process of argumentation that is at once linear and at the same time circles back on itself, the presentation of the standpoint of immediate knowing constitutes the starting point, which includes the conception of mediating knowing, the categories introduced ("Knowing [Wissen], believing [Glauben], thinking, intuiting"), and the substantive statements of immediate knowledge (VE: §§ 61–64). This is followed by a review of his claims, leading to the conclusion that every form of knowledge, although it may have the appearance of immediacy, entails mediation (VE: §§ 66–70). Next, Hegel examines the unacceptable consequences that follow from the one-sidedness of the standpoint in question (VE: §§ 71–74), which ultimately culminates in a definitive rejection of its assertions (VE: § 75). A concluding assessment situates the "Third Position" within the context of the "preliminary conception" as a whole, which, on the one hand, concludes the arc of the introduction (VE: §§ 76–77) and, on the other, initiates the transition to the logic (VE: § 78).
That this schema only has the appearance of being a logical construction, and that it is in fact flawed in its very foundations, can be provisionally demonstrated on the basis of the following features. First, it follows from the schema that the aforementioned § 65 does not figure as an element in the course of argumentation, in so far as it does not belong directly to either the argumentative sequence of the presentation nor to that of the refutation of the standpoint of immediate knowing. Secondly, we must not overlook the fact that there is in truth no clear dividing line that runs between presentation and critique. Rather, the elucidation of immediate knowing is already shot through with exactly the same objections that Hegel subsequently merely de facto repeats. It will be necessary to return later to the character of these objections and their presentation. It should already be emphasized here, however, that the suffusion of the entire investigation with moments of critique, as is particularly clear in §§ 63 und 64, occurs only on the basis of attributions that are suggestively presented but never subjected to any sort of rational scrutiny. Thirdly, a weakening of the schema can also be seen in the sections devoted to refutation, where Hegel transitions, in a manner that is significant but initially remains opaque, from empirical objections to objections of an entirely different sort, "without paying any regard to seemingly empirical bonds" (VE: § 69, 110; 118), for which he lacks—one wonders why—a unique classificatory designation. Fourthly, significant fissures also become apparent in the critical examination of the consequences that follow from the one-sidedness of the standpoint of immediate knowing. Hegel attempts to categorize these formally according to the otherwise successful framework of a distinction between content (VE §§ 71-3) and form (VE § 74), but he is unable to conceal the fact that this framework cannot quite be adapted as intended in the case of § 74. Fifthly, and finally, the starkly declaratory character of § 75 is also noteworthy in this context, given that its concluding "*assessment* of this third position" does not in any way follow organically from the previous discussion.

intratextual network becomes discernible when the outline of the text is reconstructed on the basis of § 65. In this case, what comes into view first is the fact that this section has a direct counterpart, albeit one that has been significantly displaced, in § 78, that is to say in the final section, which describes "the opposition between a self-standing immediacy of content or knowing and a mediation that is equally self-standing but incompatible with the former," as a "mere *presupposition* and an arbitrary *assurance*," and with this argument marking the transition to the logic insists that science must begin from a position characterized by the "complete *absence of any presupposition*" (VE: § 78, 117f.; 125).

The motif of arbitrariness, however, which is of exceptional importance in this context, is already elucidated in § 63. The middle and end of the text thus point back to its beginning, whose most salient feature consists in conflating the criticism of what are here explicitly referred to as the "random assurances" of immediate knowing with the criticism of the complete indeterminacy of its content—the consequence of which is that it becomes accessible to every imaginable superstition and, insofar as it "restricts itself to the idea of *God in general*, a *supreme being*," is capable of conceiving nothing but a "dry *abstractum*" (VE: § 63, 103f.; 113). This motif is immediately taken up in the following section with explicit reference to its "abstraction" and related in this context to a "proposition" that Hegel finds especially "interesting" in a "formal respect": "that the *thought* of God is immediately and inseparably bound up with God's *being* and that the *subjectivity* that characterizes thought at first is similarly bound up with objectivity" (VE: § 64, 104f.; 114. Translation amended).

From here, the intratextual network extends in two directions. On the one hand, as has already been intimated, Hegel repeats the objections to the alleged subjective arbitrariness and indeterminacy of immediate knowing in §§ 71–3, which are now presented in the context of the consequences of its one-sidedness. Here one criticism in particular—that the standpoint in question is receptive to any and every form of superstition due to its indeterminacy—is both sharpened and simultaneously given an expanded moral scope in the form of the assertion "that all kinds of superstition and idolatry are declared to be true, and the most unjust and the most unethical content of the will is justified" (VE: § 72, 113; 121). On the other hand, § 64 unmistakably takes on a special role here, a double role, so to speak, in that it is in this section that Descartes (not coincidentally) first appears on the scene. The information conveyed by this passage regarding the substantive determination of immediate knowing is reintroduced both in § 73, where it is alleged that such knowledge knows only "*that* God exists, not *what* God is" (VE: § 73, 113; 121) as well as being incorporated—and this is crucial—into §§ 69 and 70 by way of a direct reference that Hegel marks explicitly in the text. In other words, it is incorporated into precisely those passages concerned with the non-empirical case of a mediation which, proceeding from the "transition (designated in § 64) from the subjective idea to being," is contrasted, as mediation in its "true determination," with what is alleged to be immediate knowing—"not as a mediation with and through something external, but as establishing itself in itself [sich in sich selbst beschließend]" (VE: § 69, 110; 118).

The intratextual network becomes even more dense when one considers that this section not coincidentally finds its thematic counterpart in § 74, which, under the rubric of the "*form of immediacy*," underscores the lack of both mediation through another and self-mediation (mediated immediacy) and also links the absence of both in immediate knowing to the symptomatic objection to "*abstraction*," which, interestingly, here also includes the criticism of subjective arbitrariness in the sense of an abstract absolutization of the finite (VE: § 74, 114; 121). That this passage is of particular significance is shown above all by the explicit incorporation of the assertion that Hegel had already foregrounded in the *Jacobi-Review*, according to which "*abstract thinking* [...] and *abstract intuiting* [...] are one and the same" (VE: § 74, 114; 122).

Hegel stages the conclusion of the text as a return to metaphysics. What proves structurally revealing in terms of the intratextual network we have been uncovering here is the renewed recourse to Descartes, and for the following reason. Hegel, in the course of describing the commonalities and differences between Descartes and the "modern standpoint" of Jacobi, insists on "the plain inseparability of *thinking* and the *being* of the thinker" (VE: § 76, 115; 123) and thereby clearly separates the motif of indeterminate abstractness from that of arbitrariness, for which he holds only the "modern standpoint" with its abandonment of "*all* methods" responsible (VE: § 77, 117; 124). And so the circle is complete. What follows next, namely the already cited denunciation of the "wild arbitrariness of imaginings and assurances" that characterizes immediate knowing, provides a bridge to the argument of the final section of the "Third Position," in which the constitution of the standpoint in question, described here as a "mere *presupposition* and an arbitrary *assurance*," is subjected to the negation of a "consummate skepticism" that aims at "the complete *absence of any presupposition*" (VE: § 78, 117f.; 125). Keeping the aforementioned distinction in mind, it becomes apparent that Jacobi's "modern standpoint" is negated prior to the opening of the logic, but not the claim—associated here with Descartes and aimed at with Spinoza—regarding the inseparability of thinking and being.

Four Functions of the "Third Position"

On the basis of this structural sketch, we can now fully grasp Hegel's line of reasoning and consequently recognize that the instrumental construction of the "Third Position" fulfills exactly four crucial functions. Fundamental in this context is the distinction, which appears in VE: § 65 together with the criticism of the "*either-or*" disposition toward immediate and mediated knowledge, between the "true consideration" of the logical dimension and the "external reflection" that is only suitable for the "preliminary conception" (VE: § 65, 107; 115). This distinction reveals the first function of the text, namely, to contour the standpoint of immediate knowing in such a way that the turn toward the logic of essence with its "complete revision of *logic*" (as Hegel puts it in the *Jacobi-Review*) appears as an urgently necessary measure. At the same time, the reference to the operation of the logic remains aporetic at this juncture, as does, consequently, the critique of immediate knowing, insofar as it is already being considered from the perspective of logic. Hegel himself suggests as much with his remark that he will "leave this point without developing it further" (VE: § 65, 107; 115). Any elaboration of these matters would have already burst the bounds of the introduction—a performative contradiction that of course underscores the strength and not the weakness of Jacobi's position, given that an entirely new logic must be developed in an effort to overcome it. It is thus all the more telling that Hegel attempts to justify his reliance on "external reflection" by way of a reproach. Because, so the argument goes, the standpoint in question maintains "exclusively immediate knowing […] merely as a *fact*," thus refusing to consider what "matters in itself," namely, "the logical dimension of the opposition of immediacy and mediation," and "the nature of the basic matter, i.e. the concept" (VE: § 65, 107; 115), this standpoint has only itself to blame, so to speak, for the form of the critique leveled against it in the introduction.

But what is the actual target of this critique? Insofar as the method of "external reflection" is grounded by asserting the merely factual quality of immediate knowing, it might appear *prima vista* that the critique aims at the refutation of this assertion alone, that is to say, it aims to prove that there is no immediate knowing. As we have seen, however, this particular objection fails to account for the full range of criticisms expressed. And even more importantly, it becomes clear that, within the intratextual network of the critique, the refutation of the alleged facticity enables Hegel to introduce something like a "prelogical" perspective of mediation into the discussion. This perspective not only uses the "*fact*" of mediation (VE: § 70, 110; 119) to target the "*factually* wrong" assertion "that there is an immediate knowing" (VE: § 75, 115; 122), but also directs attention thereby to the genuinely interesting shortcomings that characterize the claims of immediate knowing. To put it another way (and more starkly): If the standpoint of immediate knowing were actually exclusively characterized by the fact that it asserts something that is patently false, which even the slightest effort will reveal to be completely baseless—for example the fact that my "*immediate* presence" in Berlin is "*mediated* by the journey undertaken to get here, etc." (VE: § 66, 108; 116)— then it would be utterly incomprehensible what function such an obviously trivial position could have in the "preliminary conception," not to mention why its actual refutation would be viewed the task of a new logic.[8]

The real purpose of these passages, in other words, is something else, and this brings us to the second function of the "Third Position." In proving that immediate knowing only appears to occur, Hegel aims to establish the standard of a critique that then allows him to diagnose all of the criticisms that are actually of concern and that have been raised since the very beginning in terms of a lack of mediation. This strategic advantage, however, comes at a cost that here as well threatens to unravel the whole fabric of argumentation. Namely, to the extent that the reference to the "fact" of mediation is intended to ensure that the standard is not brought in from the outside, that is to say, from the logic itself, and then applied to the standpoint of immediate knowing, then it follows from this that it can only be acquired and articulated in the form of an immanent critique. This critique, however, can for its part

---

[8] Furthermore, if one were to subject §§ 66–8 to a closer analysis, not only would the question arise as to how these trivial cases of empirical immediacy and mediation can be considered adequate to capture Jacobi's position. In addition, one would also be in a position to show that Hegel is operating with a range of very different and in no way compatible meanings of the term "mediation." Considering that these passages ultimately have an exclusively strategic function, however, it is not necessary to pursue this analysis here.

only be immanently persuasive if it can articulate aspects of the standpoint in question that are in substantial agreement with the aims of the logic, that is, with Hegel's own position. More or less hidden indications of such agreement can in fact be found, as for example in the statement, surprising in the context of the whole, that "the proposition of immediate knowing rightly seeks not the indeterminate, empty immediacy, the abstract being or pure unity for itself, but instead the unity of *the idea* with being" (VE: § 70, 110; 119), a claim that alludes to Jacobi's commitment to spirit, as is also indirectly indicated by § 74.

That this gives rise to conceptual fissures in the text is hardly surprising. After all, if Hegel had truly intended to engage substantively with Jacobi in elaborating this critique, then he would have had to explicitly reproduce the argumentative constellation of the *Jacobi-Review*, advancing the same claim as he does there, namely, that the lack of mediation means that Jacobi can provide only assurances of the freedom of spirit. Such a distinction between correct content and false form, however, would have then required a completely different presentation of Jacobi's standpoint than the one Hegel provides in the "Third Position" under the conditions imposed by the change in perspective. Whereas he does consider the question of spirit (but only under duress and even then only covertly), the critique he explicitly elaborates aims to establish precisely the opposite, namely, that a false form (the lack of mediation) is responsible for the deficient content of immediate knowing.

What thereby comes to light constitutes the third and fourth functions of the "Third position." In both cases, it is indeterminacy that, according to Hegel, reveals the desideratum of mediation. It has long since become clear, however, that in offering this diagnosis, he is pursuing two different aims. In the case of the third function, it is the motif of arbitrariness that is closely linked to the indeterminacy of immediate knowing. The pretention of subjective arbitrariness is thereby blamed for the baselessness of a standpoint that "is *indifferent to any content* and for that very reason receptive to any content," and thus "just as capable of sanctioning an idolatrous and immoral content as the opposite" (VE: § 74, 114; 122). Given that Hegel has already shown himself in *Faith and Knowledge* to be a virtuoso on the keyboard of "cauterization," it comes as no surprise that his artistry is also on display here in all of its polemical perfection. In particular, this includes Hegel's systematic refusal, on display at various points in the text, to resolve the question as to whether the standpoint of immediate knowing is merely susceptible to religious and moral abuses, that is, that this is a theoretical possibility but one that is at odds with its original intentions, or whether it is itself guilty of such abuses, and how this in turn relates to the assertion of its explicit limitation to "*God in general,* to the indeterminate supersensory domain" (VE: § 73, 113; 121).[9] In any case, it is clear what end this polemic ultimately serves. Given the

---

[9] Such a cauterization is already reflected in the blend of presentation and critique that constitutes the introductory section (VE: § 63, 103f.; 111ff.), and in which Hegel locates the use of the term "belief"—disregarding Jacobi's own distinction—in the context of its association with the Christian religion, in order to then substantiate his condemnation of the pious assertions allegedly made in response to a loss of the traditional contents of belief. Hegel, who is of course familiar with Jacobi's actual position, apparently believes that a critique of immediate knowing oriented toward religion and morality will be especially successful.

complete lack of any basis for advancing a standpoint whose arbitrariness means that it can only presuppose but never legitimate the basic distinction between immediacy and mediation, it is consequently negated, an act that provides the beginning of the logic with the "*absence of any presupposition*" it requires.

Merely eliminating all presuppositions, however, does not suffice for the introduction to achieve its intended aim; indeed, had he not ascribed of a fourth and final function to the "Third Position," Hegel would have simply been regressing back to the level of the external critique contained in *Faith and Knowledge*. As attested by the invocation of Descartes, the indeterminacy of immediate knowing that springs from the lack of mediation is also linked to the quality of abstractness, which Hegel subjects to a very different type of critique, to the extent that the beginning of the logic of being—in the sense of the immediate concurrence of thinking and being—lurks behind it. The fact that Hegel puts an affirmative spin on the inseverable connection between thinking and being in § 64 gives us a sense of the ultimate purpose of this function. Here he asserts that

> there can be nothing less sensible for philosophy than to want to contradict these propositions of immediate knowing. It could instead congratulate itself on the fact that these, *its* own old propositions which indeed express its entire universal content, have in any case become to a certain extent the universal philosophical prejudices of our time, even if in such a non-philosophical manner. (VE: § 64, 104; 113)

If one takes into account the shift that occurs shortly thereafter, however, whereby this acknowledgement is transformed into the criticism of a lack of mediation, then it becomes clear that Hegel cannot actually be concerned here with the concordance between philosophy and the convictions of a lifeworldly realism, which, insofar as these convictions are also alleged to apply to the sensuous world, he follows Descartes in rejecting as "deception and error" (VE: § 76, 116; 124).

On the contrary, it would be nonsensical to want to contradict the assertion of the inseparability of thought and being, for the reason that it evokes that substantial immediacy which constitutes the true starting point for philosophy's logical pursuits: "*Pure being* constitutes the beginning, because it is pure thought as well as the undetermined, simple immediate, and the first beginning cannot be anything mediated and further determined" (VE: § 86, 122; 136). Now that the precipice of presupposition has been avoided, Hegel is again able to risk an explicit reference to his own project. And thus we find the claim that what is presented at the beginning of the logic of being "is expressed more immediately in what Jacobi says about the God of Spinoza, namely that he is the principium *of being in all existence*" [des Seins in allem Dasein] (VE: § 86, 123; 137). In this way, the *Encyclopedia* Logic has now secured for itself the same starting conditions as those made possible by the arrangement of the *Science of Logic* presented in the *Jacobi-Review*. The change of perspective of the "Third Position" has been transformed back into the old perspective.

A Cross Check: Jacobi's Position

Repudiation and preservation (via the logic of being) of immediacy with the ultimate goal of elevation (mediated via the logic of essence)—this procedure corresponds to Hegel's general model of sublation, and sublation as made possible through semantic ambiguity is what is at issue in the confrontation with Jacobi. The success of this effort, however, remains in doubt precisely because the staging of the debate serves only instrumental purposes. What this means, in other words, is that the two central aims of the "Third Position," the repudiation and the preservation (via the logic of being) of immediacy, can carry the interests of the introduction into the logic only to the extent that they rely on a distortion of Jacobi's position. I will conclude with a brief explanation of why this is the case.

1. In order to subcutaneously extract the "Spinozistically" prepared beginning of the logic from Jacobi's standpoint, the assistance of Descartes is required, for the simple reason that he, and not Jacobi, provides the indispensable determination of thinking here. The manner in which Hegel proceeds is thus all the more significant. As if it were identical to what Jacobi terms the mediating achievement of cognizing, comprehending, or explaining, he initially introduces the determination of thinking as mediation in §§ 61 und 62 before resorting in § 63 to a subterfuge that can only be described as reckless. The problem is not only that it is Hegel himself who inserts thinking into the sequence of categories characterizing the standpoint of immediate knowing—"Knowing [Wissen], believing [Glauben], thinking, intuiting" (VE: § 63, 102; 111). Nor is it that the use of these categories is immediately reproached for its "arbitrary" orientation toward "mere psychological representations and distinctions" (VE: § 63, 102; 111), thereby knowingly suppressing the fact that Jacobi meticulously documented the whole range of his terminology and deliberately refrained from following conventional usage. Hegel's real subterfuge consists in the claim that the term "belief," insofar as it is intended to apply not only to the certainty of sensuous existence but also the immediate certainty of a metaphysical truth, attempts to grasp something that is necessarily reserved for "the spirit *that thinks*," whereby the distinction allegedly reclaimed from the standpoint of immediate knowing, the distinction between thinking on the one hand and intellectual intuition or belief on the other, breaks down entirely: "Pure *intuiting*, moreover, is altogether the same as pure thinking" (VE: § 63, 102f.; 112).

What Hegel intends to achieve with this identification of thinking and intuiting has, through our consideration of the function of abstract immediacy in the logic of being, become clear in the meantime. It is important to recognize here just how profoundly the assumption of such an identity diverges from Jacobi's actual position. First of all, to assert that thinking and intuiting are the same (and to thereby preemptively undermine the distinction between mediation and immediacy) requires that one ignores Jacobi's view of reason, which is specified, in direct analogy to sensory perception, as an organ of perception *sui generis*. Attributing thoughts to such an organ of perception, or ideas that have the status of thoughts, makes no sense, because it would involve a "transition" from thinking to being, a transition that Jacobi's direct realism explicitly rules out. Secondly, and perhaps even more importantly, the means by which Hegel attempts (despite everything) to justify his recourse to thinking prove to be completely unpersuasive, insofar as he claims that, in regard to both the certainty of God and the certainty of the "personality" of the I, it is a matter of "content that is *in itself universal*" and only reveals itself to thinking (VE: § 63, 102; 112). In fact, however, in elevating the general in this manner—and correspondingly devaluing the merely sensuously given particular—a metaphysical claim is projected onto Jacobi's position that Jacobi himself explicitly disavows. Whereas the general for Jacobi is only a concept whose formation and use originate from the mediating cognition of the understanding, he is resolute in insisting that the perceptive faculty of reason provides certainty of the existence of the singular. It is exclusively in this sense that Jacobi refers to God as personal spirit and to finite I's as concrete, irreducibly individual persons.

Against this backdrop, we can see why Hegel has to call on Descartes for assistance. Only by doing so can he stabilize his usage of thinking for the motif of abstract immediacy and, in invoking "the transition from the subjective idea to being" that can only be read out of Descartes, thereby also acquire the basis for an immanent critique that discloses the dimension of self-mediation (VE: §§ 69, 70). It is also clear, however, that in taking this approach Hegel constructs a standpoint of immediate knowing that blurs precisely the specific distinction that separates Jacobi and Descartes—after all, the program of Cartesian science draws upon intuitive evidence that no longer belongs to a distinctive organ of the intellect and that, already in the case of the I, pertains to the general case of a thinking substance rather than to any irreducibly concrete existence.[10] To put it succinctly and in terms of Hegel's project as a whole, what this means is that the very invocation of anything resembling a "position of thought toward objectivity" entails an epistemic neutralization of Jacobi that completely disregards his actual program.

2. The fact that Hegel avoids any substantive confrontation with Jacobi but nonetheless fails to guarantee a secure point of entry into the logic also has implications with regard to the second moment—the repudiation of immediate knowing as it relates to arbitrariness. The privileging of the general that goes hand in hand with the determination of thinking here leads to Hegel's denunciation of the particular as subjective capriciousness. Instead of seeing that the particular "is precisely the relating of itself to an *other* outside it," "the *finite* is posited as absolute" through the "form" of immediate knowing (VE: § 74, 114; 122)—this is the decisive criticism. It is buttressed by Hegel's insistence that this standpoint allows anyone and everyone to present their arbitrary convictions as "the criterion of truth" and conflate them with "the *nature*

---

[10] The fact that Descartes has a problem with providing certainty of the external world whereas Jacobi (as a committed realist) does not, and that Descartes considers it necessary as well as feasible to adduce a series of proofs of God here, whereas Jacobi (as a committed realist) does not, is also relevant in this context. Additionally, if one also considers here that Spinoza's *scientia intuitiva* is concerned with an insight into the essence of the individual, then one not only finds oneself confronted with a different metaphysical option, one of which Jacobi was certainly aware, whereas Hegel's commitment to the general means that he consistently overlooks it in Spinoza as well. Just as significantly, it also follows from this that Hegel's attempt to secure the beginning of the logic by summoning Descartes as a proxy, in addition to inappropriately instrumentalizing Jacobi, ultimately misses the mark with regard to Spinoza as well.

of consciousness itself" (VE: § 71, 111; 119), and it finds concrete expression in his denunciation of the moral and religious promiscuity that allegedly arises because, in the mode of immediacy, the consciousness of an individual can only ever be controlled by "natural desires and inclinations" (VE: § 72, 113; 121).

The apparent plausibility of this critique (which, by the way, already appears in *Faith and Knowledge)* results from the projection of Hegel's own preferred ontological and moral value hierarchy onto Jacobi. In doing so, however, he disregards the crucial circumstance that Jacobi's defense of the individual, undertaken in the name of freedom, in no way aligns itself with the dimension of the finite that Hegel has repudiated, but instead seeks to overturn this entire conceptual framework. In exchange for placing Jacobi's position under the general suspicion of anarchic libertinism, any serious treatment would have been obligated to acknowledge that Jacobi's concern here is rather with the development of a virtue ethics—that is to say, with the exposition of a personally binding moral habitus, which is referred to as immediate inasmuch as it does not result from a set of explicable circumstances of natural mediation.[11] And this in turn would have required—now posing an even greater challenge to the construction of a purely epistemic "position of thought towards objectivity"—a discussion of the *action-theoretical foundation* of Jacobi's project, which connects the consciousness of freedom to the original consciousness of causative action and discerns in this creative capacity for intentional beginnings the quality that sets human beings apart from other finite creatures.

It comes as no surprise that this conception of cause, which Hegel wrongly equates with Kant's category of the understanding in both *Faith and Knowledge* and in his *Jacobi-Review,* opposing it there to Spinoza's *causa sui* as a speculative concept of freedom, is not mentioned at all in the "Third Position." After all, if, according to Jacobi's position, any convincing reflection on spirit is bound to the supersensible capacity for intentional action, then it is not only Hegel's verdict with regard to immediate indeterminacy that lacks any evidentiary basis. No less dubious is his effort to realize Jacobi's intentions within the framework of a systematically mediated immediacy, the logic of which depends on drawing the difference between cause and effect into the interior of the idea, when in fact this very difference only arises through action. Perhaps this is the real reason for the stridency of Hegel's polemic: the awareness that his laboriously created construct of immediate knowing ultimately cannot gain control over the explosive potentialities of this position, which enables one, in the name of freedom, to leap out of any system whatsoever.

---

[11] See Jürgen Stolzenberg, "Was ist Freiheit? Jacobis Kritik der Moralphilosophie Kants," in *Friedrich Heinrich Jacobi*, ed. Walter Jaeschke and Birgit Sandkaulen (Hamburg: Meiner, 2004), 19–36 and Chapter 5 in this volume.

Metaphysics or Logic?
The Importance of Spinoza in Hegel's *Science of Logic*

Introduction

Hegel's *Science of Logic* has been the focus of renewed interest in recent years. This is no doubt due in part to the recent anniversary of its publication—the *Science of Logic* first appeared between 1812 and 1816, roughly 200 years ago. From my perspective, however, this external occasion is less important than the increasingly widespread recognition that the *Science of Logic* serves to ground Hegel's entire project, and that a thorough understanding of this foundation is essential for anyone who wishes to develop an adequate relationship to Hegel's philosophy. And this assertion brings us directly to the central question to be pursued in this chapter: What is Hegel's logic actually about? Is the term "logic" just another name for "metaphysics," or does Hegel's *Science of Logic* seek to distance itself entirely from all previous conceptions of metaphysics, however defined, in order to introduce an entirely new discipline?

Hegel himself seems to encourage the reader to pose this basic question regarding the meaning and the ambitions of his principal work. In the preface to the first edition, he consigns the enterprise of metaphysics—in the wake of its destruction through Kant—to an irrecoverable past.[1] Shortly thereafter, logical science is asserted to be "metaphysics proper,"[2] and finally, at the end of the introduction, Hegel claims that the objective logic "takes the place of the former *metaphysics*."[3] What, precisely, does Hegel mean by these formulations? Is the logic intended to replace metaphysics? Or is the logic, in taking the place of the old metaphysics, to be understood as a new metaphysics? Hegel's statements are hardly unambiguous, and so it comes as no surprise that several interpreters have opted for the non-metaphysical reading. According to this reading, Hegel's work must be seen as a science of *logic* precisely to the extent that its meaning and purpose consist in furthering the project of a *transcendental logic* begun by Kant.

---

[1] Hegel, *Wissenschaft der Logik. Erster Band. Die Lehre vom Sein* (1832), GW 21, 5. G. W. F. Hegel, *The Science of Logic*, ed. and trans. George di Giovanni (Cambridge: Cambridge University Press, 2010), 7.
[2] GW 21, 7. Hegel, *Science of Logic*, 9.
[3] GW 21, 48. Hegel, *Science of Logic*, 42.

Ultimately, however, this explanation fails to resolve the issue. While it is indeed the case that those who focus on Kant can point to explicit statements by Hegel indicating his indebtedness to Kant's critical philosophy, what this approach neglects is the considerable degree to which Hegel also relies on *Spinoza*. This reliance is, to be sure, not explicitly thematized in either the preface or the introduction, and even in the main text of the *Science of Logic,* Hegel tends to conceal Spinoza's influence rather than proclaim it openly. This is a peculiar phenomenon, to which I will return later. In any case, this game of intellectual hide-and-seek has ensured that Hegel's engagement with Spinoza has either been entirely ignored or dismissed as insubstantial in favor of a focus on his connection to Kant. Both responses are seriously misguided, however. A closer inspection reveals with unmistakable clarity that Spinoza's *Ethics* is of crucial, indeed constitutive significance for Hegel's project.

But what are the consequences of this insight for the question previously posed, the question regarding the true subject of the *Science of Logic?* Should it be understood as offering a new kind of metaphysics or not? At first glance, the answer seems obvious. Insofar as Hegel's text is not only concerned with the continuation and development of Kant's transcendental logic but is also just as interested in working through its relationship to Spinoza's *Ethics,* then this does indeed indicate the presence of a metaphysical horizon, all the more so given that Hegel has no interest in the concrete specifics of Spinoza's ethical theory (such as his doctrine of affects) but rather directs his attention almost exclusively to Spinoza's metaphysical groundwork in the first part of the *Ethics.* As plausible as this argument sounds, I consider it to be erroneous.

In the remarks that follow I would like to advance the contrary claim that it is precisely when read against the backdrop of his discussion of Spinoza that Hegel's *Science of Logic* reveals itself most clearly as a *post-metaphysical enterprise.* And with an eye toward the predictable follow up question of what, exactly, the expression "metaphysics" designates in this context and what I mean by the perspective of a "post-metaphysical" enterprise, I will also assert that it is only in reference to Spinoza that these two questions can be adequately clarified. In order to minimize possible misunderstandings at the outset, however, I would also like to add here that I make this claim *with a critical intent.* In other words, I consider it to be an indication of failure rather than success that Hegel's logic must be characterized as a post-metaphysical project. Two additional points of criticism are associated with this claim, which I will also address in the course of my deliberations. Firstly, Hegel's presentation of Spinoza's *Ethics* strikes me as unconvincing, and this is directly connected to the second point, namely, that his effort to appropriate Jacobi's position for his own purposes cannot be regarded as successful either.

On the Relevance of Friedrich Heinrich Jacobi

It is of course no coincidence that I mention the name of *Friedrich Heinrich Jacobi* in this context. With Jacobi, a third figure enters the stage alongside Kant and Spinoza, one who, like Spinoza, operates largely behind the scenes in the opening passages of the logic, but whose actual contribution is no less significant for that. In fact, Jacobi constitutes an essential element in the constellation under consideration, and not only because his book, *Concerning the Doctrine of Spinoza in Letters to Herr Moses Mendelssohn,* which first appeared in 1785 and then in a second, expanded edition in 1789, was responsible for elevating Spinoza to the status of a philosopher considered worthy of serious critical attention.

Beyond the basic fact that it was Jacobi who inaugurated the so-called "Spinoza renaissance," three additional factors are of fundamental relevance for developing an adequate approach to Hegel's *Science of Logic*.[4] First, Jacobi formulated the central challenge to which Hegel's logic responds and for which he seeks a definitive solution. This challenge consists in Jacobi's provocative insistence, instantiated in the double philosophy he refers to as "my *Spinoza and Antispinoza*" (Spin: JWA 1,1, 274), that we must choose between two alternatives. Either one chooses the standpoint of Spinoza and thereby decides in favor of the exemplary paradigm of his rigorous monism, an entirely self-contained metaphysics of immanence, but must accept as part of the bargain Spinoza's entirely rational and consistent conclusion that the freedom of intentional action (the *causa finalis*) is nothing more than an untenable prejudice. Or one instead chooses the standpoint of personal freedom and concludes with equal consistency that no rational explanation of such freedom is possible. As Jacobi aptly summed up this alternative (Spin: JWA 1,1, 290), the exemplary rigor and consistency of Spinoza's philosophy mean that it cannot be *refuted*. It can only be *contradicted*—by way of a leap, a "salto mortale" that demonstrates the conviction that free action is real as an "immediate certainty." It is clear that not only Hegel, but also Fichte and Schelling urgently sought to chart a path out of this dilemma, that is to say, to find a way to refute Spinoza's monism—despite Jacobi's claim to the contrary—and transform it into a *system of freedom*. In the transition from the logic of essence to the logic of the concept, Hegel explicitly raises the prospect of a "refutation of Spinoza,"[5] a goal which is of course already implied in the *Phenomenology of Spirit,* where he presents his famous programmatic claim regarding the necessity of "grasping and expressing the true not just as *substance* but just as much as *subject*."[6]

The second factor to be considered is that the influence exerted by Jacobi's reconstruction of Spinoza also stems from his linguistic creativity. Instead of simply reproducing the Latin terminology of the *Ethics*, he developed a new language to present the relations of immanence and captured the relationship between substance and mode in the phrase "*being* in everything existent" [Seyn in allem Dasein] (Spin: JWA 1,1, 39; MPW 199). In this case as well it is apparent that Hegel owes a direct debt to Jacobi's pioneering work. Not only does he explicitly invoke the phrase "*being* in everything existent" at various points in the text, especially at the beginning of the

---

[4] See the detailed discussion in Birgit Sandkaulen, *Grund und Ursache. Die Vernunftkritik Jacobis* (Munich: Wilhelm Fink Verlag, 2000) as well as Chapter 2 in this volume.
[5] Hegel, *Wissenschaft der Logik. Zweiter Band. Die subjektive Logik* (1816), GW 12, 15. Hegel, *Science of Logic*, 512.
[6] Hegel, *Phänomenologie des Geistes*, GW 9, 18. 2018. G. W. F. Hegel, *The Phenomenology of Spirit*, ed. and trans. Terry Pinkard (Cambridge: Cambridge University Press, 2018), 12.

logic of being;[7] it clearly informs and shapes the entire framework of his logic of being, which proceeds through the determinations of *being*, nothingness, and becoming before concluding with *existence*. The reason why this is important and not merely a matter of superficial terminological preferences should be clear. If one can trace Hegel's basic logical determinations back to the Spinozan-Jacobian context, then it follows that his confrontation with Spinoza, shaped as it is by the provocative prior interpretation by Jacobi, does indeed begin at the moment he first addresses the logic of being.

This is also confirmed, finally, by the third essential point. Jacobi's reconstruction of the *Ethics* is distinctive on both a linguistic and a substantive level. Rather than following the method of geometric demonstration, recapitulating the sequence of propositions and proofs as presented by the author, Jacobi penetrates directly into the heart of the work in order to capture and portray the "spirit of Spinoza" (Spin: JWA 1,1, 18; MPW 187). This essential conceptual core, around which the entire *Ethics* is organized, is described by Jacobi at the very beginning of his now famous conversation with Lessing as "nothing other than the ancient *a nihilo nihil fit*" (Spin: JWA 1,1, 18; MPW 187). This phrase as well reappears word-for-word at the beginning of Hegel's logic of being and is also productively appropriated by Hegel for his own analysis, inasmuch as it clearly provides the source for the determinations of *nothingness* and *becoming*.[8] Also relevant in this context is Hegel's indebtedness to Jacobi's reconstruction of Spinoza for an additional proposition, namely, the proposition "*determinatio est negatio*," which comes from Spinoza's correspondence and which Jacobi had already used to clarify the relation of substance to individual things, defining those individual things accordingly via negation as "*non-entia*" (Spin: JWA 1,1, 100; MPW 219f.). By this point it should come as no surprise that Hegel attributes to this proposition an "infinite importance"[9] and, beginning with his review of Jacobi's works (hereafter: *Jacobi-Review*) of 1817, even idiosyncratically intensifying it through the addition of "omnis" ("*omnis determinatio est negatio*").[10] It can be claimed without exaggeration we are dealing here with a key proposition that Hegel has appropriated from Jacobi. On the one hand, it provides the primary framework for Hegel's discussion of Spinoza. And on the other hand, he also has recourse to this proposition in deriving the basic operator of his entire logic—in the precise sense that it provides the starting point from which he goes on to develop the operation of the "negation of negation."

What becomes clear, then, even on the basis of this short overview, is something that has unfortunately still not been fully acknowledged by Hegel scholars—that Hegel's engagement with Spinoza simply cannot be adequately understood without taking Jacobi's influence into account. Both the program of the logic as a whole—the

---

[7] GW 21,100; see Hegel's logic in the *Enzyklopädie der philosophischen Wissenschaften* (1830), GW 20, § 86, 123. G. W. F. Hegel, *Encyclopedia of the Philosophical Sciences in Basic Outline. Part I: Science of Logic*, ed. and trans. Klaus Brinkmann and Daniel O. Dahlstrom (Cambridge: Cambridge University Press, 2010), 137.

[8] GW 21, 70f. Hegel, *Science of Logic*, 61.

[9] GW 21, 101. Hegel, *Science of Logic*, 87.

[10] Hegel, *Friederich Heinrich Jacobi's Werke*, GW 15, 10. G. W. F. Hegel, "Review, Friedrich Heinrich Jacobi's Works, Volume III," in *Heidelberg Writings. Journal Publications*, ed. and trans. Brady Bowman and Allen Speight (Cambridge: Cambridge University Press, 2009), 9. In the following, the *Jacobi-Review* will be cited parenthetically in the text as JR with an indication of the page number in GW 15 as well as of the corresponding page in the English translation.

refutation of Spinoza on the basis of the transformation of substance into subject—as well as the fundamental logical determinations (being-nothingness-becoming-existence) and, finally and no less importantly, the central operator of negation, which Hegel deploys from the very beginning in order to realize his logical program, are deeply indebted to this influence.

Should any doubts still remain as to the significance of this complex of issues and problems, they can be easily and definitively dispelled by considering Hegel's own remarks. In the previously mentioned review of Jacobi (a text which, because of the programmatic way in which it illuminates his intentions, I consider to be one of his most important) he presents the essential coordinates of his logical project with all the clarity one could possibly wish for. Especially revealing in this regard is the fact that he composed the review in Heidelberg in 1817, one year after having completed the *Science of Logic*—in other words, in the *Jacobi-Review*, Hegel is recapitulating his logical program while it is still very fresh in his memory.[11]

According to the review, in contradistinction to "the metaphysics of Leibniz and Wolff, which at the time of the [*Spinoza*] *Letters* was at its last breath" (JR 7; 4), Jacobi showed that "that every consistent system of philosophy must in the end lead to Spinozism" (JR 9; 7). This is the starting point that Hegel describes as "the truth," "in this initial immediacy" (JR 9; 7). But Jacobi, Hegel continues, was also completely correct in his conclusion that one cannot simply stop at Spinoza: "Since [...] in its immediacy infinite being is only something abstract, unmoving, and non-spiritual, we find that what is free, i.e., self-determining, is missing in that abyss into which all determinateness has been cast and destroyed. Immediately and for itself, freedom is *personality* as the infinite point of *determination in and for itself*" (JR 10; 7f.). The goal of the undertaking is thus to affirm the freedom in whose name Jacobi brought his case against Spinoza.

However, Hegel then critically notes that Jacobi chose the wrong path to achieve this goal. To the *immediate* certainty of freedom, Hegel opposes a logical process by which, proceeding from Spinoza, one arrives at the *mediated immediacy of freedom*. But precisely this process is nothing other than the procedure of the negation of negation, derived by Hegel from his appropriation of the proposition previously communicated by Jacobi and formulated here for the first time as "*omnis determinatio est negatio.*" "Absolute negativity," Hegel writes, "is itself the source of freedom" (JR 10; 8), and he goes on to explain what he means by this as follows:

> Yet the manner in which negation is internal to substance has in fact *thus already been said*, and systematic progress in philosophical reflection really consists in nothing other than knowing what one has already said oneself. Substance, namely, is supposed to be the sublation of the finite, and that is just to say that it is the *negation of negation*, since it is precisely negation which we took to be definitive of the finite. And as the negation of negation, substance is absolute *affirmation*, and just as immediately it is *freedom* and *self-determination*. (JR 11; 9)

---

[11] See also Chapter 14 in this volume, where I discuss the set of issues stemming from the *Jacobi-Review* and the "Third Position" in the preliminary conception of the *Encyclopedia Logic*.

There can thus be no doubt as to the starting point or the goal of the *Science of Logic*, nor of the methods employed therein. And it is also clear that the achievement of Hegel's stated aim of "systematic progress in philosophical reflection" entails the overcoming of both Spinoza's position and that of Jacobi's double philosophy. The crucial task, in other words, is to substitute "systematic progress" for the leap of the "salto mortale." To gain new insights into Hegel's project in this manner, however, is by no means the same as determining whether or not the project itself is compelling. Turning now to the text of the *Science of Logic*, I will discuss some of the problems I see here in greater detail.

Spinoza in Hegel's Logic of Being and Essence

As mentioned at the outset of the chapter, Hegel in a sense concealed the entire program of his logic, the basic outline of which I have presented above, within the text of the *Science of Logic*. The reason for this has now also been revealed. One must in fact distinguish between Hegel's *exoteric* texts, in which he *openly* discusses his aims and intentions (to which the presentation of Spinoza in his *Lectures on the History of Philosophy* also belongs), and the text of the *Logic*, where these aims and intentions are realized by way of *internal operations*. In the latter case, Spinoza's philosophy constitutes something along the lines of an unthematized presupposition of the entire logic, one that is already presumed by the starting point of the work and can only be openly expressed and overcome within the logical progression of the argument. It is thus wholly consistent with his approach that Hegel only explicitly mentions the goal of a "refutation of Spinoza" in the transition from the logic of essence to the logic of the concept.

The explicit reference that he makes at this point, however, is also bound up with his first major difficulty. Upon closer inspection, it becomes clear that Hegel retrospectively locates the alleged refutation of Spinoza at a very specific point in the logic of essence. The point in question is the chapter on the "absolute relation," which proceeds from a discussion of the relation of substantiality via the relation of causality to reciprocity, and then continues on from there to the concept as the determination of free subjectivity. Although Hegel does not mention Spinoza by name in the passage in question, it follows from this constellation that it is the *relation of substantiality* that Hegel identifies with Spinoza's philosophy here. So wherein lies the difficulty? The problem is that this reading of Spinoza does not align with the explicit discussion of Spinoza presented by Hegel in an earlier part of the logic of essence, where, in the introductory pages of the section on actuality, he addresses "the absolute." Rather than speaking of a *relation* to substance here, in the "remark" appended to the main text Hegel equates "*Spinoza's concept of substance*" with the deficient determination of an "abstract identity."[12]

---

[12] Hegel, *Wissenschaft der Logik. Erster Band. Die Lehre vom Wesen* (1813), GW 11, 374. Hegel, *Science of Logic*, 372; 370. The extent to which the presentation of the absolute corresponds to "Spinoza's concept of substance" is elaborated in the appended "remark."

In other words, rather than encountering a *single* treatment of Spinoza in the *Logic*, we are confronted with *two distinct and incompatible* versions of his thought.[13] Hegel is clearly pursuing a *dual strategy* in order to meet the challenge of Spinoza's philosophy (and Jacobi's double philosophy as well). I will turn now to a discussion of this highly problematic double strategy, taking the beginning of the logic of being as my starting point. In considering this part of the text, one cannot help but be struck by the fact that Hegel, in the revised second edition of the *Science of Logic* of 1832, significantly increased the number of references to Spinoza in the logic of being, even if, for the aforementioned reason, they continue to appear only in the so-called "remarks."[14] I also consider this modification to be the result of a strategic calculation,[15] one through which Hegel indicates—still subtly but with greater clarity than is the case in the first edition of the *Logic*—that the confrontation with Spinoza actually begins in the logic of being. Let us take a moment to consider the main features of this discussion.

The very first mention of Spinoza is both significant and at the same time highly problematic, because, according to Hegel, the initial determination of the logic, the "simple thought of *pure being*," can be attributed to Parmenides as well as Spinoza.[16] In both cases, Hegel writes, this determination has its origin in the view that "being is only being, nothing only nothing," and for this reason both figures invoke the "abstract identity" that is "the essence of pantheism."[17] This creation of a parallel between the Eleatics and Spinoza also appears in the *Lectures on the History of Philosophy*, where he writes that "taken as a whole, this constitutes the Idea of Spinoza, and it is just what τὸ ὄν was to the Eleatics."[18]

Hegel's statement is unquestionably ambiguous. On the one hand he highlights the fact that both Parmenides and Spinoza were rightly concerned with the thought of being, which in its utter lack of determination cannot be anything other than abstract. On the other hand, however, the most glaring shortcoming of these philosophies also reveals itself therein, as Hegel notes explicitly soon thereafter: "with Parmenides as with Spinoza, there is no advance from being or from absolute substance to the negative, the finite."[19] In other words, this parallelization serves as the basis for ascribing to Spinoza

---

[13] See the detailed presentation in Birgit Sandkaulen, "Die Ontologie der Substanz, der Begriff der Subjektivität und die Faktizität des Einzelnen. Hegels reflexionslogische 'Widerlegung' der Spinozanischen Metaphysik," *International Yearbook of German Idealism* 5 (2008): 235–75.

[14] It should be noted that the same applies to the references to Jacobi.

[15] In the previously mentioned essay I argue that this is the reason Hegel moves the chapter on the absolute from the logic of essence to the front of the logic of being. In the *Encyclopedia Logic*, the chapter on the absolute is missing altogether. Both points suggest that Hegel is engaged in a post hoc attempt to resolve the discrepancy between the two versions of Spinoza contained in the logic of essence, which finally becomes unmistakable at the beginning of the logic of the concept and leads to a series of unconvincing hermeneutic endeavors on Hegel's part (GW 12, 14. Hegel, *Science of Logic*, 511f.). It would certainly be interesting to know how the revised logic of essence would have looked under these circumstances, had Hegel been able to complete it.

[16] GW 21, 70f. Hegel, *Science of Logic*, 60.

[17] GW 21, 71. Hegel, *Science of Logic*, 61.

[18] Hegel, *Vorlesungen über die Geschichte der Philosophie*, TWA 20, 165 (GW 30,1, 164; 419). G. W. F. Hegel, *Lectures on the History of Philosophy*, trans. Elisabeth S. Haldane and Frances H. Simson, vol. 3 (Lincoln: University of Nebraska Press, 1995), 257.

[19] GW 21, 82. Hegel, *Science of Logic*, 71.

from the very beginning a position that Hegel refers to as "*acosmism*,"[20] to which he positively contrasts the fact that his own interest in the progress of the logic through the use of negation addresses the world in its full concreteness.

The decisive ascription of acosmism to Spinoza, which legitimizes his positioning at the beginning in the logic and simultaneously guarantees from the outset that the logical process will transcend the deficiencies of such abstraction, also informs (in terms of content if not of terminology) the lengthy statement on Spinoza contained in the "remark" on existence. As Hegel writes, in what we can now see is a direct quotation from Jacobi's *Spinoza Letters*, "the said reality in everything real, the *being* in all existence that should express the concept of God is nothing else than abstract being, the same as nothing."[21] While Hegel initially appears here to simply be repeating what he said previously, he then adds his comment on the "infinite importance" of the proposition "*Omnis determinatio est negatio.*" With Spinoza, however, as Hegel explains, "negation as such is formless abstraction."[22]

And this same deficiency is said to reveal both that and how "*the unity of Spinoza's substance*" results from the aforementioned proposition, namely in such a way that every possible distinction, whether among the attributes or the modes, not only lacks any ontological significance of its own; these distinctions cannot even be characterized as "moments" of substance, insofar as they have been established exclusively on the basis of an "external understanding."[23] With regard to the finite individual, the result is that "against this finite that would be in and for itself as such, determinateness asserts itself essentially as negation, dragging it into the same negative movement of the understanding that makes everything vanish into the abstract unity of substance."[24] Spinoza's ontology ultimately boils down to a destruction of the finite under the sign of abstract being—such is Hegel's conclusion, which corresponds to what I have termed the first version in the chapter on the absolute in the logic of essence.[25]

What are we to make of Hegel's presentation? Perhaps the only thing one can bring up in his favor is the aforementioned circumstance that he counters this version with a different one—the relation of substantiality—but this addition ultimately does nothing to improve the situation. Before I turn to this second version, I want to make

---

[20] The term "acosmism" does not appear in the *Science of Logic*, but Hegel makes prominent use of it as his description of Spinozan philosophy in many other places, including the *Lectures on the History of Philosophy* (TWA 20, 177; 195. GW 30, 2, 713) and in the *Encyclopedia of the Philosophical Sciences* (GW 20, § 50, 89; § 573, 565). G. W. F. Hegel, *Lectures on the History of Philosophy 1825–6*, ed. Robert F. Brown, trans. Robert F. Brown and J. Michael Stewart with the assistance of Henry S. Harris, vol. 3, rev. ed. (Oxford: Clarendon Press, 2009), 128. Hegel, *Encyclopedia of the Philosophical Sciences in Basic Outline. Part I: Science of Logic*, 99.

[21] GW 21, 100. Hegel, *Science of Logic*, 87.

[22] GW 21, 101. Hegel, *Science of Logic*, 87.

[23] GW 21, 101. Hegel, *Science of Logic*, 87.

[24] GW 21, 101. Hegel, *Science of Logic*, 87.

[25] With the exception of his detailed rejection of the geometric method, which Hegel undertakes in the chapter on the absolute from the logic of essence and which is missing in the revised version of the logic of being—presumably because the logic of being, in contrast to the logic of essence, does not yet thematize reflection specifically and also cannot explicitly address differently methodological procedures. This, however, makes all the more clear the difficulties confronting Hegel in his effort to find the most strategically favorable location for his deliberations on Spinoza. On this point, see also my previously mentioned essay.

clear at this point that the acosmistic interpretation of Spinoza, including the parallel between Spinoza and Parmenides that it entails, is completely misguided. After all, the fact that Spinoza considers finite things to be modes of substance and not themselves substances certainly does not entail the conclusion that they have no ontological significance. Both with regard to their essence as well as their temporal existence, they have an ontological format that is different than that of substance, but it is not one that an "external understanding" merely imposes upon substance from the outside. Rather, the essential potency of substance itself finds expression therein.

Hegel's completely erroneous account of Spinoza is—at least at first glance—all the more astonishing because it finds no support whatsoever in Jacobi. In his *Jacobi-Review*, Hegel does indeed give the impression of making Jacobi's insights his own, but in actuality this is far from the case. In fact, the decisive difference between Hegel's and Jacobi's presentations of Spinoza is already easily discernible in Jacobi's conversation with Lessing. Because the "spirit of Spinozism" is determined here on the basis of "*a nihilo nihil fit*," it does not entail the acosmism of an abstract being as it does with Hegel. What follows instead is, as Jacobi explains, that Spinoza "rejected any transition from the infinite to the finite," and "in place of an emanating En-Soph he only posited an immanent one," "an indwelling cause of the universe eternally unalterable within itself, One and the same with all its consequences" (Spin: JWA 1,1, 18; MPW 187f.).

The situation is clear: Jacobi takes aim at the heart of the *Ethics*, that is to say at Spinoza's *metaphysics of immanence*, whose essential determination is the *causa immanens*. What this means is that one must grasp what substance is and what follows from it as instantaneously and inseparably connected. There is no transition between the two, and thus it is utterly senseless to try to isolate substance from its consequences as if it were some kind of exclusive principle. Rather, the crux of Spinoza's philosophy is to be found in the precisely opposite claim that one and the same God is both *causa sui* and *omnium rerum causa*,[26] and insofar as Jacobi explicitly refers to this very passage (see Spin: JWA 1,1, 109; MPW 226), it is equally clear that his aforementioned determination of finite things as "non-entia" in no way aims to establish their ontological nullity. Instead, negation is deployed here with the sole intent of drawing attention to the ontological interdependency of "being" and "existence," of substance and modes.

All of this was readily available in print for Hegel's consideration, and, as I have shown, he did in fact make use of Jacobi as a source. But what he reads out of this source material takes on an entirely different meaning than it has in Jacobi's original, one that not only falsifies the statements of both Jacobi and Spinoza[27] but also uses Spinoza's *Ethics* to construct a decidedly un-Spinozan theory. Why would Hegel do such a thing? Part of the answer is that the unfolding argument of his *Science of Logic* is supposed to have the merit of moving past the abstract in order to penetrate the concrete, something that Spinoza was allegedly unable to accomplish. What proves

---

[26] Spinoza, *Ethics*, E I, prop. 25, scholium.
[27] This also includes the basic presentation of both Spinoza himself as well as Jacobi's reconstruction of Spinoza within the framework of *immediacy*. On the set of problems surrounding so-called immediate knowing see also Chapter 14 in this volume.

more important, however, is that Hegel's attempt to circumscribe the *Ethics* in terms of indeterminate abstract being is obviously strategic in nature. Only when Spinoza's metaphysics can be reduced, contrary to its actual intention, to a matter of "abstract identity," is Hegel able to integrate it into the logic—as its starting point—in order to then overcome this starting point in the course of his deliberations. The implications of this insight are profound, and I would thus like to underscore its crucial significance by reiterating it in a somewhat different form.

On the one hand, it is completely nonsensical to reduce Spinoza's philosophy to the determination of substance and simultaneously criticize it because "there is no advance from being or from absolute substance to the negative, the finite." It is nonsensical because Spinoza's conception of the *causa immanens* excludes the very possibility of such an "advance" and substance instead "always already" expresses itself in its attributes and modes. This is precisely the relation that Jacobi captures with his reference to "being in all existence." To that extent it is Hegel alone who bears the responsibility for destroying the relation of immanence and replacing it with abstract being. On the other hand, one also has to recognize the significance of this move and why, upon closer inspection, we should neither be surprised that Hegel distorts Spinoza to suit his own purposes nor by the manner in which he does it. In asserting, against the genuine intent of Spinoza's ontology, that there is no progression from being to existence therein, he gives the impression of making an ontological argument. In truth, however, the motivation for this assertion has nothing at all to do with ontology. Rather, Hegel is driven by an *epistemic* interest. At stake is the *interest of thinking*, which is then explicitly formulated in the logic of essence as the interest of reflection in organizing a successive development of *determinations of thought* that ultimately culminates in the *concept* as the epitome of a comprehension that has become fully transparent to itself.

That Hegel calls this interest of thinking an "objective thinking" is an indication of his distance from Kant, and from this it follows that the *Science of Logic*, to the extent that its content is "thought in so far as this thought is equally the fact as in itself; or the fact in itself in so far as this is equally pure thought,"[28] is clearly ontological in orientation. Hegel's treatment of Spinoza, however, makes it just as clear that this orientation entails a particular emphasis. Hegel's aim is the construction of a scientific onto-*logic*, in which thinking—rather than being—takes the lead role. Against this backdrop, the claim presented in my introductory remarks comes into sharper focus. Hegel does not produce a new metaphysics. What he produces is precisely what the title of his work announces: a science of *logic*.

Having arrived at this conclusion, however—a conclusion, we should note, that results directly from Hegel's idiosyncratic and perplexing effort to integrate Spinozan philosophy into his logic—we can also make an additional observation in this context. It becomes apparent, namely, that the figure of the absolute arrived at by Hegel at the end of the logic in no way offers an *ontological* alternative to substance, one that would transform its allegedly abstract rigidity and immobility into a living dynamism. What proves decisive is that Hegel's appropriation of the term logic for the title of his work

---

[28] GW 21, 33f. Hegel, *Science of Logic*, 29.

entails a radical shift: The absolute is *result* and this precisely to the extent that it is the result of an *epistemic* rather than an ontological movement. This is what Hegel calls "subject," as the terminal expression for a thinking that has developed to the point having full consciousness of itself—to self-consciousness.[29]

The Logical Alienation of Metaphysics and Its Consequences

In concluding, I would like to address some of the consequences of Hegel's construction of a scientific onto-*logic* to which I just alluded. Firstly, in terms of his engagement with Spinoza, the further progress of the logic confirms what has just been shown to be the case at the outset—Hegel's presentation simply has nothing to do with Spinoza's *Ethics*. It is, to be sure, a serious omission on the part of many Hegel interpretations to have ignored Hegel's debate with Spinoza and the Jacobian background to this encounter. By the same token, however, it also makes no sense to take Hegel's statements regarding Spinoza as valid objections to the *Ethics* or even as contributions to a serious discussion. Even if one approaches Hegel in a spirit of hermeneutic generosity, assuming the possibility of productive (mis)interpretations, one misses the mark for the aforementioned reasons, precisely because Hegel is not interested in *Spinoza,* but rather in *integrating Spinoza* into the *epistemic progression* of the logic.

That Hegel brings a second version of Spinoza into play in his discussion of the relation of substantiality, one that differs from the version I have just addressed in the sense that it does not thematize the abstract identity of substance but rather the *immanent relation of substance to its accidents,* demonstrates this interest with all the clarity one could ask for. In direct contrast to the first version, where Hegel claims that it is only an "external understanding" that imposes the distinction among attributes and finite things onto substance and thus also destroys them in turn, the second version refers to the "*absolute power*" and "*actuosity*" of substance that is manifest in its accidents,[30] an approach with which Hegel at least indicates his attentiveness to the actual statements contained in the *Ethics*. For this reason as well, we would be well advised not to take the verdict of acosmism too seriously.

In the case of the second version as well, however, although it seems more closely aligned with the *Ethics,* we are by no means presented with a convincing portrayal of Spinoza. This is already precluded by the fact that Hegel distinguishes the relation of causality from the relation of substantiality and thus asserts as the next step in the unfolding of the determinations of thought that the "absolute actuosity" of substance is "*cause*" and that its power manifests itself "*as effect.*"[31] It is clear that as far as Spinoza himself is concerned, that is, from an *ontological* point of view, these determinations cannot be separated and that the distinction between power and cause makes no

---

[29] Accordingly, from a logical perspective, Hegel's various uses of the term "God" should be treated with the utmost caution, since there can clearly no longer be any possibility of using this term to refer to the conventional *representation* of God.

[30] GW 11, 394f. Hegel, *Science of Logic,* 490f.

[31] GW 11, 397. Hegel, *Science of Logic,* 493.

sense at all. As should be apparent by now, Hegel himself is fully aware of this, and thus we are reminded us once again of his true intentions. As a result of his logical interest, he systematically pulls apart, so to speak, what for Spinoza is always already bound together, and he does this because of an *epistemic* concern with the successive development and enrichment of the determinations of thought, in a word, with a "systematic progress in philosophical reflection."

However, the most significant aspect of the intellectual performance delivered here consists in the assertion, presented in the transition to the logic of the concept, that it offers the "one and only true refutation of Spinozism," and in the characterization of this alleged refutation as an "*unveiling* of substance."[32] According to this conception, the epistemic "*genesis of the concept*"[33] does in fact have substance as its precondition, and thus two key points are once again confirmed in the context of this crucial passage—both the constitutive significance of Spinoza for Hegel's project as well as the logical reshaping of Spinoza within this project, which literally transforms the *Ontology* of the *Ethics* into a *Science of Logic*. The question whether Hegel himself believes it when he says of this procedure that "effective refutation" must "infiltrate the opponent's stronghold and meet him on his own ground,"[34] or whether this is also merely a strategic assertion directed toward the contemporary discussion, can now simply be left unanswered. It has, after all, become sufficiently clear by this point that Hegel only mobilizes the power of Spinoza's system in order to subject it from the start to a thought process that not only fails to "unveil" Spinoza's philosophy but in fact systematically distorts that philosophy at the level of its most fundamental concerns.

This observation brings me to my concluding remarks, in which I would like to draw attention to the full range of serious consequences that result from this distortion. In light of the previous discussion, it is not enough to simply acknowledge that in the case of the philosophies of Spinoza and Hegel we are dealing with two philosophical conceptions that differ from one another *in toto genere,* conceptions that cannot even be considered comparatively, since this would entail the mistaken assumption that both operate on the same plane or are oriented toward the same horizon. This observation is correct, but it does not go far enough, because Hegel's alleged "refutation of Spinoza" comes at a profound conceptual cost, such that one has to ask oneself whether it is actually worth the price. I alluded to this cost at the start of the chapter with my reference to Hegel's post-metaphysical thinking, whose *operational* profile, that is, the transformation of ontology into the "systematic progression" of an epistemically oriented onto-*logic* I have elucidated in the interim.

What, then, are the *conceptual* consequences? Once again, we find that these consequences appear with the greatest clarity in the transition from the logic of essence to the logic of the concept. In the course of the outlined progression from the relation of substantiality to the concept via the relations of causality and reciprocity, Hegel not only differentiates what for Spinoza always already forms an inseparable unity into a multi-stage epistemic development. Even more significantly, what Hegel refers to

---

[32] GW 12, 15. Hegel, *Science of Logic*, 512.
[33] GW 12, 15. Hegel, *Science of Logic*, 512.
[34] GW 12, 15. Hegel, *Science of Logic*, 512.

as the "unveiling of substance" is accompanied at the level of *content* by a successive demolition of the difference between substance and finite things present in the relation of substantiality, along with the transformation of this difference into an "*identity that exists in and for itself*"[35] as the self-relation of the subject. This structure, in which any ontological distinction between infinite and finite as well as any distinction among finite individuals themselves has been definitively overcome, is understood by Hegel as the realization of what he emphatically terms "freedom."[36]

In terms of the logic as a whole, however, this emancipation has long since begun. It has already been initiated with the use of the logical operator of the negation of negation in the logic of being, where, proceeding from the determinations of existence and finitude, the crucial insight into the "*true infinite*" is to be acquired through the sublation of the opposition between finite and infinite.[37] It is no coincidence that Hegel goes to such great lengths to develop this determination, because it is here that the conceptual center of his own approach is to be located, which he further explicates in a series of stages before it finds its fullest expression in the concept. *Prima vista*, this Hegelian holism appears to be a variation on Spinoza, but appearances are misleading in this case. In pursuing a dual strategy that reproaches Spinoza with a lack of difference on the one hand and the lack of real identity on the other, Hegel fundamentally dissolves the ontological structure of the *Ethics* in order to replace it with the complete transparency of an intentional self-relation.

My reservations with regard to this logical process are not a mere variation on the stereotypical objection that there is no such thing as an "absolute knowledge"—after all, Hegel shows in the *Science of Logic* just what type of knowledge is at issue and the extent to which it is indeed possible to achieve the desired transparency through a process of successively illuminating the determinations of thought. Rather, my reservation is based precisely on the fact that this is only possible, as Hegel has clearly understood, on the condition that the concerns of ontology are transformed into an onto-*logic*. It is my fundamental conviction, however, that the facticity of actuality cannot be fully comprehended by thought, and that the ontic experience of our own finitude will always stand in opposition to the logical thought of an identity of infinite and finite, regardless of how rigorously that thought has been deduced. For this reason, my concluding appeal is not for the adoption of Hegel's post-metaphysical thinking but rather for the option formulated by Jacobi, whose insistence that we must decide between the positions presented in his "Spinoza and Antispinoza" confronts us with no less urgency than it did his contemporaries.

---

[35] GW 12, 15. Hegel, *Science of Logic*, 512.
[36] GW 12, 15. Hegel, *Science of Logic*, 512.
[37] GW 21, 124. Hegel, *Science of Logic*, 109.

Bibliography

Primary Texts: Friedrich Heinrich Jacobi

Jacobi, F. H. *Briefwechsel. Gesamtausgabe*. Founded by Michael Brüggen and Siegfried Sudhoff, edited by Walter Jaeschke and Birgit Sandkaulen. Stuttgart-Bad Cannstatt: Frommann-Holzboog, 1981 ff. [JBW]

Jacobi, F. H. *Die Denkbücher Friedrich Heinrich Jacobis*. Edited by Sophia Victoria Krebs. 2 vols. Stuttgart-Bad Cannstatt: Frommann-Holzboog, 2020.

Jacobi, F. H. *Friedrich Heinrich Jacobi's auserlesener Briefwechsel*. Edited by Friedrich Roth. 2 vols. Leipzig: Gerhard Fleischer, 1825–7.

Jacobi, F. H. *The Main Philosophical Writings and the Novel Allwill*. Edited and translated by George di Giovanni. Montreal & Kingston: McGill-Queen's University Press, 1994 [MPW]

Jacobi, F. H. *Werke*. Edited by Friedrich Roth and Friedrich Köppen. 6 vols. Leipzig: Gerhard Fleischer, 1812–25. Reprint, Darmstadt: Wissenschaftliche Buchgesellschaft, 1980.

Jacobi, F. H. *Werke. Gesamtausgabe*. Edited by Klaus Hammacher and Walter Jaeschke. Hamburg: Meiner, 1998 ff. [JWA]

Other Primary Sources

Fichte, J. G. "A Crystal Clear Report to the General Public Concerning the Actual Essence of the Newest Philosophy: An Attempt to Force the Reader to Understand." Translated by John Bottermann und William Rasch. In *Philosophy of German Idealism: Fichte, Jacobi and Schelling*, edited by Ernst Behler, 39–115. New York: Continuum, 1987.

Fichte, J. G. *Early Philosophical Writings*. Edited and translated by Daniel Breazeale. Ithaca: Cornell University Press, 1988.

Fichte, J. G. *Fichtes Werke*. Edited by Immanuel Hermann Fichte. Reprint, Berlin: De Gruyter, 1971. [FW]

Fichte, J. G. "Foundation of the Entire Wissenschaftslehre." In *Foundation of the Entire* Wissenschaftslehre *and Related Writings (1794–95)*, edited and translated by Daniel Breazeale, 196–378. Oxford: Oxford University Press, 2021.

Fichte, J. G. *Foundation of the Entire* Wissenschaftslehre *and Related Writings (1794–95)*. Edited and translated by Daniel Breazeale. Oxford: Oxford University Press, 2021.

Fichte, J. G. *Foundations of Natural Right: According to the Principles of the* Wissenschaftslehre. Edited by Frederick Neuhouser. Translated by Michael Baur. Cambridge: Cambridge University Press, 2000.

Fichte, J. G. *Foundations of Transcendental Philosophy (Wissenschaftslehre) Nova Methodo (1796/99)*. Edited and translated by Daniel Breazeale. Ithaca: Cornell University Press, 1992.

Fichte, J. G. *Gesamtausgabe der Bayerischen Akademie der Wissenschaften*. Edited by Reinhard Lauth et al. Stuttgart-Bad Cannstatt: Frommann-Holzboog, 1964 ff. [GA]
Fichte, J. G. *Introductions to the* Wissenschaftslehre *and Other Writings (1797–1800)*. Edited and translated with an introduction and notes by Daniel Breazeale. Indianapolis: Hackett, 1994.
Fichte, J. G. "Review of Aenesidemus." In *Early Philosophical Writings*, edited and translated by Daniel Breazeale, 59–77. Ithaca: Cornell University Press, 1988.
Fichte, J. G. *The System of Ethics: According to the Principles of the* Wissenschaftslehre. Edited and translated by Daniel Breazeale and Günter Zöller. Cambridge: Cambridge University Press, 2005.
Fichte, J. G. *The Vocation of Man*. Translated by Peter Preuss. Indianapolis: Hackett, 1987.
Fichte, J. G. *Wissenschaftslehre Nova Methodo*. Edited by Erich Fuchs. Hamburg: Meiner, 1994.
Goethe, Johann W. *From my Life: Poetry and Truth, Parts One to Three*. Translated by Robert R. Heitner. New York: Suhrkamp Publishers, 1987.
Hegel, G. W. F. *Briefe von und an Hegel*. Edited by Johannes Hoffmeister. 3rd ed. 4 vols. Hamburg: Meiner, 1969–77.
Hegel, G. W. F. *Encyclopedia of the Philosophical Sciences in Basic Outline. Part I: Science of Logic*. Edited and translated by Klaus Brinkmann and Daniel O. Dahlstrom. Cambridge: Cambridge University Press, 2010.
Hegel, G. W. F. *Faith and Knowledge*. Edited and translated by Walter Cerf and Henry S. Harris. Albany: State University of New York Press, 1977.
Hegel, G. W. F. *Gesammelte Werke*. Edited by the Nordrhein-Westfälische Akademie der Wissenschaften und der Künste, in cooperation with the Deutsche Forschungsgemeinschaft. Hamburg: Meiner, 1968 ff. [GW]
Hegel, G. W. F. *Lectures on the History of Philosophy*. Vol. 3, translated by Elisabeth S. Haldane and Frances H. Simson. Lincoln: University of Nebraska Press, 1995.
Hegel, G. W. F. *Lectures on the History of Philosophy 1825–6*. Edited by Robert F. Brown. Translated by Robert F. Brown and J. Michael Stewart with the assistance of Henry S. Harris. Rev. ed. Vol. 3, *Medieval and Modern Philosophy* Oxford: Clarendon Press, 2009.
Hegel, G. W. F. *The Letters*. Translated by Clark Butler and Christiane Seiler. Bloomington: Indiana University Press, 1984.
Hegel, G. W. F. *The Phenomenology of Spirit*. Edited and translated by Terry Pinkard. Cambridge: Cambridge University Press, 2018.
Hegel, G. W. F. "Review, Friedrich Heinrich Jacobi's Works, Volume III." In *Heidelberg Writings. Journal Publications*, edited and translated by Brady Bowman and Allen Speight, 3–31. Cambridge: Cambridge University Press, 2009.
Hegel, G. W. F. *The Science of Logic*. Edited and translated by George di Giovanni. Cambridge: Cambridge University Press, 2010.
Hegel, G. W. F. *Werke in zwanzig Bänden*. Edited by Eva Moldenhauer and Karl M. Michel. Frankfurt a.M.: Suhrkamp, 1970 ff. [TWA]
Heine, Heinrich. *On the History and Philosophy in Germany and Other Writings*. Edited by Terry Pinkard, translated by Howard Pollack-Milgate. Cambridge: Cambridge University Press, 2007.
Herder, Johann G. *God. Some Conversations*. Translated by Frederick H. Burkhardt. New York: Veritas Press, 1940.
Kant, Immanuel. *Critique of Practical Reason (1788)*. In *Practical Philosophy*, edited and translated by Mary J. Gregor, 133–272. Cambridge: Cambridge University Press, 1996.

Kant, Immanuel. *Critique of Pure Reason*. Edited and translated by Paul Guyer and Allen W. Wood. Cambridge: Cambridge University Press, 1998. [CPR]

Kant, Immanuel. *Gesammelte Schriften*. Edited by the Königlich-Preußische Akademie der Wissenschaften. Reprint, Berlin: De Gruyter, 1968. [AA]

Kant, Immanuel. "Groundwork of the Metaphysics of Morals (1785)." In *Practical Philosophy*, edited and translated by Mary J. Gregor, 37–108. Cambridge: Cambridge University Press, 1996.

Kant, Immanuel. *Kritik der reinen Vernunft*. Edited by Jens Timmermann. Hamburg: Meiner, 1998. [KrV]

Kant, Immanuel. *Practical Philosophy*. Edited and translated by Mary J. Gregor. Cambridge: Cambridge University Press, 1996.

Kant, Immanuel. "Prolegomena to Any Future Metaphysics That Will Be Able to Come Forward as Science (1783)." Translated by Gary Hatfield. In *Theoretical Philosophy after 1781*, edited by Henry Allison and Peter Heath, 29–170. Cambridge: Cambridge University Press, 2002.

Novalis. *Fichte Studies*. Edited by Jane Kneller. Cambridge: Cambridge University Press, 2003.

Schelling, F. W. J. *The Grounding of Positive Philosophy: The Berlin Lectures*. Translated by Bruce Matthews. Albany: State University of New York Press, 2007.

Schelling, F. W. J. *Idealism and the Endgame of Theory. Three Essays by F. W. J. Schelling*. Edited and translated with a critical introduction by Thomas Pfau. Albany: State University of New York Press, 1994.

Schelling, F. W. J. *Monument to Jacobi's Work on the Divine Things (1812)*. Translated by Hadi Fakhoury, author manuscript, Kabiri, forthcoming.

Schelling, F. W. J. "Of the I as the Principle of Philosophy or on the Unconditional in Human Knowledge." In *The Unconditional in Human Knowledge. Four Early Essays (1794–1796)*, translated by Marti Fritz, 63–149. Lewisburg: Bucknell University Press, 1980.

Schelling, F. W. J. *On the History of Modern Philosophy*. Edited and translated with an introduction and notes by Andrew Bowie. Cambridge: Cambridge University Press, 1994.

Schelling, F. W. J. *Philosophical Investigations into the Essence of Human Freedom*. Translated with an introduction and notes by Jeff Love and Johannes Schmidt. Albany: State University of New York Press, 2006.

Schelling, F. W. J. *Philosophy and Religion (1804)*. Translated, annotated and with an introduction by Klaus Ottmann. Putnam: Spring Publications, 2010.

Schelling, F. W. J. *Sämmtliche Werke*. Edited by Karl Friedrich August Schelling. Stuttgart/Augsburg: J. G. Cotta'scher Verlag, 1856–1861. [SW]

Schelling, F. W. J. "Stuttgart Seminars." In *Idealism and the Endgame of Theory. Three Essays by F. W. J. Schelling*, edited and translated with a critical introduction by Thomas Pfau, 195–268. Albany: State University of New York Press, 1994.

Schelling, F. W. J. *System der Weltalter. Münchener Vorlesung 1827/28 in einer Nachschrift von Ernst von Lasaulx*. 2nd extended edition. Edited by Siegbert Peetz. Frankfurt a.M.: Vittorio Klostermann, 1998.

Schelling, F. W. J. "System of Philosophy in General and of the Philosophy of Nature in Particular." In *Idealism and the Endgame of Theory. Three Essays by F. W. J. Schelling*, edited and translated with a critical introduction by Thomas Pfau, 139–94. Albany: State University of New York Press, 1994.

Schelling, F. W. J. *System of Transcendental Idealism (1800)*. Translated by Peter Heath. With an introduction by Michael Vater. Charlottesville: University Press of Virginia, 1978.
Schelling, F. W. J. "Treatise Explicatory of the Idealism in the 'Science of Knowledge.'" In *Idealism and the Endgame of Theory. Three Essays by F. W. J. Schelling*, edited and translated with a critical introduction by Thomas Pfau, 61–138. Albany: State University of New York Press, 1994.
Schelling, F. W. J. *The Unconditional in Human Knowledge. Four Early Essays (1794–1796)*. Translated by Marti Fritz. Lewisburg: Bucknell University Press, 1980.
Schelling, F. W. J. *Werke. Historisch-Kritische Ausgabe*. Edited by Thomas Buchheim et al. Stuttgart-Bad Cannstatt: Frommann-Holzboog, 1976 ff. [AA]
Schlegel, Friedrich. "Jacobis Woldemar" (1796). In *Kritische Schriften und Fragmente*, edited by Ernst Behler and Hans Eichner. Vol. 1, *1794–1797*, 177–91. Paderborn: Schöningh, 1988.
Schlegel, Friedrich. *Philosophical Fragments*. Translated by Peter Firchow. Minneapolis: University of Minnesota Press, 1991.
Schlegel, Friedrich. "Über F.H. Jacobi: Von den göttlichen Dingen und ihrer Offenbarung" (1812). In *Kritische Schriften und Fragmente*, edited by Ernst Behler and Hans Eichner. Vol. 3, *1803–1812*, 158–69. Paderborn: Schöningh, 1988.
Schulze, Gottlob E. *Aenesidemus oder über die Fundamente der von dem Herrn Professor Reinhold in Jena gelieferten Elementarphilosophie*. Edited by Manfred Frank. Hamburg: Meiner, 1996.
Spinoza, Baruch de. *Ethics*. In *The Collected Works of Spinoza*, edited and translated by Edwin Curley. Vol. 1. Princeton: Princeton University Press, 1985. [E]
Spinoza, Baruch de. "The Letters". In *Spinoza. Complete Works*, translated by Samuel Shirley and edited by Michael L. Morgan, 755–959. Indianapolis: Hackett Publishing Company, 2002.
Wolff, Christian. "Rational Thoughts Concerning God, the World, and the Human Soul, and also All Things in General (1720)." In *Early Modern German Philosophy (1690–1750)*, edited and translated by Corey W. Dyck, 95–134. Oxford: Oxford University Press, 2019.
Wolff, Christian. *Vernünfftige Gedanken von Gott, der Welt und der Seele des Menschen, auch allen Dingen überhaupt*. In *Gesammelte Werke* I,2, edited by Charles A. Corr. Hildesheim/Zürich/New York: Georg Olms Verlag, 1983.

Secondary Literature

Adickes, Erich. *Kant und das Ding an sich*. Berlin: Pan Verlag Rolf Heise, 1924.
Adolphi, Rainer. "'Geschehen aber zu denken ist immer das Schwierigste.' Zu den Problemen des Prozeßansatzes in Schellings Freiheitsphilosophie." In *Schellings Weg zur Freiheitsschrift. Legende und Wirklichkeit*, edited by Hans Michael Baumgartner and Wilhelm G. Jacobs, 252–71. Stuttgart-Bad Cannstatt: Frommann-Holzboog, 1996.
Adorno, Theodor W. *Negative Dialectics*. Translated by E. B. Ashton. New York: The Continuum Publishing Company, 1992.
Allison, Henry E. "Kant's Concept of the Transcendental Object." *Kant-Studien* 59 (1968): 165–86.

Aristotle. *Nicomachean Ethics*. In *The Complete Works of Aristotle*, edited by Jonathan Barnes. Vol. 2. Princeton: Princeton University Press, 1984.
Beiser, Frederick C. *The Fate of Reason. German Philosophy from Kant to Fichte*. London: Harvard University Press, 1987.
Berlin, Isaiah. *Against the Current: Essays in the History of Ideas*. London: Hogarth Press, 1979.
Boehm, Omri. *Kant's Critique of Spinoza*. Oxford: Oxford University Press, 2014.
Boethius, Ancius M. S. *The Theological Tractates. The Consolation of Philosophy*. Edited by Eric H. Warmington. Translated by Hugh F. Stewart, Edward K. Rand, and S. J. Tester. Cambridge: Harvard University Press, 1973.
Bollnow, Otto F. *Die Lebensphilosophie F.H. Jacobis*. Stuttgart: Kohlhammer, 1933.
Bowman, Brady. "Notiones Communes und Common Sense. Zu den Spinozanischen Voraussetzungen von Jacobis Rezeption der Philosophie Thomas Reids." In *Friedrich Heinrich Jacobi: Ein Wendepunkt der geistigen Bildung der Zeit*, edited by Walter Jaeschke and Birgit Sandkaulen, 159–78. Hamburg: Meiner, 2004.
Bowman, Brady. *Sinnliche Gewißheit. Zur systematischen Vorgeschichte eines Problems des deutschen Idealismus*. Berlin: Akademie Verlag, 2003.
Buber, Martin. *Das dialogische Prinzip*. 6th ed. Gerlingen: Lambert Schneider, 1992.
Damásio, António R. *Looking for Spinoza. Joy, Sorrow, and the Feeling Brain*. London: William Heinemann, 2003.
Derrida, Jacques. "Faith and Knowledge," translated by Samuel Weber. In *Religion*, edited by Jaques Derrida and Gianni Vattimo, 1–87. Stanford (California): Stanford University Press, 1998.
Derrida, Jacques. "Heidegger's Ear. Philopolemology (Geschlecht IV)." In *Reading Heidegger. Commemorations*, edited by John Sallis, translated by John P. Leavey Jr., 163–218. Bloomington: Indiana University Press, 1993.
Derrida, Jacques. *The Politics of Friendship*. London/New York: Verso, 1997.
Falke, Gustav. "Hegel und Jacobi. Ein methodisches Beispiel zur Interpretation der Phänomenologie des Geistes." *Hegel-Studien* 22 (1987): 129–42.
Frank, Manfred. *"Unendliche Annäherung." Die Anfänge der philosophischen Frühromantik*. Frankfurt a.M.: Suhrkamp, 1997.
Frank, Manfred, and Gerhard Kurz, eds. *Materialien zu Schellings philosophischen Anfängen*. Frankfurt a.M.: Suhrkamp, 1975.
Gabriel, Gottfried. "Von der Vorstellung zur Darstellung. Realismus in Jacobis 'David Hume.'" In *Friedrich Heinrich Jacobi: Ein Wendepunkt der geistigen Bildung der Zeit*, edited by Walter Jaeschke and Birgit Sandkaulen, 145–58. Hamburg: Meiner, 2004.
Habermas, Jürgen. "Faith and Knowledge." In *The Future of Human Nature*, translated by Hella Beister and Max Pensky, 101–15. Cambridge: Polity Press, 2003.
Halbig, Christoph. *Objektives Denken. Erkenntnistheorie und Philosophy of Mind in Hegels System*. Stuttgart-Bad Cannstatt: Frommann-Holzboog, 2002.
Halbig, Christoph. "The Philosopher as Polyphemus? Philosophy and Common Sense in Jacobi and Hegel." In *International Yearbook of German Idealism* 3 (2005): 261–82.
Hamilton, William. "On the Philosophy of Common Sense." In *The Works of Thomas Reid*, edited by Sir William Hamilton, 6th ed. Vol. 2, 742–803. Edinburgh: Maclachlan and Stewart, 1863.
Hammacher, Klaus, ed. *Friedrich Heinrich Jacobi. Philosoph und Literat der Goethezeit*. Frankfurt a.M.: Vittorio Klostermann, 1971.
Heidegger, Martin. *Being and Time*. Translated by John Macquarrie and Edward S. Robinson. Oxford: Basil Blackwell, 1962.

Henrich, Dieter. *Der Grund im Bewußtsein. Untersuchungen zu Hölderlins Denken (1794 – 1795)*. Stuttgart: Klett-Cotta, 2004.
Henrich, Dieter. "Der Ursprung der Doppelphilosophie. Friedrich Heinrich Jacobis Bedeutung für das nachkantische Denken." In *Friedrich Heinrich Jacobi. Präsident der Akademie, Philosoph, Theoretiker der Sprache*, edited by Dieter Henrich, 13–27. Munich: Beck, 1993.
Henrich, Dieter. "Die Anfänge der Theorie des Subjekts (1789)." In *Zwischenbetrachtungen. Im Prozess der Aufklärung*, edited by Axel Honneth et al., 106–70. Frankfurt a.M.: Suhrkamp, 1989.
Henrich, Dieter. "Fichte's Original Insight" [1967; Fichtes ursprüngliche Einsicht]. In *Contemporary German Philosophy*, edited by Darrel E. Christensen et al., translated by David R. Lachterman, 1: 15–53. Pennsylvania: Pennsylvania State University Press, 1982.
Herring, Herbert. *Das Problem der Affektion bei Kant*. Kant-Studien Ergänzungsheft 67. Cologne: Kölner Universitäts-Verlag, 1953.
Horstmann, Rolf-Peter. *Die Grenzen der Vernunft. Eine Untersuchung zu Zielen und Motiven des Deutschen Idealismus*. Frankfurt a.M.: Anton Hain, 1991.
Horstmann, Rolf-Peter. "Gibt es ein philosophisches Problem des Selbstbewußtseins?" In *Theorie der Subjektivität*, edited by Konrad Cramer et al., 220–48. Frankfurt a.M.: Suhrkamp, 1987.
Ivaldo, Marco. "Wissen und Leben. Vergewisserungen Fichtes im Anschluß an Jacobi." In *Friedrich Heinrich Jacobi: Ein Wendepunkt der geistigen Bildung der Zeit*, edited by Walter Jaeschke and Birgit Sandkaulen, 53–71. Hamburg: Meiner, 2004.
Jaeschke, Walter. "Freiheit um Gottes willen." In *Schellings Weg zur Freiheitsschrift. Legende und Wirklichkeit*, edited by Hans Michael Baumgartner and Wilhelm G. Jacobs, 202–22. Stuttgart-Bad Cannstatt: Frommann-Holzboog, 1996.
Jaeschke, Walter, ed. *Religionsphilosophie und spekulative Theologie. Der Streit um die Göttlichen Dinge (1799 – 1812). Quellenband*. Philosophisch-literarische Streitsachen 3.1. Hamburg: Meiner, 1994.
Jaeschke, Walter, ed. *Transzendentalphilosophie und Spekulation. Der Streit um die Gestalt einer ersten Philosophie (1799 – 1807). Quellenband*. Philosophisch-literarische Streitsachen 2.1. Hamburg: Meiner, 1993.
Jaeschke, Walter and Andreas Arndt. *Die Klassische Deutsche Philosophie nach Kant. Systeme der reinen Vernunft und ihre Kritik 1785 – 1845*. Munich: Beck, 2012.
Jaeschke, Walter and Birgit Sandkaulen, eds. *Friedrich Heinrich Jacobi: Ein Wendepunkt der geistigen Bildung der Zeit*. Hamburg: Meiner, 2004.
Kaplow, Ian. *Analytik und Ethik der Namen*. Würzburg: Königshausen & Neumann, 2002.
Kierkegaard, Søren. *Concluding Unscientific Postscript to the Philosophical Crumbs*. Edited and translated by Alastair Hannay. Cambridge: Cambridge University Press, 2009.
Kobusch, Theo. *Die Entdeckung der Person. Metaphysik der Freiheit und modernes Menschenbild*. Freiburg/Basel/Vienna: Herder, 1993.
Koch, Oliver. *Individualität als Fundamentalgefühl. Zur Metaphysik der Person bei Jacobi und Jean Paul*. Hamburg: Meiner, 2013.
Koselleck, Reinhart. "Einleitung." In *Geschichtliche Grundbegriffe. Historisches Lexikon zur politisch-sozialen Sprache in Deutschland*, edited by Otto Brunner, Werner Conze and Reinhart Koselleck. Vol. 1, XIII–XXVII. Stuttgart: Klett-Cotta, 1979.
Larmore, Charles E. *The Practices of the Self*. Translated by Sharon Bowman. Chicago/London: University of Chicago Press, 2010.

Lauth, Reinhard. "Fichtes Verhältnis zu Jacobi unter besonderer Berücksichtigung der Rolle Friedrich Schlegels in dieser Sache." In *Friedrich Heinrich Jacobi. Philosoph und Literat der Goethezeit*, edited by Klaus Hammacher, 165–208. Frankfurt a.M.: Vittorio Klostermann, 1971.

Locke, John. *An Essay Concerning Human Understanding*. Edited by Peter H. Nidditch. London: Oxford University Press, 1975.

Montaigne, Michel de. *The Complete Essays*. Edited and translated by Michael A. Screech. London: Penguin Books, 1991.

Otto, Stephan. "Spinoza Ante Spinozam? Jacobis Lektüre des Giordano Bruno im Kontext einer Begründung von Metaphysik." In *Friedrich Heinrich Jacobi: Ein Wendepunkt der geistigen Bildung der Zeit*, edited by Walter Jaeschke and Birgit Sandkaulen, 107–25. Hamburg: Meiner, 2004.

Pätzold, Detlef. "Die Vernunft und das Absolute." In *Handbuch Deutscher Idealismus*, edited by Hans J. Sandkühler, 25f. Stuttgart/Weimar: Metzler, 2005.

Pluder, Valentin. *Die Vermittlung von Idealismus und Realismus in der Klassischen Deutschen Philosophie. Eine Studie zu Jacobi, Kant, Fichte, Schelling und Hegel*. Stuttgart-Bad Cannstatt: Frommann-Holzboog, 2013.

Pogge, Thomas. "Erscheinung und Dinge an sich." *Zeitschrift für philosophische Forschung* 45 (1991): 489–510.

Prauss, Gerold. *Kant und das Problem der Dinge an sich*. 3rd edn. Bonn: Bouvier, 1989.

Ptassek, Peter, Birgit Sandkaulen, Jochen Wagner and Georg Zenkert. *Macht und Meinung. Die rhetorische Konstitution der politischen Welt*. Göttingen: Vandenhoeck & Ruprecht, 1992.

Rohs, Peter. "Der Pantheismus bei Spinoza und im Deutschen Idealismus." In *Subjektivität und Anerkennung*, edited by Barbara Merker, Georg Mohr and Michael Quante, 102–21. Paderborn: Mentis, 2004.

Rohs, Peter. *Fichte*. 2nd revised edition. Munich: Beck, 2007.

Sandkaulen, Birgit. *Ausgang vom Unbedingten. Über den Anfang in der Philosophie Schellings*. Göttingen: Vandenhoeck und Ruprecht, 1990.

Sandkaulen, Birgit. "Das Nichtige in seiner ganzen Länge und Breite. Hegels Kritik der Reflexionsphilosophie." *Hegel-Jahrbuch* 2004 (2004): 165–73.

Sandkaulen, Birgit. "Die Ontologie der Substanz, der Begriff der Subjektivität und die Faktizität des Einzelnen. Hegels reflexionslogische 'Widerlegung' der Spinozanischen Metaphysik." *International Yearbook of German Idealism* 5 (2008): 235–75.

Sandkaulen, Birgit. *Grund und Ursache. Die Vernunftkritik Jacobis*. Munich: Wilhelm Fink Verlag, 2000.

Sandkaulen, Birgit. "'Individuum est ineffabile.' Zum Problem der Konzeptualisierung von Individualität im Ausgang von Leibniz." In *Individualität. Genese und Konzeption einer Leitkategorie humaner Selbstdeutung*, edited by Wilhelm Gräb and Lars Carbonnier, 153–79. Berlin: Berlin University Press, 2012.

Sandkaulen, Birgit. *Jacobis Philosophie. Über den Widerspruch zwischen System und Freiheit*. Hamburg: Meiner, 2019.

Sandkaulen, Birgit. "Selbst und Selbsterhaltung. Spinoza im Blick der Neurowissenschaft." *Studia Spinozana* 15 (2006 a): 231–44.

Sandkaulen, Birgit. "Spinoza zur Einführung. Fichtes Wissenschaftslehre von 1812." *Fichte-Studien* 30 (2006 b): 71–84.

Sandkaulen, Birgit. "System und Systemkritik. Überlegungen zur gegenwärtigen Bedeutung eines fundamentalen Problemzusammenhangs." In *System und Systemkritik. Beiträge* zu einem Grundproblem der klassischen deutschen Philosophie, edited by id., Kritisches Jahrbuch der Philosophie 11, 11–34. Würzburg: Königshausen und Neumann, 2006 c.

Sandkaulen, Birgit. "'Was geht auf dem langen Wege vom Geist zum System nicht alles verloren.' Problematische Transformationen in der klassischen deutschen Philosophie." Deutsche Zeitschrift für Philosophie 50 (2002), 363–75.

Schneider, Ulrich J. *Die Vergangenheit des Geistes. Eine Archäologie der Philosophiegeschichte*. Frankfurt a.M.: Suhrkamp, 1990.

Siemek, Marek J. *Von Marx zu Hegel. Zum sozialpolitischen Verständnis der Moderne*. Würzburg: Könighausen und Neumann, 2002.

Sommer, Konstanze. *Zwischen Metaphysik und Metaphysikkritik. Heidegger, Schelling und Jacobi*. Hamburg: Meiner, 2015.

Spaemann, Robert. *Personen. Versuche über den Unterschied zwischen ›etwas‹ und ›jemand‹*. Stuttgart: Klett-Cotta, 1996.

Stekeler-Weithofer, Pirmin. *Hegels Analytische Philosophie. Die Wissenschaft der Logik als kritische Theorie der Bedeutung*. Paderborn: Schöningh, 1992.

Stolzenberg, Jürgen. "Was ist Freiheit? Jacobis Kritik der Moralphilosophie Kants." In *Friedrich Heinrich Jacobi: Ein Wendepunkt der geistigen Bildung der Zeit*, edited by Walter Jaeschke and Birgit Sandkaulen, 19–36. Hamburg: Meiner, 2004.

Strawson, Peter. *Individuals: An Essay in Descriptive Metaphysics*. London: Methuen, 1959.

Sturma, Dieter, ed. *Person. Philosophiegeschichte – Theoretische Philosophie – Praktische Philosophie*. Paderborn: Mentis, 2001.

Sturma, Dieter. *Philosophie der Person. Die Selbstverhältnisse von Subjektivität und Moralität*. Paderborn/Munich/Vienna/Zürich: Schöningh, 1997.

Sturma, Dieter. "Präreflexive Freiheit und menschliche Selbstbestimmung." In *F. W. J. Schelling. Über das Wesen der menschlichen Freiheit*, edited by Otfried Höffe and Annemarie Pieper, Klassiker Auslegen 3, 149–72. Berlin: Akademie Verlag, 1995.

Timm, Hermann. "Die Bedeutung der Spinozabriefe Jacobis für die Entwicklung der idealistischen Religionsphilosophie." In *Friedrich Heinrich Jacobi. Philosoph und Literat der Goethezeit*, edited by Klaus Hammacher, 35–81. Frankfurt a.M.: Vittorio Klostermann, 1971.

Tugendhat, Ernst. *Vorlesungen über Ethik*. Frankfurt a.M.: Suhrkamp, 1993.

Vaihinger, Hans. *Kommentar zu Kant's Kritik der reinen Vernunft* 2. Stuttgart/Berlin/Leipzig: Union Deutsche Verlagsgesellschaft, 1892.

Vaihinger, Hans. *The Philosophy of "As If": A System of the Theoretical, Practical and Religious Fictions of Mankind* [1913; Die Philosophie des Als Ob]. Translated by Charles K. Ogden.1925. Reprint, Petoskey, MI: Random Shack, 2015.

Walther, Manfred. "Konsistenz der Maximen. Universalisierbarkeit und Moralität nach Spinoza und Kant." In *Motivationen für das Selbst. Kant und Spinoza im Vergleich*, edited by Anne Tillkorn, 109–32. Wiesbaden: Harrassowitz Verlag, 2012.

Westphal, Kenneth. "Hegel's Attitude toward Jacobi in the 'Third Attitude of Thought toward Objectivity.'" *The Southern Journal of Philosophy* 27 (1989): 135–56.

Willaschek, Markus. "Phaenomena/Noumena und die Amphibolie der Reflexionsbegriffe." In *I. Kant. Kritik der reinen Vernunft*, edited by id. and Georg Mohr, Klassiker Auslegen 17/18, 325–51. Berlin: Akademie Verlag, 1998.

Windelband, Wilhelm. *Lehrbuch der Geschichte der Philosophie*. 1912. Reprint, Tübingen: Mohr Siebeck, 1993.

Zöller, Günter. "Das Element aller Gewißheit. Jacobi, Kant und Fichte über den Glauben." *Fichte-Studien* 14 (1998): 1–41.

Proof of First Publication

Jacobis Philosophie. Über den Widerspruch zwischen System und Freiheit. Hamburg: Meiner, 2019.

Leitmotifs

1. "Life and Work." Previously unpublished.
2. "Jacobis 'Spinoza und Antispinoza.'" *Philosophia OSAKA* 8 (2013): 23–36.
3. "Fürwahrhalten ohne Gründe. Eine Provokation philosophischen Denkens." *Deutsche Zeitschrift für Philosophie* 57 (2009): 259–72.
4. "Wie 'geistreich' darf Geist sein? Zu den Figuren von Geist und Seele im Denken Jacobis." In *Geist und Psyche. Klassische Modelle von Platon bis Freud und Damasio*, edited by Edith Düsing and Hans D. Klein, 143–59. Würzburg: Königshausen & Neumann, 2008.
5. "Zwischen Spinoza und Kant: Jacobi über die Freiheit der Person." In *Freiheit nach Kant: Tradition – Rezeption – Transformation – Aktualität*, edited by Saša Josifović and Jörg Noller, 208–33. Leiden: Brill, 2018.
6. "Dass, was oder wer? Jacobi im Diskurs über Personen." In *Friedrich Heinrich Jacobi. Ein Wendepunkt der geistigen Bildung der Zeit*, edited by Walter Jaeschke and Birgit Sandkaulen, 217–37. Hamburg: Meiner, 2004.
7. "Bruder Henriette? Derrida und Jacobi: Dekonstruktionen der Freundschaft." *Deutsche Zeitschrift für Philosophie* 49 (2001): 653–64.
8. "'Ich bin und es sind Dinge außer mir.' Jacobis Realismus und die Überwindung des Bewusstseinsparadigmas." *International Yearbook of German Idealism* 11/2013 (2016): 169–96.
9. "Das 'leidige Ding an sich.' Kant – Jacobi – Fichte." In *Kant und der Frühidealismus. System der Vernunft. Kant und der deutsche Idealismus 2*, edited by Jürgen Stolzenberg, 175–201. Hamburg: Meiner, 2007.

Critical Relations

10. "Ichheit und Person. Zur Aporie der Wissenschaftslehre in der Debatte zwischen Fichte und Jacobi." In *System und Systemkritik um 1800. System der Vernunft. Kant und der deutsche Idealismus 3*, edited by Christian Danz and Jürgen Stolzenberg, 45–68. Hamburg: Meiner, 2011.

11. "Fichtes Bestimmung des Menschen – Eine überzeugende Antwort auf Jacobi?" Lecture presented at the conference *Transcendental Philosophy between Metaphysics and Politics. In Memory of Marek Jan Siemek*, Warsaw, May 2018. Previously unpublished.
12. "Dieser und kein anderer? Zur Individualität der Person in Schellings Freiheitsschrift." In "Alle Persönlichkeit ruht auf einem dunkeln Grunde." *Schellings Philosophie der Personalität*, edited by Thomas Buchheim and Friedrich Hermanni, 35–53. Berlin: Akademie Verlag, 2004.
13. "System und Zeitlichkeit. Jacobi im Streit mit Hegel und Schelling." In *Systembegriffe um 1800–1809. Systeme in Bewegung.* System der Vernunft. Kant und der deutsche Idealismus 4, edited by Wilhelm G. Jacobs, Jürgen Stolzenberg, and Violetta L. Waibel, 299–316. Hamburg: Meiner, 2018.
14. "Dritte Stellung des Gedankens zur Objektivität: Das unmittelbare Wissen." In *G.W.F. Hegel, Der "Vorbegriff" zur Wissenschaft der Logik in der Enzyklopädie von 1830*, edited by Alfred Denker, Annette Sell, and Holger Zaborowski, 166–91. Freiburg: Karl Alber, 2010.
15. "Metaphysik oder Logik? Die Bedeutung Spinozas für Hegels Wissenschaft der Logik." *Studia Hegeliana. Journal of the Spanish Society for Hegelian Studies* 1 (2015): 139–54 (In Spanish translation).

Index

a nihilo nihil fit 19–20, 32, 238, 243
absolute, the 43, 46, 55, 75–6, 81–2, 89–90, 190 n.26, 195, 240–2, 244, 245
acosmism 242–3, 245
act, action 20–2, 24–7, 31, 36 n.10, 39–44, 58, 63–5, 67–71, 84–9, 112–13, 120–2, 126, 137, 177, 233, 237
    intelligible 72, 187, 198
actuality 6, 19, 39, 42, 70, 72, 115–16, 194–5, 197–8, 208 n.14
actuosity or agility 184, 206 n.8, 245
    blindly actuose being 26, 194
admiration 58 n.17, 70, 73
Adolphi, Rainer 197 n.59
Adorno, Theodor W. 121 n.22, 132–3
Aenesidemus (Schulze, Gottlob Ernst) 117, 131 n.7, 132–4, 138
affection 137–8
    in Fichte 146–7
    Kant's theory of affection 132, 134–6, 140, 141 n.37, 142–4
agency, agent 21, 23, 25–7, 34, 41–3, 58–9, 84, 175, 183, 185
Allison, Henry E. 141 n.37
animal 43–4, 69, 79, 126, 172, 174, 177, 180
    animal rationale 41, 53–4, 56, 67
appearance (opposed to the thing in itself) 117–18, 132, 138–41, 145, 147–8, 214
arbitrariness 69, 102
    as Hegels criticism of Jacobi 57, 220, 223–4, 226–7, 229–30, 232
Aristotle 36, 64 n.9, 73, 94, 96, 98, 99–103
Arndt, Andreas 153 n.3, 165 n.40, 171 n.6
atheism 23–4, 30
atheism controversy 12, 16, 161, 170, 179 n.32

being (Sein)
    absolute 6, 178 n.30, 195
    being-for-itself 125–8

being in everything existent (Sein in allem Dasein) 19, 81, 107, 230, 237, 242, 244
being in Hegel 224–32, 237–44
Beiser, Frederick C. 36 n.12
belief 34–6, 116, 118, 144, 171,176–80, 231
    and knowledge 30, 32, 34, 37–8, 42
    as practice 34, 36
Berlin, Isaiah 36 n.12
Boehm, Omri 61 n.1
Boethius, Ancius M.S. 168, 186–7
Bollnow, Otto F. 42 n.23
Bowman, Brady 36 n.10, 114 n.12, 124 n.26
Bruno, Giordano 26 n.14
Buber, Martin 86

Cassirer, Ernst 121
categorical imperative 62 n.5, 64–6, 68, 80, 87, 201
causa finalis 33, 36 n.10, 175, 204, 237
causa immanens 19, 24–6, 32, 34, 38, 243–4
causality, causation, action-oriented 21, 58, 62, 113, 121–3, 126, 137, 205
    as category of the understanding in Kant 58, 117, 121–3, 132–3, 142–4, 205 n.6
causa sui and causa rerum 194, 198, 243
    in Schelling 188–91, 194, 198
cause, final, as concept of practical experience 6, 20–1, 25, 205 n.6, 233
    absolute 27, 59
cause and effect 25–6, 113, 119–20, 123, 205, 233
    confusion of ground and cause 26–7,194–5, 205
    distinction of ground and cause 6, 26, 69, 205 n.6
    principium generationis 205

certainty
  double of self and world 109–13, 115–16, 118–20
  immediate 35–6, 39, 42, 44, 57, 107, 116, 125, 144, 216–17, 237, 239
  sensuous in Hegel 113–14
Claudius, Matthias 10–11, 16 n.1, 43
cogito-sum 76, 80, 107, 224
cognition 36 n.11, 40–1, 43 n.24, 49, 52 n.12, 54, 88, 124, 161, 163, 207, 232
common sense 35 n.8, 114
conatus 71, 124, 196, 209
conditioned, unconditioned 27, 43 n.24, 52–5, 57, 59, 72, 125, 127
consciousness 54, 106–7, 114, 126
  in Fichte 164–8
  personal 84–6, 88, 109
  practical, existential 42–4, 57, 59, 64, 67, 70, 78, 84, 86, 112–13, 205 n.6
consciousness paradigm. *See* representation model of consciousness
construction 53, 58, 109, 115, 158–9, 164–5, 167–8, 170, 210, 212
contradiction, practical. *See* refutation vs. practical contradiction
controversy concerning divine things 12, 17, 161

Damasio, António R. 33 n.7
deed 58, 70, 179
  deed = deed 170
Deleuze, Gilles 33
Della Rocca, Michael 25 n.13
demonstration 16, 22, 36, 91, 238
Derrida, Jacques 37 n.14, 93–103
Descartes, René 24, 32, 57, 76, 80, 105–10, 174 n.15, 191, 219, 224–7, 230–2
desire 41, 67–70, 71–2, 189, 200
determinatio est negatio
  in Hegel 222, n.5, 238–9, 242
  in Jacobi 238
  in Schelling 199–201
determinism 63, 68–9, 175
Diderot, Denis 4, 7, 48
Dilthey, Wilhelm 42

double philosophy 6, 15–18, 24, 26–7, 211, 237, 240–1
drive 41, 71–2, 196, 199

egoism 66, 156, 181, 192, 199
  speculative (*see* speculation)
empiricism 50, 67 n.13, 112, 123 n.25, 215
Enlightenment 9, 39, 47
  Berlin Enlightenment 9, 16, 32, 36
  French Enlightenment 4
essence 192, 196, 199, 209, 232 n.10
  essence and existence 25, 189, 243
existence (Dasein) 5, 51, 54–7, 107, 239
  and coexistence 67, 69
  to disclose and to reveal (Dasein enthüllen und offenbaren) 23, 27, 36–42
  essential or real vs. actual in Spinoza 25, 209, 213
  finite, temporal 24, 86, 88, 205, 206 n.10, 207–8
experience 162, 166, 172
  of human praxis 22, 24–5, 26–7, 42
explanation (Erklärung, erklären) 20–4, 26–7, 36, 41–2, 53, 57, 59, 127–8, 145, 172–3, 184, 204–5, 207–8, 214, 237
explanatory gap 70

f/act (Tathandlung) 91, 108, 179
faith
  in Mendelssohn's critique of Jacobi 31, 34
  rational faith in Kant 34, 36
Falke, Gustav 93 n.3
fatalism 22–3, 30, 61, 66, 90, 129, 173 n.11, 198, 204
feeling of honor 70
feeling of our own existence 57, 64, 88, 107, 113, 126, 161, 198, 200
  in Fichte 157–68
feelings, moral. *See* admiration, feeling of honor, gratitude, joy, love
fetish 43–4
Fichte, Johann Gottlieb 11–12, 16, 17, 18 n.3, 22, 26, 37–8, 46, 49, 52 n.12, 56, 68, 76–7, 80–2, 86, 91, 93–4, 96, 105–9, 111, 117, 119, 121, 127, 129,

131, 133–6, 145–9, 153–68, 169–81, 184, 207, 211, 212, 217, 237
fideism 9–10
finite/infinite 24–5, 42, 54–5, 59, 67, 75, 77–8, 85, 203–9, 211, 213, 217, 221, 227, 232, 239, 241–4, 247/ 160 n.24, 168, 206 n.8/10, 207, 210 n.21, 247
    Spinoza's rejection of transition from the infinite to the finite 19–20, 243
finitude 27, 42, 55, 59, 78, 86, 88, 123 n.25, 183, 201, 203, 208–9, 211, 247
force (Kraft) 173–4, 176, 179–80, 192
freedom 3–4, 18–24, 33, 36, 43 n.24, 55–9, 61–73, 126–8, 170–81, 183–5, 198–201, 233–9, 247
friendship 73, 93–103
Frank, Manfred 108 n.3

Gabriel, Gottfried 37 n.13
geometric method 18–19, 32, 242 n.25
Gettier, Edmund 35 n.9
God, personal, as spirit 26–7, 31, 59, 71, 77, 82–3, 91, 184, 191, 193, 195, 221, 232
God in Spinoza. *See* substance
Goethe, Johann Wolfgang 3–4, 7–8, 10–12, 17, 29, 99 n.22
good, the 64–5, 69–71, 72–3
gratitude 58, 70, 73
ground 139, 141, 147
    confusion of ground and cause (*see* cause)
    ground and consequence 25–6, 194, 205
    ground and existence in Schelling 185, 188–93, 194, 197 n.59, 198, 201
    non-ground in Schelling 190–3, 199
    (principle of) sufficient reason as union of ground and cause 53, 57, 172, 205 n.6

Habermas, Jürgen 22, 37
Halbig, Christoph 216 n.1
Hamann, Johann Georg 7, 10–11, 39, 135 n.15
Hamilton, (Sir) William 35 n.8
happiness 65, 72

Hegel, Georg Wilhelm Friedrich 4, 8, 12–13, 15, 17, 19 n.5, 20 n.6, 22, 26, 29, 33, 37–40, 45–9, 57, 65, 72–3, 75, 76, 81–2, 90–1, 93–4, 99, 107, 111, 113–14, 121, 123, 127, 153–4, 178, 181, 200, 203–4, 207–11, 213–14, 215–33, 235–47
Heidegger, Martin 42, 102, 190 n. 26, 192
Henrich, Dieter 15 n.1, 86 n.17, 105, 108
Herder, Johann Gottfried 7, 10–11, 17, 77, 81–5, 99 n.22, 174 n.15
Horkheimer, Max 121 n.22
Horstmann, Rolf-Peter 108 n.6, 123 n.24
humanity 80, 87, 177, 186
    humanity as it is 7
Humboldt, Wilhelm von 7, 99
Hume, David 112, 123 n.25

I, absolute 75–6, 108, 184
I-hood (Ichheit) 56–7, 77–8, 109, 158–61, 164, 166–8, 179
I and Thou 109, 118, 120
idealism 111–12, 114–15, 175–6
    transcendental idealism 112, 117, 121, 129–49
identity 40, 56, 68 n.15, 83, 84, 88 n.21, 105, 119, 167, 184, 185–7, 191–201, 207–13, 217, 231, 240–1, 244–5, 247
    what-identity 84–91
    who-identity 84–91
imagination in Spinoza 203–9
immediacy, mediation 39, 114, 118, 130, 215–33, 239
immediate. *See* certainty
individual 56, 87, 108, 122, 124, 127–8, 158–61, 166–8, 181, 187, 198–200
    organic 125
individuality 56–7, 88 n.21, 125–8, 156, 158–9, 160–1, 166–9, 183–201
intuition 64, 113–19, 221–2, 231
irrationalism, irrationality 10, 23, 36, 118 n.17
Ivaldo, Marco 162 n.27

Jaeschke, Walter 153 n.3, 165 n.40, 171 n.6, 188 n.17
Jean Paul (Richter, Johann Paul Friedrich) 11, 153, 156
joy 64–5, 71–2

Kant, Immanuel 5–6, 9–10, 12, 16–17, 22, 24, 29–30, 33–4, 36, 38, 43 n.24, 46, 48 n.6, 49–51, 54–6, 61–6, 68–9, 71, 76–7, 80–1, 84, 87, 89, 105–9, 112, 114, 116–18, 120–1, 122–5, 129–48, 153, 155, 162–3, 166–7, 170, 178, 186–7, 201, 207, 211–12, 214, 215–16, 233, 235–6, 244
Kaplow, Ian 79, 85 n.15
Kierkegaard, Søren 39–40, 154
Koch, Oliver 62 n.6, 76 n.2, 114 n.13, 161 n.6
Koselleck, Reinhart 9
Kreines, Jim 25 n.13

Larmore, Charles E. 127 n.28
Lauth, Reinhard 93 n.1
Lavater, Johann Caspar 10, 77, 82
leap 22–3, 42, 90, 154–5, 170, 217–19, 221, 237, 240
Leibniz, Gottfried Wilhelm 32, 83, 112, 124–7, 160 n.24, 167, 239
Lessing, Gotthold Ephraim 9, 16–17, 20–1, 29–30, 32–3, 82
life 40–2, 53, 106–7, 126–7, 164, 168
  and speculation (*see* speculation)
  living nature (*see* nature)
lifeworld 21–2, 24–5, 114, 121, 127, 171, 181
Locke, John 50, 51, 67 n.13, 77, 83–5, 89, 117, 123 n. 25
love 58, 68, 70, 192–3
  pure love 65

materialism 173–4
mechanism 63–4, 68–9, 123, 164
mediation. *See* immediacy
Mendelssohn, Moses 5–6, 9–10, 16–17, 29–35, 37–8, 44
metaphysics
  of action 39–44, 72, 89
  of immanence 24, 32–3, 204, 209, 237, 243
mine-ness 113, 127, 159, 167, 181 n.38
monism 19–20, 23–6, 81, 84, 160, 170, 173, 175, 178, 179 n.32, 180–1, 184, 237
Montaigne, Michel de 94–5, 97, 100–2

moral feelings. *See* feelings
moral law 68–9, 72, 80, 87, 96

Nagel, Thomas 168
name 88–9, 95, 97–8, 102–3, 156
nature
  biological, living 54, 56, 67, 123–4, 127, 178, 180, 186
naturalism 12, 33, 66, 68–9, 85, 125, 127, 171, 174, 178–80
necessity 31, 58, 69, 101, 123, 137, 147, 176, 194, 196, 198–9, 211, 217
negation 200–1, 207, 221, 239, 242–3, 247
  see also determinatio est negatio
Nietzsche, Friedrich 33, 54
nihilism 12, 68, 117, 119, 160, 163, 170, 175–8, 181
non-ground. *See* ground
non-philosophy (Unphilosophie) 155, 160, 217
Novalis (Hardenberg, Georg Philipp Friedrich von) 10, 17, 153–4

One-and-All 81–4, 89–90
other, otherness 56, 88–9, 128, 194
Otto, Stephan 26 n.14

Parmenides 241, 243
Pätzold, Detlef 30 n.3
person 61–73, 75–91, 153–68, 175, 183–201
  first-person 109, 119, 128, 159, 171
personalism 81, 87, 89
personality 56, 75, 78–80, 83, 87, 90, 109, 158–61, 164, 167, 179, 183–201, 220, 232, 239
personhood 75, 77–8, 80–5, 89–90, 168
perspective
  observer 40–2, 113, 120, 128
  participant 22, 42, 124, 181
philosophy of one piece. *See* system
Plato 20, 35, 51, 64 n.9
pleasant, the 64, 70 n.17
Pluder, Valentin 114 n.13
possibility 6, 54, 70, 72 n.19, 141–2, 160 n.24, 197–8
potency, potentia 66, 71, 174–5, 192–3, 196, 243

power 61, 71, 120, 124, 175, 178, 180, 192, 196, 245
practice, praxis 6, 21–2, 24, 34, 36, 40, 73, 103
presentation (Darstellung) as opposed to representation (Vorstellung) 36, 94–5, 111, 118
principium generationis. *See* cause (principle of) sufficient reason. *See* ground

rationalism of Wolff and Mendelssohn 10, 17, 30–4, 50
rationality, 20–4, 36, 44, 50–6, 67, 69, 90, 125, 160. *See also* adjective reason
  historiogenesis of 53
  limits of 23, 217
realism 105–28
  committed, genuine, resolute 112, 143–5, 148
  empirical in Kant 112, 116–17, 136–40, 143, 148
  epistemic 113–19
  practical 119–28, 171, 176–80
reality 21–3, 25–6, 31, 36–9, 43, 58, 77, 106–7, 112, 114–20, 124, 132, 140–7, 163–4, 170, 176–8, 195, 205, 213, 242
reason in possession of man or man in possession of reason 10, 44, 48–52, 67
  adjective or discursive 20, 22–4, 44, 50–8, 67–8, 71, 160, 168, 217
  intuitive, practical, substantive 44, 50, 54–5, 59, 210, 231–2
reflection 37–9, 41, 47, 85–6, 88–9, 208–9, 213, 219, 228, 239–40, 244
  reflection theory of self-consciousness 86–7, 105–7, 109, 111, 167
refutation vs. practical contradiction 22–3, 33, 42, 129, 154–5, 204, 221, 237
refutation of Spinoza in Hegel 237, 239–40, 246
Reinhold, Karl Leonhard 17, 111, 117, 132
religion
  Christian 5, 15, 16, 30–7, 38–40, 43–4
  as ethical practice 64–5

religious materialism 5
representation (Vorstellung) 106–7, 115, 118, 119 n.20, 121–2, 126, 139–47
  model of consciousness 105, 110–12, 114–17, 119–20, 124
revelation 36 n.11, 115–20, 144
Richard of St. Victor 88 n.21, 187
Rohs, Peter 154 n.6, 160 n.23

salto mortale. *See* leap
Schelling, Friedrich Wilhelm Joseph 12, 16, 17, 22, 26, 38, 46, 61, 72 n.19, 75–82, 85, 90–1, 108, 111, 118–19, 123, 125, 127, 130, 154, 155 n.8, 178, 181, 183–201, 210–14, 217, 237
Schiller, Friedrich 11, 64
Schlegel, August Wilhelm 211
Schlegel, Friedrich 12 n.15, 39, 93, 95, 99, 153–4
Schleiermacher, Friedrich 17
Schneider, Ulrich J. 32 n.5
Schopenhauer, Arthur 41, 119 n.20, 132, 196
science 47, 52 n.12, 57, 59, 82, 91, 128, 160, 162–3, 226, 232
self 56, 84, 87, 115, 160–1, 187–201
self-activity 42, 70
self-consciousness 46, 56, 105–11, 128, 166, 245
  see also reflection theory of self-consciousness
self-determination 72, 126, 186, 199 n.67, 220, 239
self-preservation 41, 66–72, 85, 124, 196–7, 199, 209
self-relation 47, 55–7, 59, 161, 196–7, 247
selfhood (Selbstsein; Selbstheit) 59, 80, 84, 86–7, 88 n.21, 89–91, 96, 107, 119, 161, 187–8, 192–3, 195–7, 199–200
sensibility 123, 137–44
Siemek, Marek J. 181 n.38
singularity 87, 95 n.10, 96, 98, 100, 208
skepticism 111, 117, 215, 227
Sommer, Konstanze 190 n.26
soul 49, 55–7
  beautiful soul 64, 72–3
Spalding, Johann Joachim 170

speculation
   speculation/cognition and life in Fichte
      148, 155–6, 162–6, 180
   speculative egoism 117, 145, 148
Spinoza, Baruch de 5–6, 8–11, 15–27,
      29–34, 36 n.10, 38, 42–3, 61–2,
      65–8, 71, 81–2, 85, 89–90, 112,
      124–5, 127, 129–30, 153–5, 160,
      170–5, 178–81, 184–5, 189–96,
      198–200, 203–14, 217, 220–4, 230,
      232 n.10, 233, 235–47
Spinoza controversy 6, 8–11, 16, 161
Spinoza renaissance 9, 11, 15, 66, 237
spirit 49, 55–9, 71, 87
   in Schelling 185–7, 200
Stekeler-Weithofer, Pirmin 216 n.1
Stolzenberg, Jürgen 62 n.6, 233 n.11
Strawson, Peter 77
striving 66–8, 70, 71, 73, 85, 124, 196,
      209
Sturma, Dieter 76 n.2, 199 n.67
subject 46, 56, 80, 98, 105, 110, 217,
      221–2, 237, 239, 245–7
substance in Spinoza 19, 26, 61, 88 n.21,
      170, 173–4, 179, 184, 196, 205–6,
      217, 220–2, 237, 239
system 18–27, 43, 153–6, 159–60,
      164 n.34, 170, 184, 203–14, 220,
      237
   philosophy of one piece 18, 130,
      155 n.8, 168, 211
   of reason 22, 33, 129–30, 170

taking hold of (vernehmen) 59
temporality, time 25–6, 58, 88, 90, 113,
      121–2, 203–14
   eternal time 25–6, 205–10, 212, 214
theism 90, 191
theism controversy. *See* controversy
      concerning divine things
thing in itself 10, 129–49
Timm, Hermann 36 n.10
totum parte prius esse necesse est 35, 90
transcendental object in Kant 139–41
true, the, truth 5, 23, 27, 35, 41, 44,
      52 n.12, 58–9, 70 n.17, 221–2
Tugendhat, Ernst 65 n.11

useful, the 64–5, 69–70

Vaihinger, Hans 131–2
virtue ethics 64 n.9, 73, 233

Walther, Manfred 71 n.18
Westphal, Kenneth 216 n.1
what vs. who. *See* identity
will 20, 24, 33, 36, 41–2, 67, 69, 72, 160, 168,
      170, 175, 177, 179, 189, 196–201
Willaschek, Markus 132 n.9, 142 n.44
Windelband, Wilhelm 132–3, 142
Wittgenstein, Ludwig 37 n.13
Wolff, Christian 17–18, 32 n.5, 33, 50–1,
      110–11, 114, 117, 239

Zöller, Günter 144 n.47, 162 n.27

www.ingramcontent.com/pod-product-compliance
Lightning Source LLC
Chambersburg PA
CBHW062122300426
44115CB00012BA/1779